C000253692

Ponderings VII–XI

Studies in Continental Thought

EDITOR
JOHN SALLIS

CONSULTING EDITORS

Robert Bernasconi	James Risser
John D. Caputo	Dennis J. Schmidt
David Carr	Calvin O. Schrag
Edward S. Casey	Charles E. Scott
David Farrell Krell	Daniela Vallega-Neu
Lenore Langsdorf	David Wood

Martin Heidegger

Ponderings VII–XI

Black Notebooks 1938–1939

Translated by
Richard Rojcewicz

Indiana University Press
Bloomington and Indianapolis

This book is a publication of

Indiana University Press
Office of Scholarly Publishing
Herman B Wells Library 350
1320 East 10th Street
Bloomington, Indiana 47405 USA

iupress.indiana.edu

Published in German as Martin Heidegger *Gesamtausgabe 95: Überlegungen VII–XI (Schwarze Hefte 1938–1939)*, edited by Peter Trawny
© 2014 by Vittorio Klosterman GmbH, Frankfurt am Main
English translation © 2017 by Indiana University Press
All rights reserved

No part of this book may be reproduced or utilized in any form or by any means, electronic or mechanical, including photocopying and recording, or by any information storage and retrieval system, without permission in writing from the publisher. The Association of American University Presses' Resolution on Permissions constitutes the only exception to this prohibition.

The paper used in this publication meets the minimum requirements of the American National Standard for Information Sciences—Permanence of Paper for Printed Library Materials, ANSI Z39.48–1992.

Manufactured in the United States of America

Cataloging information is available from the Library of Congress.

ISBN 978-0-253-02471-8 (cloth)
ISBN 978-0-253-02503-6 (e-bk.)

1 2 3 4 5   22 21 20 19 18 17

CONTENTS

Translator's Introduction

This is a translation of volume 95 of Martin Heidegger's *Gesamtausgabe* ("Complete Works"). The German original appeared posthumously in 2014.

The volume is the second in the series publishing Heidegger's "Black Notebooks." These are small (ca. 5 × 7 in.) notebooks with black covers to which the philosopher confided sundry ideas and observations over the course of more than forty years, from the early 1930s to the early 1970s. The notebooks are being published in chronological order, and the five herein correspond to the years 1938–1939. In all, thirty-three of the thirty-four black notebooks are extant and will fill up nine volumes of the *Gesamtausgabe*.

Heidegger gave a title to each of the notebooks and referred to them collectively as the "black notebooks." The first fifteen are all "Ponderings." Their publication began in volume 94 with "Ponderings II" ("Ponderings I" is the lost notebook). The present volume includes the second five "Ponderings," VII–XI. The publication of the extant "Ponderings" concludes in volume 96 with "Ponderings XV."

As can be imagined regarding any notes to self, these journal entries often lack polished diction and at times are even cryptic. Nevertheless, the style and vocabulary are mostly formal, not to say stilted, and are seldom colloquial. This translation is meant to convey to an English-speaking audience the same effect the original would have on a German one, the degree of formality varying pari passu with Heidegger's own. A prominent peculiarity of the style I was unable to render in full, however, is the extensive use of dashes. Heidegger often employs dashes not merely for parenthetical remarks but for any change in the direction of thought. Sometimes dashes separate subjects and predicates, and some dashes even occur at the end of paragraphs. Due to differences in English and German syntax, I could not include all the dashes without making for needless confusion and could not place them all at the exact points that would correspond to the original sentence. This admission is of course not meant to imply I did capture the varied styles of the notebooks in all other respects.

The pagination of the notebooks themselves is reproduced here in the outer margins. All of Heidegger's cross-references are to these marginal numbers. The running heads indicate the pagination of the *Gesamtausgabe* edition. I have inserted myself into the text only to alert the reader to the original German where I thought it might be helpful (for example, as indicating a play on words I could not carry over into English) and to translate any Latin or Greek expressions Heidegger leaves untranslated. I have used brackets ([]) for these interpolations and have reserved braces ({}) for insertions by the editor. All the footnotes in the book stem either from me, and these few are marked as such, or from the editor and are then placed within braces.

I am indebted to Shane Ewegen for a careful review of the penultimate version of this entire translation and for helpful suggestions on improving the text.

Richard Rojcewicz

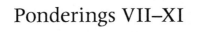

Ponderings VII–XI

PONDERINGS VII

The essence of the Germans:

That they may be chained to the *struggle* over their essence, for only inasmuch as they take up this struggle are they the people they alone can be.

Suitable for this struggle is only that which, with unwavering confidence[1] in its essential pride, is able to suffer the highest question-worthiness of what is most question-*worthy* (beyng[2]).

One who encounters the distorted essence only negatively will also not ever be equal to the essence.

(Cf. p. 84.[3])

---

1. [Reading *Zutrauen* for *Zeitraum* ("time frame"), in accord with the corrigenda to this volume posted on the German publisher's website.—Trans.]

2. [Archaic form of "being" to render *Seyn,* archaic form of *Sein.*—Trans.]

3. [All cross-references cite the pagination of the notebooks themselves, indicated here in the outer margins.—Trans.]

Nothing is in vain—least of all nothingness itself; for in it beyng delivers itself to its most unique uniqueness.

Like an errancy, beyng is riven through beings.

Those who have arrived too early must not depart too late.

Anyone who thinks ahead to future decisions must create a plight—and must know that.

To be German: to project the most intrinsic burden of the history of the West and to bear that burden on one's shoulders. (Cf. p. 81.)

Rare in history are those thrusts (p. 19) which, although unrecogniz-able by their own era, permeate all beings and come to be in another spatiotemporal field of another beyng. It is still more rare for these thrusts to be recognized; the recognition consists in clearing the way for the trajectory of these projections and making ready those who project. Historiology almost always snatches up, i.e., parries, the pro-jections.

Because historiology as a "science" arises out of a determinate form of Western history—out of the modern essence of history—histori-ology is therefore not a mere inconsequential superstructure taking cognizance of history by history—but instead is one of the essential paths on which history is "made." This historical role of historiology is still not recognized, let alone grasped in its bearing for the decisive phase of modernity. Why does history employ the triviality of histo-riological science in order to achieve such an effectuation as must be presumed in the parrying of those thrusts? Does the history (of be-ings) indeed consist in the parrying of such thrusts of beyng?

Is it essential to the thrusts that within them that which thrusts, in   2 thrusting and projecting, should conceal itself in self-refusal? Do we first surmise on this basis something of the *history of beyng*, whereby the essence of this history may be called the negative force of the hesi-tation of what is concealed and undecided of the appropriation into the decision?

2

The history (of beings) as the parrying of the thrusts of beyng. Such a parrying is "culture," which not accidentally deteriorates into the gigantic form of the organization of lived experience. "Schmeling[4] lives [*erlebt,* "has a lived experience of"] the world"—if only this were a mere inconsequential journalistic cliché, if only the journalistic cli-ché were not the most real reality and by no means simply a fleeting turn of phrase.

And if only those who play at being indignant over this did not take part in the same game.

---

4. {Max Schmeling (1905–2005), German boxer, world heavyweight cham-pion 1930–1932.}

For "culture" as an organization of lived experience is the reason that these, apparently combating one another, are of the exact same essence: *cultural politics, cultural concern, Christian cultural assimilation.*

The third—is the most dangerous. Here everything is processed and united, and yet what is creative—the uprightness of venturing the ex-
3   posure to the projective domain of the thrusts—is radically | *denied.* But this denial is very well concealed, and this concealment is justi- fied as a measured assimilation most comprehensively. The doom of the West is that which assumes the insidious semblance of saving it from "downgoing": *cultural Christianity*—of course, this "saves" it from "downgoing" by making such "downgoing" impossible in denying it the necessary presupposition: the greatness of historical beyng out of venturing the truth of beyng.

3

The apologetic undertakings of cultural Christianity, long ago (since Irenaeus) entrenched in the West, constitute a *preliminary form of modern historiology.* The latter must not at all be associated with Thucydides, but rather with Augustine and the *civitas dei* ["city of God"],[5] which then finally gives rise to the most Christian modern realm of the highest cultural *values* and which once again confirms what it merely wants to "revalue." Therefore, cultural Christianity— because historiology derives from it—can also make use of historiol- ogy and do so with a special virtuosity. This Christian way of *"rewrit- ing"* history necessarily sets a precedent followed in modernity, the
4   more modern modernity becomes. | (As already Karl Marx rewrote and turned upside down the Christian Hegel and Hegel's historiol- ogy—which both Marx and Hegel call "historical philosophy.")

4

Because the Catholic Church as "Catholicism" worked out the grand- est Christianizing of modernity since Trent, now everything want- ing to have a modern future must necessarily become "Catholic." This happens most effectively when a "conversion" to the Church is *not* nec- essary but at the same time the struggle *against* the Church remains possible, a struggle which, according to the modern decisionlessness in all things, naturally cannot once more be against the "Church" but is only against curialism (operated out of *Rome*) in "politics."

---

5. {Augustine, *Sancti Aurelii Augustini De civitate Dei libri 22* (Leipzig, 1877.)}

5

There was once a German thinking which surpassed by far the concept of the state that grasps the state as an apparatus of offices and authorities; and this despite the modern essence of such thinking, whereby it will not in the end avoid this concept of the state.

Is the "apparatus" character—the institutionalization of an institution—overcome or even only reduced | if another institution is placed beside the first, or must then not both sides unite into a still more decisive form of an "institution" and let the apparatus character come to count as what it basically is, the metaphysical essence of modernity? Is an institution sublated in its functional character or first fully confirmed and reinforced, if its bearers have taken on as their essential ontological form that of the operative instituter and organizer? (The executors merely constitute a determinate extreme form of these and are not at all "barbarians" we should romantically feel indignant about.—)

6

There are still childish romantics who gush over "empire" ["*Reich*"] and even over the "imperial" university, in the sense of Stephan {sic} George's idea of "empire." Whence the anxiety, of those who are supposedly free of anxiety, in face of the empire as the gigantic devices of the party apparatus and the state apparatus in their unity? Can the metaphysical essence of modernity and thus of the proximate future generate a more powerful unity than *the apparatus of the unity of apparatuses*? One who here perceives mere alienation and yearns to go back to a past—such as that of the Middle Ages—which never was | is forgetting that indeed in the gigantism of this ap-paratus (in German: equipped-for [*Zu-rüstung*]) the gigantic possibilities of "*lived experience*" are opened up and no lived experience is to be denied anyone, and he is forgetting that, in this equipping-for, "culture" is first secured and equipped as the organizing of lived experience. Therefore, even the constant professing of culture is not a "catchphrase," and the doorman at a movie theater has a perfect right to see himself as a "bearer of culture."

One does not know what one wants if on the basis of concern for *culture* one believes one must persuade oneself into an opposition to "National Socialism."

To be sure, the space of this concern and the number of those who fill it are growing more steadily and faster than the responsible ones could foresee—despite all the indications of it. And this space is already roofed over and guarded by Christian cultural activity, which is of course deceived if it intends to renew Christianity thereby—. Yet this intention is perhaps only a mask—one wants mastery in cultural activity—not in "politics."

What if Christian cultural activity were *then* only the dark side 7 (passing itself off as the bright side) of that which | Bolshevism pursues as the destruction of culture—the dark side of the process by which modernity arranges for its own consummation and struggles to equip itself for it?

Thus the *most proximate* decision is only this: *which of the gigantic equippings of the modern world-picture will be instituted as the victorious one.*

The fronts and the forms of this struggle over the decision are not yet established. We must not consider the struggle simply as a future incident by calculating in advance in a *historiological* way. Instead, we need to know, through ever greater meditation, the essence of modernity in the whole of its *historical* course, assuming the Germans are still open to the carrying out of a decision through which, in the consummation of modernity, the plight of a transition is awakened. Then those must be ready to whom the plight of history is not a woe, nor a joy, but a thrust of beyng itself.

7

The *future thinker* must know the *distorted* essence of beyng. Therefore, he can never become a denier, but also never an affirmer, of "beings" and a fortiori never what common thinking would deduce from this | 8 neither-nor: a doubter. Then is all that is left to him the cleverness of the dialectician, who can let all "sides" of beings count at once and at the same time eliminate them, bringing everything into balance in the absolute (wherein he knows *himself*—more surely than even Descartes—to be well *sublated*) and not merely into the oppositionality of the representational subject-object relation?

In the transition to the other questioning, however, "dialectics" must be abandoned; for "dialectics" belongs entirely to modern thought and is a calculative mode of representation transferred back into philosophy out of science and thus by necessity formed unconditionally. It is no accident that for its own assurance dialectics has taken refuge in the Christianizing of the world-picture.

(The unconditionality and certainty of the subjectum [*Subjektum*] already belong together for Descartes—cf. *Meditationes* II and *III*[6]—although he did not yet attain, on the basis of the essence of subjectivity,

---

6. {René Descartes, *Meditationes de prima philosophia* (Leipzig: Meiner, 1913.)}

the purely modern systematization of this connection. The same connection is displayed in what is essential to German Idealism, for which *anthropological* ontology is at the same time onto*theology*. And this connection gains a new configuration in the essence of all | "worldview.")   9

The future thinker must be able to scorn, right from the start and in a decisive way, precisely this refuge and this escape that comes from balancing, because he experiences the errancy of *beyng*, and such errancy is essentially richer and "more in being" than any correctness of any lived experience of beings. Whoever even only for moments and short periods can, in paving his own way, traverse the errant paths of beyng effectuates concomitantly the transposition of modern humans into that which is refused them, yet without thereby sublating the self-refusal into a possession.

Nevertheless, almost every word of beyng is delivered over to reinterpretation in metaphysics, and the attempt to indicate the essence of beyng through "finitude" has attained exactly the opposite, insofar as this attempt, with the help of a very crude and facile dialectics, was acquainted with the fact that indeed the finite always presupposes and co-poses something infinite—whereby what might be attained is already half accomplished: the proof of the existence of "God," i.e., of the Christian cultural God of the "Christian worldview."—

8

To the "artist"—thus today someone who somewhere restrains himself and "works" only through indiscernible and long | indirection—   10
how foreign must be everything that is covered by the activity of the now empty crafts and by the use of the customary forms of production and exhibition, that procures for itself a sham validity, and that by "struggle" gains for itself a historiological framework in "happenings."

9

How often does the *scholar* justify to himself what he himself at times surmises, namely, the goallessness and groundlessness of his occupation, justify it by taking comfort in the thought that what he produces will some day for someone somewhere be a "building block"—for which edifice? The *scientist* is "better" positioned in this regard, and he can already more decisively separate his activity from the rest of "life" and especially from "psychic lived experience." The methodicalness of research gives "existence as a scientist" a justification and indeed even claims to be an affirmation of life, since research does

make humanity "at home" in beings. And in that way then a "joyful-ness" penetrates science and its administrative institution—the uni-versity—and indeed has already reached such a superficiality of self-interpretation that people are not reluctant to see here, in this newly
11   secured pleasurableness | of "otherwise" undisturbed research, the fulfillment of what Nietzsche called "joyful science." But perhaps sci-entists would be uneasy about their marvelous state if they had to ex-perience something of that "joyfulness."

10

The mere creating and bringing into play of an apparent productivity is without truth, unless we know what basically has precedence over history. For example, where is the ground for the fact that our essen-tial poets and thinkers remain so ineffective and must at once seem inferior in relation to the emptiest mediocrity of pen pushing, pro-vided the latter is currently relevant? Can we even speak of an infe-riority where no struggle or distinction is at issue, but where mere for-getting maintains the upper hand instead? The constantly unfettered mania for novelty, the ever greater impotence of recollection, the pre-dominance of the mediocre, the increasing facility in the production of the now ordinary "cultural assets," the revaluation of the traditional "cultural assets" into mere pieces of the exhibition of cultural-politi-cal organizations—all these are already *consequences* of a deeper pro-
12   cess, | one making Germans into secret enemies of their own con-cealed essence. They are already so the moment they withdraw from meditation. If other peoples renounce questioning and save only their past, then that does not contravene their basic attitude, since they are not tasked with questioning. But what if the inherited defect of the Germans to gaze at what is foreign were overcome in what is nearest and current, what if we develop our own taste, etc., for which never-theless we merely copy others in what is most essential, most unique, and most our own and set everything and the first thing on "politics"? All peoples lose ever easier what is most proper to them as this is more uniquely their own and is incomparable and can be grasped and con-figured solely in never-wavering self-meditation.

And wherein lies that which alone makes us, the Germans, into a people? Legendarily, the "people of poets and thinkers." But "poets and thinkers" are only the precursors of those creative persons who will once in the history of the West place beings into the decision of beyng again and thus allow the flight or advent of the god to become
13   the | event through which that history first becomes history: the struggle for and the downgoing of the essential occurrence of beyng.

There is no universal operative "principle" by which every people is a people; instead, every people is raised to the structure of its essence through *its* history and its essential position toward and in history, through *its* "principle." And the "principle" of the Germans is the struggle over their most proper *essence*. Only for that reason is the struggle over their "substance" a necessity. But the saving (and securing) of the substance *is* neither itself already the struggle over the essence, nor can this struggle, as something supervenient and later, be left for the time the "substance" has supposedly been ensured; for the "substance" "is" what it is only if it is borne and determined by the essence, i.e., with regard to the Germans, by the struggle over their essence. For us to kindle the flames of this struggle, what suffices is neither opposition against what is to the West nor opposition against the *Asiatic* East, especially since we remain, even in relation to the latter, in the undecidedness dominant in everything essential. It would be a half-measure, more disastrous than any | other undecidedness, for us to renounce the Western democratic-liberal spirit and yet persevere in the essence of modernity, instead of now already and now precisely outgrowing modernity in an essential volition, and despite the necessities of modernity, bringing it to its end. The principle of the Germans is so originarily a struggle—as the struggle over their essence—that this struggle must arise purely out of their proper power of decision and cannot even be based on mere oppositions to others, let alone dissolve into such oppositions.

Moreover, because we are assigned to this most proper struggle over ourselves, we must also accept the danger of flight from this most difficult of all struggles and must endure the various forms of that danger. Everything essential always moves on a thin edge and does so all the more decisively the more essential it is, yet this edge is just as difficult to find as to abide by. Correspondingly, the dangers increase, and so does what is most dangerous about them—unrecognizability. We seem to cast off an inherited defect—the running after otherness and the glorification of the foreign simply because it is foreign. Yet how close is not the outcome | both that we, hardly having become sure of this renunciation, now believe confrontation is no longer needed and also that this unneediness extends at last—i.e., here, at first—to the confrontation with ourselves, such that, for example, we already no longer tolerate any attempt to bring Hölderlin's words about the Germans to the ears of the Germans.[7]

14

15

---

7. {Friedrich Hölderlin, *Gedichte-Hyperion-Briefe, Sämtliche Werke. Bd. 2* (Berlin: Propyläen, 1923), p. 282ff.}

What will it signify if one day we should no longer be strong enough to endure meditation? What is happening if a people is destined to a struggle over its essential law and yet is mired in a lack of freedom toward itself? Where is the courage of the hero if we, without knowing it and without wanting to know it, remain struck with terror due to the obscurity of our essence? Whither has self-respect and innermost "honor" escaped, if we make all questioning innocuous and impossible through the now easy characterization of it as "unreliable"? Is there still an essential pride which can be entrusted even to that which is not immediately "self-evident" and useful? When could the struggle over our essence come to pass, if we renounce all the conditions | leading to this struggle?

16

11

The greatest danger threatening our essence, i.e., threatening the struggle over our essence, is that we might one day finally come to affirm everything that was denied in the first shock of the revolution, ostentatiously foster all "cultural values," even place a "value" on "refinement," and from the initially unavoidable excess of one-sidedness swing over to an excess of balance.

12

"*Culture.*"—Why should not a worthy baker who by chance gains a "lived experience" of the Norwegian coast while on a sea voyage get the idea that he is actually the first to discover that country? And why should not a respectable laundress who for the first time has an opportunity to gain a "lived experience" of Schiller's *Kabale und Liebe*[8] persuade herself that the genuine "culture" of the people would now properly commence with her visit to the theater? On the "principle" of this sort of formation of conviction and opinion all the results of "cultural politics" depend. | Such politics, however, is by no means merely an extrinsic application of the previous "culture" to domains formerly indifferent to it, nor is such politics a mere expansion of the effective field of "culture" and a distribution of "cultural assets" to those who used to be deprived of them—on the contrary, this politics carries out an essential transformation of "culture" as such in a direction already co-posited by the essence of culture.

17

---

8. {Friedrich Schiller, *Kabale und Liebe: Ein bürgerliches Trauerspiel in fünf Aufzügen* (Mannheim: Schwan, 1784.)}

Culture now means: to "cultivate" culture; thereby presupposed is a further region within which culture can be taken into service.

As soon as culture is transformed into the *cultivation* of culture, the cultural *values* themselves move away from the purview of representation—even *these objectifications of goals* become superfluous, and thereby the meditation on goals or even the thought of setting goals becomes completely alien. The most uncanny sort of goallessness commences with the transformation of culture into cultural politics.

It is not that we would have no "goals"—we *have* them so unconditionally that no recollection of them is even needed; on the contrary, the point is that *in* and *through* this sort of possession of goals and "certainty" about goals, goals themselves become superfluous and turn away from themselves, and that this process has its proper ground in the fact that in general I the human being as subjectum interprets humanness as "culture." That the *certainty* of goals in the form of "cultural politics" can *be* the most extreme and most obstinate form of goallessness is grounded in the essence of modernity. Only the recognition of this connection allows us to enter the domain of the incalculable—inasmuch as we mean the latter as something *essential* and not simply as the denial and limit of the calculable, for *in that way* even the incalculable is still something calculated. As long as we think in such a way, we arrive only at seeing a forced "paradox" in the proposition that the certainty of goals is goallessness. There is no longer a place for para-doxes in this thinking which is heedful of the history of being. A "paradox" is merely the reverse side of the dialectical absolute metaphysics of the unconditioned, and therefore by necessity remains mired in the basic position of that metaphysics.

13

Errancy is the most concealed gift of truth—for in it is bestowed the essence of truth as the stewardship of the self-refusal and as the purest preservation of beyng in the unrecognizable protection of what always is. To be sure: errancy I is here not "error," an established mistake, the failure of truth as correctness—but instead is that which belongs to the "there"—of Da-*sein*.[9]

Errancy never becomes more established through the possession of "truth" so as thereby to be grasped and possessed—instead, it can be

---

9. [*Dasein*, in the most literal sense "thereness," is Heidegger's term for the beings we ourselves are, thematized specifically as places (*da*) where occurs an understanding of what it means to be (*sein*) in general. The hyphenated term stresses this thematizing of humans in relation to being.—Trans.]

traversed only *in being errant*—but how seldom may one "be errant," how often and how exclusively must we content ourselves with rectifying what is incorrect and, well secured outside of errancy, organize activities with the help of which we bring forth "results."

14

Philosophy—out of "beings" and out of what most of all are beings, to be delivered over to beyng, for the sake of a capacity to recollect beings.

15

The incalculable: if this were only the irrational, then rationalism could ultimately triumph over it. But the *in*calculable is that which first provides an abode for calculation and for its limits—and opens itself only to those who no longer "reckon" with the incalculable but instead undergo its thrust as an appropriation into beyng—and who are prepared for thrusts. (Cf. above, p. 1.)

20

16

Today nothing is easier than "results"—but also nothing so inessential. What is going on in an age in which results appear not only as testimony to truth but as truth itself, in the sense of the true and "real"?

17

That we *have* a federal institute for history[10]—say rather historiology—why? For the same reason that *denies* us a thinker of history and allows Christian historiologists to *proliferate*.

18

Every *certainty* has the remarkable "intention" to detach the one who is certain from that against which the certainty makes certain, and from what it makes certain, and thereby to take the edge off his emp-

---

10. {The "Federal Institute for History of the New Germany" was founded in 1935 by Bernhard Rust, minister for education, refinement, and popular culture. One of its areas of work was called the "Research Division for the Jewish Question."}

tiness. This state then appears to be steadfastness and yet is even less than uncertainty—for it is a destruction of being.

19

In the *sciences*, there are fortunately no errings, only mistakes and incorrectness. The depth of a *philosophy* is measured—in case there is measurement here—by its power to be errant. Since, however, errancy can never | be willed and fabricated but instead arises out of   21
beyng itself as captivating, and can never be evaded, therefore the power to errancy on the part of a thinking says something about the nearness of that thinking to beyng.

20

What can easily be confused by an age that finds pleasure in facts and joy in deeds.
        What counts as "nearness to reality" is to take the extant states of a present time as they are and in the equally immediate mastery of them to prove one's own ability and one's own power of accomplishment and with this proof of power to claim that the "truth" of one's own comportment is demonstrated. (For example, the current state of mad "traffic"—whose whence and whither (in what is essential!) never come into question—must precisely be mastered. One does not see that the madness is thereby affirmed more radically than in leaving it alone. One reckons with facts—e.g., if drunkenness and increasing inebriation are obviously "causes" of traffic accidents, then one does not think of preventing inebriation but instead takes inebriation as a fact and simply demands that | a person in a drunken state   22
not get behind the wheel, which is precisely what the drunkard all the more wants to do and does do.)
        This nearness to reality by way of facts cannot and should not be discussed here through a pompous "moralizing." The task is merely to point out a *confusion*: it is one thing to acknowledge, apart from considering being, the present states of "beings" because "beings" *are*, but it is quite another thing to consider, and come to terms with, beyng and the essence of an age, for this meditation regards and affirms not something present-at-hand, but on the contrary, something that has been in its futurity. This meditation does not seek nearness to the "facts" because they are facts but rather binds itself to the history of beyng and *asks* which decision is compelled by that history. The fanatics for facts are the "idealists"; they live on their "ideal" of removing present-at-hand difficulties, provided it is only a removal and

thereby something comes into "operation." The ones remote from fac-
tuality are the "realists"; they take things as they *are*, i.e., according
to the way beyng is announced in the things—announced, to be sure,
only in long meditation. The "idealists" will maintain they are the
genuine realists, but the "realists" will renounce counting as "idealists." Therefore I an agreement is impossible here, and the confusion
will not at all be suppressed as such with insight or through the unavoidable public predominance of the pseudorealistic idealists (also
called "heroism"). But grasped in terms of the history of being, this
cannot be stopped, since modernity pursues therein the fulfillment
of its essence.

21

All *meditation* yields the risk of leaping over essential preliminary
stages of what is historically necessary, and the risk is greater the more
essentially the meditation proceeds. Therefore meditation must have
the power to leap back while yet remaining in the leap ahead and to
incorporate expressly into the forward leap that which is overleapt.
"The self-assertion of the German university"[11] errs inasmuch as it
overleaps the essential lawfulness of "today's" science. It errs again by
believing that, in overleaping, it could come back to "science," whereas
precisely with modernity even "science" is at an end and we do not
know the mode of future knowledge and the configuration of that
knowledge—we know only that a mere "revolution" in beings without
a transformation of beyng creates no originary history but simply entrenches what is already present-at-hand. Therefore even the first
step I toward the preparation of a transformation of beyng did not need
to wait for "National Socialism," as little at that questioning claims to
count as "National Socialist." Here realms are brought into relation
which have no *im*mediate bearing but which at the same time mediately and in various ways press toward a decision concerning the essence and destiny of the Germans and thus press toward the fate of
the West. The mere calculating of "standpoints" can find only "opposites" here, and even ones which do not at all "repay" taking heed of
them, since indeed the ascendancy of the National Socialist worldview is decisive.

By essence this worldview cannot think at all beyond that victory,
and does not even want to, for if it understands itself it must posit it-

---

11. {Martin Heidegger, "Die Selbstbehauptung der deutschen Universität,"
in *Reden und andere Zeugnisse eines Lebensweges*, GA16 (Frankfurt: Klostermann,
2000), pp. 107–117.}

self as "unconditional" in accord with its appropriate "self-consciousness." A pope who gets involved in discussions over dogma is not the "vicar" of Christ on earth—but on the other hand the pope is the head of the Church only if he at the same time takes care that, according to the changing course of events, the Church allows itself   25 everything possible, even what runs contrary to it, so that I in correspondence with the course of Western history, Christianity as cultural Christianity might be preserved in "culture." Thereby the spiritual welfare of the faithful is especially well protected. Protestantism founders by not grasping how the fulfillment of the unity of "faith" and "cultural creation" necessarily requires a double-entry bookkeeping, for the mastery of which the accountants need a long education. In the modern forms of humanity—in worldview—the unity of "faith" and "culture" comes to the fore in an acute way, not only due to its dependence on Christianity. Schools and educational establishments as deliberate institutions, "surveillance" of education into a worldview as a stern activity—these are not arbitrary and artificial or violent fabrications—but are essential necessities of a worldview that has entered into the decisiveness of its "self-consciousness." Meditation is anathema to this worldview and is necessarily looked upon as shackling.

22

In times of transition, impatience often inclines those who are best to demand at once and always something *"positive"* and thus to furnish the "positive" with a false importance and to seek it I in the wrong—   26 because still preliminary—place. Such a striving—which is readily called "healthy"—betakes itself to the proper path only if the transition out of what has been into what is coming is so comprehensive that all the doings and thoughts of the transitional ones have to maintain themselves already *outside* the either-or of positive-negative, optimism-pessimism.

Few are able to suffer the solitary hardness and ambiguous confusion of a long age of transition—no one is able to endure it—because to want to "get over" it by means of some expedient would indeed be a flight from it.

23

Language.—Not all linguistic usage is the same. There is the ordinary use of language which, as ordinary, dominates everydayness; and then there is the concealed lawfulness of words, which has arisen out of the history of beyng.

For questioners, the public "linguistic usage," especially that of an era which has lost all reverence for words and can no longer by its own means regain such reverence, *never constitutes what is primarily binding.*
27   Questioners I must first be compelled back into the essentiality of words, must create language before it is again taken up into "usage."

If, for instance, one understands "activity" [*Betrieb*] merely as "bustling about" [*Betriebsamkeit*], and the word can be taken thus, then one has renounced meditation on why there is such "activity," where it has the ground of its essence, and how the distorted essence might not in the end be essential for a determinate essence. Why should words not also retain their essential weight, so that something meditative would enter into their employment and above all into what they designate? Since we move too much in the domain of calculation, we demand univocity of linguistic usage in the sense of something "standardized"; we believe we can exploit the purity and "assets" of language, and we fail to recognize that its essence is abyssal and demands a very free and superior relation to it.

Why do the French have an academically governed language?

24

The *"negative."* The greatest, closest at hand, and easiest misinterpre-
28   tation looms over all thoughtful negation, which is taken as I mere rejection and prohibition, if indeed not as an expression of irritation and exasperation.

In truth, negation is the battle over the most essential affirmation of the full essence of beyng and is the attempt to extricate oneself from what is the most "oppositional" (as it may seem) into something other and "positive." This is so because everything positive, if stated immediately and hardened into a doctrine, is misinterpreted a fortiori—not only that, but even it itself most tenaciously contributes to the misinterpretation of beyng. The most trenchant mark of the usual misinterpretation of the thoughtful "not" and "no" is the way every saying of "nothingness" is misused; i.e., "nihilism" is devalued as merely "negative," rather than at least being grasped "positively."

25

"Spiritual education," if there is such, can aim only at awakening humans and gathering them up, *as* awakened, so that they are able to make *demands* and are able to do nothing else. Demands arise from a claim—but toward what must a claim extend in order to actually demand a demand, i.e., *excessively* demand it? And from where is the claim supposed to come, if not out of rootedness in an essential plight? But where are the | *creators of plight* in this age? Must not an "educa-   29 tion" aiming at such a thing appear to the age as nonsense incarnate? Certainly; but that is not a reason to be indignant against the age. On the contrary—in this situation, which is perhaps already a dire situa- tion or the first gleaming of one, we must meditate on the fact that "education" is already familiar to us only in the form of the age and must become a failure to those who create a plight, a failure that de- velops immediately in institutions and makes us precisely unfit to un- dergo the plight.

26

Do claims arise out of *importunities*? But who are the importunate ones? What courage must first come to the spirit if the bloodline is still supposed to flow and the flow is to have a direction and the di- rection a power to configure space?

The courage for the truth of beyng—, the courage for what is most question-worthy—for the experience that beyng itself is the appro- priating eventuation—the importunity itself does not come from hu- mans but toward them, provided they find their way out of this en- tanglement in subjectivity.

But that cannot be compelled—even education is | too weak for it.   30 Only this remains: to extricate oneself into beyng, to point, with the least obtrusiveness, toward the history of beyng, indeed in general only to extricate oneself into *history*.

27

If the *human being* posits himself as subjectum but does not grasp the subject in terms of subjectivity (self-consciousness) and finally re- nounces *unfolding this* (cf. the course of German Idealism), if a subjec- tum is taken only to be something extant as present-at-hand, and if this that is present-at-hand is understood "biologically," and if the bio- logical is "concentrated" only on blood as what is genuinely present- at-hand, and if this that is genuinely present-at-hand becomes the genuine bearer of heredity and of "history," then all this is perhaps very comprehensible and even new for a thinking that now becomes ever cruder and more extrinsic. But what is more decisive about this interpretation of the subject is the peculiar "decisiveness" with which the human being is here set out into a mere extrinsic presence at hand

and the way that that step taken by Descartes, who *never asks* about
the truth (meaning) of the *sum qua esse* ["the 'I am' as being"], is made
31   definitive and the very forgottenness of being remains in forgottenness (cf. p. 57). But from here—where all this has come into its appropriate greatness as gigantism—how is any favor to be accorded
even only to the presentiment that the human being could and should
be transformed and that this transformation must come from beyng
itself and *therefore* must affect the human being not merely *as* a being
but *in* his beyng? This concealed humanity possesses its ground and
essence in the unique circumstance that humanity in itself has *to be*
the grounding of the truth of beyng. How empty, abstract, and unreal
must "beyng" sound over and against that presence at hand of "blood."
How far from beyng is the human being as subject—*as* relational
center for all beings—so far that the human being cannot any longer
know his own origination as subject and above all *cannot want* to know
it, and so far that this sovereignty of the subjectum arose on the basis
of a not yet concluded history of beyng, in which φύσις ["nature," "the
self-emergent"] allows its counteressence of "machination" to pre-
dominate. Anthropology is the preventive measure instituted by
32   modern humanity in consequence of which the human being arrives
at *not* wanting to know who he is. Yet this not-wanting takes the form
of believing it has already recognized what humanity is and what arrangements might preserve humanity as this humanity for "eternity."
There must be one person who has contemplated the gigantism of this
self-sequestration of humans against themselves and against every interrogative struggle over their essence in all the directions of that
struggle, in order to be overtaken by the assault of what is un-
German or not even related to the German. Such an assault comes to
a head in this improper conception of the human being as subject and
furthermore in the form that this is understood precisely as what is
most German.

28

We have been talking much in recent years about the doom of "intellectualism" and about the harms semi-refinement has wreaked on
the spirit of our people. The possibility of an anthropological way of
thinking of the characterized kind is in fact the strongest proof for
the "rightfully" maintained supremacy of semi-refinement, of the inability to think any more and of the unwillingness to question any
more, and for the ignorance regarding how much the Germans still
"actually" think.

29   33

Knowledge and action.—Let it be conceded that thinking can by itself "effectuate" nothing immediately, especially if "effectuation" and "reality" are gauged according to the number and extent of changes in what is present-at-hand. Let it be admitted that we need those who act. But let us also for a moment meditate on what a *lack* of thought and knowledge *effectuates; these* "effects" are still more gigantic than all the results of action, and they are also more necessary, if indeed the essence of modernity cannot avoid its consummation and must even maintain a "greatness" in this consummation.

All such "ponderings" *never* have the aim of simply establishing "states of affairs," of looking on the "dark side," or even of "criticizing," without being able to commend an effective means of change. Instead, the point is always only to *think out* from the reference to what is closest, out into beyng itself and its simple basic movement. In turn, the purpose of that is not to acquire a mere "metaphysical" *insight* instead of insight bearing on the critique of culture. To the contrary, the goal is always *meditation*—the self-transposing of humanity into the domain of the truth of beyng—which means: exposure to the plight and to the need of a transformation, one which is already older than all historiological | incidents and also younger than the newest achieve-   34 ments. For, *this* transformation of the human being from subject to the grounder and steward of Da-sein is the necessity of beyng itself— and that has always required such a transformation, because beyng in itself is only the "between" in whose openness the gods and humans become recognizable to one another and fitted together in order to raise up beings as a whole to the glory of the god and at the hazard of the human being.

In *which* basic movement of beyng does our—historiologically unrecognized—history vibrate? What is modernity itself in the short span of Western history with its few simple thrusts of beyng? Is modernity the liberation of the *distorted essence* of beyng (the liberation of the machination arising out of this distorted essence) into the affiliation with the essence of beyng? And if this essence—thus consummated in its first beginning—will launch the *other* beginning, in whose course the simplicity and stillness of beyng first create an excess of appurtenance *to the struggle* over the gods and humans, in the age of which not only are the *old* tables of "values" smashed, but so   35 are all the "new" ones, because the wretchedness of "values" | no longer finds shelter in the spatiotemporal field of the truth of beyng— then this, by refusing itself (as the event of appropriation) in the abyss of its intimacy, bestows itself into its essence which is older than its first essence. Let us learn thereby that the basic movement of beyng (a movement which trembles qua modernity) is *de-divinization:* the unfolding all the way to the end and the entrenchment of decisionlessness about the god.

A *god* is only the one and the ones that tear humans away from "beings" and that compel beyng as the "between" for themselves and for humans—those gods that must have first arrived if a people is to find its essence.

But the god is never an "object" of Christian tactics or of political expedients or of "incantations" drunk on "lived experiences," incantations in which such "objects" could perhaps become "perceptible."

30

Modernity—the age that is more and more sure of its essence the more exclusively it thinks only of what it does. But "it does" only what the fullness of subjectivity must do—preserve itself in meditationlessness—perhaps l to the point of self-destruction. Meditationlessness, however, is not mere blindness; on the contrary, it is gigantism in calculation, and precisely that is what requires gigantism in the unleashing of the drives to violence and to destruction.

31

Philosophy—perhaps we have already been too long and too exclusively accustomed to seeking and finding, in what is said and accomplished and thus publicly produced, the unconcealing of what is concealed. And perhaps that is why our claims on the concealed and ultimately on the height and essence of concealedness are very ordinary, superficial, and crude. How could we then still be surprised if humans know little of the event of reticence and above all want to know nothing of it? They had to encounter here a power which has long since convulsed their everyday activity and security without acquainting them about it. Yet there could come into history a moment which required of humans a few who expressly carry out this reticence—even if only for an instant, in order to procure for history a now necessary transition. It could l be that humans would for a time even need to involve themselves in a knowledge of this moment and, unified with that, in the renunciation of "deliberately" (and with the assistance of definite measures) arranging and compelling the impending transition according to what dominates as ordinary. Admittedly—when and where are to be found those who are clear enough

in their essence and strong enough in their anticipatory volition in order to carry out that deliberate renunciation even only for a while—for so long that the possibility of a tradition of carrying this out is grounded along with a generation of concealed stewards of the stillness? In the sphere of these necessities, thinkers must think ahead all the way to the ground of the decision on silence and on the acceptance of the insidious ambiguity of such silence (which seems to be exasperation, or anxiety in the face of expressing oneself, or the consequence of "foundering," or a sign of arrogance—and what it *is* cannot be known, unless one were compelled to it oneself and had to become someone necessary). But this silence—not at all equivalent to going "unpublished"—can indeed have power into the future, provided the domain of history is not definitively obstructed on account of humans no longer receiving the call to make themselves at home in the I abyss. For, the few great transformations of history occur only   38
in the respective brief clearings of the simplicity of beyng, and beyng, due to its uniqueness, ever again requires an overcoming of dammed-up beings and only seldom finds among humans an audience for this requirement.

In this *absence* of the thrusts of being, there arises the possibility of what is insistent, loud, and usual about the beings taken as "extant"—i.e., taken as "history," ordinarily so called. If now a people (one which, like the Germans, has an extraordinary mission in relation to the saving of the truth of beyng) sets out to make what is most ordinary the law of its "life" and completely repudiates its destiny—or, more clearly, renounces the struggle over that destiny—then this process itself is *so* unusual that meditation must tarry here and must ask whether something necessary is not happening. Meditation must do so because those who are offered something essential must along with this distinction also take on the unusualness of a collapse and of errancy. Then the one thing can no longer be avoided, namely, that the human being awaken for the still-concealed essence of I history, which   39
essence now appears to be overpowered in the collision with the superior force of historiology in the broadest sense. History will never be saved by caring about perpetuation and the "future," i.e., the mere continuance of what was hitherto, which is precisely where progress belongs. History is saved only if the *"saving"* is in itself the creative justification of what is still ungrounded—i.e., only if the *truth* of beyng co-configures the *essence* of history and the *knowledge* of that essence.

The assault (ever attempted anew in long endeavors) of innermost thinking, to allow the truth of beyng for the first time to become necessary merely as a question and to become compelling in its necessity, gives the few attempts to say something about it an "intrinsic" stamp which can never be pursued and traced in an utterance.

Perhaps the conclusion ought to be that the stillness of the history of beyng must remain something merely surmised. But that which in this way appears insecure to our *calculation* is in itself the unshakable abyss of something simple: the fact that at times beyng lets a god come to be and casts the human being into the trembling of this coming to be, whereby the human being might recollect beings in their onto- logical truth (not in their most proximate and ever most proximate objectivity). Accordingly, we must experience the plainness of an ex- 40   tant thing in our unconcern | in order to surmise the keenness of a tumult of beyng—and we must perceive a last blowing out of this storm in order to find things entirely in their enclosed repose. We must abide at once in the storm and in repose and thus must be sober, in order to know the affiliation of each to the other as the echo of the truth of beyng.

32

"*Dialectics.*"—It became dominant for the first time, and not acciden- tally, ever since Plato grasped beingness as ἰδέα ["idea," "that which is most properly seen"]. Heraclitus and Parmenides do precisely *not* know "dialectics"; if we "read" them in that way, we are merely fol- lowing the Platonic and then the Hegelian interpretation. The effect of "dialectics" on ordinary opinion and speech consists in our be- coming less and less capable of carrying out, or of even knowing in advance, what dialectics precisely seems to accomplish: *the overcoming of oppositions*. The dialectical overcoming is insidious in that it is pre- cisely compelled back *into* the oppositions and their entrenchment (all dialectics "lives" on that) and precisely does not ask whether that which bears an opposition might not be of a completely different es- sence and be the origin of oppositionality only as the oppositionality of representation. Dialectics is the constant compulsion of the prin- 41   ciple excluding the thinking of the | (represented) beingness of beings from the truth of beyng. The overcoming of oppositions qua sublation serves to secure the pre-posited *unity*—out of *this* and for its sake, ev- ery step must be thought out.

This "unity" is that of the "system" and *as* system. Genuine dia- lectics becomes possible only in modernity and more precisely only after Kant—by way of insight into the "transcendental"—grasped *sub- jectivity* and thus also the representational relation to the object such that now the subjectum itself could *essentially* enter into the dialectical movement, specifically so that *this* movement unfolded subjectivity in its absoluteness.

German Idealism carried out "movements" of thought, ones we still do not grasp in their uniqueness for the history of being since we see them as a simple whole on the basis of the modern interpretation of beings and truth. We must here await future thinkers who will creatively face this German assault on the whole of beings and will not remain held fast in historiological interpretation. Since thinkers had to be held fast in such interpretation hitherto, the age of German Idealism is now roundly condemned—apart from empty cultural-political veneration of it. The consequence is that | for some time a thought-   42
ful overcoming of "dialectics" on the basis of its greatest and most necessary forms will have no necessity. And that means: the essence of modernity is hardening itself in the absence of this necessity. Yet such hardening is the retardation of the history of being and of the decisions of that history. And this retardation—what if it were a—premature and unrecognized—form in which the truth of beyng—the truth of the self-refusal—announced itself?

33

After Hölderlin and after Nietzsche, there is no more poetizing among the Germans, and no more thinking, which essentially—as grounding history—could be a revolt against God if thereby the last power of the last decisions is not risked. But on that account even the avoidance of these decisions and thus the suppression of poetry and thinking will become a habit, indeed even a required institution.

And when we speak of "solitude" we still all too readily place back into the familiar and usual the only poets and thinkers who will matter in the future, as if they merely stood out from the familiar and usual, whereas they are inserted into a history, one in which not only is there a struggle "over" | something (over the common good *ahead of*   43
the individual good, over the preservation of the "substance" of the populace, etc.) but in which the *struggle* over the most concealed essence of the Germans is itself grappled up to that which is to be struggled *for*. But *this struggle over the struggle for the essence* is not the exaggeration and complication of an egoism that is grinding itself down; on the contrary, it is a reversion to the constant simplicity and broadly anticipatory repose in revering the still-concealed destiny. Therefore, risking oneself in this struggle possesses a restful clearness about oneself and about one's public inconspicuousness. Therefore, even those who are preparing for this struggle will experience nothing of it itself.

Therefore, from every side they will be denied every concurrence—even only as an apparent help. Therefore, a few—nowhere registered—must risk themselves for the last decisions of questioning—they must not merely fall out from their times—which, in view of today's cleverness in the historiological disposal of all mixed cuisines, is not difficult—but, above all, they must not fall into their times. If they succeed in this that is most difficult, then they have thereby become ones who indeed *are* "*there*," even if they cannot be identified. And *they* will "encounter" only those who are capable of the *same,* namely, being "there." And this "encounter" | will be not a resting in the reciprocally bestowable present time but, rather, a calling to oneself out into the future, a passing by on the paths of the history of beyng, and such a history reaches far back.

44

34

If the essence of the Germans requires of them a struggle over their essence, and if this struggle therefore itself must first be *gained* in a struggle and not merely struggled through, then what sort of madness is smirking out of the now instituted educational procedure according to which the only poets who may be read in a "German lesson" are those who have essentially promoted "ethnicity" ["*Volkstum*"]? Which of us will then presume, in a "time" that is so confused, to settle for "all eternity" what is German and what is a people and do so at a time which is perhaps itself only the consequence of an essential misunderstanding of what is German, a misunderstanding due to nationalism? And even if one could say something about the German essence, how can one pretend to have grasped the entire essence? Whence this raving blindness which now sets about spoiling the most concealed German possessions? Why must in this way all education become immediately a mutilation of the essence? It is because the moment of history has still not | been grasped, since the present is eternalized and history is disavowed.

45

35

People?—Is that a community of "blood," of "fate," of "work," of "disposition"? How and why blood, fate, work, disposition—unless the human being is taken as subjectum and unless this present-at-hand thing is parceled out into bodily, psychic, and spiritual properties, with a view to make the human being himself and his preservation the goal and thereby to grant all these properties the same weight?

Is this then not the "masses"—raised to "personality"—and the condition—scarcely thought and grasped—posited as the unconditioned? Is everything not all too easy, because it has selected for itself an inferior opponent? Does it not border on doom, because it is in part "meant" well and in the best possible way? But can it be avoided as long we persist on the edge of a-historicality?

36

Kant—he must certainly be stricken from the history of the Germans—for what did he accomplish on behalf of the "ethnicity"? Even if we credit him with the "categorical imperative" and its "national" amplitude, | he still thinks this imperative in terms of "humanity"   46 rather than ethnically. Wherefore still Kant? Wherefore still "thinkers" at all, except to mention them at cultural-political rallies, so that one does not expose oneself to ridicule?

But, seriously—wherefore still Kant? For the sake of the intellectual exercise involved in reading his works? For the sake of demonstrating historiologically that there was once this work among the Germans and that it had a "historical" effect on the subsequent centuries? Yet how inconsequential is all this—or, despite everything, does there still happen in this work something futural, something so "present" that it concerns the current present time in the latter's concealed essence? Insight into the *transcendental* subjectivity of the subject— is that not an essential step by which the *subject* as such is set forth more profoundly and thus more ominously and thus more intensely? Does this thinking not make visible a domain which the overcoming of modernity must still traverse explicitly, if this age is not to perish through blind self-mutilation?

Wherefore still Kant? As *one* still untrodden path in order to keep meditation on modern humanity at the correct depth? For only through | Kant—is there prepared the longest still unexhausted pos-   47 sibility—to keep the conception of the subjectivity of the subject far from the cruder mistakes of psychological and biological interpretations—i.e., to set anthropology back into a metaphysical plane on which the confrontation with it first becomes difficult and thus first becomes a struggle. But the latter must arrive, because struggle is the only form in which we find ourselves in our essence and because this struggle must be a struggle of meditation.

Why therefore Kant? Because he is a German thinker who in the most German way thought of "humanness" as Western—i.e., in his sense, thought of the essence of the human being? Why therefore

Kant? Because he is an impetus in our history, one of those thrusts which first gather their power when they come to strike—which first return to their uniqueness historically and more richly, the less they are made "relevant to the present"—for some short-sighted present—in this or that way—in being utilized or in being rejected.

37

The *contemporary* opponents of an epoch always gaze only into the past and yet behave like successors. But the coming future of the | West is grounded not through them, who are opponents only of what is at hand, but through those who become *resisters* in the collision of the thrusts arriving one day out of a convulsion of beyng. The thrusts need resistance in order to pull themselves together in their highest power and in that way to conquer. These resisters must be steadfast *in* their time outside of this time. And they must be able to endure being taken for mere opponents, who indeed are of the same kind as those they are taken for. And the error is complete when the resisters have the opponents as their "followers." But the resisters must also already know whence the thrust of beyng will come to them; they must foster a preparedness for the truth of beyng. And this truth itself having thus remained unfamiliar, they must first disclosively question the truth.

48

A great errancy will have to arrive in order to create a space against what is flat and spaceless. Only the *errant* ones, who leave all correctness and incorrectness equidistantly behind, may traverse the spatiotemporal field of beyng with the passion, constancy, and decisiveness required | so that a clearing might come to beyng at all. In this clearing, beyng openly refuses itself and thus, through this thrust of self-withdrawal, impels the creative ones to the place where to them beings emerge as the preservation of beyng. So that beings might become this preservation, the truth of beyng must find a grounding. So that this finding might occur, there must be the errancy which is kindled out of the burning hearts of the errant ones and which gleams precisely in the guise of night. How should the new day arrive, if the night is withheld from it and everything is suppressed into the twilight of decisionlessness? It remains undecided whether this twilight is the one of the evening or of the morning, but this twilight all the more eagerly poses as the light pure and simple, in which each understands each and by which all are made familiar with all.

49

38

The sharpest opposition seems to have the greatest power of over-coming, and such oppositions are given to expressing themselves in an "antithesis." But opposition is never that which overcomes; everyone who overcomes must have first overcome the opposition it-self. For he will understand that "antitheses" necessarily fall short of what I he alone can strive for. The question of the truth of beyng is   50 never and never will be the "antithesis" to the question of the entire metaphysics of the West: what are beings? It is rather so originarily *different* that it can no longer stand "against" metaphysics but instead stands *"for"* it, although not in immediate affirmation but in virtue of a transformation into a simpler necessity. "Antitheses" *can* therefore say essentially more than they seem to say; that holds for broad stretches of the thinking Nietzsche carried out, although he remained caught in an "inversion."

39

The *"philosophy of existence"* is a modern philosophy which does not grasp the "subjectum" "ethically" as mere "personality" but does place all science and likewise all metaphysics (although in different ways) in the service of an "appeal" to the "subject"—the required "commu-nication" merely confirms this "subjectivism." Without actually knowing it, the "philosophy of existence," in its conception of "sci-ence" and of "metaphysics," drives the *representational* relations to be-ings into an extreme and brings everything into a state of suspense that can be saved only in the "encompassing." The I "existential ana-   51 lytic" of Da-sein, carried out in the context of the *question of being,* de-termines "existence" on the basis of *Da-sein* and in no way determines the human being as subject through existence—that should be clear to anyone who has sought to ask the question of being and has not merely clung to the word "existence." The *ecstatic* character assigned to everything "existential" makes radically impossible any conjunc-tion of this "existential analytic" (which pertains only to the question of being) with the essentially subjectivistic "clarification of existence." But how often today does not the impossible become possible! The "philosophy of existence," whose genuine form has been attained only by Jaspers, must be immediately recognized in various respects as modern.

Already the articulations of its "systematics," which basically be-comes the Kantian one, along with the mid-position of existence or of the "clarification of existence," characterize the fundamental atti-tude. Since in no fundamental attitude of modern philosophy can his-tory become the essence of thinking, therefore historiology must ful-fill the systematics and lead to the greatest possible manifold of historiological-psychological treatments of the previous tradition of thinking. The encompassing in all these "philosophies" derives not from an extrinsic goal | of completeness, but from the deeply hidden historical undecidedness as regards the essential questions and their history. The character of such thinking requires a compromise with the past, and that signifies a dissolution of itself, provided in general a proper core did develop into a formative power.

52

40

Nietzsche's solitude.—How one takes and judges this solitude is a touch-stone for the character and depth of one's grasp of Nietzsche's ques-tions. We are inclined to see in this solitude a withdrawal from the contemporary public domain, in the sense that Nietzsche could not feel at home in it. We also appeal to the notorious incomprehension on the part of his contemporaries to help explain an "extreme" case. But this solitude—even though it is not as originary as Hölderlin's—which is why, seen externally, it appears milder—is of a completely different provenance. This solitude must remain foreign to us as a first illumination of the approach of thinking into the domain of beyng—the fact that to it was attached an excessive form of human and per-sonal isolation, i.e., apartness, | is only the consequence of that orig-inary *solitude toward being. This* solitude is a counterintimation of the uniqueness of beyng.

53

41

Meditation—does not simply mean any sort of reflection or reflected-ness and certainly not the entertaining of misgivings; on the contrary, it is the leap ahead into the truth of beyng. This essence of meditation is uncommonly similar to the uniqueness of the moment of medita-tion. But meditation is easily mistaken as a mere description of the "present situation" or as readily leading precisely those who are se-rious into a "pessimistic" mood. Already because, as a questioning, it disturbs our rest, places us before something insurmountable, and requires a transition—and ultimately, despite all this, appears to be uncreative—meditation then seems something we should root out, not cultivate.

Yet now since above all the distorted essence is taken negatively and everything empty is taken as a nullity, and since we are too small and too poor in resistance to experience therein—in what is apparently mere negation—the self-refusal and to grasp this itself as beyng and raise it up into knowledge, therefore in the age of de-divinization and of undecidedness those who meditate do in fact seem to be deformers and underminers, and their nearness to beyng remains hidden.

42

54

Simplicity and solitude.—Solitude, in the way that it is not a consequence but a ground, does not individuate and does not communalize; instead, it grounds and bears the affiliation to beyng. And therefore solitude is the precondition for being struck by simplicity and for making visible its law.

Simplicity tolerates no historiological calculation and comparison.

Simplicity renounces the encompassing.

Simplicity is quite inexhaustible and thus requires what is most difficult: the capacity to turn back to oneself.

Simplicity can never "simply" be found in beings, but rather is the sudden bestowal of those unrecognizable bestowers that, as the errant, resistant, and steadfast ones who create a plight, have long enough and in a confused way prepared the stewardship for beyng. (Cf. Ponderings VIII, p. 38.)

43

History—who could decide whether the truth of beyng does not hide itself merely to a few concealed ones and like a forlorn gust of wind in a lonely valley blows about over the earth and for a moment lets all affiliation eventuate and lets the god be recollected by humans and humans be needed by the god?

If the *claim of humans*—the still undecided and ungrounded stewards of the truth of beyng—*on beyng itself* were not to be fulfilled so basely and pettily and thus so easily and cheaply in each case by beings, if the struggle over the truth of beyng were a fire and not a forlorn spark of a yet hidden ember, if the human being were not shielded from beyng by beings and by what to him count as beings, then the human being would have already long ago struggled up to a height of the all-consuming downgoing. Instead, we find the prospect of a more

55

and more secured duration and monotony of human claims and human goallessness.

The constant external threat, which has long since instituted itself into the gigantic as regards economics and war, does not speak against this duration. On the contrary, "catastrophes" of *this* kind, self-abradings of states and peoples, are merely a transitional form in the continuance of what is still left over and is ever smaller, namely, the ever more comprehensive, open, and covert "hostility" of all against all in the beings and protections of the *same* institutions and with the means of the *same* measures. All of this indicates that the genuine struggles over beyng are more and more disappearing as possibilities and that only | oppositions within beings maintain the upper hand and claim for themselves the essence of "struggle" (p. 125). Indeed this goalless reciprocal abrasion is becoming the basic form in which the claim of humans on beings is made valid and is even fulfilled. *Beyng*—i.e., always the appropriation of humans as ones who ground truth in the passing by of the god—remains so originarily refused to the human being that he never succeeds in knowing this refusal and totters in machination as the distorted essence of beyng, since machination becomes for him everywhere the organization of his "lived experience." But what does it signify that the human being—appertaining to beyng—more and more retracts his claim on beyng? Must he be driven to this, the more unconditionally he makes himself the center of beings? If yes, then why is this so? The human being as the *center of the lived experience* of beings as a whole behaves as this central being for beyng—and indeed does so all the more unconditionally, the less the individual takes himself as an individual and the more the commonality of his community moves into the sphere of what is immediately intelligible and constantly (and without meditation) remains close to him in everyday doings and undergoings (work—results—pleasure—birth—death—everything on the plane of everyday | lived experiences and thus as the course of the stream of life, a course that reifies itself in the "bloodstream" and therein makes itself still more graspable and more real).

Humanity as race and as breeding stock can claim to be what of all beings is most a being and can prove this claim / in the sphere of its intelligibility / at any time as correct (cf. above, p. 38f.). This correctness is the "guarantor" of the "truth" of all beings thereby determined and available to lived experience and thus is itself *the* true being pure and simple—and accordingly is "being" ["*das Sein*"]. Not only does the human being as human being, *animal rationale,* become the *subiectum* [*Subjectum*] of all beings, but within the subjectum [*Subjektum*] the *animal* is again declared the proper *subiectum* of the subject. Thereby an extreme form of "subjectivism" (metaphysically understood) is attained, a form which can be completely dissociated from "egoic-egotistic" subjectivism and can struggle against it, but which nevertheless not only permits, but even requires, the "subjectivism" of communal "lived experience." Now for the first time "subjectivism" is on all sides complete and round, and only in this roundness of the subjectum can the human being without resistance start rolling and from "within" set himself rolling—specifically such that the question of *whither* he I is rolling has lost all meaning for the one who is rolling. The subjectum is for itself its own unique space and time—this unconditionality is expressed by the subjectum declaring itself to be "eternal."

This "subjectivism" is intrinsically connected to the one of German Idealism. And German Idealism has already pressed on to the unconditionality of the subject—but has sought this unconditionality in reason (spirit) as absolute self-consciousness. *One* counterpart to this unilateralness is Marxism, which makes "matter"—the sensuous (the immediate)—absolute. The other counterpart springs from opposition to both Marxism and spiritualism. This one makes the body and blood the absolute *subiectum*—but in such a way that it now attempts at the same time to sublate the previous unilateralness and draws an arc from the voice of blood and of the necessity of breeding all the way to "lived experience" and to the community of breeding stock.

As soon as we consider the subjectivity of (modern) humanity the most intrinsic historical force, we will not fall victim to the superficiality of seeing in the just-indicated development of absolute subjectivism merely an artificial "dialectic" or even merely the pressing forward of some accidental "worldviews."

What arises in this development of the unconditional subjectivism of a racial people or of a racial struggle and properly drives and bears this subjectivism is most assuredly *not* a *creative* upsurge of *self-transforming* humanity, but rather is the force of pressure of the powers which drag down in present-at-hand humans who are arranging for what is present-at-hand about them. This "dragging down" is here meant only *metaphysically*, not as a moral or "cultural" evaluation.

The human being presses into domains in which his urges and passions can unfold as such. But this does not mean licentiousness becomes his law. On the contrary, there arise quite new drastic forms of "discipline" which at the same time in other respects do not exclude complete unruliness, especially since these forms no longer feel this unruliness as such.

There always remains, precisely in such stages of development, the likelihood of "regressions," namely, that the past might seize upon

what is pressing forward, and *thus the retardation of the history of modernity, despite all the increasing velocities, might become ever greater, the stagnation more insistent, and the endurance of this mixture of all possibilities of subjectivism ever surer.* Only when we begin to understand, as regards
60 *this* dominance of the subjectum, | how the subject, as center of beings, brings itself so to speak completely before beyng and before the truth of beyng—only then will we be able to know the plight into which humans must first be thrown in order to find themselves in their essence—namely, their stewardship over the truth of beyng.

44

After Hegel's great "logic,"[12] any sort of "theory of categories" is for all relatively well-prepared scholars in philosophy only a matter of diligence and of cleverness in devising variations. To be sure, an essential difference remains and cannot be sublated: for Hegel, this "logic" *has* its absolute metaphysical ground and *is* this ground itself in the whole of the Western history of metaphysics. All later theories of categories, theories believing they can strip away absolute idealism as an antiquated scaffolding in order then to retain the "categories in themselves," like nuts for cracking, are perhaps "more correct" and "more complete," but for that very reason are also philosophically without necessity and without truth.

It is to be expected that philosophical erudition, on account of increasing anxiety in the face of philosophy and from its own predilection for what is as benign as possible, will devote itself even more eagerly than before to the drawing up of "theories of categories."
61 Philosophical erudition takes its "necessity" from | what is present-at-hand—historiologically transmitted—about "philosophy" and about what goes under this name. All accomplishments are appraised through incorporation into what is present-at-hand "about philosophy"—by good fortune, *there is* precisely this sphere of spiritual occupation and of eagerness. And one is not supposed to know anything here of the "justification" of philosophy itself.

It is easy to understand the reckoning which takes the following line: today "we" (who?) have no creative philosophy and must resign ourselves to that; but we can indeed, through steady spadework, establish a certain level and awaken interest, such that then, out of this best possible average of what has been handed down by the historiology of philosophy, one day creative thinkers might again come forth.

---

12. {Georg Wilhelm Friedrich Hegel, *Wissenschaft der Logik*, erster und zweiter Teil. (Leipzig: Meiner, 1923).}

At work here once more is the usual mistaken inference according to which the best possible average ensures the highest possible "peak performance." The opposite is the case, quite apart from the fact that philosophical erudition never produces philosophy *if* the latter does not already originate elsewhere. This "if" is completely unavailable to traditional philosophy—in the sense of historiological learning. The latter *can* be very essential—but only provided thoughtful questioning has already arisen. And that? It is decided in beyng itself.

45

All well-intentioned "apologetics" *for* "philosophy" which seek to demonstrate how pressing is our *need* for philosophical "education" everywhere in "science" and in the clarification of a "worldview" are doing a disservice to *philosophy*—because indeed every "service" done for it is a disservice. "Philosophy" does not belong within the purview of service and serviceability. One is defending here something one neither "possesses" nor knows, and with the best intention one is adding to the confusion, for the decisions now lie elsewhere, not in the deliberations over measures within strictly organized cultural activities. The proper mistakes are rooted in an inability to recognize the domains in which the decisions belong. Thus here: not whether in a "cultural" respect "philosophy" is needed or not, whether for this purpose it is required in one way or must be pursued in a different way—instead: whether "culture" still has a futural sense at all, whether philosophy belongs to "culture" at all, rather than already intrinsically disavowing the essence of "culture," i.e., simply passing it by.

Consequently, what is essential even to this pondering over "philosophy" is not to figure out and propose a way to rescue its sinking prestige—but rather | to recognize how completely in this very domain—where indeed the "whole" is supposed to be thought—every opinion is already ruled by a misunderstanding (indeed altogether by a lack of any understanding) of the domains of decision and of what it means to meditate on them. This is a process whose ramifications no one can yet survey. To know of this process, however, means to be ready for appearances which are bathed in a gigantic—i.e., almost unrecognizable—ambiguity. Thus, alongside the crude repudiation of all philosophy, there could emerge endeavors which might amount to a renewal of philosophy and to an "ascent" of "philosophical" interest. Yet it would still be an illusion—indeed not an accidental one, but a necessary provision in the service of the *retardation of all decisions*—to believe that only in consideration of this event in the history of being does meditation on the variegated and neglected activity of philosophical erudition have impelling power. And those who take part in such activity have the most difficult access to this meditation—it is *even unnecessary* for them—since they are to remain tranquilly what they appear to be and are to carry out their "function" as well as can be and thereby become an "expression" of their times, which indeed

64   is the highest that can be attained according to the standards I of modernity.

A history of humans will of course arrive, provided they are once again thrown into history, where the "expressions" of an age have become quite inconsequential because everything expressed is for its part no longer capable of giving anything and justifies itself only subsequently as an appendage. But if *to be an expression* poses as the "principle" of configuration, then it is already proven that somewhere or other emptiness—specifically in the form of decisionlessness—has become *generative*. In this situation, humans then have their reasons to veil their impotence in the semblance of the opposite. Humans of the modern age will now wander ever more often in the marginal domains of this situation. The inconsequential incidents of such secondary domains, wherein even "philosophy" moves, are nevertheless mostly sharper indications of the genuine concealed history than are any sort of incidents of the "day" that produce a sensation; for the latter are not only "redacted" four or five times before they receive their public aspect—they are above all in themselves only semblantly transparent to the ones who partake of them—and are basically already immeasurably meaningless—and with their help the human masses

65   everywhere receive for a time their small and I brief troubles and amusements.

46

The necessity of philosophy—appropriate to the essence of philosophy is only that thoughtful questioning which ever out of itself newly makes philosophy necessary in a novel—unusual—necessity and thus never appeals to the presence at hand of philosophy and of its "history" but instead calls philosophy originally into beings. This holds primarily of the other beginning; yet is this beginning not what it is in virtue of its opposition to the first beginning? Is not here—if anywhere— the necessity of philosophy historically proven? Historically yes—but not historiologically; yet "historically" means: the essence of history is itself newly determined (on the basis of the event) through inceptual questioning in the other beginning. The other beginning indeed *follows*—historiologically calculated—upon the first; but historically it is only through the *other* beginning that the "first" *becomes* the first.

What nevertheless here seems to be torn apart is in itself the *same*: the question of being in the form of the first beginning and in the form of the other beginning.

The question—of the truth of beyng—passes over any determining of beings in their distinctiveness—but *Da-sein*? Da-sein is precisely not a being, and humans first come to be on its basis—Da-*sein* the unsupported and unguarded—the productive leap of the "between"— | here the plight of beyng as event of appropriation is compelling—in   66 Da-*sein* for the first time the essence of beyng opens up—otherwise the history of the first beginning would never come into the open; never could beingness be disclosed as constancy and presence, and the latter as "time," unless a first clearing of the "there" were grounded in Da-*sein*.

But—here also is the moment of greatest danger—that this grounding might expand into a doctrine and lose every power of carrying out a grounding—a power which the grounding preserves only if the thrusts of the grounding are able to create for themselves their own history. Yet how long already have the ones who first prepare been settled in their abode—where indeed they still could say—that is, name—poetically what they saw coming and *what therefore* still is *coming*—without their finding what was coming *toward* them as the future.

47

History—if a clearing track of beyng shoots through beings and if this track in its obliteration remains there imperceptibly, so as always to offer beings an errancy and a wide space for humans to feel at home, humans who in flight from their essence place beings before beyng and thereby gain temporary satisfaction. Historiology and all | remem-   67 brance move in the obliterated tracks of beyng, without ever recognizing them as such. If humans would once have to watch over a still glowing track of beyng and promote beings through that track—then which collision would have to be there with which gods? History—the absence of beyng? (Cf. Ponderings VIII, p. 36.)

48

Plato's ἐκφανέστατον[13] ["that which most gleams forth"] is still the last dying illumination of the concealed glow of φύσις. All glow is dark. And if appearances give up this darkness, they then lose their ground

---

13. {Plato, *Phaedrus*, 250d.}

and in order to maintain their constancy must adhere to the causes and means of their production. The ἐκφανέστατον becomes the "sensuous." And now morals and science have their booty. The former distrusts the sensuous, the latter explains it. And the rescue of sensibility can then succeed only in a countermove against morals and science, i.e., in dependence on them, and the sensuous is then debased to merely "affirmed" "life" in itself, from which every echo of beyng has been stolen.—

And it is becoming difficult and ever more difficult—provided any attempts are still made—to overcome the deformations. Perhaps quite other modes and powers of the most intimate affiliation must awaken

68   first and seek their track, if the I human being is to find his way to Dasein and beyng is to become the hearth fire between earth and world. We turn aside all too readily into the customary, whose customariness we then mask from ourselves with the help of a worn-out ideal. And yet scattered here and there are the rare ones who surmise something else and who know only this is of help, not a return to what was.

Ever since φύσις was disempowered, all greatness in art has been confused and is becoming all the more confused as skill and ability are spreading and becoming more prevalent and historiological cognition is made easy to handle.

49

A question: to what extent does the historiology of art participate in the destruction of the history of art? Or does the historiology of art arise only when the inner destruction of the history of art has already commenced? In the nineteenth century, these "movements" appeared to be clearer—but how did matters stand previously? Since when is there *historiology*? Since the Church Fathers—i.e., since the end of Greek antiquity. Thucydides is not a "historiologist."

Everything extreme has its beginning in refusal and renunciation; these both swing over themselves in the I rarest assignment. In the

69   farthest remoteness lies the measureless proximity. This spatiotemporal field is the truth of beyng, as soon as beyng has become the event of the appropriation of Da-sein through the god.

50

Revolutions (p. 77)—are upheavals in something already present-at-hand but are never transformations into something completely other. They can prepare transformations but can also undermine them. The history of Western humanity is running on toward a point which can be crossed only by decisions whose type had to remain alien to the previous history (cf. "Of the Event—The Decisions"[14]).

The first and thus longest *decision* concerns the decisive itself: beyng. Whether the human being—appertaining to beings and since then constantly consigned to beyng—once will build his essence out of beyng itself and out of the grounding of its truth or whether the darkening of beyng will take its end through the instituting of beings *in* beings as producible, and the abandonment of beings by being, united to the forgottenness of being on the part of humanity, will bring about an end state. The uncanniness of this state consists not in monotony but in the endlessness of what is apparently ever new. Yet this | uncanniness can no longer be experienced as such, because the human being has come to be at home in everything—perhaps even in boredom itself, a boredom veiled to him primarily in the form of the highest activity and limitless use of all the means available to institute beings. Whoever thinks out to the extreme (and thus nearest) point of decision of history must have in view the possibility of this end of endlessness in the same, so as to know how little the upheavals are capable of here, since more and more they can only roll back into the past and into its already long since historiologically calculated tradition.

The first and longest decision must begin by separating that between which the highest decision must ground the space providing its interval and its field: beyng and beings. This decision would not be the longest and thus also the oldest, if it did not already come into the open in some form, even if disguised and concealed. Ultimately—grasped in the train of the previous (metaphysical) thinking—it is the "distinction" between being and beings (the ontological difference). What in this way seems reduced to the level of "logic" is in truth, however, already thought in the sense of the *projection* of Da-sein—which immediately | forbids considering the distincta (being and beings) as two representable objects and leaving them in the homogeneity of such objects.

In the ground-laying distinction lies a knowledge of the (obviously still unmastered) decision. That decision must—in the projection of beyng—decide *for* the *truth* of beyng against the priority of beings as regards the measure for the interpretation of beingness. Yet thereby the decision is not against beings; instead, merely a free domain is won for the question of how beings as a whole come to be on the basis of

70

71

---

14. {Martin Heidegger, *Beiträge zur Philosophie (Vom Ereignis)*, GA65 (Frankfurt: Klostermann, 1989), pp. 90–95.}

beyng and are vibrant therein. Indeed with this "question," which harbors the necessity of the sheltering of truth in beings, the space of the first decision is already again abandoned. The "between" for beyng and beings—; yet this "between" is not a third added on to the two distincta. Instead, because what is at issue here cannot be a mere differentiation and because beyng remains completely other than all beings, though at the same time their abyss, beyng itself is that *"between."* This is so true that it can still be grasped—perhaps first of all—in a remote consequence: only where beyng holds sway, is there "space" and "time," and a fortiori | only where beyng holds sway, is there that originary space-time, namely, the "between" which has chosen itself as beyng itself for truth (clearing of its own hiddenness). Through this first—and longest—decision, beyng itself is brought onto the "catastrophic" course of its history and becomes manifest in that history through this course; and "metaphysics" proves to be the opening move of the course of beyng.

72

51

Inasmuch as the essential happens in fundamentally different domains, *historical* knowledge in itself needs to be transformed. Therefore, historical meditation must preserve an inner freedom for the respective unique necessities. To a historiologist, everything proceeds on a few, ever interconnected levels. The historiologist counts on the explanatory *context;* the historical thinker seeks in each case—almost in a desultory way—the origins of what is necessary—he thinks in an apparently contextless way.

52

Hard by the edge of nihilation runs the way indicated by beyng for thinking. And if thinking is first assigned to the decision about beyng, and is so from afar by | beyng itself, then the moment must come in which truth itself demands the grounding of its essence. Here every support and protection will be denied—every foothold in beings disrupted, because a foothold is contrary to truth, which bursts open to the clearing in whose open realm, as in a still gaze, everything finds the preservation of its essence—becomes a being. But how long must the aloof genus of thinkers still search, in order to touch upon portions of *this way?*

73

Or is the history of thinking rather an eager and merry flight from this way and from the point of decision to which the way presses on?

53

The importance you place in beings is already determined by the sustenance deriving from the essence of truth. This sustenance is assigned to its affairs out of the vibrant power of beyng. But whence beyng, if no origin in beings satisfies it?

54

When movements are presumed to be the paradigms of history, the first result is ossification. What is ossified gives refuge to what is empty and evident—the evident I develops into the measure of the "simple."   74
And yet the simple is what is abstruse and withdrawn from all calculation—and hides more often than it offers itself.

55

Art—what is happening if art itself is made the object of a "festival" and this festival is "raised" to an institution? It is indubitable proof—perhaps already very superfluous—that art has come to an end—indeed must be at an end. How much more forcefully could still-concealed beyng manifest itself if we were already able to admit this end and see what it signifies—instead, we becloud the senses and the mind with "historiological" notions bearing no historical necessity and simply justifying historiologically that which is current as the youngest and newest historiological matter.

If a people can no longer celebrate its gods—but instead must encounter its "religion" as a "lived experience" in festivals instituted for that purpose, then even the de-divinization has withdrawn from this people, a people which is only the plaything of an untrammeled machination covered over by the fleeting exchange of one establishment for another.

56   75

In what way and with what aim may we today still think "about" the arts? By asking whether we must not venture—to be exposed once to "beings" *without* artistic activity and thereby raise to the light of meditation the superficiality of all "lived experiences" in their swagger and thus unmask, in his contingency and abandonment by any necessity, *everyone*—even the historiologist of art—who finds validation and an occupation in artistic activity. Should not *this* venture compel us into the nearness of beyng and make us place in question all cultural activity? In truth, this activity is striving for precisely what in its *own* manner a groundless "cultural Bolshevism" promotes and for what were once necessary *ways* to a determinate and delimited course that is called to a downgoing (i.e., called to greatness) but are now internally complete *goals* and *"values"* as occasions to withdraw from the historical decisions and simply make secure the human being as subjectum. Because the step toward this lies in the essence of modernity, though it was taken explicitly for the first time in the nineteenth century in the entire breadth of the *historiological* organization of history, there must arise—indeed very soon—a time I in which the twentieth century will have to resolve itself to defend precisely the nineteenth. Without this defense, the twentieth century would misinterpret and mistake its superficial organizations and projects.

76

Richard Wagner's *victory* in the twentieth century leads "compellingly" to a defense of the nineteenth, and this defense furnishes at the same time that which all historiological organization of history requires: a foil, a background, against which the proper "progress" is brandished.

57

Style (cf. Ponderings IV, p. 72[15]) is a mode of self-consciousness and thus is a phenomenon of modernity. So did the Greeks, e.g., not have style? Yes and no. What we call style (self-certainty of creative law-giving) they did have—seen from our point of view—; but they did not have it *as* style. What *we* take to be style—what was that for them? Did it at all enter their experience? Note the characteristic *expansion* of the concept of style from the arts to cultures and thereby in general to the subjectivity of the human being. Ultimately, the *desire for style* provides the clearest indication of the predominance of self-institution, which must necessarily transfer itself into a *mode*. Why was the concept of style essential precisely I in the arts? Even Nietzsche is caught in this notion of style. "Culture" as "style," i.e., art, i.e., τέχνη.

77

57[16]

Revolutions (p. 69) can never overcome a historical age, for they merely want to give validity within the age to what was previously suppressed

---

15. {Martin Heidegger, *Überlegungen II–VI*, GA94 (Frankfurt: Klostermann, 2014).}

16. [This misnumbering published as such.—Trans.]

and misunderstood. Revolutions strive to arrest the age precisely for the first time through and in its completion. Revolutions expand the semblance of a new beginning of history, yet that is only a mask concealing an ever greater entrenchment in the historiological—a bringing forth of the past in a "new" coat of paint and with altered purposes, uses, and allocations. The "sense-bestowal" is other—but the other merely wants to save the past and can therefore only be a consequence of it. Revolutions link up in what is without history and thereby always stimulate historiology. The more completely a revolution catches hold, all the more unambiguous does this process become.

58

Everything that grows must be able to remain at its location and to wait for its times. But we readily take growth as applying only to "life," and perhaps growth does have its essence there. Yet how are we to name that which *historically* comes to be and in this I becoming,   78 which differs from development, properly *is*? That which is primarily grounded in its location and therefore is by essence more constantly rooted in it than anything "alive" (cf. Ponderings VIII, p. 55f.); this "more constantly" not a matter of mere degree, but of essence. The projection of a constancy wherein this projection itself stands: the "growth" of the decisions which are foreign to everything merely alive.

A good number of "philosophers" are known in the historiological tradition, for "philosophy," like any essential way—e.g., art—of the productive strife of beyng, allows a field of work and of effectivity, in which what is decisive occurs only in name and yet is said to be "permanent." The *number* of thinkers is inconsequential—; but not inconsequential is whether at any time the unique one "finds *himself*," the one who saves what is most rare in its rarity and in each case receives the thrust of beyng and lets the trembling of this thrust vibrate through beings. If this is so, what do we then know of beings? How aloof and washed up on an empty shore is then what is ordinary, wherein the human masses seek "the world"? How firmly preserved does everything essential then remain for the few? *How* solitary must the gods then first be? And I is the thinking of the thinkers supposed   79 to know something of that? Yes—but know of it only if this thinking would possess the nobility of affiliation in the appropriation of beyng out of the ultimate reticence. The genuine thinkers—we do not know them and do not know the ways by which they have perhaps spoken to us—do not belong among the "number" of the philosophers. Why *can* it even be decisive to recognize this? Because history has perhaps again reached the point at which humans are needed by the gods, and this need requires for its upsurge a space of impact far outside of every-thing ordinary and sure. Since this *can* be, since history, which we know and pursue only in its historiological guise, stands within *this* possibility, therefore philosophy—as the preparation for that think-ing—is necessary. The grounding of philosophy could never be accom-plished historiologically, as the demonstration of a continuance of an extant usage. The necessity of philosophy arises only out of the most extreme historical possibilities, insofar as history is rooted in the truth of beyng.

Therefore a *possibility* grounds what is most necessary and most unique? Yes—and here all "logic," which indeed never even questions the *essence* of thinking, I let alone grasps it, leaves us wanting. Under this historical necessity for the proper disclosive thinking of beyng, there also stands, even if barely touched by the determining disposi-tion of that necessity, every historical preparation for such thinking. This preparation cannot even be justified on a historiological basis. *Its* historical ground can only be the history of thinking—not as the past but as the history of the *first beginning*. That beginning indeed appar-ently lies back in the past, but as having been it is the still futurally occurring first decision of being in favor of beings in the form of the self-emergence (φύσις) of beyng qua beings themselves. This decision does not cancel—but instead opens up—the possibility that humanity might be needed as that which grounds the truth of beyng. But the hidden appointment of the human being to be the perceiver of beyng (out of which then comes the "rational" living being, and this ratio-nality ultimately lays claim to the essence of the subjectivity of the subjectum) already includes that which is most possible of the high-est possibility, namely, that this possibility might incur the loss of it-self and so raise what is possible of its essence out into the extreme and tear what is incalculable of its impact away from every condition: that now for once the human being is needed and, prior I to this, be-ing as event of appropriation becomes the indigence of the god.

Is our history already struck by an intimation of this possibility? To be sure, not yet struck, but if we may conjecture here, then per-haps indeed predestined. For how else are we to understand—think-ing ahead to the truth of beyng—*the fact that* Hölderlin and only he has founded this intimation of beyng for the Germans and that therefore his utterance is still without those who *interpret* it in the knowledge that they must place themselves *out* into that extreme possibility of the history of beyng in order to venture what is most unapparent in the *thinking* of beyng and of the essence of its history and, in the bravest coolness, *shatter* the predominance of metaphysics through saving the concealed essence of its question (What are beings?) in the question of the truth of beyng? Seen from the point of view of modern Western humanity, however, the preparation for this possibility of the thrust of being is the most difficult burden which is to be taken up historically and transformed into the weight of Dasein.

But to take it up requires something still more preliminary: to project this possibility before oneself, to make the transition out of modernity.

59

82

If the opponent is made immediately into an enemy, and the enemy is already made into the "devil," then all opposition is deprived not only of anything creative but even of the space for a struggle. The elimination of the struggle produces an ossification of the will in the sense of a willing out beyond oneself. The ossification allows a sinking down into a-historicality. Moral conduct still remains as the way out for keeping value consciousness awake in the diminishing certainty of the attitude. On this basis we can recognize the presuppositions upholding those processes through which the essence of struggle is disturbed and thus a struggle over the essence is made impossible. The essence of struggle arises out of the essence of those who ground.

60

Those who ground.—They must indeed quite surpass the gods; for to the gods and to their effortless success, the abyss (beyng) is denied. Only humans who are aware of the abyss, who steadfastly know the abyss, can be ones who ground, and they will be such only as long as they stand firm in this *surpassing* of the gods. The surpassing, however, is not | the highest. Therefore, all who ground go to earth on the great- 83
ness of the surpassing; to them alone is the downgoing kept open. What is groundless, however, stays in the constancy of things that are always attainable, ever wished for, and continually used. Therefore one who grounds needs the discrepancy—the extreme *as the essential occurrence of beyng itself;* in the abyss of beyng all tumult and all jubilation are gathered—for where else could a space arise for the struggle, if not in the all-consuming rupture, out of which alone, as its *origin*— not assimilation (dialectics)—can "unity" be disclosively thought.

61

The excess of the stillest hours—in the secluded quarry from which the blows of the tools reverberate off into the evening and the *frag-*

ments indicate the boulder growing into the depths, where only the breaking leads to the earth and all forming becomes a petty game— fragments, if, in cracking, something new collapses under others and finds itself in its own weight.

84   But those who are destined to belong among the breakers must no longer be ones who smash, as little as they can still be formative. Those who *break* are ones who create a plight, who in advance grant a place for the truth of beyng. For that, this "between" must be broken open and the hardest boulder sought out. But over and against the essential occurrence of beyng, what is harder than these beings which in the course of the abandonment by being institute round about themselves the semblance of beyng? And where is this instituting of a greater volition than in the place at which it has secured for itself, as the carrying out of the consummation of modernity, all present and future means of calculative cultivation and planning of its forms of achievement and raises the securing itself to its thrilling performances and declares them to be its own cultural creation?

It is in the depths of this process of the essential consummation of modernity, in the least visible of the most public of Western publicness, that the abandonment of beings by being is to be sought out.

Those who break, who must break open the "between" in beings,
85   against | the disguised and confused throng of beings, may gain a foothold only in the extreme decisions and speak back only out of these decisions and in their spaces. The result is nevertheless a new ambiguity in the discourse and attitude of the breakers and a constant danger of confusion. Never before was this as essential as it will be in the future, namely: what one does *not* and does *not any longer* do and what one does not and does not any longer make the "object" of one's utterances. Such a "no" requires the highest decisiveness of essential knowledge out of a meditation leaping farthest in advance. But this "no" also belongs intrinsically to all who simply from *un*decidedness leave everything as it is and so in their own way promote that gigantism of the retardation of the decision. But this tacit "no" of those who are decided has indeed its own power of silence by which those who know recognize themselves, not as emptily confirming one another but as *opponents* predestined to one another.

The coming forth of these deciding ones who break and ground has its own time and withdraws from historiology.

86   *62*

Schelling—grasped historically on the basis of the history of being (i.e., here, in the overcoming of metaphysics), he stands between Leibniz and Nietzsche. Diverting him into an apparently Aristotelian-Christian positive-negative philosophy is just as inessential as deriving him from romanticism. Both are *historiologically* important and perhaps for now so persistent that in this regard Schelling might still influence the appraisal of German Idealism in modern thinking. For indeed modern thinking still faces a task which apparently contradicts it and could look like its sublation but is in fact only its ultimate confirmation: that life—"nature" and its nonliving beings—i.e., the "earth," is made an object of theory and of conceptual interpretation and description (in the context of a renewal of Goethe's "world picture"). There could then commence a "choosing" in favor of the "elements"; Paracelsus and Boehme and all the polar opposites of modern thinking could recur and now, as formerly happened to Kant, Descartes, Hegel, and Spinoza, could be assimilated by scholars into henceforth irrational erudition | in the field of philosophy.   87

This bogging down of "philosophy" must still be endured; to let it simply pass by essential thinking is, for those who question, a matter of inner decidedness and not a task. But in public activity of culture this last bogging down of "philosophy" will spread in an especially obstinate way. And that for two reasons: *first,* the learned conceptual systematics and description of what is *not* graspable mathematically appears to be especially "close to life" and "profound."—This investigation into the counterrational—into what cannot be calculated—seems to take seriously the incalculable, whereas in fact the noncalculable—that at which calculation stops—is merely made into an object of *correspondingly* modified calculation. The entire enterprise is reactive and thus dependent on modern thinking; in other words, it is only the necessary consummation and exaggeration of that thinking, along with a claim to be "profound" and even to be an overcoming. *Second,* this learned systematizing of what is asystematic enters the advisable nearness of those worldviews which, on the basis of an extreme *calculation,* degrade the *"intellectus"* and attribute a priority to "life." (Richard Wagner and Ludwig Klages as mixtures of a unilaterally understood Nietzsche with Bachofen.)

Furthermore, the Aryan transformations of the basic tenets of psy-   88
choanalysis; and everything which ekes out a validity through opposition to the concept, to what can be explained. With the help of these achievements, philosophical erudition will again take on the semblance of "living" and "nature bound" thinking and thus, as one might suppose, the semblance of "actual" philosophy. In this process, to be sure, that is what is more incidental and unimportant. What is necessary lies precisely in the fact that the limit-domain of calculative thinking and of modern metaphysics is now altogether incorporated

into the domain of erudition and of systems of cosmology. This bogging down (the expression does not signify decay and failing—which
already lie in the essence of philosophical *erudition*) promotes possibilities of "lived experience" in a new and proper enterprise and thus
proves to be the genuine and timely instituting of a "thinking" that
has long since lost its questions. If "life" and "earth" and "nature" have
become objects of an apparently noncalculative thinking (which is
nevertheless all the more merely calculative), then the representa-
89 tional domain of the subjectum is completely traversed | and concep-
tually instituted even for science and "philosophy." And then the last
impulse toward questioning is eliminated, for we now dominate even
the indomitable and at the same time believe we have submitted to it.
One might suppose that Western metaphysics will be investigated and
made useful historiologically according to this, its reverse side, and
will be so all the more as these researches provide an opportunity to
uncover "sides" the rationalists have neglected. But—you lawyers of
bogs and mists—who will aver that precisely those rationalists and
masters of thought were not *closer* to what you here immediately "live"
and in "concepts of lived experience" give out as universally "best"?

But Leibniz and Schelling and Nietzsche—and every essential
thinker of Western metaphysics—must not be misused in this way.
They will not be, if our thinking is open to the history of being and
from the question of beyng takes a course that can no longer encounter the distinctions rationalism-irrationalism, optimism-pessimism. Questioning out of beyng is of a different origin than is every
questioning of beings, wherein also belongs pararational "thinking,"
whose telling "effect" is already secured.

90 Even here, publishers will find their servants. But for individuals
who know and preserve, in view of the increased—because necessary—bogging down, what counts is primarily only one thing: to keep
visible the history of metaphysics in its basic conditions as regards the
history of being—for the sake of the necessities of the transition.

And the other thing: over against the semblant depth of the bog, to
make necessary the plight of clarity and of light; for otherwise beyng
remains absent—since it must disdain the abomination which makes
confusion a principle and a means for "lived experience."

63

What is incalculable.—The hardest "reality," the one of historical force,
is not the reality of incidents and not the reality of the resolutions on
which the incidents rest; instead, it is the reality of *the fact that* beings,

remaining without the truth of being, propagate the semblance of beings and spread this semblance over everything like an impenetrable
net. What is this itself, namely, the *fact that this is history*? How should
we explicate *the fact that* this history of being does not contest beings
and lets them "carry on" in their machination? And when we have
explicated it, what I does such knowledge afford us? Is this history in-   91
deed only an obscure sign of the solitude of beyng itself, a solitude
about which we so seldom agree (and of which humans know so
little)? How solitary is the light bathing the things that grant themselves their luster in it and replace it with the abundance of their
forms? What does it help to "explain" this light, whereby we do not
so much encounter the light, but its darkness, and merely calculate
that which is without light? Are not the light and the clearing that radiates out from it becoming even more unique and solitary, such that
they avert every respect in which they are supposed to be posited but
in this averting merely become *still* more granting and in the brightest light make themselves known as darkness? Then the night would
never be before the light nor after it nor only an accompanying "epiphenomenon" but instead would be the light itself in its solitude—the
deepest night. Here the light is to us, however, no longer merely an
"image" of beyng—but itself a reverberation of beyng (φύσις—φάος)
["nature—light"].

   And *the fact that* now, as never before, beings are abandoned by
beyng—could that not even become an upsurge of beyng, wherein
the indigence of the god I comes close to us and in this indigence so   92
does the god himself? Contrary to the highest expectations directed
otherwise, i.e., expectations of progress in beings, that could be the
moment a unique thrust convulses the already long since dormant
history of the gods, alters all measures and values, and lets the past
end in its own emptiness. What is *incalculable*—must it not be what is
closest, closer than everything close—the thoroughly overlooked, the
unexpected in all expectation, as what cannot be expected? What is
incalculable—that is accepted by the one who calculates when he con-
fesses it as something he does not and never can attain, that which
flees before *him*—yet as such and even as such it is still the calculable,
whose calculation merely cannot be fully carried out. The incalculable—is not a being and occurs "only" as beyng itself, with which all
calculation can "do nothing" [lit., "begin nothing"], not because
beyng is worthless for a beginning, but because calculation and explanation never grasp the beginning. Yet how *far* does calculation now
not extend through all humanity, since for the longest time the human being and ultimately even the semblance he calls "God" have be-

93   come "outposts" within calculation, | and everything is perhaps well
hidden, and ever better hidden, through the virtues and accomplishments supported by a person of the most amiable will? Then how
overly close—and yet how utterly unattainable by calculation—is the
incalculable? How acute is the extreme decision of the leap into beyng
and away from the calculation of beings?

     Yet this *is* "only" for the knowledgeable ones, those who, in order
to rescue this history of beyng for beings, must renounce historiology
for a long time and forgo all narration and calculation, since at issue
is the *transition*. And *if* now there are such ones, who venture into
beyng, who in the brightness (which has already become the grayest
pallor) of the most ordinary day still only see the light as darkness, if
a poet walked down the street, unrecognizable to the people of pen-
pushers, and if this poet could be only of an essence already poetized
in advance—i.e., if he had to fall prematurely—and if, unrecognized
by the poet, a thinker walked without a path, in advance thinking a
thinking as the thinking of beyng, and if in this way the essence of
history—differently than before—had first to be grounded in advance
of all happenings, then indeed to these who ground only their own
essence could appertain. That is so, provided this essence had to abide
94   in | the deepest concealment and the entire abyss remained in the
background of each of the intimating words of those who ground,
whereby they testify they do not know the way but only surmise the
place necessarily originating all the ways on which the determination
of the human being would be sought.

     But this "place" is not a present-at-hand location—instead, it is the
chasm of beyng along with possibilities of the simplest decisions. And
the first decision concerns whether humans are to *belong* to beyng, to
the indigence of the god, or are to calculate beings henceforth and *secure* themselves as that which most is—either as a people or as a splin-
ter of an inexact species. This decision, however, has as its ground the
possibility of the distinction between beyng and beings (cf. p. 111).
And that distinction does not depend on thought and representation;
instead, it arises from beyng itself—whether beyng resolves itself on
its own proper truth (clearing) or not. The god and the human being,
indeed separate and different—belong to beyng as the banks to the
river. But the bridge is Da-sein.

95   Yet every image allows {?} errancy and the | artless {?} repose of a
mere view. We thus again and again evade the "nearness" of beyng in
the historical uniqueness of that "nearness": we remain without the
truth of beyng, pursue what is calculable, and do not grasp—on account of its excessive nearness—what is incalculable. And those who

grasp it are unable to lead it in its space, into the "space" in which guise it itself essentially occurs. All leading here would be a leading astray, for beyng, itself the liberation of beings into their open realm, can belong only to the liberated—to those who bind themselves to the *first* necessity. And they do so by making the indigence of the *god* (the fact that he needs beyng) their own plight and thus set their essence out from all calculation and come to know the plight of the lack of a sense of plight.

64

A-historicality can be prepared only through the deterioration and unruliness characteristic of historiology. It is attained when historiology becomes institutionalized in all human occupations and becomes unrecognizable as historiology. The newspaper and the radio are such institutions, and what they themselves erect and institute can still not be calculated today, for these possibilities already surpass all "fantasy," because the institutions by their very essence become ever more invisible and unintuitable, although they chain themselves ever more exclusively to that which is next coming to presence and disappearing.

Why does a swift *forgetting* belong inevitably to calculation and to   96 the certainty of its precedence? Does not even calculation need the incalculable that is appropriate *to it,* that is here then always something belonging to the past? If the instituting and calculating have forgotten *what they,* shortly before, produced in all intelligibility and with a great noise and how they thereby led astray, then they are taking this *forgetting* as such to be the ground of their accomplishments, ones which are now suddenly "irrational." Why should calculation not make its computations even with the help of this counterfeiting and—recover its expenses? The "irrational," the "lived experience," has still always been the finery of those rationalists and calculators who would not like to be considered what they can indeed only be. Thus all calculation has an "interest" in historiology, with the help of which this calculation makes us forget what is determined and ever and again makes something else count as what is properly "historical" (historiological—worth mentioning out of the past). That is the reason historiology is established on prehistory—just as "prehistorical" notions determine the "picture" of "history."

How can a people be brought to recognize goallessness as the "sense bestowal" of the essence of that people? What must transpire so that this may be taken up?

Hölderlin and Nietzsche—The History of Beyng.

We readily name together Hölderlin and Nietzsche, but we should do so only if we know what differentiates them. In what respect must they be differentiated first of all? In that respect which touches what alone compels us to name the one and not pass over the other. And what is that? It is *the history of beyng*—not the historiology of metaphysics and certainly not the historiology of "literature."

The history of beyng: how beyng loses its first, scarcely dawning truth, the truth belonging to it itself (ἀλήθεια in φύσις) ["truth," "unconcealment" in "nature," "the self-emergent"], and so must misplace its "essence" into the superficiality of *beingness*. How beingness allows beings to become things brought forth as created; how what is brought forth by the creator God becomes a representation in the human being considered as subjectum; how representedness, as the essence of beings (objectivity) raises to supremacy the ever more and more hidden and machinational distorted essence of beyng (φύσις—τέχνη).

These few strokes will for a long time keep the essence of beyng far from its own truth, the truth arising out of it and thus belonging to it. Being is indeed always still I thought in terms of already established beingness and yet, ever since the first loss of its essence (in the Platonic ἰδέα), has become something accessory (a priori). Ever since this degradation to an accessory, one which then nevertheless appears as the *condition* of possibility (of an *object*, to be sure), beyng refuses itself in its essential occurrence, without this refusal becoming surmised as such and grasped in its ramifications.

Meanwhile, however, for the first time and almost as an aside in this history of beyng, something else was gained through struggle: the plight of the lack of a decision regarding the advent and flight of the gods—whereby, in naming them, one helped them appear in this plight and thus helped make the whole of beings questionable in the history of its beyng. Hölderlin withstood this plight, i.e., brought it into the open domain through a downgoing. His "position"—if it may be called so—in the history of beyng is a unique one and determines the essence of his poetry as well as the fact that he must poetize "the" poet (namely, the one of the forthcoming history of beyng).

But as happened to beyng in the first beginning of its history, so now similarly the plight of its undecided truth seems to be hidden and forgotten through the emergence of I modernity. Except that in the interim the other one (Nietzsche) in various disguises and disruptions paved the way to a meditation on the history of the "ideal" through an exertion toward an ultimate, all-inverting (and *only* inverting) consummation of metaphysics. This consummation became the *pen*ultimate step in the necessity to make the question of beings worthy to be asked once again on the basis of an originary decision in favor of beyng, whose truth first requires a grounding. And so the essential occurrence of beyng was disclosively thought as the "between" in which that plight of the lack of a decision can establish itself as the necessity of a decision. Thereby the history of beyng enters the transition out of the end of metaphysics into the other beginning. Only the history of beyng provides the ground for naming Hölderlin and Nietzsche together and at the same time for grasping them in their incomparability to each other; for the fact that both had an essential relation to the Greeks, and both, even if in fundamentally different ways, recognized the "Dionysian" and the "Apollonian," and both critiqued the Germans, etc., is only a consequence, merely grounded in various ways, of the destiny of Hölderlin and Nietzsche in the history of being.

The pair become least visible, however, if we seek to interpret them reciprocally, the one through the other, and I thereby bring into play   100
the activity of historiological comparison. Yet that is tempting, since it could here produce especially rich "results." If these are what is to be bestowed on us, then it would be more worthy to forget Hölderlin and Nietzsche again for now. Perhaps that is even provided for. The cores of cultural politics have been found. With good instinct, Hölderlin and Nietzsche are banned. We must nevertheless indicate—as incidental as all this may seem—the danger in such a procedure. The danger is to be found not where the implicit suppression of both (naturally with the necessary lip service) is underway, but rather where both are called as witnesses by all who want to go backward, whereby Hölderlin and Nietzsche are first *mis*used in the proper sense.

Yet such an indication can perhaps scarcely accomplish anything here—unless it is thought for a long time to come, which the history of beyng appropriates in order to bring the truth of beyng to a decision and thus release to those who belong in this history their determinant force.

66   101

The "object" of philosophy. Here the whole exertion of thought concerns the postulation of that which is to be disclosively questioned.

Nay—such questioning accomplishes nothing other than this postulation; for with the latter and through it that which is questioned disclosively comes to be determined.

The long accompaniment, which fell to the lot of philosophy through "science," has at last led even philosophy to take as its object something present-at-hand, which is to be elaborated at once and from various sides and by many researchers. Quite to the contrary, however, only one thing is necessary: to make ever more importunate, through the thoughtful disclosive questioning of beyng, the *objectlessness* of philosophy and thus to compel a situation in which only the one decision matters, namely, whether a thinking is strong enough to endure in objectlessness and to renounce all supports offered in the form of the apparently necessary elaboration and advancement of individual "problems," or whether one sees in meditation on that which is to be disclosively questioned only preliminaries and also something programmatic which is to find its justification precisely for the first time in the executed system. But I now—in the long time of the transition from metaphysics to the history of being—what is required is only the experience of what is most question-worthy, and this circumstance has its sole ground in the fact that this that is most question-worthy is not merely by accident unrecognized, misinterpreted, and forgotten, but instead is by its very *essence* withdrawn from modern humans and is so precisely when it overpowers them on account of an excessive nearness in their humanity. Unaccustomed to the inexhaustibility of what is simple and intent on the changing results of what is constantly new, modern humans are not capable of experiencing, in the objectlessness of thinking, that captivation which sweeps those who are thinking into Da-sein and thus appropriates Da-sein as something steadfastly undertaken.

We know practically only incidentals of the excessive demands placed on thinking by what is decisively not an object and altogether not a being. And the rarity of philosophy must indeed have its ground in the fact that humans, even if beyng has *once* carried them away into its essential occurrence, immediately seek for shores I where they might build onto their conceptual formation and even declare that formation to be the river itself. For a long time—in the course of the history of metaphysics from Plato to Nietzsche—thinking has been banished to what is superficial, and in this domain thinking itself (the forming of objectively representational assertions about things present-at-hand) swaggered as the guideline for the determination of beings and did so even and precisely where, beyond the supposedly new consideration of beings, they were raised to objects for a subject, and ultimately the subject itself, as finite subject-object, was entrusted to the absolute subject, i.e., to pure indifferentiation and identity as its ground. Whence is a preparedness supposed to arise here for a leap into the essential occurrence of beyng itself, especially since even metaphysical thinking has become unfamiliar to most and has remained only as an object of historiological reportage on the opinions and standpoints of philosophy? Within the predominance of this way of "thinking," every attempt to tell of beyng thrusts into an atmosphere of misinterpretation, whether the confrontation with such attempts corresponds to their intention or not.

Yet there are perhaps grounds even more abyssal barring us I from the truth of beyng: language, not "in itself," for such never exists, but indeed the fate of language itself, namely, that language has entered a configuration and a form of effectiveness in which it no longer responds to beyng, although the essence of language has its first and unique determination therein. Meanwhile, language has made itself familiar to us as a tool. Even if the misinterpretation does not go so far as to consider the word a mere imitation and sign of a mental representation of something present-at-hand, even if—indeed ultimately presupposing the view just mentioned—we ascribe to linguistic expression an emotional value, nevertheless the essential delimitation of language and consequently all theories of language are caught fast in a domain that cuts language off from the originary relation to beyng itself.

104

67

Will the essential gaze of essential humans into the plight of beyng (beyng as the indigence of the god) ever be strong enough to master the demonic spirit of calculating and instituting? Only if beyng bestows itself into the essence of the event.

68

105

Is *this* now the sole *decision:* complete destruction and disintegration or else the constraint of a total compulsion? Will this decision determine peoples to be peoples and save them as such? Or is this decision still one *within* the modern essence of history, and does it merely decide how modernity is to be brought to its end? Accordingly, is this decision indeed *no* decision, since it does not place the *essence* of the age into discord with another one and thereby place the age itself for the first time in a light which shines out over it? Is it no decision, because it also must leave undecided the further working of those forces which, peculiarly mixed together, determine the West especially in its modern form, the forces, namely, of "Christianity" and "culture" as Christian culture and as cultural Christianity? And *why* must all this remain undecided, and for how long? As long as the necessity of the genuine decision cannot assert itself out of the plight which is superior to it? But that will endure as long as the beings of this history are not thrust into the domain of the trembling of beyng, as long as beyng itself refuses itself, and as long as this self-refusal is not experienced as the most essential occurrence of the essence—as self-with-

106   holding. | In other words, as long as meditation does not concern itself with this issue, become meditation on the decision, and at length create the first paths on which thinking is made ready for the thrust of beyng, a thrust which must affect individuals.

But what if at the same time the saving and securing of the human masses have progressed so far that only a blind "decision" between masses counts as a goal?

69

The danger of thinking.—The genuine danger is not that thinking might suffocate through superfluity and have to stop. Instead, it is that thinking might let itself be pressed onto the erroneous path of instituting itself as a counterinstitution, that thinking might expect to satisfy the demands of utility, of immediate effectivity, of the community, of the public, and of lucidity.

What is the attitude required of creative ones in an age now in the process of setting the institution of the form of effectivity *prior* to the effectivity—prior to the clarification of the goals of the institution and the gathering of its powers? We take this question too lightly if it is

107   made to relate only to | current circumstances and is thereby answered by saying that all questioning and every meditation are pointless. Instead, questioning must pave a way in front of itself for its own history.

The essence of history / determined through the truth of beyng / must precede history—; judged in this way, a light first shines on the still *obscure priority* of the institution and of calculation over that which does the instituting—; the essence of the necessities of the transition, an essence that indicates itself in its distorted essence. The most extreme abandonment of beings by beyng is itself the most proximate (and yet to that which is abandoned the most remote) intimation of beyng. We must first bring into the purview of a meditation the prevailing, though obscure, priority of the institution as something question-worthy, especially because this priority must still change in its essence due to the circumstance that what is to do the instituting, over and against the institution, loses in weight and essential power through the priority, such that the priority deprives itself of all sense.

The sign of this lies in the indifference toward every institution, in the form of an indifference that nevertheless precisely allows the institution to prevail and that indeed becomes a unique form of letting something prevail. What is transpiring here? And *how* do we need to comport ourselves in this process? If we experience it as a sign of | beyng: does something necessary meet us here? Does this experience   108 compel us to essential transformations of humanity, ones of which we do not know to whom their execution is kept open, yet ones we today already, by knowing to bring them into a *truth*, start on their way inasmuch as we search for the paths on which we might press on to a possible preservation of this truth?

70

Human destiny—in all its institutional forms and their trappings—is driven out so far into machination that a metaphysical decision (consequently a moral one related to "ideals" and "values") does not achieve anything, because it already can no longer incorporate into its decisional space this essence of humanity.

The modern essence of humanity has entered that phase of its history which delivers this essence over to beings so exclusively that the abandonment by beyng is beginning to provide an intimation of beyng itself; the sign of a decisive transition. What does it mean | that the   109 human being, who as modern seems to have brought himself into the definitive possession of his goals and their calculation, now already stands outside every interpretive possibility whose horizon would still be drawn from the past? Or that the human being, the more exclusively he considers himself in terms of calculation and function, although without knowing this or even being able to know it, is now becoming a stranger in the midst of beings, wherein he believes himself at home? Or that the human being is hunting for a historical moment in which this foreignness will overtake him and then either will undo him with its horror or will set him out into the plight *of actually being* the foreign one in the abode of the gods? This either-or is the decision concerning whether or not in that historical moment an open domain is prepared in which the human being can experience and take up the strangeness as such and what is strange about it. This history of humans, commencing with the transition out of modernity, brings them for the first time explicitly into the historical space of being itself, whereas they previously had taken beyng only as the most outer husk of beings and as a being itself.

A hindrance—but not a danger—could soon develop for the think-ing of beyng, from the fact that the "earth" and what belongs to it are declared to be the *objects* of "philosophy" and that the Goethean rela-tion to nature is degraded to a guideline for philosophical erudition.

This "spiritual" penetration of "nature" is more erroneous than any sort of crude "biological" interpretation, whose calculative attitude comes to light at once. But this hindrance is practically summoned up by the prevailing mania for "lived experiences" and will find imme-diate confirmation of its semblant truth in that which is called "life." (Cf. above, on *Schelling*, p. 86ff.) The danger threatens the earth itself, because such a spiritualization of it presents a form of devastation that cannot at all be halted immediately, since it is instituted and promoted by the ruling humans for their own security.

Once again lying historically far ahead of all this is what Hölderlin calls "the earth," which receives a mere *historiological* elucidation if we conflate it with "Gaia" [Γαῖα, "Earth"]. Historically—i.e., as bearing future humanity—the earth can come to be only if humans are pre-
111   viously thrust into the truth of *beyng* and if, on the basis of a | disclo-sive thinking of beyng, the gods and humans themselves enter into the site of the battle over their destinies, from which battle the world first flashes up and the earth regains its obscurity.

72

Thinkers are distinguishers whose *distinguishing* is wafted along on the wind of *decisions* that come from afar. Thinkers run—with open eyes—against this wind and against the thrusts concealed in it.

Thinkers distinguish being over and against beings and do so by becoming the first to be decided ones on the basis of the essence of beyng itself. (Cf. p. 94f.)

Yet thinkers distinguish beyng from beings only if beyng as the event of appropriation has separated the gods from humans and has become the separability of this separation. In this way alone can beyng appropriate thinkers to the decided distinguishers and retain thinking itself as *its own* essence in the most proper essential occur-rence and secure for philosophy an unconditioned origin in what is most question-worthy. The distinction, taken in its complete empti-ness and breadth but also in its obscurity and groundlessness, is the
112   one between being and | beings. And the decision is an essential thrust of beyng itself, as soon as beyng has come into the truth of its essen-

tial occurrence as event. The distinction between being and beings looks like a finding. Indeed:

Future thinking will need to think out *only* to the following: that beyng, against all appearances to the contrary, at first has nothing to do with "beings" and that beyng must be grasped in its full truth and always made the springboard of every question. That we can never be practiced enough in this strangeness. But also that no one may be absolved of the operative mastery of the steepest paths of the concept and of the rigor of the simplest word—in order for what is strange to remain strange in the purest configuration of what is simple. But that the mastery of the use of weapons springs from the struggle itself and in advance is determined by the attitude of struggle even in the mode of the forging—not merely handling—of the weapons (question—concept—word and silence).

Accordingly, where the technique of thought is merely something learned historiologically and where only historiology stands altogether before all history, then even the most agile | "mastery" of his-   113
toriology produces an entrenchment of the presumptuous blindness of erudition in philosophy, and this erudition always appeals first of all to "beings" and "facts."

73

Thoughtful configuration:
  1. the ordered presentation of what is named.
  2. the paving of a way of questioning.
  3. the movement of a thrust of beyng.

The third includes the first two, correspondingly transformed in themselves, but could never be attained by the first two or replaced by them. All erudite philosophy moves in the first and also takes questioning in the scientific form of "problems." The second is already determined by surmising the third and in the transition remains the extreme of what we can reach; perhaps it must even, from the lack of a genuine power to put a stamp on its own necessity, take refuge in the first, although *this* expedient involves many misunderstandings. (Cf. *Being and Time*.[17]) The third, on the other hand, could enter the neighborhood of "poetry," although it is fundamentally different from poetry. Yet this fundamental difference shows itself at first only to rare eyes and is still hardly to be dispelled of confusion. Nietzsche's thinking maintains itself in this | confusion, one not to be overcome imme-   114

---

17. {Martin Heidegger, *Sein und Zeit,* GA2 (Frankfurt: Klostermann, 1977).}

diately, visible least of all to the thinker himself, and providing *him* the power of his creativity. But if interpreters make the notion of a "poet-philosopher" the principle and theme of their interpretation, they thereby in advance are renouncing every exertion needed to comprehend Nietzsche. As long as we do not see these distinctions of thoughtful configuration clearly enough, or even surmise them, we will also not remove the history of Western thinking from the mania for historiological explanation, the mania which has already made the greater part of such explanations so readily available to knowledge and to the exploitation of cognition that a historical meditation, transposed into the domain of the thrust of the history of being, no longer has any effect. For indeed this meditation, if things go "well" with it, is considered at most a new sort of *historiological* interpretation, and this somewhat forced recognition is its definitive condemnation. But least of all should the distinctions of thoughtful configuration be made objects of a "typology" of "types of thought." Meditation on these distinctions can arise only from—and be determined by—an already strong intimation of beyng itself. Everything depends on whether philosophy raises itself into its essence and whether philosophy finds those few who for moments have become

115   equal to this process and I no longer are slaves to public opinion.

74

Clarity.—The clarity of what can be explained, of what cannot be doubted, of what is noncontradictory, is not an essential clarity, for the latter can gleam only where darkness resides and as the ground of thought is compelling and thus where darkness does not disappear through clarity, but unfolds itself instead.

75

"Binding to nature."—Everywhere, on different paths, and in various durations, contemporary humans demand the "real," or else they are sympathetically talked into this demand by a few. This *demanding could* indicate a process on whose surface contemporary humans continue to move, without recognizing the level of their path as the surface of another one. It *could* be so, but everything else indicates it is *not* so. Above all, confusion reigns as to what the reality of the "real" is supposed to be, whether or how it offers itself as a standard. What we seek under this name must of course be the opposite of what we flee as the unreal. And again the question is whether the "unreal" is not given this appraisal merely because reality has not been decided.

Thus a perplexity—not at all recognized as such—could indeed pre-   116
vail in both respects: we do not know what we are fleeing and leave
undecided what we are seeking. *This* lack of knowledge, not the simple
lack of possession of something like a present-at-hand reality, but
rather the more deeply grounded not wanting—and not being able—
to know the reality of the real, would then be the secret goad prompt-
ing that flight and that demand and postulating closeness to reality as
the aim of seeking and as the condition for "life". But that not being
able—and not wanting—to know reality would in turn need to be
grounded in a lack of the possession of the truth of beyng. And this
lack of possession could already bring into play the consequence of
beyng itself, namely, its withdrawing from beings and its giving itself
up in the appearance of this naming and opining. But the demand for
"reality" would then be not an endeavor to work consciously against
this abandonment by being but, instead, would be a bustling about to
increase and entrench, unconsciously, that already sovereign semblance of "beings" as well as the semblance that humans could possess what is real. The fact that this is *so*, that consequently the demand
for closeness to "life" and to "reality" presents the opposite of what it
pretends, and that here the *evading* of beyng I is not only carried out   117
in general but is expressly pursued and instituted—the simplest
"proof" for all this is ready to be perceived anywhere today. But that
it is *not* perceived and can no longer be perceived is a part of the proof.
And what is that? It is the fact that one avoids questioning and detests
question-worthiness like something menacing and harmful and that
questioning is thus immediately and falsely transformed into uncertainty, skepticism, weakness, and cowardice—in order to keep in re-
pute and in "power" *still* more tranquilly that avoidance of beyng—of
course, without any knowledge or intimation of this—under the semblance of a closeness to beings.

How so? Do not needs for clarity and for answers to questions announce themselves everywhere? Does not an uncertainty, acknowledged or not, permeate the human masses? And is this supposed to
be an avoidance of questioning and of question-worthiness? Yes indeed—for this amounts only to a snatching at what is unproblematic.
The fact that such snatching seizes onto *nothing* does not already make
it a passion and a craving for what is question-worthy qua the essence
of beyng, since this essence holds sway beyond rest and unrest. Such
snatching, that knows how to conceal itself in the guise of "spiritual"
"interests," leaves what is question-worthy ever again on the side of
the things to be disavowed. And what these demands for reality mean
by the anticipatory I confirmation of its possibility and justification is   118
precisely the opinion that the "real" (and a fortiori its reality) could

be encountered and grasped at any time and in any way—and needed
for that would only be, so to speak, a diverting of the previous highways of the common pursuits in what is taken as "life." Such a diverting, which can, however, only be a change of highways, is the requirement and care for a "binding to nature." And in the ambit of their
purview such requirements even have their "good points," and this
makes every contrary misgiving a malevolent subversion: as certain
of itself as this pursuit of a guarantee of "closeness to life" *seems* to be,
that is how far it *is* from all meditation, such that the condemnation
of any misgiving arises "compellingly" at the least hesitation.

And yet—how do matters stand as regards this "binding to nature"
and the institutionalizing of such a bond? Forest and brook, moun-
tain and meadow, air and sky, sea and isle are now taken as distrac-
tions, as sedatives, as objects of recreational activities that have their
fixed forms of pursuit and their corresponding institutions. At most,
the just named is taken as "landscape," which after a brief sojourn or
hurried tour is brought to mind and perhaps stowed in the memory
119 as matter for later | amusement. Nowadays, landscapes are even as-
saulted from historiological, folkloric, and antiquarian curiosity and
mania for comparison, and this is thought to be superior to the mere
enjoyment of nature. Both mixed together, on the basis of this perhaps still uneven {?} capacity for enjoyment and also on the basis of
historiological cognitions, produce the illusion of henceforth belonging among the indigenous ones and of contributing to the production of indigenousness.

This enjoyment of nature and the curiosity regarding the landscape
are no longer relegated to the circumstantial endeavor of individuals;
the accessibility of "nature" is functionally instituted—(the institution is itself a branch of business in which farmers and farmsteads—
in case they can still be called so—already participate, even though
these are properly supposed to be "objects" of this joy in "nature").

A corresponding literature promotes and develops the capacity for
lived experiences of this enjoyment of nature, i.e., for the correct use
of the offered opportunities, and ultimately a theory of the "earth"
and of "nature" "underpins" this literature both "theoretically" and
in terms of "worldview." City existence becomes the measure of this
activity regarding nature, an existence which with its functional forms
and its pleasure spots not merely goes on alongside but at the same
time institutes itself into "nature," so that perhaps occasionally the
possibilities of enjoyment reciprocally increase and also mingle together. The assimilation of the activity regarding nature is easier in-
120 sofar as nature itself becomes landscape, | and landscape an "object of
commerce." Villages are no longer farming settlements but instead

have become cities that include agricultural pursuits; the latter demand the corresponding incorporations into more general life—; the
most isolated "farmstead" has already been destroyed *from within* by
radio and newspapers. This destruction, however, is once again covered over inasmuch as now the "farmers" take up the old modes of
"clothing" and "games," etc., modes introduced by city dwellers
"bound to nature." The "farmers" for their part pursue these modes
as an activity regarding nature and show them to others—tourists—
on request. In all this, even a good deal of "taste" develops; i.e., something grown old is with great cleverness set up as functionally available. One even has one's "joy" and recovers one's expenses, one comes
to know oneself, the landscapes bring themselves into a traffic inter-
change, and everything stands ready for the arbitrary mixtures and
dosages of this activity with regard to nature.

Who surmises the uprooting of the last, sparsest growths that once
were? Who *wants* to surmise at all that here something is happening
which would be completely misinterpreted if considered merely as the
loss of the "good old days" and regretted by way of calculation? The
fearfulness of this outwardly pleasurable activity with regard to na-
ture can be grasped only if | without emotional fanaticism we think   121
it back into that process of the abandonment of beings by being which
unfolds its authority in the gigantism and relentlessness of the advance
of calculation and bustle. This is the reality no one sees and no one
wants to see, because these progressives of the new age at bottom depend most tenaciously on the misinterpreted old ones and are the "romantics" in the proper sense. *Anyone who, like them, takes history only
historiologically can also not experience the "real" in its proper presence nor
here most of all.*

Yet at issue now is by no means a correct or incorrect determination
of reality—rather, what alone counts is the steadfastness of humanity
in being. Only out of this steadfastness do the *decisions* arise which
displace humans into the abyss of freedom and lay down between the
gods and nothingness an open domain—in which what is called "nature" finds its way to its essence again, and so does what alone guards
the genuineness of that essence out of the affiliation to a world.

But *this*—that beyng might again be mindful of humanity, that humans themselves, through the need of beyng, might again become
needed (struck by the need and claimed by it)—*this* cannot be accomplished and instituted by the human being. Only through great up-
heavals is an appropriation of Da-sein possible out of the | indigence   122
of the god. Yet these upheavals do not happen within beings (simply
as "revolutions") (cf. p. 69ff.). Even an occurrence such as the "world
war" was not capable of anything, despite the "hells" into which hu-

mans were then drawn, despite the sacrifices and also the upswings, which were mostly accomplished in secret. The world war was not capable of anything, if we think out to the essential upheaval of humans; on the contrary, it became a preparatory school for basing the trappings of the self-instituting human being still more decisively, completely, and readily on the self-securing of his current essential state. Will then such occurrences, even if still more horrible and destructive, ever be at all capable of an essential upheaval of the human being? No—; something must eventuate that touches the human being in his essence and first makes him one who can know that he must *venture* his *essence* and cannot hold obstinately to it if beyng is to incorporate him into the abyss of its essential occurrence. But as long as the human being merely wanders about amid beings and puffs himself up as their center and pursues them, he will never enter the space of a possible venture, for this space opens only with the *distinction between being and beings*.

123   76

Anthropology.—An age in which not only the representation of the human being but also that of beings as a whole has become anthropological in the strict sense of this word must have anthropomorphized the human being in a unique way. What does it mean to anthropomorphize the human being? It means to take him the way common opinion takes everything it considers a being, namely, as something present-at-hand, wherein, among other properties, even spiritual ones are present-at-hand, and if they are not, then indeed they can be produced at any time. The human being is thereby forced into a mode of his own representations, and this mode allows him most easily to avoid his essence and to insert himself simply into the rest of beings, though indeed as their relational center. Basically, however, this anthropomorphizing of the human being means only one thing: the human being is withdrawn from the relation to being. Emphatically expressed: whether the human being has a goal or not is not a possible question, for he himself, in some form or other of his mass being or individual being, is the goal.

This anthropomorphizing of the human being lies like a thick fog over "humanity." Because the human being nevertheless has everything (culture, etc.) at his disposal and even more completely and
124   quickly than ever before, in this "world" never could anything | strike him that might overthrow him. This anthropomorphized human being can assimilate anything. Is a transformation still possible here? Starting with the human being, no; beyng will have to swing out in

preparation for striking, and much will need to undergo eradication. "Evolutions" and "developments" of current states are merely particular forms of movement *within* this anthropomorphizing. Even if "anthropology" is abandoned and another self-interpretation takes its place, the essential state of the human being could still not change. Even if individual peoples meditated on their past and out of that reckoned up new "ideals," this historiological way would only be a new form in which the decisions withdraw and the preparations for them are neglected.

This anthropomorphizing of the human being indeed rolls him up entirely into his self-certainty, yet it at the same time presses this self-certain human thing to the edges of the abysses at which this thing, in case it could awaken from itself, would never be able to find its way about—never could the human being be able to know nothingness, that concealed reminiscence of beyng, and even the negativity of nothingness would be withheld from him.

77

125

All "struggles" over doctrinal opinions and doctrinal propositions, "struggles" for a "religious" or "political" dogmatics, might be unavoidable in the transition; but they *are* not struggles, since they lack the freedom by which they would increase in relation to an opponent. The lack of freedom extends so far into the essential that such "strugglers" can never choose the opponent, i.e., place themselves into question thereby—the saying that freedom springs from necessity is now misused, where the necessity is lacking because so is the genuine plight, but where the arbitrariness in the calculation of aims is instituted with ever less restraint.

(Cf. p. 56.)

{Index}

Abandonment by being
[*Seinsverlassenheit*]: 84, **90ff.,**
115f.
Anthropology [*Anthropologie*]: 31,
123ff.
"Antitheses" ["*Antithesen*"]: 49f.
(cf. [Ponderings] VIII)
Art [*Kunst*]: 67f., *74ff.*

Beauty [*Schönheit*]: 67f.
Beyng [Seyn]: 1f., 8f., **33ff.,** *49,*
55ff., **68f.,** *83,* 97f., 102, *112*
"Binding to nature"
["*Naturverbundenheit*"]: 115f.

Calculation [*Berechnung*]: 96
"Catholicism" ["*Katholizismus*"]: 4
Certainty [*Sicherheit*]: 20
Clarity [*Klarheit*]: 115
Configuration [*Gestaltung*]: 113
"Culture" ["*Kultur*"]: 2f., 16ff., 105

Decision [*Entscheidung*]: 7, *68f.,*
94f., *105f.,* **108f.,** 111f., 121
Descartes: 30
"Dialectics" ["*Dialektik*"]: 8, 40
Distinction [*Unterscheidung*]: 70,
111, 122

Earth [*Erde*]: 110
Errancy [Irre]: 18f., 20, 48f.

"Facts" ["*Tatsachen*"]: 21ff.

Germans [*Deutsche*]: 11f., 32, 44f.
God [Gott]: 35

Historiology [*Historie*]: 3f., *20, 68,*
77, 95f.
History [Geschichte]: 1f., 54, 66,
72, 77f., 95ff., 121
Hölderlin: 42f., 52, 81, **97ff.,** 110
Human being [Mensch]: 30f., 55ff.,
108f.

Incalculable [*das* Unberechenbare]:
19, 91f., 96
Institution [*Einrichtungswesen*]:
106f.

Kant: 45ff.

Language [*Sprache*]: 26f., *104*

Meditation [*Besinnung*]: 23ff., 33f.,
53
Metaphysics [*Metaphysik*]: 50, 97ff.
Modernity [*Neuzeit*]: 4ff., 18, 34,
35f., 105

Nietzsche: 42f., 50, 52f., 77, 97ff.

Opposition [*Gegensatz*]: 49f.

Para-doxon: 18
People [*Volk*]: 45, 96
Philosophy [Philosophie]: 19, 20f.,
36ff., **61ff.,** 65, **78ff., 84f.,** *86f.,*
101f., 114
"Philosophy of existence"
["*Existenzphilosophie*"]: 50f.
Ponderings [*Überlegungen*]: *33*
"Positive" ["*Positives*"]: 23f.

"Refinement" ["*Bildung*"]: 30
Resisters [*die Widerständigen*]: 47f.,
55
Retardation [*Verlangsamung*]: 59
"Revolutions" ["*Revolutionen*"]:
69f., 77, 122

Schelling: 86ff.
Science [Wissenschaft]: 10f., 20
Solitude [*Einsamkeit*]: 52, 54
Struggle [Kampf]: 82, 111
Style [*Stil*]: 76f.
"Subjectivism" ["*Subjektivismus*"]:
56ff.

Theory of categories
[*Kategorienlehre*]: 60

PONDERINGS VIII

a   Beings—the solitude of beyng, a solitude gone astray into what is publicly present-at-hand.

The present-at-hand: what is available to production and to representation, is sighted in such availability, and is admitted only into the horizon of this sight. The seizing of such beings develops into an institution. Out of the latter arises the certainty of public opinion, which spreads an invisible shield over the present-at-hand and accepts the prevailing of a *semblance* of being. "Nature" and "history" are incorporated into this sphere of beings, are altogether seen, i.e., explained, only within that sphere, and are made handy for the public hand of calculative instituting. Everything surpassing the things that are proximally present-at-hand and explainable is always only a transfiguration of what is explained. Every reaching out to being, from the publicness of the present-at-hand, extends at any time only to a transfiguration which, as its means become more exciting and captivating, is all the more definitively the blockage of all the paths to something originary. Everything that transfigures descends into the past. Only something originary decides a future of humans and points them toward the bridge to the acceptance of another essence.

If the gods are once again from afar underway on the long bridge toward humans, then the human masses, who desire everything and miss nothing, must be securely blindfolded against what is merely a being, so that the curiosity of seeking lived experiences will not block the bridge nor thwart what is coming. Therefore the one who knows cannot deplore—and must not reproach—the raving of the blind and of those without a sense of plight; the one who knows must practically be able to send a greeting to the age of the calculation of his own regulated needs—for that is at issue to the incalculable, to the obscure intimation of a departing god, and such intimation perhaps—we do not know—announces the Last[1] god.

The *decision* of the approaching ones, whereby they become future ones or else presently past ones: do you belong among the proclaimers of what is merely a being—or *are* you someone who holds beyng in silence? (Cf. p. 39.)

A genuine knowledge of the essence of *history* as well as steadfastness in history—must be prepared for anyone who, heedful of the abandonment of mere beings by being, has to accomplish the transition into the completely other age. For this transition can be carried out only from the highest knowledge, since such knowledge must break the power of *historiology*—representational calculation—and in order to do so must first recognize it *as* a deranging power. Yet to such a knowledgeable transition, there still remains enough of what cannot be known, and indeed the transition alone is the preparation for the truth of what is concealed.

Whoever has surmised the essence of history—the appropriation of the human being into Dasein, the appropriation arising out of beyng as event—will know clearly enough that as a consequence of "metaphysics" all "historical philosophy" serves only "historiology" and makes history familiar, even according to "laws," levels, and "types."

In addition, however, we must know the essence of history, in order to be able to keep safe the truth that what genuinely and purely "Happens" has always to remain what is most concealed.

---

1. [Regarding capitalized adjectives, see the editor's afterword, p. 354–55.—Trans.]

1   *3*

The coldness of the bravery of thinking and the night of the errancy of questioning lend to the *fire of beyng* the pure jolt by which its heat and its light blaze up. Coldness and night are the concealed coffers in which what is simple is preserved from touch. But we too readily and too frequently avert coldness and night; we tolerate them only as the negatives of warmth and day, for we think out of the comfort of everydayness. And everydayness can be so insistent because in the "beings" and "realities" it offers we believe we have also already found being itself.

The devaluation, in the double form of the averting of the negative, also deprives us of the possession of heat and light. We prefer what is lukewarm and overcast and make that the center for the semblance with which we then reckon in the oppositions of light and dark, warm and cold. We are very little aware that the domains in which we encounter these oppositions are decisive. Therefore we so easily fall into 2 the play of "antitheses," which counts as | an expression of insights. And yet the "antitheses" are inextricably duped through the undecidedness of the domains in which they are encountered. But how are these decided?

We must question back all the way to the distinction between beyng and beings in order to find a foothold for meditation here. This distinction, however, is not an opposition; if the distinction (and what underlies it) is originarily the inceptual, then opposition is never first. Then coldness and night do not negate; but neither can an affirmation—addressed to them—touch the miraculous fact that they preserve what is simple in its first decisiveness. We relate both, together with their oppositions, to our sense organs and believe we have thereby explained something. This prejudice is nevertheless only the ungrasped consequence of a much more originary pre-judgment whose inceptuality already forbids us from calling it a pre-judgment— this more originary pre-opinion is the mania to explain being through beings, which thus for the longest time will prevent an interrogative knowledge of being. But the night belongs to beyng and is not merely an "image" of it, a sensibilizing of something nonsensuous: how is the 3 night supposed to sensibilize—| if it is itself nothing sensuous and therefore also nothing nonsensuous—, indeed altogether nothing objective that could be represented—nothing of a being—but instead is an essential occurrence of beyng. What we ordinarily call night and from an old tradition recognize in a remainder of beingness, is never the first—but only something hackneyed we now employ to indicate darkness. Yet this reference to the "night" allows only an approximate intimation of how much our language as language—not merely in its separate "expressivity"—is alienated from beyng—must have become alien—because perhaps already the first—*historically* essential—words could not persist in the power of the beyng which is to be said, and they consequently fled into beings.

We still know nothing of the essential affiliation of beyng and language; grammar studies and linguistic philosophy are in fact themselves already consequences of the disempowerment of beyng through beings. But when will we grasp the absurdity of linguistic philosophy and realize that philosophy itself can arise again only out of a complete essential transformation—better: out of an essential discovery—of language. A poor and very preliminary paving of the way for this essential discovery of language | is the carefulness of speech in every   4
attempt at "thinking." For here language is above all never the "expression" or "means of formulation" of a thought, but rather is the originary conjunction of thinking and what is thought; from this conjunction, the mere instrumental use of language then extracts "the thought," which in turn is precisely only then a "thought" to which we must assign a "reality," so that it might "count" in the world of calculation and lived experience. The most desolate destructions of the earth, which now delineate their frantic progressions, are merely something incidental over and against that invisible and inaudible process, imperceptible in every direction of "lived experience," of the complete uprooting of language.

In the proliferation of oratory and journalism, and these again in the form they take on the radio, this process finds not its causes but rather only quite remote and crude consequences of its ultimate massification in the gigantism of its complete concealment.

Therefore "today"—in these centuries—thinking is impotent; better: the power of thinking—in case thinking would be ventured and is ventured—lacks resistance and impact. For never can what is unquestioning and the age that is completely unquestioning summon up resistance | against what is most question-worthy. The most prox-   5
imate domain of resistance is only the questionability of all beings, and our age can have no courage for this questionability, since the age would thereby have to place itself in a decision that is equally contrary to everything "doctrinaire" and machinational. The thinking of beyng could strike up against beings and become perceptible; but what if beings have become nonbeings and in them everything has become

evident? Of what avail would here be the fire of beyng? It would avail nothing here—but only *there* where the human being sets out to find his way back to the simple decisions from which beings arise as the preservation of beyng. This "there" displays another beginning of history, and such a beginning will come, provided the commencing a-historicality of historiological humanity does not introduce the complete end of humanity and accordingly, as an a-historical age, is not only obliged to this process but makes it altogether inaccessible and ungraspable.

Every "revolution" is not only too weak to stand up to this process and overpower it, but is radically unfit to do so. But what does stand *against* this process is, as a volition of the transition, the thinking of beyng, which must know in advance this one thing, namely, that | only beyng itself in its essential occurrence is able to project such a thinking and no planning or calculation or even "willfulness" is of any help—today's humanity is here at most capable of merely not resisting. Of course—that already requires a persistence in meditation on the one necessity of questioning; this necessity is not to be measured with any gigantic amount of today's "consumption of energy," because it derives from a different essential volition of humanity, i.e., from a different truth of beyng.

This truth requires that bravery of thinking and that errancy of questioning which have left all doubt behind because they know this single thing with regard to the concealed essence of humanity: the human being is the one thrown into the truth of beyng and so is consigned to the possibility of the projection of that truth, but in this thrownness he is himself a being and, *because* he is this, is excluded from pure steadfastness in beyng—beyng as the "*between*" of the unique encounter of gods and humans. Thence stems the possibility of bravery and errancy—because the human is that being who, on the basis of this being, stands in the truth of beyng and yet is never | able to be beyng. Therefore, in rare moments of history that compel an essential transformation of humanity out of the essential occurrence of beyng, and that brings the human being more originarily into errancy and thus into the nearness to the truth of beyng, *everything* must be *ventured* in thinking: not primarily the whole of beings and their extant ground—but rather the uniqueness of beyng and the fact that beyng *is*. But the human being—seen in that originariness—is the unique being that is consigned to beyng and at the same time remains removed from it, and out of this intermediate position can find the uniqueness of a grounding of the truth of beyng, a grounding we call *Da-sein*.

Only one who is inextricably caught in the propensity to the great ventures of questioning can become a grounder of the truth of beyng. Only he is able to see what now *is historical,* which is altogether different from what historiology will establish today and tomorrow.

4

What is now happening is the *ending* of the history of the great beginning of Western humanity; in this beginning, the human being was called to the stewardship of beyng, although this calling was immediately transformed into the claim of representing beings in their machinational distorted essence.

Yet the end of this first beginning is not a stopping; instead, it is a genuine commencement, which, however, remains withdrawn from itself in its truth, because it must order everything according to mere surfaces. For only from instituting the surface and from dancing on it can today's human being, such as he knows himself (namely, as subjectum), find himself confirmed. And he needs confirmation, because he has long since abandoned the venture of beyng and abandoned himself to the cultivation and calculation of what is present-at-hand. The knowledge of what is now happening as this end remains therefore denied first and last precisely to those who are selected to start this ending in its most final form (gigantism) and to pose the a-historical, in the guise of the historiological, as *"the"* historical. From here, there is no transition to the other beginning. The transition must recognize the a-historical as the most superficial gray dregs of a concealed history, so that the transition, by way of a broad interrogative leap ahead, might save humanity into history. 8

In the a-historical, that which belongs together only within it comes most readily into the unity of a complete commixture; the apparent buildup and renewal and the complete destruction—these are the same—the groundless ones, those addicted to mere beings and those alienated from beyng. As soon as the | a-historical "holds its own," the licentiousness of "historicism" commences—; groundlessness in the most varied and opposed forms—without these recognizing themselves as of the same distorted essence—falls into an extreme hostility and a mania for destruction. 9

The "victor" in this "struggle," which contests goallessness pure and simple and which can therefore only be the caricature of a "struggle," is perhaps the greater groundlessness that, not being bound to anything, avails itself of everything (Judaism). Nevertheless, the genuine victory, the one of history over what is a-historical, is achieved only

where what is groundless excludes itself because it does not venture
beyng but always only reckons with beings and posits their calculations as what is real.

5

One of the most concealed forms of the *gigantic,* and perhaps the oldest,
is a tenacious facility in calculating, manipulating, and interfering;
through this facility the worldlessness of Judaism receives its ground.

6

A changeover into the gigantic is still in store for "everydayness" and
the "they." The "inauthenticity" of Da-sein still moves at present in
what is harmless. But there are still harmless, childish ones who cal-
culate and who believe | that the instituting of the "community of the
people" will overcome "everydayness" and the "they" (as supposed
symptoms of the urban world of decadence). The blindness of such a
belief arises from a growing incapacity to think beyng rather than establish beings.

7

Treitschke calls the time of German Idealism "the days of philosophical arrogance."[2] Should we then be surprised if ordinary au-
thors and "publicists" belittle that age and to the Germans defame
"philosophy" as a "sin" and as an essential mistake? The fact that at
the same time German "thinkers" are "celebrated" on occasions when
it would serve cultural-political ends goes together very well with
that derision, for both stem from the same muddy source of a-historical ignorance.

8

In "historiological" ("psychological" and "biographical") ages, what
most crudely block the way to the truth of the works and partial works
of the creative ones, and thwart every formation of space, are the creative ones themselves, their presence at hand as "living beings" of their
public which already considers them historiologically before they can

---

2. {Heinrich von Treitschke, *Deutsche Geschichte des 19. Jahrhunderts,* 5 vols.
(Leipzig: Hirzel, 1879ff.) The twenty-third chapter discusses the "arrogance of
speculation."}

even start to become historical. The fact that Hölderlin was taken away so early and remained a mystery to his "times" and to the "public" | and was misinterpreted as a "romantically" miscarried "classicist"— all this may be seen as latent proof that his poetry harbors a truth reaching far in advance and off the beaten path, perhaps even harbors the sounding of the essence of the future truth itself.

But why are those gone away able to contribute more to pave the paths for questioning beyng than those merely ensnared in beings? It cannot be because now their "work" stands for itself; on the contrary, the departure itself casts over the partial work something inexhaustible and suggestive, such that to it every semblance of something piecemeal keeps its distance and bestows a peculiar mode of the grounding of truth. Of course, this occurs only if the departure is not again explicated merely "historiologically"-"psychologically" and misused as a means of explaining the "work." But what is known today is only the historiological concept of the work, not the historical.

And where one wants to get beyond the historiological view of the work, one arrives at "aesthetics" (the work as arouser of lived experiences). But since "aesthetics" is linked in a genuinely psychological (rather than historical) way to the "aesthete," and the latter is understood as the mere individual enjoyer, the work is then taken "politically." But this is only a particular designation for the exaggeration of aesthetics and for the | silent enjoyment of the individual in the instituted arrangement of the lived experience and enjoyment of the "community." This proliferation of aesthetics is only a consequence of the *historiological* mode of thinking. Therefore the talk of the work can also fit in with the newly arisen political aesthetics and then refers again merely to what is over and against the creators and the enjoyers. Every interpretation of Hölderlin (borne solely by the unexpressed task regarding the history of being) is irremediably subject to misunderstanding in the domain of feeling of public aesthetics, even before such interpretations are tested. Or could they overcome aesthetics? For that, historiology would have to be overcome first, which in turn requires the destruction of the a-historicality.

All of this says only that here any sort of intention immediately based on an "overcoming" can accomplish nothing and acts against itself, assuming that in it a presentiment of the necessity of a historical beginning is operative. Then we must come to see that that departure of the poet is not a historiological incident; instead, it derives from the essence of beyng itself. But this represents the decision as to whether we can belong to beyng or want to remain mere slaves of beings. But whether this decision does or does not become necessary | lies concealed in the freedom of beyng. Yet we can surmise concealment and

11

12

13

from that presentiment know the self-refusal, only if what is simple has struck us and placed us into the open domain.

The contrary of freedom is not compulsion, but the semblance of freedom in the form of training. But where the calculative institution determines the quality of an order, there education must become training. And to be trained toward the supports and expedients of the institution is then called "character"; the latter makes this knowledge dispensable and takes questioning ultimately as an object of derision, which is the most ordinary form of possessing what is most ordinary, namely, approval. Approval fills the void of publicness and places itself, as the semblance of publicness, before the silenced voice of the people, who know themselves only historiologically and—in case historiology is still too bright for them—seek their essential confirmation in the pre-historiological and definitively renounce history.

9

Historiology—is the properly explanatory determination of what is at hand, what is "present." Only incidentally does historiology relate to the past (cf. p. 28). To take something historiologically therefore means to make it intelligible as present day and in the accessibility | of someone of today. Historicism is not the dissolution of everything into the historiological, in the sense of the immediately past and enduring, but is rather the calculation of history in regard to the present with the means of today. The more poor in history an age becomes by its very essence, all the more eagerly does it pursue historiology, which becomes the basic form of the self-consciousness of the age. Historiology is thus a sibling of "technology"; both are fundamentally the same. This is at once the reason the modern natural sciences and human sciences—on the level of their proper essential fulfillment, i.e., superficiality—prove to be identical, such that one cannot even speak of a relationship here. It might seem remarkable that today no one yet sees this sameness of essence and that, on the contrary, such a "profound" oppositionality has opened between the two groups of sciences that any sort of agreement is excluded. But precisely that is a sign of the sameness of essence; for agreement can never take place as regard content and objects, because it already exists unrecognized in the essence, i.e., in the mode of procedure, indeed in the procedure as such. And this sameness allows precisely a manifoldness in the objects that becomes ever more inconsequential | over and against the equal—i.e., equally gigantic—mastery of everything in calculability and explanation. That is why the sciences fuse more and more into everydayness and become as inconsequential and yet at the same time as useful as a bake shop or a canal system. In other words: the sciences

maintain a directedness toward the representing and producing of beings and move within a (to themselves always inaccessible) truth
about beings as such and about the possible articulation of beings into
regions. This articulation can have validity in the sciences themselves
only as a distinction of their respective objects (nature vs. history).
The sciences never research the essence of beings, but instead claim
and exploit an essential determination in their own way. The essence
of beings—being—is altogether not *subject to research,* taking research
as the mark of the scientific relation to beings.

Only when being and the question of being fall victim to forgetting
do we pay heed to research in its process and in its results. Research
then assumes the role of "spiritual" creativity; "art" and "science" are
named together. Sciences are decisionless; I they are unable to make   16
necessary and develop any essential decision. They are labile in their
direction of work and in their application. Only because the previous
"cultural" idealism (for which "science" constituted a value for itself
and in itself, next to "art" and "religion") remained unclear about the
essence of this "culture" and about its modern character could the
transition from "science in itself" to "political science" become something like a shock. Soon thereafter, everything settled down and the
term "political science" was no longer heard, demonstrating only that
this transition changed nothing at all and could not change anything
that would have been allowed to touch the previous science in its essence. This "transition," which is actually not such, but only more of
the same with a certain twist, would be suited to let the current state
of affairs be recognized *as the same* as the previous one, so that the
prayer leaders of the "new" science would lack an excuse for arrogance
and the partisans of the "old" science would be deprived of a reason
to "mourn" something that had disappeared. But we avoid recognizing this; and that means we are *still more* scientific in the previous
sense than we were before. We do not want to *know* anything of ourselves; instead, we merely pursue a reciprocal confirmation of a I state   17
already entered—i.e., we take ourselves historiologically and in that
way arrive at a historiology of science. Indeed even these ponderings
and considerations, over and against the urgency of the results and
usefulness of research, remain entirely on the margin of the pursuit
of science.

But even this that is marginal and decisionless, this veneer of spirit,
must still be drawn into an institution, in the form of a "docent
school."[3] The original idea seeking to gain validity under this name
has already been perverted to its opposite. A docent university could

---

3. {Cf. Martin Heidegger, "Zur Einrichtung der Dozentenschule," in: *Reden und
andere Zeugnisse eines Lebensweges* (Frankfurt: Klostermann, 2000), pp. 308–314.}

have only *one* task: to place in question the whole of modern science and thus the whole age, or in other words to introduce such meditation in those who are serious and knowledgeable, and to do so from various sides, in order to prepare a situation in which "science"—without detriment to its continuation as research—would no longer be taken historiologically, but instead would have to be submitted to a decision with respect to its historical bearing. This "docent university" would require a freedom in contrast to which the much-discussed "freedom of science" could present only the distorted essence. The "academies," however, aim at the reverse: they pursue the instituting

18   of a "dogmatism"; they bring about a further indoctrinating | of the university, under the *semblance* of a higher meditation. Even this raging mania for "academies"—not only in the sciences, but in all pursuits—is pure historicism but at the same time is a proliferation of what was formerly despised as merely "academic," a proliferation into the horizon of those who had been excluded: soon everyone will be a fellow of some "academy" or other.

What was once a concern of the few, and not always the preeminent ones, and what used to harbor a challenge, has now on a "historiological" path (through the historicist pursuit of culture) become a self-evident mass state of affairs. It is in such processes that we can first recognize the "power" of "historiology" and surmise the extent of its destruction of history. Historiology receives the ultimate entrenchment when the "refinement" and the "possibility of the lived experience" of the "cultural assets" become the right and even the political duty of everyone. The interlacing of historiology with technology is carried out with necessity and on the basis of the essence of modernity and of the modern determination of humanness. This interlacing allows the pursuit of culture instituted in it to take on the semblance of universality and greatness and to steer under full sail

19   around the uncharted abysses of history. | Here lies the root of the impotence for a historical downgoing. "Historicism" becomes the basic form of the unfolding of "nihilism"; for the latter attains its irresistible force only when what was formerly great and essential starts to be flattened down to the level of the masses and thus an immediate degrading of what is great and essential cannot be avoided.[4] Where "culture" is functionally instituted and the promotion of culture is bruited about in a "slogan," the avoidance of a decision regarding beyng is already in train.

The exclusive and "passionate" affirmation of "life" and of beings hides the most dangerous nihilism. Over and against "life" and beings,

---

4. [Reading *nicht* ("not") *vermieden* for *vermieden*.—Trans.]

this nihilism is merely a semblance that bears the "not" and the "no" and the "nothing" like a shield before itself, where what is Godless and worldless and groundless is plain as day. The essence of historiology cannot be read off from or limited to "historical science"; the latter is much rather merely a relatively conventional form and technical entrenchment of historiology. Equally insufficient is the identification of historiology with historiological consciousness (i.e., consciousness of the past). The metaphysical presupposition of historiology is the determination of the human being as *animal rationale*—the givenness of the human being as a "psychologically," "biologically," "morally," "aesthetically" representable present-at-hand thing that "develops."

10   20

Language.—The Germans will not grasp—let alone fulfill—their Western destiny, unless they are equipped for it by the originality of their language, which must ever again find its way back to the simple, uncoined word, where the closeness to beyng bears and refreshes the imprintability of discourse. But at first the German language will be sacrificed to Latin-Italian phrasemongering, to journalistic flattening, and to "technical" "standardizing." The mere elimination or translation of foreign words is insignificant if such a purification does not arise from an incisive necessity of discourse, for it will then merely conceal the just-mentioned mode of the destruction of language.

11

Heroes who seek publicity, or even need it, in order to confirm themselves before it are not heroes; for they have already renounced the first condition of the highest valor: solitude. It follows that *we* cannot at all know the genuine heroes, provided the word "know" could have any place here.

12

Historicism is always accompanied by a superficial appraisal of the "present," although it indeed ought to have available all the threads I leading into the past and making the present explainable, i.e., histo-   21 riologically determinable. Thus one believes one is now showing a special regard for the present by equating it with late antiquity and thereby thinking of decadence and end, exorbitance and presumption. But this equating—even if weakened to a mere corresponding— is not only historically impossible—it also and above all produces no

meditation on the present, for such meditation can never be "negative"—which that one is, however—not even if the age should historically be an ending. Admittedly, even a "positive" evaluation does not
promote meditation, for such evaluation is basically only an interpretation deriving from a countervolition and is reactive—finding everything "good" or indeed "not bad" and requiring "expectancy"—even
here a historiological calculation, except with a change of sign. Meditation on an age in which meditation itself historically belongs must
entirely avoid the evaluative opposition of "negative"-"positive," indeed must stand altogether outside of "evaluation." This "outside"
leads to the margin of decisionality—indeed so definitively that decision as such now comes up for decision. Decision as such: whether the
22   ground of the human being I is to be taken from the truth of beyng or
from beings. The first case produces the necessity of a transformation
of the human being into Da-sein; the other—previous—case yields a
(perhaps ultimate) entrenchment of the human being as hitherto, the
animal rationale in the form of the "subject."

13

If the crowd is supposed to determine what "spirit" and "culture"
are, then the sovereignty has fallen to *"psychology"*—which investigates and explains the "spirit" and "Spiritual creation" as present-at-
hand things. Of what sort the "psychology" is, whether explanatory
or descriptive, individual or social, "rational" or "biological," remains
of subordinate importance, because in each case *humanness* is not at
all disclosively questioned. What is pursued is only an explanation of
the extant human being.

For even the "spirit" and the "spiritual" (the "mental" and the "animating") are of the same debasing and ontologically obstructive sort
as the "psychic." The most superficial of all kinds of "psychology" and
"anthropology"—thus also, however, the most common kind and the
most impressive to the "people"—can be found in the "typologies";
there the so-to-speak *calculating* with human exemplars is carried to
an extreme. And since typologies always work together with oppositions, and since "oppositions" (mere oppositions which never recol-
23   lect their own I ground) are what is most commonly understandable
to the usual way of thinking, therefore the consideration of the human being now reaches the level of the "ordinary." Such "typologies"
are mere plunderings from Nietzsche's thought, *without* its genuine
impetuses and abysses, and so this activity of "psychology" takes on,
for those who know, the character of buffoonery, whose buffoons
must admittedly be reckoned among the most boring human "types"

which are to be pursued. If "psychology" is completely built up as an institution in which knowledge of the human being is functionally secured, then this "development" is not in itself surprising. If the human being has become incapable of placing himself out into the essential decisions (i.e., of venturing his own determination out of the essence or distorted essence of beyng and of rising and falling on that venture), then he comes into the hands of the sciences of the human being (anthropology, biology, and psychology). And then there "develops" the semblance that the human being is looking into himself, whereas in truth he is only (even in "depth psychology") creeping along on the surface of himself as a present-at-hand object and poking his nose into the properties of that object.

This semblance of going into oneself engenders the next, to the effect that it will one day be discovered thereby what a human being "is" and accordingly ought to be. But how I can the *being* of the human being ever become known, if all questioning of being is thwarted and the *being* of the human being (*animal rationale—ens qua subiectum et obiectum* ["rational animal—a being as subjectum and objectum"]) is settled beyond question? Yet that mad straying of anthropology and psychology into such a manifold semblance allows a first glimpse of the reason all common "thinking" must be greedy for such science— namely, because the latter confirms the apparent justification of that "volition" *not* to know who one is and yet to pretend one possesses secure knowledge of how to lead others. All psychology therefore always only plays the bailiff for the warding off of every *question* of the human being under the flag of "anthropology," "psychology," and "biology."

That double semblance (of going into oneself and of knowing the *being* of the human being) drives ultimately into a third (or is driven by that third?), to the effect that a knowledge of beings as a whole could unfold out of cognitions about the human being as the center of beings. According to this illusion, "psychology" must become *the* science of the various "worldviews," not only in the sense that "psychology" itself presses in that direction and thus replaces "philosophy" or at least poses as the "scientific" form of philosophy, but also that the "worldviews" themselves make it their ambition I to see themselves grounded "scientifically." It concurs very well with the way of "thinking" of the "worldviews" that they at the same time covertly or openly battle "intellectualism" and "science."

These connections between "psychology" and "worldview" as well as the battle of "science" against philosophy were thoroughly rehearsed in the 1880s and 1890s—the heyday of the most ordinary liberalism—and now "live" their resurrection in the forms of the gi-

24

25

gantic. All of this is arched over by the Christian-pagan cathedral of organized Wagnerism and by the romantic renewal of all romanticism. Herder and Wagner as cardinals of this Church, in which even Catholicism provides the side chapels, while the German powers of Protestantism (the attitudinal, formational, and patrimonial components) are rubbed away.

But everything that could be mentioned about "psychology" would remain insignificant if taken as a historiological characterization of current states of affairs. Essential is history alone, which is merely disguised by those states—; "psychology" and its pressing forward into the public comprehension that accommodates it are merely corollaries of the end of metaphysics in the sense of the priority of beings and of the pursuit of beings over beyng and | its truth. Psychology must remain ignorant of that which it serves; only in this way can psychology develop the zeal and the claim it needs in order to consider itself important enough. For within the processes of the consummation of modernity, psychology ever remains something supplementary which idly poses as the foundation.

Yet "psychology" is not meant here in the sense of that "department" within the "school of sciences" at a university, in which guise it had its origin and ever since has "lived" and still "lives" only on regressive feelings and "reactive" undertakings. "Psychology" as understood here concerns the self-interpretation of all "lived experience." And it is also understood in its sovereignty over everything we must call ink spilling, which includes "poetry" and "journalism." Psychology is the institutional form of the modern spirit, whereby the "spirit" itself derives from the humanity of the Middle Ages and of late antiquity and institutes "culture" as its functional form. Furthermore: only as occurrences of the abandonment of beings by being and as witnesses to the lack of a sense of plight of modern humanity, drunk with needs, can the states of affairs be known, provided a truth and an essentiality are supposed to inhere in those states.

27   *14*

Historiology as Devotion to Beings.—Science (research) as a "religious" attitude (cf. p. 116).

There might insinuate itself here the opinion that "historiology," in opposing history, is ever to be evaluated negatively. But first and foremost, historiology is not the "opposite" of history; each is of such a different essence that they can never be brought into opposition. But that does not exclude their differentiation. Historiology, in an age that delineates it through its sovereignty, can become the basic form in which beings as a whole are thought, everything previously great (un-explainable) is retained in memory, called into it, and everything present is pursued in that way. The future is here only an expedient for what is present, a detour quickly abandoned, but indeed traversed in order to come back to the present. Historiological memory thinks of everything and, thanks to this possession, brings to the human being a feeling of wealth and belonging, so that he—unnoticed only by himself—finds himself confirmed as the promoter of the highest human goods.—In the absence of the gods (who are indeed no longer missed), the lived experience of the historiological organizations | of lived experience becomes a devotion and thus the form of the consummation of religion; e.g., the *organization* of the Wagnerian festivals *as* organizations. It is no accident that thereby still the abdominal music of Wagner and much else that is "romantic" in the usual sense is also played, for the genuine and essential romanticism is nothing other than the devotional instituting of the devotion to "lived experience" (music, medieval German, and art as religion).   28

All of this presupposes that the human being has become the sub-jectum. Romanticism is an essential phase of modernity and is possible only in it. The significance of romanticism for the configuration of the nineteenth century will be recognized only if grasped as essentially as it is in the excellent—though romantic—book by Richard Benz,[5] who is himself a genuine and farsighted romantic. Only in the essence of the sovereignty of historiology do the "elements" of romanticism flow together. The fact that this essence of historiology does not explicitly manifest itself is merely a confirmation of that confluence. The historiological work of the romantics and its effect on the configuration of historiology as a science in the nineteenth and twentieth centuries are *primarily consequences* of that sovereignty of "historiology" (cf. above, p. 13ff.).

Today, however, since historiology | has already been penetrated by a historicism (p. 20f.) and instituted anew to something complete, it is first becoming the genuine devotional form that makes a "religion" which has no need of gods the object of religious lived experience. An age in which culture as such (and thus also the nineteenth-century theory of culture—as well as religion as a cultural value) becomes the object of lived experience must know itself in possession of the "true" "religiosity"; its "God" is the lived experience of religion itself. The calculability of the prevalence of the *instituting* of all procedures and representations gives this religiosity at the   29

5. {Richard Benz, *Die deutsche Romantik: Geschichte einer geistigen Bewegung.* (Leipzig: Reclam, 1937).}

same time its own fitting "Church." And everyone is underestimating if he does *not* seek in this decisive age (one that consummates modernity) *the gathering up* of romanized antiquity, of the romantic Middle Ages, and of the modernity viewed on the basis of the nineteenth century, in order thereby to recognize the most modern form of the historiological calculation of the entire previous Western "history." Insofar as ecclesiastical Christianity, in its various configurations, claims a corresponding (apologetic) gathering up of the "truth" of the previous history, it must attempt today—in league with the powers of disarrangement and uprooting—a "confrontation" with this consum-

30 mation of modernity in order perhaps to draw even this latter | into its own "truth" or—which would be even more dangerous—to lure it into a complete fusion with this Christianity.

The continuing uniformity in the instituting of representations and procedures as well as all the apparently unsurveyable oppositionality within the content do not exclude such an unobtrusive "victory" of the now long since uncreative and Godless Christianity and Romanism. Thereby historiology, which arose out of *Christian apologetics,* would return to its origin and would consummate its sovereignty. Whether and to what degree the Roman Church thereby remains superficially extant is of minor importance. The subsiding of this extrinsic configuration could at most obscure the capacity of this institution for change and concealment. In the complete sovereignty of historiology (i.e., in the sovereignty of modernity), everything past comes to *a* constant presence, one that is available immediately and easily, according to need, so much so that *this* presence can no longer know, and no longer even wants to know, that *it* is the past itself: what is plightless in the form of the highest activity and of the disavowal of every possibility of history. The human being is then so definitively

31 caught up in beings that beyng | must be completely isolated from him.

Yet only then does there draw near the moment of the first decision, the decision that grounds history. No one knows the when and how of this moment; only its *that* and its origin out of the most free freedom are *known* to those dispersed ones who bear the beams for the narrow bridge of the transition from the increasing decisionlessness into the still fleeing decision. This knowledge is not a "belief," inasmuch as what is thereby meant is only the supplementary and thus dependent resistance to an explanatory representation. This knowledge is steadfastness in the truth of beyng—; not communicable to calculation nor "unreal" according to the measures of the reality of everything instituted and of the "deeds" and "accomplishments" subordinated to it. Such knowledge in itself—i.e., precisely in its being struck by beyng—is both the *measure* of what is worthy of decision and the *intimation* of the preliminary decisions:

are you one who merely amuses or annoys your contemporaries;
are you one who can still recollect what is great and simple;
are you one who is becoming an impetus to meditation;
are you one who is creating for beyng a path of its history?—
But where historiology reigns, the mania for effectiveness and the
need for validity are in good company with "cultural work"—the
forms opposed to "devotion."

15   32

By coming to understand a *philosophy*—supposing there is such a thing
as philosophy—one has not yet grasped it, i.e., thought out beyond
it into its conceptuality; on the contrary, one has simply degraded
it below itself. The "lay person" is of the opinion that philosophical
thinking is "abstract," and the "expert," the philosophical scholar,
benefits from that opinion. In truth, however, philosophical thinking
is neither abstract nor concrete but, as the thinking of beyng, cannot
at all be assessed according to the modes of the representation of beings. (Cf. pp. 40–41.)

16

Historiology and culture.—The essence of today's culture is cultural politics. This politics pursues the continuation of a "romanticism" under
the star of Richard Wagner, a "romanticism" drawn into the massive,
the ordinary, and the loud and specifically instituted and planned for
that purpose. Those who still retain enough taste, refinement, and
judgment might then believe they could assist the construction of a
total German culture through a historiological transmission of the
genuine romantic movement. Here even *Christian* cultural politics, the
oldest of its kind, might hope to be a participant one day very unob-
trusively. All these endeavors regarding culture calculate historiologically. And as indeed historicism seizes upon what is populist [*volks-
haft*[6]] as its object, I it then already appears to be justified, through this   33
content, as the prescriptive mode in which a people is brought to itself and into the possession of its "truth." This communal [*volklich*]
historicism now places all creativity in the shackles of a binding to the

---

6. [Heidegger employs in these notebooks primarily three adjectives derived
from the noun *das Volk*, "people": *volkhaft*, *volklich*, and *völkisch*. I have rendered
them respectively as "populist," "communal," and "folkish" and have placed the
German term in brackets at each occurrence. The term *völkisch* has racial over-
tones. It is up to the reader to determine Heidegger's attitude toward the over-
tones of each term.—Trans.]

people, under the semblance of having finally discovered and pointed out the true soil of the roots of culture. What does not correspond to these (very confused and mixed) representations of the historiology of what is populist [*volkhaft*] and proper to a people [*volksmäßig*] is then—historiologically calculated—alien to a people [*volksfremd*].

By essence, all creativity from the very first shatters what is historiologically familiar, since precisely as a creating it ventures out into something indeterminate and other. This venture, however, arises so strictly from the genuine communal [*volklich*] rootedness that there is neither talk of it nor any sort of reference to it, because indeed the venture transforms the communal [*volklich*] for the first time into its previously unknown and historiologically unusual essence and therefore—historiologically—remains strange and "shocking." The venture of creativity is then completely and necessarily led into danger and off to the side, provided the "*truth*," in which the human being is supposed to create a ground for himself historically, must first be brought into the open realm through a questioning of what is most questionworthy. Indeed the historiological measures for the instituting of a populist [*volkhaft*] culture seem to overcome the admittedly ever ambiguous (genuine and ungenuine) internationalism. But the latter is merely dissolved into a wretched mishmash of something specifically national, I historiologically accessible. The arithmetic of the mixing within the various regions (e.g., the one of art) can even feign a creativity, where in truth the power of a genuine emulation is already lacking, the power that, differently than historiological imitation, does presuppose one's own historical force. The planning with respect to a total culture is then still overhasty and indeed superfluous if it lacks a prior clarification and grounding of whether in general a "culture" can still have historical force and can bear a history, inasmuch as precisely "culture" presupposes a determinate humanity, the one that has given itself the goal of a *pursuit* of beings and of their regions and in this goal sees in advance the complete assurance of its proper essence—i.e., modern humanity.

If now, however, not in virtue of progress but for the sake of being, modernity strives for its completion and end, and if thereby a history opens up to which "culture" must be inappropriate and above all must be insufficient as a form of human accomplishments and attitudes, then all endeavors regarding a communal [*volklich*] total culture will fall into the situation of pursuing the contrary of what they want. Indeed, precisely as cultural endeavors they *are* already definitively in the shackles of the historicism to which all that remains is to entrench a mishmash of the past into an eternal present and to introduce an a-historicality.

But a still higher danger comes to history through I historiology,   35
insofar as the latter (what pertains to its concept) has established itself as the unobtrusive basic form of everyday representation and
opinion: the danger that everything creative, scarcely having ventured out in public, rather than transform anything, might itself be
changed into the past, not in the crude form whereby it is explained
as having already been and is thereby rendered harmless, but rather
in that insidious mode according to which the change into the past
and the fusion with it do at the same time concede and appropriate
something new, whereas in truth they are opposed to every decision
and essential transformation. But even if what creates history overcomes the resistance of the historiological (the historiologically current and fixed), it still faces a danger belonging to it essentially and
not on account of the sovereignty of historiology. The creative ones
themselves slip the standards of judgment into the hands and heads
of those who will later overcome and condemn and who, through the
unavoidable entrance into the public and usual, will cover over the
inceptual originariness of what is created.

Here "inceptual" originariness [*Ursprünglichkeit*] does nevertheless
not mean "originality" [*Originalität*]; the latter is a "historiological
category" of calculation based on what is then present. The inceptually originary is what grounds history, because it contains the nonre-
currence of the necessary decisions in the uniqueness of a configuration, and in erecting the future transposes past things to itself in the
originary essential truth. But if such I decisions are carried out and   36
taken over, the originary withdraws behind that which it itself decided and henceforth will disregard. This withdrawal of what is decisional and originary is not a flight from current beings; on the contrary, it merely testifies to an affiliation with beyng, to an issuing forth
out of the event. To enter into *history*—to become historical—means
to issue forth out of beyng and out of the withdrawal from beings, to
appertain to beyng, to refuse oneself as something concealed and out
of this self-refusal to appropriate humanity into Da-sein. History is
the appropriation of the concealedness of beyng (Ponderings VII, p.
66f.); *only* what issues from beyng enters into history—historically
thought. Historiologically thought, "to enter into history" means to
be assigned to what is past and settled and thus to be ever ascertain-
able historiologically. We know little enough of history, and that little
amount is even the unessential. Only *the fact that* we *know* little of it
decides the freedom for history and the dominance over historiology.
Such *knowledge* is the root of that still passion of the creative reverence
for what is unique and great. The Germans most of all lack this passion; what satisfies them instead is the learned or commanded, loud

and brief, adulation of whatever is at the time erected historiologically. Constancy and steadfastness in what is essential arise only out
of the lucidity of reverence.

37   The power for reverence cannot be inculcated, but the seed of its
growth devolves upon the human being when he is unsettled of beings and jolted into an unsettling by beyng, i.e., when he is released
for the assault of freedom and delivered up to the danger of what is
most question-worthy. But as long as the revering power is lacking,
historiology can let its arts play unhindered and unweakened.
Whether historiological cognitions thereby decrease or increase is im-
material. History is closed to historiology, and "culture" as cultural
politics is the last obstruction on the way to history. The better the *historiological* refinement, the more suitable is the cultural politics. The
more decisive the endeavors of the latter, the more indispensable remains the former. Therefore the "necessary" preservation of the historiological human sciences belongs just as necessarily ("compellingly") in the x-year plan of cultural politics as does the defense of
the natural sciences through the needs of the economic and ordnance
plans. "Metaphysically" seen (i.e., truly seen in terms of the history
of beyng), historiology is of the same essence as technology, and that
means above all that *technology is the historiology of nature.* Only thereby
is the most originary concept of historiology attained as well as the
abyssal distance to history. Accordingly, a knowledge of the essence
of the connection between historiology and culture is necessary—for
those who know.

38   *17*

Only a fool would believe that a transformation of humanity—i.e.,
here, a transformation of a people or even of the West—is to be sought
overnight or indeed at all. But even more wretched are those who
could never know that such a transformation, although not ascertain-
able historiologically, *is* and will be historical, according to that deeper
essence of history (p. 36) in which the concealment of beyng eventuates, such that this event remains concealed. Therefore even in the
self-knowledge of those who know, outside of historiological chro-
nologies and cultural changes and outside of the vacuous monotony
of an eternity which always remains too weak, the same uniqueness
of beyng is to be attained as the same through struggle. To know the
essence of history, i.e., to stand creatively in the truth of the essence
of history, to be constant in this steadfastness, means to be historically futural. This future has nothing in common with the historiologically calculated attachment to the forthcoming or not forthcoming

"better" times, an attachment that wavers back and forth between enthusiasm and despair. The self-knowledge of those who know, however, does itself belong to the essential occurrence of beyng; this self-knowledge is indeed never the "community" of the chosen ones but is instead the solitude of the solitary ones (Ponderings VII, p. 59), out of which everyone who essentially grounds knows himself appropriated by beyng as an intermediary in beyng itself, beyng qua the "between" for gods and humans. From this "between," the strife of world and earth I arises, and a truth to be preserved in beings is attained by way of strife.   39

18

Concerning the decision.—What is now to be decided is not the will of a generation versus that of a previous one, not the "spirit" of a century versus a passing century, not the essence of an age versus a forthcoming age, not Christianity versus a new "religion," and not two millennia of Western history versus an alien history; on the contrary, the decision is between the all too familiar and already mastered *beings* and the concealment of *beyng*. Will beings assert themselves, or will beyng shine a ray of its essence and allow humans to find themselves back into an originariness? At the beginning of Western history, this originariness was already announced to humans, obscurely enough, only to become lost forthwith: to attain for themselves through strife their essence as grounders and preservers of the truth of beyng. This decision between beings and beyng (not a logical either-or) is determined by the acuteness of its originariness in relation to what is unique of a unique historical destiny of a people. Only from the spatiotemporal field of this decision does the essential structure of a people arise, and all historiological-biological attempts to investigate and explain the conditions of a people amount to a pursuit of that blindness which makes humans unsuited for the appropriation by beyng and too small for the greatness of history.

In this decision I between beings and beyng, what is contested is   40 the familiarity, mastery, and correctness of beings versus the concealment of beyng. At the same time, what is contested between them as the space of the decision is the essence and essential force of correctness versus concealment, both of which in their own respective way belong originarily to the essence of truth (i.e., to the essence of the clearing of the concealed). Therefore, in that decision, as something necessary for its own decidability, what is co-decided is the essence of truth. Accordingly, insofar as we know of the decision and are compelled by its necessity, we are thrown into the question of the essence of truth. In the face of this question, what founders is all snatching at the "true" and at "truths," because such an effort, without an essential grounding of truth as such, lacks a basis and a path. But the essential grounding dovetails completely with that decision and is therefore not a supplementary and correspondingly otiose question regarding the Common features of "truths" already possessed (cf. lecture course 37–38[7]). Yet *this* question of the essence of truth already no longer allows "what is true" to be sought only or even primarily in beings (as the realities); such questioning is in itself already a transformation of the human being into his previous position toward beings and toward himself. Here for the first time the power of thinking (the thinking heedful of the history of beyng) manifests itself, and

41 this thinking can never be | "abstract," since it is never concrete and thus is not subordinate to any "logic" as a "norm."

And yet this thinking (the preparation of philosophy in the other beginning) is for itself a mere puff of wind if one supposes it could and should compel beings out of their rigidity and do the same for the humans turned only toward them. Decisive for the decision is never the immediate alteration of beings, but rather the mediate grounding of that originary essence of the human being out of which he responds to the uncompelled open domain of beyng and brings that domain to language through poetry and thought so that at the same time the essence of language might find its fixed ground. Accordingly, no longer sufficient for the preparation of the decision, let alone for its execution, is any effort toward a "better" art, one "bound to the people"; what suffices here is, at most, meditation on the essence of art and on what sort of essence that must be in order to bring the truth of beyng to sovereignty. But this essence is itself historical, and the essential capacity and essential height of art depend on its relation to beings and on its negative relation to beyng. Along with the essential historicality of art, there is also decided, however, which of its familiar and still unfamiliar "genres" are destined to ground the history of beyng. (Purely calculatively, to pursue *all* art equally means—leaving out the

42 pursuit itself—to misunderstand the essence of | art in its destiny to ground history.) The decision about the essence of truth includes one about the essence of art and thus furthermore one about the prescriptive determination of the decisive "genre" of art.

The decision is historical in the essential sense of deciding between history and a-historicality. A *historiological* consideration (regarding, e.g., the present *situation* of the West and of the peoples of the West)

---

7. {Martin Heidegger, *Grundfragen der Philosophie: Ausgewählte "Probleme" der "Logik,"* GA45 (Frankfurt: Klostermann, 1984).}

therefore never even attains the "level" or, better, the space of the decision; historiology as such belongs to that *about which* the decision is
to be made. Such meditation recognizes that the term "situation" is
already no longer sufficient to appraise what is unique of our "Da-
sein" (which is no such thing as a "situation") even only in its basic
traits for the decisive meditation; that is because we no longer find
ourselves in a position within historiologically determinable beings,
but instead know ourselves in the decisional space between beings
(and everything historiological) and beyng (and history). This is a
"place" which is supposed to become the origin for the space-time of
a standpoint or, better, of the paths necessary in that space-time (the
paths of the history of beyng, the transition). This "place" is perhaps
the primal home of the essence of solitude, assuming I solitude, sib-   43
ling to the essence of beyng, offers beyng its first and constant abode.

19

Eternity.—A remarkable error dominates human thinking, to the effect that eternity could be explained by timelessness, whereas the essence of eternity can be nothing other than the deepest oscillation *of
time* in its refusing and bestowing, preserving and losing.

20

To seize the most intrinsic determination, hardly surmised and seldom graspable, in its own proper center of gravity while renouncing
every foothold and letting all crutches and supports fall into the void
is perhaps a presumption, but without it nothing necessary comes to
fruition.

21

Standpoint.—Our standpoint, our place to stand, is not a "place," not
a present-at-hand and immediately assignable location in the space of
beings (such a location is suitable to the *subiectum*). Our stance is place-
lessly the steadfastness [*Inständigkeit*] of the granting of the place of
the "between" for gods and humans, without knowing the former,
without reaching the latter in their appertaining essential originariness. Our "standpoint" judges every recourse to "culture," to its goals
and their demands, as an evasion of the decisions. Our standpoint
makes I visible the conditionality of all care about the "substance" of   44
the people, especially if this "substance," as the unconditioned, is
placed before everything. Our standpoint does not deny the compan-

ionship of all this as required for the continuation and unavoidable consummation of the age—but nothing of it lies in its most proper horizon, not even the greatness of a historical Dasein. Beyond this—outside of every appraisal of greatness—there lies concealed in the age, the one that is transitional of itself, a decisional plight which in all previous history never existed and never could exist.

The decisional plight—the plight that this decision is still not recognized in its necessity and even less is being prepared—does not pertain to just any decision developed out of determinate cultural circumstances, conditioned by determinate political relations, and called forth by the situation of the peoples, but instead concerns *the* decision of decisionality itself: whether once again a history can come to be out of the ground of the first deciding (cf. p. 39ff.), i.e., whether all beings can again be delivered up to beyng, whether beyng can be grounded out of the uniqueness of its essence. This decisional plight traverses the age and does so in concealment as the first indication of a transition. Hence the disorder of the complete goallessness of
45   everyone; hence the confusion in the standards I for proceeding and judging; hence the obstinate adherence to the "situation" and to its immediate alteration; hence the hurried snatching up of all historiologically recognizable and attainable goals and measures; hence the pressing of the untrammeled masses into domains of knowledge, enjoyment, and lived experience, domains that have become accessible in the meantime; and hence the inability to go back or to get out of the rut. All this, according to its external appearance and impact, is so gigantic and irresistible that thereby all the more does what is most concealed seem to be a nullity, provided an indication of it is ever allotted us.

Not the masses themselves, but the institutions in which they are caught up are now pressing into historiological self-consciousness and thus becoming dominant. The aptitudes of the peoples are now "taken in hand" and incorporated into gigantic plans. *Historiology* penetrates everything, so that even *historical* meditation can become unsure whether it is maintaining the ground of its questioning. Therefore, it must be asked whether even greatness and what is great, wherein what is historical of history seems to be gathered up, are not merely "historiological categories," hidden forms of calculation without an origination in beyng itself. At the very least, the concept of greatness is still ambiguous. Either this concept refers to something protrusive which is looked up to and in relation to which a distance is experienced; and then the calculative and historiological are still providing the measure. Or else greatness means the incomparable and I that
46   which does not at all admit of comparison, does not offer any oppor-

tunity for satisfying the mania for comparison—as deriving purely out of beyng—; but *in this way* then what is great can no longer be named such—not only because the name is insufficient, but because what is in this way grasped as "great" refuses to be made public and in such refusal hides its essence.

22

The compulsion to inversion and to mere opposition indicates most pointedly that the modern age must now inevitably undertake and carry out its essential consummation. Within this consummation, historiology can still attribute to the age a rich—unprecedented—development, so comprehensive that unprecedentedness is raised to a "principle" of development. Yet confirmed thereby is only that the age of the "subjectum" least of all extricates itself from itself but must carry out everything that goes further and everything forthcoming as an ever-increasing entanglement. As long as this age thinks only in oppositions, it will not be able to set itself loose from itself and certainly not be able to place itself above itself. But why can it attain only oppositions and inversions of its "goals" and "values" (cf. Nietzsche)? Because to it—as self-certain—l beings themselves are unproblematic and truth is not a question. Therefore, the age can admit no space outside of itself for something question-worthy, and precisely what seems to be the most radical self-breeding and planning is most obstinately thrown back upon itself. The compulsion to this thoroughly veiled and disguised egoism is rooted in the unexpressed and undisturbed sovereignty of "metaphysics."

23

"What does not kill us makes us stronger,"[8] says Nietzsche very often. Perhaps we may also ask: what about that which does kill us? This that kills is even more rare than what does not. *But what kills us—has made us strong.* Yet how seldom do we venture that which kills us; how much more do we seek becoming stronger rather than *being* strong— if by the latter we understand steadfastness in essential decisions. Here the "finitude" of beyng is radically undergone, that finitude which is not the limitation of an infinity, but instead is the abyssally grown determinateness of what is decided—*what must kill* so that to it again a decidedness might newly suffice—especially when at issue is the pos-

---

8. {Cf., for example, Friedrich Nietzsche, "Götzen-Dämmerung," in *Werke*, vol. 8 (Leipzig: Kröner, 1919), p. 62.}

48   iting of a beginning. That I requires above all a complete detachment
     and the broadest leap in advance.

     The decidedness from which both arise at the same time (but which
     is never a matter of "mere" volition) opens up, through the detach-
     ment and the leap in advance, that "space" of the spatiotemporal
     transition which does not know any voids but instead is riven in its
     most concealed stretches by the lightning bolts of that which is ques-
     tion-worthy and which demands to be preserved in what once again
     stamps itself on beings. The space of this decidedness and the diffu-
     sion of such space constitute that about which it is to be said essen-
     tially—not accidentally—that it *kills* "us."

24

     Sciences can never proceed by way of decisions and also never need to;
     it is *about* them that decisions are made, and the deciding powers and
     institutions are historically diverse. The sciences are not only able to
     incorporate this diversity at any time *but* also do always take their im-
     pulses from such more or less explicit decisions, and this proves not
     the "supratemporality" of the sciences *but* instead their procedural and
     operational character. Progress in the sciences therefore consists not
     in the gaining of new results *but* in the simplification and ever greater
     self-evidence of the course of the operation. In time, therefore, even
     the demand for cognitions deriving from the pursuit of the operation
49   will diminish, I and in correspondence so will the claim on the indi-
     viduals who keep the scientific "operation" in motion. Perhaps two
     years of military service is a better preparation for the sciences then
     four semesters of "studies" which still in the conventional way pro-
     vide instruction on sundry topics or even a "philosophical" formation.
     A type of work and comportment, which *is* only insofar as a decision
     comes to be made *about* it, requires the capacity for an inconspicuous
     and contented slavery which had its appropriate counterweight in the
     other readily available forms and institutions of pleasure and relaxa-
     tion. Even these are securely and wholly aimed at not endangering
     the thoughtlessness.

     The "technical schools" have long since overtaken the "universi-
     ties"; the latter can exist only by being assimilated into the former.
     From this assimilation there arises an assemblage of the university
     sciences around the technical school as a nucleus which in turn has
     as its center the military-technical faculty. The Berlin "university
     town"—talk of a university is here an "anachronism" required for
     "cultural-political purposes"—speaks clearly enough for anyone who

has ears for it and who does not at all "regret" this development of the sciences, but instead welcomes it as indirectly helping to clarify the things that used to be called "spiritual." If we may speak here at all of danger, then only of the one residing in the fact that the "scientists" again notice too late what is happening with them and that thereby once more a "romanticism" of the "spirit" lets its | belated endeavors   50 fall as disruptions on the path of the functioning of science. These "disruptions" can, to be sure, only very fleetingly impede the smoothness and univocity of the research. One should (and will) therefore—when the time of insight has arrived—establish saloons in the vicinity of the research institutes in place of the entirely superfluous and merely "decorative" "docent academies." From these saloons the researcher obtains the "invigoration" needed to carry on the work. All spiritual activity is here a lie.

The "idea" of a "docent academy" was to be sure once thought as an actual "revolutionary" form of an assemblage radically pressing on to an overcoming and making it a duty to *question*. Why, however, does everything essentially thought shift here into its opposite as soon as it is merely compelled directly, hastily, and uniformly into an institution mostly imitative of others? This ossification makes no matter to the endeavors and undertakings of science, but that "idea" of a "docent academy" was a philosophical one—not for the use of pedants in philosophy and an occasion for putting on airs—; philosophical: i.e., thinking out toward an originary *decisive* overcoming of the current essence of science and thereby merely preparing and cultivating a new growth, but not forcing it overnight. Yet how can such a project be brought into the vicinity of an | official position? That is   51 impossible and in due time was thwarted.

To be sure, even the inner possibility of that idea of a *docent university*, as it should be called, is over and done. And at bottom it was in fact *not decisively* thought; it—even it—arose from a belief in an ability to effectuate something essential through a—indeed mediate and patient—engagement. Even here, "science" was seen too much from the inside, rather than in its exclusive affiliation with the age, whereby only one course is left open for philosophy: to pass by. The sciences are what is decided about. On the other hand, philosophy—rare and hardly recognizable—is what does the deciding; that means: philosophy does not develop decisions of just any arbitrary sort about just any arbitrary objects—it unfolds the essential decisions of what is Essentially decisional—of what primarily—i.e., throughout the entire history of metaphysics—manifests itself merely as the *distinction* between beings and beingness. Indeed never is this distinction grasped *as* such, which would already call for meditation on its origination out of the decision (event), and that would signify: the end of metaphysics in the sense of the first *decided* transition.

A consequence of the *decisional character* of philosophy is manifest
52   in the possibility of a *"critique"* in the manner of Kant. | To be sure, such a critique moves only on the ungrounded soil of the distinction between beings and beingness in the sense of the modern interpretations of being as objectivity. The original unity of the ground of the possibility of the distinction (the transcendental imagination) was *scarcely* pursued down into its root (cf. Kantbook[9]). In the relation of philosophy to the sciences, it is still a false echo of the transcendental mode of questioning to seek—through an immediate philosophy of the sciences—of their constitution and conditions—to effectuate something essential with respect to them. Primarily, and thus solely, "the" science must be grasped *historically* (in terms of the history of beyng) in its modern essence; the consequence then for philosophy is to let the sciences work themselves out in their particular essence and to abandon altogether the modern coupling of the sciences and philosophy. This coupling existed already in Greek antiquity, but in another sense—even if the possibility of the modern relation has its roots precisely there.

25

The greatest slavery consists in being unwittingly dependent on, and led by, one's own slave.

53   26

Whoever must get over and done with something essential (Christianity, culture, "science," "university," Western metaphysics, worldview, mania for lived experience, desire for immediate education—not desire for "effectivity") and never repudiates anything at one stroke but still overcomes it on the basis of something most powerful, only he enters the path of those standpoints whereby essential decisions become necessary. Because the capacity for *change* and the historical presuppositions for that are becoming ever smaller, because everything is becoming ever more rectilinear and planned, and because the topplings [*Umkippungen*] remain absent, therefore the creators, beyond their appropriate rarity, are becoming still more rare.

---

9. {Martin Heidegger, *Kant und das Problem der Metaphysik* (1929), GA3 (Frankfurt: Klostermann, 1991).}

Since everyone thinks only in the historiological way and esteems only what can be explained, therefore each *toppling* and certainly a series of them and this series certainly as *intrinsically* conditioned are already an objection and enough of a reason to infer an uncertainty. But in truth a series of necessary topplings testifies solely to the uniqueness of a creative obligation which still does not know its essence, nor whither and how far it is going. *Goal*-lessness is not the same as goal-*lessness*. The mere confusion and interswirling of many goals can be named in that way, but so can the creative superiority over every goal-setting | production and operation.   54

Among the thinkers, the ones who do not merely experience topplings but also hang in the balance [*auf der Kippe stehen*] are Leibniz, Kant, Schelling, and Nietzsche. And precisely they allow us to establish most easily that in scarcely recognizable and ever changing configurations *the same* is sought and carried through. But this "sameness" cannot be detached and installed beyond change as something constant; it is not merely what remains the "same" in change but is what hangs in the balance, and so is what in itself can never be the same. But within metaphysics the "balance" is always a conditioned one—conditioned by the unquestioning foothold in beings (in their priority). But what if this priority drops out? Which toppling is necessary *then*? Any transfiguring or surpassing of beings is intuited in its apparentness; every standing on the ground of facts proves to be a blind tottering. The genuine wandering, which must first make its way to the bridge of beyng and requires secure bridges, is now beginning. Decisions give the way a configuration, but they never follow one another in succession; instead, they overlap and in the overlapping become all the more constant. Nothing has the retroactive power they do.

27

55

In the concealed light of the essence of decisional history and of the errancy of that history, the movement of life is still sheer rigidity in the synchronism of life's constantly recurring paths and forms. Whence the error by which we see in life what is *most in motion,* i.e., "becoming," which we even contrast with "being" (i.e., beings as the present-at-hand, what is present)? Only from this opinion about being itself, according to which we understand life merely as the greatest possible and incomprehensible change of the ever-different present-at-hand things and thus place life (the apparent otherness to being) in the horizon of precisely this being itself—only thereby can we attribute to what has life a superiority with respect to "moved-

ness," over and against other beings, which at the same time have been degraded to present-at-hand things. Indeed the *essence* of motion is itself grasped in terms of οὐσία (δύναμις—ἐνέργεια) ["substantiality (potentiality—actuality)"]. But life and what is alive are perhaps still more essentially rigidity than is the lifeless, which lacks even that possibility. As long as Western humanity is arrested in metaphysics—and
56   is so all the more, the less this can be known—for so long I will life, and the transfiguration into something alive and the accompanying praise of "life" count as an acquisition of the higher, genuine "being." Even Nietzsche—perhaps because he, precisely in inverting Platonism, was more thoroughly a metaphysician than hardly any other Western thinker—fell prey to this valuation of "life." Moreover, this valuation clearly has on its side the approval of Common opinion, and closeness to "life" is then here a "reality," i.e., a being pure and simple. All "materialism" (and what pertains to its kind) is still a harmless aberration opposed to this noisy metaphysics of "life," a metaphysics claiming to touch what is highest.

Yet "life" is indeed distinguished by the certainty of *growth*, which we understand not merely as enlargement but also as the development of the aptitudes, especially with the consolidation of the whole organism; at the same time, we understand this Self-consolidating development as a striking of roots, and the *incorporation* of a surrounding field (of beings) as a conditionality of the organism. Nevertheless, even if the full riches of possible configurations and of their variants and counterturns are also taken into account, in all living things the first disposal of the essence of such beings would retain a rigidity. The liv-
57   ing thing would lack an openness I to beings as such; nowhere is a trace of *truth* the ground of this being.

But where a being is borne by this, namely, *that* what bears has become a *releasing* into the decisionality of beyng, where such releasing first makes necessary the attachments and the detachments, the twistings free and the overcomings, where this releasement at the same time contains everything decided and tolerates no jettisoning, where truth (as a clearing in beings and *toward* beings) has always already woven into beyng all illumination and every sound, all verve and every hardness, there the closeness to "life" never decides about what is real and its reality. There what counts is only the fall of the Da-sein in the human being into the abyss of beyng, and what counts as well is the power to venture the truth of beyng in a free conjuncture of the abyss to a ground which then as a being of that beyng preserves a necessity for beyng. Here, in the essential occurrence of truth, where the clearing of beings to the concealment (of beyng) first lets beings be what they can be out of the "number" of their hidden possibilities,

here arises human *history*, the interplay (which projects in advance and yet at the same time binds to something unalterable) of decisions which never extinguish, but rather inflame, one another and which arise out of the plight of beyng itself. Here every escape | into trans-   58
figuration fails, every escape into that forcing up high which *has* no height but only deludes itself of one on account of a supposed distance from something lower.

To *have* height means to *be* above. But *this* way of being no longer knows any above and below and cannot be explained through the distinction of lower and higher; for abysses are nothing that extend downwards as seen from a secure place above. On the contrary, abysses are just as much above as below—if this perspective is allowed at all. Abysses are what is ungrounded but what bears a grounding of the origin (of the appropriation of gods and humans to the emergence of the strife of world and earth). Here alone do motion and becoming prevail, and these are never attained by living things, in which are possible only displacement and the intake and expulsion of the same. The more exclusively we adhere to representation and Representational explanation, the more strictly does this determine in advance all sight and everything visible, and all the more in motion and in becoming will appear to us that which in its vicissitudes does not disintegrate but still remains even therein intact, like the lapsing of a living thing. The latter therefore has its essence in the species, and the "individuals" merely provide—in order to be expended—a thriving by way of constant perdition.

This is of course already no longer explainable *mechanistically*, or much rather: | it is *still not* attributable to the changes of mere locomo-   59
tion. But we cannot explain the motion of living things on the basis of a higher motion, in case we may speak here of motion at all. The impossibility of explaining a living being is for it the genuine safeguard of its essence, since it is that being which is what it is without a basis in a truth of beyng but which remains ungrasped even if it should be thoroughly explained; for a living being surveys and incorporates a range of things it itself is not and does so such that this incorporation "has" the incorporated neither as something external nor as something internal in the sense of an appropriation. Appropriation occurs only where the being stands in the proper domain of its essence, i.e., is delivered up to the *preservation* of its essence and where this delivering up is itself the most proper being of this being. If the living thing is once explained and perhaps even determined, then that *incorporation* (which we must call the appriopriation that lacks a proper domain) is abandoned and forgotten, and the "living thing" has then become a mere class of what is lifeless. But then the progress of sci-

ence consists not so much in the successiveness of the living thing as in the definitive *renunciation* of experiencing the living thing as such.
60   This renunciation, however, is not taken as a renunciation; instead, science accounts it a profit and indeed the one toward which science has been steering for a long time. The unrecognized and ever less recognized and ultimately not at all recognizable renunciation of the experience of what is alive disseminates itself as the secure intention to intuit now even life itself. For this a typical example will best oblige here, namely, the fact that scientific progress, which from the viewpoint of modernity is beyond doubt, is not based on a penetration into beings (i.e., into the truth of their beyng), but rather on an ever further withdrawing from beings into the superficiality of their objectivity, whereby the superficial becomes ever more manageable and the "principles" of explanation ever more paltry and empty, i.e., ever more decisionless and general.

Technology as the historiology of nature is becoming the form of the "knowledge" of any being whatsoever, is taking possession also of the historiology of history (of the past), and is expanding into the basic form of the relation to beings. Every claim to beyng is wiped out, but the supreme illusion of freedom (the illusion of dominating everything) arises at the same time; the most intrinsic ambiguity of the abandonment of beings by being has attained its now completely un-
61   recognizable | sharpness. In the limitless sphere of technology, everything is "alive"—; this life is the substitute for the attained a-historicality, and the latter is then taken to be history. By way of many detours and transformations, τέχνη has won a victory over the inceptually still preserved ἀλήθεια (cf. Plato's *Phaedrus*[10]). The anthropomorphizing of the human being has reached its goal.

The highest form of explanation and thus still remaining explanation [*Erklärung*] is transfiguration [*Verklärung*]. For this a-historical but thoroughly historiological human is by no means a temperate calculating being; in him romanticism celebrates its supreme triumph. *Music,* wordless and truthless yet thoroughly calculated and indeed touching "life" and the body, is becoming "the" art which gathers all arts in itself and around itself. That is to say, art is becoming τέχνη in the sense of technology, politically ordered up and politically calculable, one means among others for making manageable what is present-at-hand and for doing so indeed in the mode of transfiguration.

---

10. {Cf. Martin Heidegger, "Platons Phaidros: Übungen im Sommersemester 1932," in *Seminare: Platon—Aristoteles—Augustinus*, GA83 (Frankfurt: Klostermann, 2012), pp. 85–148.}

"Lohengrin" and ever again "Lohengrin" and armored vehicles and air squadrons all belong together, are the same.

But the fact that such apparently diverse things are the same in form is only the paltry start of a "development," the start of a series of unprecedented incidents in view of which the human being confirms his anthropomorphizing ever more securely and feels | ever more hale.   62
Even "catastrophes" such as the "world war" are endured and one day are found to be useful, although from them nothing decisional could arise. The devastation can no longer be experienced as such in its culmination. Yet ever still shines in an unrecognizable night the light of decisional history in whose abyss, traversed by the gods, the gigantism of a-historicality, in the semblance of "vitality," still remains a mere superficies of the distorted essence which the essential occurrence of beyng never gets rid of, because beyng in itself—as the indigence of the gods—has already *decided* all plights (transformed into needs) of the representational and productive human being in the distorted essence of those plights. Therefore, however, the human being, as the being assigned to beyng, is given the possibility of becoming a decider and of venturing for once *the* decision between beings and being or of evading it again, as always (cf. Ponderings VII, p. 77ff.).

Only those with knowledge of the abysses of beyng recognize the foregrounds and backgrounds of the "history" established by historiology. But this knowledge is itself steadfastness in the truth of beyng, |
and such steadfastness establishes a unique standpoint (that of the   63
transition) (cf. p. 43ff.). This standpoint demands a meditation which has recognized in their inevitability all the things a "cultural critique" still entices us to deny; therefore, this meditation does not "criticize" them, but instead grasps them as the distorted essence and already gains from them a predelineation of the essence of beyng itself, the disclosive thinking of which must be ventured in the transition. Such a venture, if it amounts to anything at all, can amount only to a shimmer cast for a moment by an illumination of the history of beyng over the darkness of a-historicality which for itself in the glare of its self-certain pleasurability has revalued all nights into everydayness. If the thinking of beyng—the most unapparent in the apparentness of the gigantic extravagance of beings—is truly *of* beyng, appropriated by beyng, then it indeed surmises these intimations, but does not know the hour of their history, can therefore never be instituted immediately in what is "alive," loves errancy qua the landscape of truth, and detests the correctnesses which once again confirm the present-at-hand and link up to beings such that beyng would remain forgotten.

28

The oldest thinkers were permitted to say immediately the truth of beings. The newer ones were able to express the correctness of human representations. The future ones will have to learn the disclosive thinking of beyng. The "school" for this learning is Da-*sein*.

                                          29

Art—what we so name and know historiologically in its history—is possible only on the basis of the metaphysical decision which has made itself self-evident as the distinction between beings and beingness, the sensible and the un(super)sensible, the "real" and the "ideal," explanation and transfiguration. The metaphysical distinction indeed rules in the most manifold forms—mostly now unrecognizable—over the current and forthcoming instituting of "life" and "reality." We *use* these forms in order to teach, and to "enact," the "ideas" and "values" of a worldview as such. The distinction itself, however, is so worn out that no one is shocked by it any longer or even suspects that it might still harbor an unasked question. (Philosophical erudition procures some sort of connection to a historiologically given "metaphysics" or to a mixture of various metaphysical doctrines and utterly lacks de-
65   terminative power, I which in any case has been made otiose by the self-evident character of the distinction. And if in order to be up to date philosophical erudition now also discovers "life" and the "people" and "action" and "utility," then even this is only a pedantically supplemental application of the inversion of Platonism.)

In the meantime, art has been a party to the diffusion of the metaphysical distinction into what is current and massive. Art is the production of what used to be a "work" and now—as a consequence of historicism—is still so called, and this production is historiologically traditional and historiologically ever more skillfully incited and gathered up, is familiar to the many, and is often not at all "bad." Corresponding to its self-evident metaphysical ground, "art," as a "higher" means of cultural activity, has become naturalized, together with the assurance of being called to beautify and ease "life," and together with the claim to fit in when compared to what came earlier. Yet that which is groundless and decisionless and consolidates the metaphysical distinction to something hardly noticed but all-bearing is also the reason the pursuit of art, especially with the historicism growing around that pursuit, is not impugned by the already glimpsed end of (metaphysically borne) art. If, nevertheless, the end of metaphysics is not the end of thinking but is only the consummation of the history of the first beginning of thinking, and if thinking becomes the thinking of beyng, and if the metaphysical distinction is disrupted in the leap | into its origin (the decision), what will then step into the place of that which metaphysically was art? Must not here something more origi- 66 nary and more uncanny (since compelled by beyng itself) announce its necessity? Must not here, for the sake of responding to beyng, first of all precisely a detachment from all artistic pursuit be demanded as well as a detachment from every *historiological* consideration of the history of art? Are there still ways of meditation here? Can the history of art at least mediately intimate indeed not how we should begin to arrive again at art but at most how we must be prepared for a thrust of beyng itself?

Or must now everything arise immediately and entirely out of the other beginning and all that is transitional be seen precisely *as* transitional? Must now the other of "art," what corresponds to "art" in terms of the history of beyng (must then a correspondence belong to it at all?), not be grounded on a hard *knowledge* and demand such knowledge—a long constancy of a few in questioning the *one thing* (the decision)? In view of these necessities, of what avail would be *"musical education"* and in general that which is "musical," even in the form of the pushing forward of "music"? But perhaps that is inevitable qua the distancing of the masses from the deformity of beyng. "Music" in the broadest sense is perhaps a holding out in a fragile | semblance 67 of a "vitality" that makes us more and more self-satisfied and averse to any experience of the plight of beyng. With the help of beings (the abundance of "lived experience") an evasion of beyng?

Every formal valuation of the current artistic activity and of the historiological renewals of the history of art, every renovation of the *content* of artistic activity through the suppliance of new "ideals" and "values"—all this is necessarily caught in the past, and yet it would be inconsequential were it not for the fact that thereby the decision about art is neglected and so is even "art" itself as a decision. The question of the "Origin of the work of art"[11] wants to provoke meditation on art in this domain of decisionality and to prepare a historical moment for the essential change of art from the "metaphysically" borne one to another sort of art. Yet here it is still possible that art will no longer find *any* resonance and that then all the more constantly, cleverly, and calculatively will artistic activity become something ordinary. Then *the sheltering of the truth of beyng in beings* will designate a process

---

11. {Martin Heidegger, "Der Ursprung des Kunstwerkes," in *Holzwege*, GA5, 2nd ed. (Frankfurt: Klostermann, 2003), pp. 1–74; Martin Heidegger, "Vom Ursprung des Kunstwerkes: Erste Ausarbeitung," in *Heidegger Studies* 5:1989, pp. 5–22.}

whose future configuration will remain just as obstinately hidden to us as self-refusal (qua the essential occurrence of beyng) illuminates itself to us and *unsettles* us from lostness in beings and through this unsettling determines the disposition of Da-sein.

68   If someone is merely effective and even very effective, but thereby "is" always only that which all others already "are," then he lacks everything proper to uniqueness, which is to say, proper to an originary affiliation with beyng. And if "art" has become a means of expression and a confirmation and representation of this *effectiveness,* then it has reached its ultimate utility, and the exploitation of its *essence* is complete.—But what is meant by the other of art? *The setting into work of truth.* Truth, however, means here the truth of beyng and compels beyng itself (what is of its essence) to unsettle us out of the priority of beings (and thus of metaphysics). But the "work" is the working "of" beyng (in the specific sense of the genitive proper to the history of beyng), not the presentation of beings. The "working" of "beyng," however, cannot be the result and consequence of a cause, but is instead the effectuation of the "between"—displacement into the spatiotemporal field of the decision between gods and humans—beginning of history.

69   *30*

Spengler—in him Nietzsche's inversion of Platonism becomes the mere sovereignty of mere "facts" over and against the impotence of "truths," which for Spengler means the "generalities" of mere opinion. The glorification of "facts," which perhaps presents the most bleak and at the same time most blind "romanticism," although the latter is for Spengler highly contemptible, leads ultimately to an extolling of Rome and Caesar—this is a unilateral Nietzsche, merely taken more *historiologically* and decisively than the biological and swampy Nietzsche of Klages. It would be fruitless to start by ferreting out Spengler's self-contradictions. His blindness toward that which nevertheless confers a power to shock on his presentations (and on his alleged "experiences," which indeed are merely extracted from the historiological "literature") is permanent. Spengler can be taken only the way he must be taken according to his own "doctrine," namely, as a symptom of his era, an era he of course sees only from his own "perspective," which he maintains is the "absolute" perspective.

In Spengler's doctrine, neither "pessimism," nor "relativism," nor "zoologism" ("humanity is for me a zoological greatness"[12]) is the

---

12. {Oswald Spengler, *Pessimismus?* (Berlin: Stilke, 1921), p. 14.}

"danger." Here nothing at all is dangerous any more; there is only the very | fixed consistency of succession, whereby the rudest slap in the   70
face no longer has any meaning, since everything merely comes down to the operation of "facts" and their fatedness. "The entire nineteenth century does not contain one single question which scholasticism had not already discovered, thought through, and brought into an illustrious form as one of its own problems."[13] Spengler's enthusiasm for "facts" seems to stop here, for otherwise he would have to know (yet what actually is "knowledge" for a scribe of "facts"?) that "scholasticism" not only was completely unfamiliar with any "problems" but was even so far removed from the nineteenth century, so different, that it never could have chanced upon the "problems" of that century. Such statements of Spengler's, like the one just cited, may make an "impression" on unknowledgeable people of "facts" (technicians and bank directors), and they may be recorded with a smirk by chaplains trained in apologetics, but they indeed merely demonstrate the a-historicality of this prototype of all contemporary "historiologists." Before all else stands this statement: "There is no actually new thought in so late a time."[14] What amazing {?} honesty and modesty! Yet what immediately follows are enumerations, | many lines long, of what   71
Spengler has "created as new." But the self-contradiction—it does present itself so crudely—is here without significance, for such is proper to this sort of "philosophy" which surrenders to "facts," to beings, insofar as something like that can at all be conceded to it. This *complete* immersion in Platonism (that it is an inverted Platonism makes no essential difference), this ignorant proclamation of the abandonment of beings by being, removes from, or better, *denies* this way of thinking any dangerousness. Consistent with this innocuousness is then the strategy to take as an "opponent" in each case only something weak, ordinary, supplementary, and uncreative—; one derides inconsequential "academic philosophy" and yet remains oblivious to even the very first presuppositions of, e.g., a confrontation with Kant (even here Spengler is a worsened edition of a unilateral Nietzsche). What is at least astonishing, however, is that the immersion in Platonism thunders against "romanticism" and derides everything that is called "projection" and labels it idealism, i.e., "dawdling." How is | Platonism, especially if it is still standing on its head, supposed to   72
recognize itself in what it forgets and never could conceptualize, since to it the "concept" can only be a "concept"?

---

13. {Ibid., p. 8.}
14. {Ibid.}

This thoughtless thinking, oblivious to any danger or plight, could never grasp projection as what originarily opens up the truth of beyng and thus is neither a mere "program," nor a "perspective," nor a mere notion floating "above" "life."

Yet how does it happen that Spengler does often hit the mark in his critique of the times and proceeds so surely in his reproaches? Even here Nietzsche is speaking—but again only a superficies of Nietzsche and never Nietzsche's genuine "nihilism," which cannot be severed from his "metaphysics" and thus from Platonism. The a-historicality of Spengler, this "philosopher of history," is perhaps illustrated by nothing so clearly as by his opinion of having said something about Hölderlin when ridiculing the fact that—moreover, in a very dubious way—the circle around the poet George sought in Hölderlin an image of the Hellenes instead of affirming Roman civilization.

73   Yet—all misgivings about | Spengler carry weight only if we concede that in him *a genuine power of his era* was put into words. This power, despite all the scholarly opposition it endured, has affected precisely those who afterwards rejected, and believed they had overcome, Spengler's pessimism and his "disposition of decline." Spengler helped, even if very superficially, to make available to tradespeople at least a superficies of Nietzsche's thinking. That the consequence was a currently all-the-more-assured disdain of "philosophy" is no wonder, since Spengler is precisely an "expression" of today's "cultural soul" in his incomprehension of what eventuated philosophically and metaphysically in Nietzsche's thinking. Yet for this very reason it is precisely misbegotten to believe Spengler can be "disposed of" by way of scholarly refutations; he is not to be disposed of, as long as the domain of meditation on Nietzsche's thinking is not put forward, and without this the talk of "disposing" is senseless. Can anyone know *history* and even want to speak of it in a binding way, if to him the human being is a "zoological greatness"?

74   *31*

History and the priority of the untruth of historiological explanation: with the help of "facts," it can always be shown that "great historical events" have influenced "artists" and "thinkers" and have led to "works." But *it can never* be "shown" in a corresponding way that the executors of those events were possible only on account of poets and thinkers. Therefore, what is proved is the secondary role of poets and thinkers, if not indeed their superfluousness. To be sure. But for who? For those who believe history can be explained through "facts." Yet the height of the mistake is reached when the venerators of "facts" are convinced of having grasped the fatedness of history over and against the "causalism" of a derivation from "ideas" and "programs." The genuine fatedness of history is manifest precisely by its withdrawing from this prostration before "facts" and by denying it any knowledge of the origin of the "facts," an origin which is admittedly not to be sought in "ideas." And "fate"—what if this concept is only the last expedient of historiology—a way out into what has no way, the renunciation of all | meditation?   75

32

Modernity, in accord with its distinctive position in regard to humanity, is driving toward a decision incorporating the entire previous, metaphysically borne history of the West. Therefore, no incidents, accomplishments, and movements of the present age can be taken and promoted for the sake of themselves and their goals—everything must be undertaken in its modern character and at the same time tacitly unfolded toward its transitionality, its possible power of preparing a transition. Why? Because all Western goals have been exhausted, and everything further can only be a jumbled modification of what already was. And this is so because the position toward beings can calculate out of these only still other beings (for production and "lived experience") and could never open up another source, unless this position is radically convulsed. And that is so because only beyng itself can bestow originariness on beings; but beyng can never be found as beings can, especially not by an age in which beings | have long since   76
become mere objects of calculation and lived experience.

Thus beyng discloses itself only through its essential separation and remoteness from all beings, which of course must not be thought in the sense of the metaphysical distinction between beings and beingness. This essential separation arises only from a decision whose decidedness must develop long in advance out of a preparedness to be assaulted by beyng itself and to be transformed in essence. But such preparedness surely means to think ahead and carry forward everything into the transitionality of the decision between the abandonment of beings by being and the essential occurrence of the truth of beyng. This will happen neither through "programs" nor through their "actualization"—but only through meditation (cf. above, p. 64ff. on art). And from this meditation arises the capacity to renounce what previously was usual and what even in the future will primarily be esteemed as the ideal (culture and the like).

What this involves above all is a capacity to endure the reputation that such renunciation is merely something "negative" and "despondent," whereas, quite to the contrary, it is the *first* and *for that reason* most difficult step of meditation, the step by which far in advance and

77   yet *without* programmatic calculation and comportment the | possibility of a completely other standpoint (p. 43ff.) is prepared. This longest step toward the transition and toward the secure bridge is the most inconspicuous and the most unavoidable. It is also incomparable to any previous "cultural accomplishments" and "edifices of thought." It cannot be calculated historiologically, because even the knowledge of the closure of all previous settings of goals arises from meditation on the truth of beyng and on the abandonment of beings. This is because the transition, which is now becoming necessary, does not proceed on the level of historiological beings, but instead precisely abandons that level, whereby a decision arises only as a leap.

This leap, however, is not at all arbitrary, because over and against the expired possibilities of beings and the fostering of beings (culture), it leaps over only to the one unique thing, beyng and its disclosure, or in other words because the verve of the leap appropriates the leaper only on the basis of beyng itself and its essential occurrence. On the "standpoint" this decision (as breaking through the metaphysical distinction) reaches in the leap, for the first time the two extreme and unique possibilities of Western history become visible:

1. the complete (although covered over by historiology) a-historicality;

2. the long, inconspicuous preparation of a grounding of the truth

78   of beyng, on which ground once again the gods | and humanity are brought to an encounter, one that expands a spatiotemporal field within which the opened up and the closed off attain equiprimordially to the essential occurrence of beyng and precisely as beings find themselves delivered over to preservation.

The preparing of this decision between these extreme possibilities thereby brings them, precisely *as these* possibilities, for the first time into meditation and into the presence of the confirmation of the steadfastness in enduring their unfolding. The preparing of the standpoint of the preparedness makes itself at home in the—historiologically calculated—uncanniness of a tarrying for what is completely other, which is always too essential to behave at any time as something "new."

And yet the *renunciation* of the apparent pursuit of the promotion of culture, i.e., the renunciation of a prowling about in the previous "religious," "artistic," and "political" goals of the metaphysically degenerated West, is the least thing this preparing must endure. More difficult, and thus to be known in advance, is the incommensurability of meditation with everything gigantic, which in the meantime

has precisely started to exhaust its possibilities. This incommensurability with the reigning standards signifies here a compete disappearance, or better, I an absence of any appearance at all, over and against   79
what alone is taken as appropriate to these standards.

This inconspicuousness—the still hidden indication of a completely other kind of "greatness," one which perhaps even essentially exceeds this designation—this inconspicuousness possesses nevertheless the power of a sui generis appearance in "intimations" which become familiar even to historiological calculation (from which nothing escapes), if only in the form of a complete misunderstanding—this is the case, e.g., with the event of the premature departure of Hölderlin. This event surpasses all the incidents of the Napoleonic age and all productions of "classical" and "romantic" art—surpasses everything which has followed in "history" since that event. But the very inconspicuousness of that event could not take effect prior to historiology; one explains it "genetically," perhaps even "Christianly," and perhaps can adduce corresponding "instances." One here explains an incident and ends with a regret that in this way posterity was deprived of the possession of a completed oeuvre. One observes a breakdown and does not surmise the decisional power of this that is inconspicuous, because one calculates the work itself I only on the basis of its contemporaries,   80
from which it is to be set out in relief in its particularity.

Nor do we surmise that here the first convulsion of the West—of its foundations, i.e., its metaphysics—eventuated and that this convulsion can indeed be dampened but never extinguished, because it is so essential that it has already created for itself a completely different mode of continuance (namely, by way of inconspicuousness) and has grounded its stability in a capacity to wait. While, around the same time, *historiology* started to expand and form itself into a fixed institution as research and science, the inconspicuousness of a quite other *history* began. While "Christianity" received, through German Idealism, its justification in absolute thinking (Hegel) or as the counterfactuality to this (Schelling's later philosophy), the historical decision about it was already made by the assignment of its God among "the gods," i.e., by the commencing flight of the gods as the granting of a place for a quite different "metaphysically"—i.e., no longer in the previous Western way—graspable, pursuable, and configurable opening up of a quite different time—one withdrawn from all calculation I   81
and therefore "long." While all art (with the—very concealed—convulsion of all metaphysics) in essence proceeded to its end, and mere—at present very superior, capable, and knowledgeable—artistic activity commenced with force and became the "total artwork" in correct directedness toward an operational program, and while the historicism

of Herder and of romanticism started to delineate the cultural form of the nineteenth and twentieth centuries, already a quite different discourse and poetry withdrew into inconspicuousness.

But woe—if now, with all the easy means of historiological calculation, we wanted to calculate precipitously the current and future state of the age presently coming into sovereignty, and if we had to be completely mistaken about the inconspicuousness and about the law of *its* effectivity (the commencing philological study of Hölderlin, the appraisal of Hölderlin as *one* guide to the Greeks, the degradation of his poetry by interpreting it in terms of "fatherland," and the Christian-Catholic apologetic exploitation of it in connection with, and at once against, the above). Woe—if we should forget that the intimation assigns to us a long meditation, out of which we let the work repose in its highest safekeeping—its inconspicuousness—until we have

82   thought into it, on the basis of our own exertions of I preparation, the essential *decision* whose direction of development we must first truly recognize and disclosively think—i.e., disclosively question—on the basis of the experience of that convulsion. Woe—if, instead of becoming transitional ones, we escape into a historiological revering and extolling of the poet and his "work" and thereby, in the most insidious form, merely pursue the obstruction of that convulsion.

Indeed the law of what is inconspicuous remains in force even here—over and against historiological calculation, no matter how concerned and seriously "well" intentioned it is to prepare historical meditation and no matter if it is at the cost of renouncing a possibly first needful "interpretation" of this poet. Woe still—if we should intend to make—or even "underpin"—a "philosophy" out of this poetry whose place and time are yet ungrounded, even if founded.— Woe, if we should forget that *thinking* is now all the more assigned its *most proper and most inceptual task,* one that is "older" than metaphysics, namely, the question of being as the question of the truth of beyng, as *one* preparation of a preparedness for the decision about history and a-historicality.

83   It is impossible and at the same time unnecessary to bring this questioning into an explainable historiological relation to that convulsion of history through Hölderlin. Only this do we know: the asking of the question of being, in overcoming metaphysics, opens up *one*—very narrow—path toward experiencing a little of that convulsion and leading the convulsion (in such limits within the peculiar law of a course of thought) to the preparation of the quite different standpoint. Poetizing and thinking enter into an essentially transformed, incalculable relation. When and how both become manifest as Da-*sein* within self-altering beings, without publicly existing and "operating,"

no one knows and no one wants to know, i.e., none of those who have experienced even only the smallest of the necessities of the transition and of its preparation. For genuine meditation adheres neither to the past nor to what is coming, in the sense of what can be represented historiologically—and it concerns the present situation even less. On the contrary, it grasps the times in their most simple essential traits (priority of the human being, world-picture, abandonment by being, commencing a-historicality) and recognizes these traits in their affiliation with the history of beyng.

33

84

Philosophy—if we consider how few have so seldom grasped essential thinking in its concealed volition and how bridgelessly this thinking stands toward "beings," despite its allegedly determinable "effects" on ideas and actions, then the question of "why" might almost seem superfluous.

And in fact it is so; for the thinking of beyng will not only be useful for nothing, it can also "effect" nothing, because it exhausts itself in being a beyng: in standing as Da-*sein* within the essential occurrence of beyng itself. Yet does this signify more than a superfluity, for which beyng occasionally claims a thinker? Indeed—we have no standards to evaluate such occasional steadfastness in beyng; thus *the thinking* of beyng would have to be compelled at times by beyng itself, and "only" thereby would beyng essentially occur. Perhaps an age such as "modernity" is entirely deprived of the possibility of recognizing as even in the least "essential" what is goalless and is entirely withdrawn from calculation, indeed deprived of the possibility of finding being in such steadfastness at all.

Yet perhaps this is I also the time the essence of philosophy must   85
be experienced more knowledgeably, because beyng over and against beings is pressing on toward a decision. Beyng itself *is* and only beyng is—and as beyng it *is without* a goal. Such a "without" means here: the setting of goals must remain remote as something inappropriate and debasing. The truth of beyng is to be grounded, because this truth belongs to beyng. *Whether* and how on such a ground something else—a preservation of beings—might be built is unessential to beyng, since the essential occurrence of beyng has already surpassed—and so can dispense with—every preservation of beings.

Because beyng is only the abyssal ground, it has no goals and averts every setting of a goal. Never can the overcoming of nothingness become a goal of beyng, because nothingness is first empowered to its nullity by beyng, and out of this nullity beyng saves itself in its unique-

ness. To be sure, the human being (as more steadfast in Da-sein) becomes ever more essential thereby, namely, that only beyng is. The
more essentially the human being is appropriated by beyng, the less
86   important he becomes I as one being among others and before others.
(The impossibility of the subjectivity of the *subiectum*.) But at first and
presumably still for a long time henceforth, the human being will be
conceptualized as *subiectum* in the midst of beings. This concept [*Be-
griff*] is not an empty general representation, but the totality [*Inbe-
griff*] of firm structures in which humanity moves. Indeed it seems
that now for the first time human subjectivity comes to terms with its
most proper and still unexhausted essential implications, inasmuch
as the human being is utterly intent on leaving nothing to "accident"
and incorporating everything "without remainder" into the plans and
calculations of reason. But that means calculatability itself is posited
as *the goal,* and goallessness, even in the sense of something superior
to goals, must count as utter abomination.

The thinking of beyng thereby first moves up into its incontestible
strangeness; a historical moment is prepared in which the extreme
oppositions of the supreme decision stand face to face. Therefore the
idle talk of a returning late Roman age—omitting all its other impos-
87   sibilities—violates I the genuinely historical meditation which recognizes in today's age not something "late" but at best—if we may be
permitted such calculation—something early, i.e., something that still
has a long aftermath ahead of itself. Too clearly, too decisively, too
manifoldly, and too lengthily are already prepared all the signs indicating that now for the first time in unitary force with the full expenditure of all powers and wishes, the age of a *consummate subjectivity* is
commencing, in that every trace of a "subjectivism," i.e., of an apparently merely egoic subjectivity, has been obliterated. The unique historical moment of the forthcoming "history" of what is a-historical is
determined by the fact that meditation and meditationlessness, as
basic dispositions, are attaining their highest simultaneity and
through their doubled decidedness bestow on the age (of transition)
a sharpness foreign to history thus far, the sharpness of a discord at
once reticent and covered over.

The superficial form of this simultaneity makes meditation seem
goalless and thus useless. That means meditation disappears from the
public eye and can no longer count as an exception; such an appraisal
88   still presents the smallest concession on the part of I what is usual and
proper. But meditationlessness appears as the first impact of the clev-
erest calculation and the relentless enterprise which occupy the public
sphere and altogether admit that sphere as a unique domain of "Da-
sein," whereby this designation itself vanishes. Yet the human being

of consummate subjectivity is anything but a calculating machine; the "age of technology" does precisely not make "technology" into a goal, but rather into a means of meditationless calculation.—And because technology in this way becomes the easiest to use and understand, it causes neither a "materialism" nor a poverty of feelings. Quite to the contrary: the human being—having become the consummate subject—is able for the first time to unfold completely and to institute that which since some time ago the prescient spirit of language has called "lived experience." Now the human being is first brought beyond the mere whim and particularity of individual solitary experiences and is set into universal needs and their claims: to feel one's feelings and enjoy the passions (this last word *not* taken in the Christian, disparaging sense). The enjoyment of the feelings, however, since all feeling is a *self*-feeling, includes | the felt enjoyment of oneself—   89
precisely the enjoyment of the human being as subjectum. Since the human being feels himself in his *feelings,* it appears to him that in them he is encountering something other than himself and yet again himself in this other. Lived experience, as the enjoyment of feeling, becomes in this way an enticement for the human being to secure this subjectivity ever more exclusively, because indeed subjectivity is raised in *feelings* at the same time into an other, wherein the human being is released from his own "ego." To be able to feel the feelings, to dissolve into their enjoyment, is the supreme lived experience.

"Art" undertakes the management and the corresponding organization of lived experience (as a feeling of the feelings), whereby the conviction must arise that now for the first time the tasks of calculation and planning are uncovered and established, and thus so is the essence of art. Since, however, the enjoyment of the feelings becomes all the more desultory and agreeable as the feelings become more indeterminate and contentless, and since music most immediately excites such feelings, music thus becomes the prescriptive type of art (cf. romanticism, Wagner, and—Nietzsche). Music bears in itself a proper lawfulness and also a calculability of the highest kind, yet that does not at all contravene—but merely manifests—how decisively it is that pure | number and the sheer feeling of the feelings are compatible and   90
require each other. All types of art are apprehended musically, in the manner of music, i.e., as expressions and occasions of the enjoyment of the feelings (feelings of achievement, glory, power, communion). Poetry, in case such ever arises beyond mere ink spilling, becomes "song" and the word merely a supplement to the sound and to its flow and rhythm. "Thoughts," especially if they disturb meditationlessness, are prohibited; moreover, one disposes of the genuine thoughts (λόγοι) in the calculation and planning that can "effect" something. The in-

terpretation of art in terms of lived experience is elevated to the role
of the measure for all active and productive human comportment
(τέχνη); comportment is most highly honored when judged to be "artistic" (the state as a "work of art"). In the manner of art is also configured the apprehension of culture and of cultural politics—these are
organizations of lived experience as expressions of the "life" of the or-
ganizers. Culture, pursued in that way as political culture, becomes
the basic form of the planning and of the management of the lived experience of consummate subjectivity.

The feeling of the feelings as *self*-feeling in the sense of the creators
91   of the feelings I proves to be the "living" form of self-consciousness
and thus at the same time decides about the mode of genuine "knowledge"; this knowledge is precisely *such* feeling. The corresponding habituation and feeling-habit are named "instinct" or "character." Only
myopia and faultfinding could believe that here an arbitrary "worldview" of a few sufficiently violent ones would be coming into effect.
In truth, what is carried out here is the consistent bursting forth of
the essential volition of the subjectivity of the subject—the subjectivity which already in the first beginnings, under the characteristic
title *cogitationes* ["thoughts"] (Descartes), focuses all modes of "consciousness" on *sentire*—self-feeling. The worldview now becomes the
unique prescriptive one which, in definite political and folkish
[*völkisch*] castings, points only to its decisive champions. Basically,
however, even the opponents and the reactionaries are borne by this
worldview that takes the human being as subject; i.e., for them the
meditationlessness of calculation merely disguises itself in what is historiologically handed down and then presumed to be superior, en-
dowed as it is with a nongenuine, because uncreative, pomp.

Nevertheless, because hardly anyone would suppose or even only
concede a meditationlessness in the sovereignty of the calculation of
92   everything, or I in the unlimited capacity for every form of the lived
experience of everything and for self-feeling in everything, or in the
disposal of the fastest and most efficient communication of all lived
experience to all who do not have an immediate lived experience of
it, therefore the self-consciousness (in the basic form of propaganda)
pertaining to the subjectivity of the subject is unconditionally certain
of itself, so certain that every other mode of knowledge is rejected as
impossible, indeed is not even heeded any longer as a possibility. The
age of consummate subjectivity is, according to the predetermined beginning of the sovereignty of the *certitudo* of the subject, the age of
complete questionlessness. Not only do questions related to an essential transformation disappear, but questioning as such—in the sense
of the decision toward something most question-worthy—remains

absent and no longer attains the power of one alienating limit to another.

A person unable to see any greatness in the certainty of this consummation of subjectivity lacks every precondition for historical meditation. Admittedly, required here is insight into the *kind* of greatness possible for subjectivity as such and solely for it, I if the greatness   93 of the age is to be assessed historically. The same insight also provides the knowledge that this age will never grasp or tolerate the essence of meditation. The age of subjectivity is the extreme form of the inversion of all (thus far surmised) being into the explainability of beings— being becomes finite or infinite objectivity for the thinking subject. Thereby this subject undertakes the disposal of being and makes itself appurtenant to and subservient to the calculation and lived experience of "genuine" beings (the subjectum)—and being is itself the last service of the beings evaporated in mere thinking—hence still being as such.

Thereby, however, the possibility of meditation (the possibility of questioning the truth of beyng) is decided. The thinking of beyng escapes the *essence* of the age—nay, it cannot once escape, because it never could have been domiciled therein. Where is its origin? In beyng—but when "is" beyng? Questioning in this way, we have already decided in favor of meditation, in favor of preparation for goallessness, which is not to be measured according to effects nor newly disclosed from effects. And yet we stand in the I age of meditationless-   94 ness and carry out the type of representation, opinion, behavior, and usage characteristic of this age. Or do we stand in the transition? And what here is the thinking of beyng? How do we comport ourselves to lived experience and to the subjectum? To feel the feelings counts as the "highpoint" of lived experience (music therefore the "absolute art"). Feeling is thus an occurrence in the human being, something the subjectum "has" or something that can be stirred up in the subjectum. And how should this conception of feeling, like that of every other property of the human being, not be "natural" and find immediate confirmation in the view of everyone?

But perhaps to be "natural" (i.e., straightforwardly "understandable") has now become something uncommon, ever since the human being experienced and conceptualized himself as the *animal rationale.*" This interpretation of the human being, grown out of the basic conception of beings as φύσει ὄντα ["beings by way of nature"], entrenches at the same time that opinion about beings; body, soul, and spirit appear, in light of οὐσία, in their differences and unity, and the feelings (παθήματα) become things present-at-hand concomitantly (συμβεβηκότα in the *widest* sense) in something present-at-hand. The

feelings should consequently be appraised and in general differentiated according to what they effectuate and how they themselves |
were effectuated (to be effectuated: to appear as present-at-hand in consequence of something else already present-at-hand). The human being is thus a thing in which these effectuated and effective feeling-effects occur—he is their bearer, enjoyer, and user in one. These nexuses were later researched and explained in the manner of exact science by physiology and psychology—and the genuine "progress" these cognitions offer consists in the entrenchment of the already given basic conception of the human being and of beings in general. Any other possibility—over and against this "natural" conception of the human being—seems excluded, and if it did announce itself, then immediately so as—to be natural.

But why should this single *uncommonness*, which has become the ground of what is now "natural," remain unique, nonrecurrent? Uncommonness is always a sign that in its domain its corresponding possibilities are closed up and are covered over thereby for a long while. That uncommonness (the interpretation of the human being as *animal rationale*) is, however, already deprived of the right to uniqueness, because it arose on the ground of a quite *definite* history of beyng, a history we are only now beginning to know as the disempowerment of φύσις and the collapse of yet ungrounded ἀλήθεια. The beginning of the history of being was overpowered by the | priority of beings which was necessarily enabled by that beginning itself, and that priority then further made itself irresistible through the interpretation of protrusive beings in the sense of constant presence. The most inceptual possibilities of the first beginning of the history of beyng were blocked off; they can never again be liberated in their initial form.

Through them, however, right from the very beginning, the uniqueness and obviousness of so-called "nature" are convulsed, although this convulsion can no longer be sensed, on account of the prestige of "nature." But if now the "naturalness" of the interpretation of human "nature" has reached its end state in the consummation of the subjectivity of the subject, then thereby is prepared a decision whose first judgment must concern whether a decision is actually forthcoming or whether that end state also perpetuates decisionlessness as what is "natural," i.e., preserves decisionlessness with a capacity to endure as long as in general the a-historicality of humanity persists. Thanks to this a-historicality, the human being establishes himself as the technological animal and places himself back into the present-at-hand and extinguishes the last shimmer of even the *semblance* of beyng, placing beyng not only into its darkness but even into that which is without darkness since it is a fortiori without light (cf. above, p. 39f.).

Yet the decisive decision can only become the one in which beyng | itself, in its decisionality as event, determines what is to be decided: either the sovereignty *of beyng* or else a new variation on the priority of beings (i.e., a new modernity). With these decisions concerning the history of beyng, a concomitant decision is made about the human being and indeed about the mode of his *essential* determination and essential configuration, not only because the human being *also* pertains to beings but because an essential relation to beyng remains his assignment. This relation, obscured and *modified* in the *animal rationale* and in the *subiectum*, appears ever again and remains unrecognized. This decision in the history of beyng, however, thereby also concomitantly decides about the definitive form of humanness in modernity, i.e., about "lived experience" as the feeling of the feelings, and indeed once again not insofar as the feelings merely belong as powers and properties to the human dowry, but inasmuch as they would make up the *humanness* of the subject. This decision about the feelings as such, however, does not concern the mere apprehension and "concept" of "feeling" and thus something like the correctness or incorrectness of psychological doctrines and of psychology as such. Instead, the decision in the history of beyng distinguishes the one and the other mode in which the human being is a human being in feelings and in the act of feeling—; that means: whether he is the bearer, organizer, and enjoyer | of the feelings (which are something present-at-hand in him)—or whether what one has long since and naturally recognized as feeling is productively transformed in accord with beyng to that which, rather than reside present-at-hand in the human being, radically bears the being of the human being and above all carries out his essential determination, i.e., excludes the *animal rationale and* the subject as modes of humanness.

Being and Time[15] indicates the preparation of the decision toward *this* possibility by using the term "disposition" ["*Stimmung*"] to name the "feelings." (At issue in that book is not a modification of the psychological-anthropological explanation of the emotional side of the human being, but rather a fundamental and different essential grounding of the human being in Da-sein, a grounding determined *purely* out of the question of being. The execution of this decisively recognized task was as defective as could be—but what is decisive re-

97

98

---

15. {Martin Heidegger, *Sein und Zeit*, GA2 (Frankfurt: Klostermann, 1977), p. 178ff.}

mains the quite different questioning out of a quite different horizon.)
Disposition (cf. winter semester 37–38[16]) disposes the human being
to his originary vocation of assignment to the stewardship of the truth
of beyng. To be disposed does not mean to wallow in dispositions qua
feelings and to feel these feelings; instead, it means: in appertaining
to beyng, to *be* the "there" qua the clearing of concealment as such.

99   To feel feelings is | to adhere obstinately to subjectivity; but to be dis-
posed is to be transported into the open realm of the truth of beyng,
such that beyng is thought not superveniently as the last pallor of what
is represented as present-at-hand, but rather is first, constantly, and
steadfastly experienced as the event (cf. *Beiträge*[17]) and not objectively
represented. The disposed human being receives the vocation of his
essence out of the basic disposition attuned to the event of appropriation. And the vocation is one toward Da-*sein*, toward being a ground
for the truth of beyng. The essence of the human being now arises as
essentially occurring out of beyng, and such essential occurrence is
originary history—because arising out of the event itself.

But it would be at variance with this thinking that is heedful of the
history of being if we were to calculate in advance the consequences
and effects of its course—this thinking must persevere in each of its
moments and must *know* the concealed momentariness of its future
history as that which refuses itself and thus originarily is already "extant." The grounding of the truth of beyng is goalless, because every
goal and all setting of goals would have to degrade the essential occurrence of beyng to the level of a means, as if the source of a river
could ever be a means of that river. If being simply and, moreover,
unrecognized as such, streams steadily on, without a break, out of the

100   sphere of the beings of concern at any time, | then the human being
persists in his humanness (of the *animal rationale*), and it appears to
him (the subject) that belonging together with this humanness are
also all beings (objectivity) and everything real (everything effective
and effected).

Nevertheless, the human being of such an essence is an excluded
being—excluded from the decision about the origin of his essence. Yet
the excluded one is found sublated in beings, through which this being steers amid good and ill, fortune and misfortune. It could appear
as a goal to *this* human being to secure the greatest "prospects" of his
essence in their full breadth and duration. Thereby the "history" of
this more and more historiologically (a-historically) developing hu-

---

16. {*Grundfragen der Philosophie*, p. 151ff.}

17. {Martin Heidegger, *Beiträge zur Philosophie (Vom Ereignis)*, GA65 (Frankfurt: Klostermann, 1989).}

man being would be adjusted to constantly "new" and "newer" times, the setting of goals would increase in calculability, and the prestige and authority of beings—merely because they are "real"—would have to grow until——beings undergo, precisely through the calculative mastery, a complete shrinking into objectlessness and can acquire thereby no impulses or paths to their preservation. The untroubled commonality of the prestige of beings in the sense of things present-at-hand, merely because they are present-at-hand, can be broken—if at all—only through the Flashing disappearance I of beyng on the   101
basis of the human capacity to experience beyng.

34

"Nature" and the "natural" are precisely what φύσις was at the beginning, for characteristic of them is the wholly astonishing, unusual, and unnatural. Over and against this, we can see what "natural" means today and has long meant: what is straightforwardly self-given to sound common sense—what, for a long habituation in the experience of beings, a habitation whose origins are no longer known, is understandable in the sense of that which arises out of itself. The appeal to the "natural" creates an impression of immediacy and of a relation to beings that is drawn directly from the sources. In truth, this that is "natural" owes its privilege to an entanglement of representations and opinions in the unquestionableness of being, and such unquestionableness opens all the floodgates to the pressure of what has become historiologically self-evident. The "natural" is the historiologically ordered, whose artificiality has become so refined as not to be noticed as artificial any longer, least of all where the procedure and the valuation are intent on bringing into effect something new over and against something outmoded.

35

102

"*Classicism*" is an essential consequence of historicism, specifically insofar as the latter could *disdain* itself in its sheer calculative character. It attempts to do so through the calculative acceptance of an "ideal" in the semblance of having by itself discovered this "ideal" and helped it to its essential validity. Thereby historicism presses everything decisive, and the mutual strangeness of everything originary, away from all originariness and replaces the lack of originariness with an obstinate adherence to the ideal. The suppressing of what is decisive and the fleeing from the leap—into the possibility of having to renounce (that, e.g., art has now become impossible)—signify the lack of a relation to *history,* that lack which is proper to all classicism and which also places what is decided ever still in the momentary possibility of downgoing. In contrast, classicism again takes and proclaims its bond to the "ideal" as an "eternal" task. The historical never proclaims but, rather, *is.* The thoroughly Historiological comportment—aimed at calculative representation and production—within classicism consists primarily, however, not in its making the "classical" its ideal but in establishing *in general* something "classical" in the sense of the | utterly exemplary and prescriptive.

103

History knows no "classical" periods because, as arising out of the essence of beyng, history, like beyng, is only what it is and never—unless against its essence—allows itself to be misinterpreted and misused as a goal or a value. But because our notion of beings has for the longest time—ever since the transition from ἀλήθεια to ὁμοίωσις ["correspondence"] and to the correctness of λόγος ["discourse"] qua assertion became *historiological,* so also *all comportment to history* has the character of classicism or, which is the same, the opposite character, that of romanticism. Through this historiological comportment to "history," the prescriptively exemplary entrenchment and the self-enjoyed transfiguration of its past become equally possible, and in each case history is the object of representation and production and never is being [*Sein*] itself, which challenges a being [*Sein*] of humans—i.e., their standing and falling in one moment and for one moment.

Classicism and thus also romanticism, as historicisms, are considered on the basis of their own tradition and promulgation and have already prepared the measure and the rational explanation of all "historical" phenomena (an explanation of their dependencies and lines of descent). Classicism does not exclude a "creating" but does presuppose that the being of | beings is unquestionably unproblematic. But as soon as we approach a historical moment which demands and *is* indeed *the* decision between the origin of beings and the originariness of beyng, then the overcoming of every sort of classicism and romanticism, i.e., the overcoming of their essence, must issue forth as a historical necessity. And thus everything depends on historical meditation, assuming we intend not to let the moment of beyng pass by but to situate ourselves toward that moment and to know that *such* a transition, which is comparable neither to a change of generations nor to a turn from one "millennium" to another, requires even less, indeed not at all, the constancy of a "cultural edifice." Nor does this transition demand the tempo of "revolutions" with the dubious advantages of contrast against what is overthrown. Instead, it demands the momentariness of great renunciations, the power for the inconspicuousness of no longer doing the usual in acting, appraising, and—think-

104

ing. Thus the transition demands the hardness needed to bear the semblance of indifference and "pessimism." All this only in order to venture a leap into the domain of history here or there and to make Da-*sein* visible, I by which name "something" is designated that is ap-   105
propriated only if the truth of beyng liberates itself for the stillness of the concealed power of beyng. All evasions into historiology, all adherences to the past, sink into unreality. In Dasein the abandonment of beings by being is ventured as the beginning of a decision with which history commences and historiology ends.

All overt and covert "classicisms" betray themselves as misuses of history by historiology, processes whose greatness and riches are not at all grasped by the pejorative term "misuse," since here the term is meant in the metaphysical sense and signifies the edifice of beings and of their representation over and against beyng and the self-refusal of beyng. Therefore the term must be thought on the far side of historiological and "philosophical" valuations.

36

History and decision.—Every genuine act and above all every being [*Sein*] require the possibility of a constantly renewable *collectedness* which is not a mere closure, but instead is a finding of one's way to the source out of which every step draws its necessity. This collectedness is I the most inconspicuous of what must happen if history is to   106
come to be. Yet right in the midst of the gigantism of public edifices and institutions a destruction can elapse that inconspicuously uproots the possibility of—and above all, the need for—that which is most inconspicuous. Between construction and destruction and within their simultaneity, a private and uncannily still decision is being prepared, and that indicates we are approaching an essential moment of Western history with a tempo unfamiliar to us. Perhaps this decision could never be established historiologically and remains concealed in the knowledge of those who save what is inconspicuous, so that on a new day of history it might, altered and unrecognized, radiate through the Dasein of the Germans.

37

Nobility—arises only where what is noble has pre-founded its possible arena in a noble realm. The start of this founding lies with those who are able to *be* the saviors of what is inconspicuous. But what is most inconspicuous is inconspicuousness itself, that particular Da-sein I
which in its steadfast accomplishment is not acquainted with thoughts   107

of *results* and so can never be enticed to extol itself on account of its results and proclaim them in public as things at hand and certainly not on account of a concomitant contortion of what is "ordinary" as the effective background of future progress. Everything noble, without its express knowledge or intention, is far removed from any act of comparison, presumption, or disparagement. Inconspicuously—and without "effecting" it—nobility brings into being what is silent and is rooted in necessity. Never does nobility require assurance that it is distinguished from others.

38

The "ideal" of a "respectable press" rests on an essential misunderstanding of "publicity," since the latter obtains the dubious ground of its existence from unrespectability. That "ideal" rests on a delusion or else consciously or unconsciously makes itself the culmination of unrespectability. One can and perhaps must proclaim this ideal, but one should know that it is and remains precisely an ideal of the *"press."*
108   Any moral indignation over it I is childish.

But if one could abolish the "press," then publicity and its possible disfigurement would be eliminated at one stroke (especially if we include the "press" of the ear—namely, radio). Yet that would mean abolishing modern humanity in the midst of the most beautiful approach run to the consummation of this humanity. So all that remains is an actual organizing of this ideal of a "respectable press." Whether a few individuals *know* the significance of such a press is, calculated according to the configuration of modernity, inconsequential. But perhaps from such knowledge a history might once arise. Yet this possibility is nothing for blocked eyes and ears. It has already settled accounts with all calculation.

39

The folkish [*völkisch*] principle manifests its gigantic modern significance when grasped as a variant and offspring of the sovereignty of the *sociology* of society. Is it an accident that National *Socialism* has done away with *"sociology"* as a *name*? Why did Jews and Catholics pursue sociology with special partiality?

40

"Science" on the basis of Da-sein and as Da-sein signifies a very dif-
109   ferent attitude which presupposes a passage through I research as

something of everyday ineluctability and which thus masters research on the basis of a knowledge immersing all beings in the fire of beyng. Future science, ignited by the transition into another standpoint— radically different from the modern one—is no longer determined by a representation which, in accord with its directedness toward research, acquires functionality as its essence and more and more renounces *knowledge*. Instead, this standpoint is determined precisely by knowledge, i.e., by a questioning steadfastness in the truth of beyng.

41

Greatness.—We must boldly, though soberly, think in such an essential way that we recognize all "greatness" and the possible notions (different according to the epoch) of greatness as *historiological* concepts. Historiology finds in its field of objects "greatnesses"—i.e., historiology measures them, since it is a comparative-calculative *explanation* of humanness, even—and precisely—where historiology presents itself, as it were, merely in an intuitive way. But greatness exists where it is not simply something measured but also raises itself to become the standard, related to measure and valuation, so that greatness ever still I objectifies, and it dissembles historical being—i.e., being itself, which is precisely history. The revering of greatness indeed seems to bring us closest to history itself, but always only in representation and in the calculation of ideals. Yet such historiology is indeed furthest removed from the venture and affirmation of the abyssal and from what is intrinsically question-worthy in history. Greatness is not an essential structure of history. But history still keeps itself as far from us as does all beyng dissembled through the sovereignty of beings. What is great and what is small, as well as their intermediary, the common, lie outside of history, for which reason, however, they govern the calculations of "historiology"—not merely those of the "science" of this name—but also all "lived experience" of "life" and of "reality." 110

42

How may we ban the frantic and unrestrained cleverness of the prattle that ever more successfully avoids speaking of the greatest and simplest works of thought and poetry? What is undertaken by such an overly clever age with respect to the few essential questions in the inconspicuous form of an I unobtrusive discourse? The age passes right over them. And that is indeed most appropriate, for we grasp what is simple and essential only if a still more essential simplicity prevails. 111

But customarily—i.e., from long habituation—"grasping" is entangle-ment in calculations that jut far out. "Historicism," which bears and stamps all the comportments, opinions, and evaluations of today's hu-manity, cannot be banned. It *must* stop, "thanks" to the devastation it itself effectuates. The essential ground of this necessity resides in the circumstance that what is historical never "effectuates" and certainly does not act on what is historical—instead, here *are* only peculiar creations of the space-time of being, and being—solitude itself—in a solitary way places what is solitary over and against what is solitary.

43

Youth.—"Who has the young has the future"[18]—a familiar saying, whose frightfulness is therefore not surmised. Who is here the "who"? An age that is appointed to a beginning and that, according to its abys-salness and originary maturity, must be inaccessible to the young, or at most a horror to them, will never "have" the young. But perhaps, in repelling, it will startle a few of them | to hold themselves ready for the momentariness and closed transitionality of maturity—of the knowledge of beyng. An age that is tasked with the consummation of an age and that thereby must superficially use progressiveness and success as its own confirmation, does have "the" young, i.e., those who in their youth have already become "old," insofar as they elevate "youthfulness" to a principle. Where the end of an age extols itself in the raiment of its last and lengthy advancements, the Concealed his-tory thwarts all the necessities of the beginning and thus also those of "maturity" (for maturity is not end and consummation—but is in-stead the now solitary beginning with all its concealed possibilities). The "young," who make youthfulness a principle, can become en-thused only over what is of the end and over its superficial consum-mation which is accessible to everyone and which everyone can carry out. To "have" these young people means to bewitch a generation that demands blindness and insight at once and that dismisses every claim which could tear through it convulsively.

"Who has the young has the future." Certainly—but which future? Only the one which is precisely | anticipated by these young people themselves already and so is no longer a future. On the other hand, whoever "has" the future, in that he *is* futural, can never have the "young"; instead, he "has" the once "mature," in that he unknow-ingly—since they must remain unknown to him—thrusts them from

112

113

---

18. {Remark originally attributed to Napoleon Bonaparte.}

himself and into the necessities of a beginning. To be futural means to appertain to the origin of history—to appertain to beyng—as to the indigence of the gods, in order to be thrown into the stewardship of Da-*sein*. That saying is a rule—and why not the most intelligible one?—of historiological calculation and therefore testifies to an obliviousness with regard to all history.

44

What those who come forth out of the end of metaphysics would perhaps like to reserve for themselves as the *last* approach-run to thinking must become what is *first* in the way the question of the truth of beyng is configured. In the face of the end of metaphysics, thinking became more and more a running behind the sciences, an acceptance of beings in the form of objectivity, a form that established the ordinary way of representing in all domains and separated these out as regions | of culture. Moreover, philosophy itself, in the course of the   114 history of metaphysics, distributed its "problems" to specialties which direct the "elaboration of the problems" even if a scholarly philosophy is abominated. This habituation of thinking to fixed tracks, each of which is blockaded by the appurtenant domain of objects, turns every attempt to think originarily, on the basis of beyng, into an alien procedure and does the same with the attempt to remain steadfast in the essential occurrence of beyng. Nevertheless, the danger of misunderstanding does not lie with those who follow such a procedure and demand "intelligibility," but with those who perhaps one day will let themselves be misled into slighting the essential strangeness of all thinking of beyng and into pressing for agreement. Consequently, the former never need a vacillating affiliation with the essential occurrence of beyng, since this occurrence often manifests its extraordinary power "only" in the form of the highest isolation.

45

The decay of thinking is not due to a decrease of "refinement" and education, nor can this process simply be depreciated as decadence. | The   115 decay pertains to the essence of modernity and has its source in the detachment of thinking from that which truly is to be thought—namely, being. This detachment has its concealed ground in the circumstance that in general thinking was never able to come to terms with the truth of beyng, but instead, as representational, immediately introduced the objectification of being (into beingness). Ever since, the human being developed out of his essence (*animal rationale*) toward the *subiectum*—but he also became at the same time more and more, and more ignorantly than ever, incapable of venturing beyng.

Instead, the detachment of thinking from being (for basically, thinking does indeed still think being) releases humanity to the most uncanny conventionality in the imposition of beings and in the enjoyment of present-at-hand things. The certainty of such dominance nevertheless penetrates into ever greater preliminaries, and the unsteadfastness of change, the inability to endure in a rooted steadfastness, pertains to the unrest of the calculation which has usurped the essential character of thinking. The decay of thinking is to be overcome only through a transformation of the relation of humans to being. Overcoming is here, as it is wherever it strives to be genuine, necessarily irresistible substitution. But how to replace an age, and even the one of a unique (metaphysical) history?

116   *46*

"*Historiology*"—the ancients distinguished "historiology" not in opposition to the natural sciences (roughly the ἐπιστήμη φυσική) but in opposition to μῦθος ["myth"]. Indeed historiology (ἱστορεῖν ["investigate"]) did precisely introduce (something every opposition accomplishes) a definite interpretation of μῦθος. Thereby μῦθος is the fabulous—a "telling of marvels"—ἡ δ' ἱστορία βούλεται τἀληθές ["whereas historiology desires the truth"] (Strabo, XI, 5[19]). Historiology desires what is correct, what is in actuality, but this is not thought in terms of the critical function of historiology in the sense of the critique of sources—for the cited determination refers historiology not to the past but instead simply to the unconcealed, that which is not veiled in any way. The subsequent narrower concept of "historiology" is founded on this one; thereby the ἀληθές ["true," "unconcealed"] is *already* elaborated through the procedure of inquiring, finding out, becoming versed in various ways in the sense of τέχνη—producing—*more* in the sense of setting forth, adducing, rather than "manufacturing." Thus ἱστορία here signifies enlightenment in the fundamental sense; the later *historical* phenomenon of the "Enlightenment" is defined by its directedness *against* the *Christian* μῦθος.

---

19. {Strabo, *Strabonis Geographica*, vols. 1–3, (Leipzig: Teubner, 1866).}

47

History—if we quite decisively refuse to determine the essence of history on the basis of the relation to historiology as the latter's object, and if we also do not go back to some | reality lying "behind" this object, whereby we would still take historiology as the guideline, but if instead we grasp history on the basis of beyng (not on the basis of some region of beings), then the determination that is heedful of the event says that 1. beyng steps into its truth and only in that way essentially occurs, 2. this essential occurrence is concealed, 3. knowledge of history is possible only as a grounding of the truth of beyng.

History is there where no one surmises it; it stands in a rare illumination which is itself concealed. The historical can harbor a wrathful spitefulness, which is not to be confused with the historiological concept of "moral" baseness and mere vulgarity.

The essence of history can be determined from temporality *only* if, as is the basic intention of *Being and Time,* time is grasped in advance with a view toward beyng as an indication of the truth of beyng. But if "temporality" is meant in the sense of the ordinary understanding of human comportment and activity as taking place within time, then the referring of history to time is not only trivial but is even erroneous. Yet the particular concealment proper to all history can occasionally be grasped in the form of a trackless disappearance and submergence into ineffectuality, although even here misinterpretations easily slip in because "effectivity" is indeed not essential for history.

Hölderlin is historical in the sense of that ineffectuality.

48

Descartes.—The attack on Descartes, i.e., the counterquestioning *appropriate* to his basic metaphysical position, a questioning rooted in a fundamental overcoming of metaphysics, can be carried out only on the basis of an *asking of the question of being. Being and Time*[20] (1927) attempted the first such attack, which has nothing in common with the earlier and subsequent "critique" of "Cartesianism." Through the choice of the opponent, this attack for the first time places that opponent in his incontestible greatness within the history of Western thinking. This attack knows that "refutations" accomplish nothing here and that instead through the originariness of the attack the attacked one comes all the more to stand in his historical unshakable-

---

20. {*Sein und Zeit,* p. 119ff.}

ness and therefore can all the less count as "disposed of," if indeed a
future of thoughtful questioning is still open to the West. Therefore
this attack (although it has since been exploited to an equal extent by
Jews and National Socialists, yet without being grasped in its essential core) has no commonality with the currently ebullient and impu-
dent carping at Descartes from "folkish [*völkisch*]-political" viewpoints
119   by overzealous and still untenured | lecturers in "philosophy." Nor is
it necessary, even if many would like to see it done, to set onself publicly against such literature. What is essential here, and thus to be
thought into the future, is only the *insight* into the ground which allows such refutations of Descartes to become a badly played comedy:
these ideological viewpoints—the appeal to "life" and to the "differently" determined "human being"—are in fact thoroughly indebted
to Descartes. In other words, they accept—to be sure, altogether unwittingly—the Cartesian postulation of humanness as "subjectum."
They entrench Cartesianism in a way whose crudeness guarantees
that Descartes will always be more and more intelligible to the
"people." Of what avail all the obscure and pompous "refutations," if
they take nourishment from—and even let themselves be confirmed
by—the dominant *forgetting of being,* whereas the attack can be ventured only on the basis of an *asking of the question of being*? The asking
of this question then, of course, would have to bring to light unintentionally the triumphant "opponents" of Descartes in their wretched
behavior, which admittedly would only be *one more* historical insignificance.

120   49

Being and Time.—There is no dispensing with *Being and Time.* Admittedly and fortunately. Woe if it were otherwise. Essential questioning would then be abandoned, and the necessity of thinking would
become an occupation that "makes progress," and this manufactured
progress would be brought to the attention of contemporaries and supply the universal idle talk with new "matter." If there were somewhere
a sign that that questioning is being *asked*, then *perhaps*—but only perhaps—it would be necessary to pursue the questioning. But in truth
the thinking and saying of beyng are determined by *beyng* itself; but
what if beyng—observed in public and in the age of the first onset of
modernity—demanded silence and an education toward the capacity
to keep silent? And what if such education harbored its own mode of
historical transmission, and what if one could now learn "more" from
silence than from all prolix "literature"?

50

"Metaphysics." Is it, as Hegel believes, only **"remarkable"** "if a people loses its metaphysics,"[21] or, instead, is it worthy of *questioning* whether a people ever already | had possession of *its* "metaphysics," i.e., ever   121
developed it? But this question provokes another one as to whether a "people" must possess and develop its *"metaphysics"* in order to create actuality for the essence of that people—or whether a people *might* not be destined to *overcome* metaphysics as such and grasp itself in its own essence on the basis of a more originary assignment to being. To ask this means to meditate at the same time on the extent to which humanity must grasp itself as "a people" and on the place from which the necessity of *this* self-knowledge arises. The loss of metaphysics will be considered merely remarkable by anyone who takes its reacquisition to be self-evident and has accepted *metaphysics* itself as the highest knowledge of being. But if we must venture out into what is unasked in these questions, then every foothold in the past disappears and every recourse to what is merely calculated and believed about the tasks fails. Not only the "interpretation" of being but also, and above all, already the *truth* of being (every interpretation is supposed to be able to move in this truth) are now question-worthy, and metaphysics as such becomes unsubstantial and remains—unless taken up into the history of beyng—an object of "spiritual-historical" calculations.

51   122

Once and for all: I have nothing to do with the "philosophy of existence" and especially nothing to do with the version of it propounded by Heyse.[22] I will leave it to this "thinker" to consider whether his gruel has anything to do with me, a gruel cooked up out of misunderstandings of *Being and Time* which have been rewarmed seven times and overly salted with the "intellectual assets of National Socialism."

Very much to the contrary, however, I have a great deal to do with the seriousness of Karl Jaspers's attitude and meditation. Nevertheless, an abyss indeed separates his *Philosophy* from the questioning I carry out in *Being and Time*—a circumstance that has no effect at all on my revering him and feeling grateful to him.

---

21. {Georg Wilhelm Friedrich Hegel, *Wissenschaft der Logik*, erster Teil (Leipzig: Meiner, 1923) p. 4.}

22. {Hans Heyse, *Idee und Existenz* (Hamburg: Hanseatische Verlagsanstalt, 1935).}

Pascal in one place calls the human being a "thinking reed."[23] Perhaps Heyse, whose very own clichés inspire him to a remarkable "posture," is one such "reed"—except that he does *not* think. His ink spilling is worth the mention only because it derives from a state of these modern times which has already lost the power of thoughtful meditation and has replaced it with mere inflated phraseology, so much so
123   that I everyone finds this to be in order and no one can any longer sense a genuine need for something else. *This* insensitivity, in whose "sight" a "living," "spiritual" "wrestling match" plays out, is the best protection against the admittedly ever smaller danger that such a barbarity of "thinking" will one day see itself compelled to evade its own uncanniness—whereto?

To the protection of political reality. It is *not* this reality and *not* the mere (still only imitative) decadence of thinking that can testify to the extent of the alienation from authentic thinking; instead, it is simply *this*, namely, the fact that such decadence covers itself over and even poses as an ascent, with the help of a reality originating elsewhere. It is *not* the springing up of such concoctions—which arose (prior to 1933) from quite different "goals"—that is worthy of note, but the preparation of oblivious people, a preparation that takes "seriously" a thing one can still precisely call "seriousness" in the field of thinking. Nothing that happens here is the "fault" of today's humanity; on the contrary, it is only the broadest and shallowest aftermath of a concealed event lying much further back.
124   Therefore one may at most *establish* one's standpoint against this but must never throw oneself into a confrontation. Indeed, even that establishment can count only as the establishment of one's own meditation and never serve as a public disavowal of it, for even such disavowal could be used only to provide the pursuit of "spiritual life" with "novelties" and to confirm this pursuit in its alleged indispensability.

52

The actual danger for *genuine* thinking (i.e., for the thinking compelled out of its own essence *by its proper to-be-thought*, namely, beyng) is never the crude disdaining and "rejection" of philosophy. Moreover, today when philosophy no longer "is," these are not "accomplishments" and not gains. The endangerment of thinking commences only where "thinking" and "philosophy" are affirmed or are demanded in the guise of "spirit as power," i.e., where in the configuration of a cul-

---

23. {Blaise Pascal, *Pensées* (Paris: Hachette, 1904), no. 346ff.}

ture all these established pieces of equipment are eagerly procured and where, in calculating such activity, something "quite in order" is carried out, so that even the immediately past time moves into the shadows. Here commences the sovereignty of the ambiguous. Here confusion becomes a weapon.

53   125

Descartes's "rationalism" means that the essence of being is determined out of the certainty of thinking, out of the self-certainty of thinkability. Being now explicitly receives the previously suppressed or only crudely grasped character of calculability—producibility—in the widest sense. This interpretation of being becomes the basic condition of modernity and of modern humanity. Yet this basic condition first attains its full power only when this age sets out toward its proper consummation. The history of today's humanity stands at this temporal point.

Therefore it is an almost insane misunderstanding of the current age, and of the worldviews proper to it alone, to attempt on this basis (e.g., on the basis of a "National Socialist" pseudophilosophy) to take up the cudgels against Descartes's "rationalism," presumably only because Descartes is French and a "foreigner."—Instead, the proper greatness of today's worldviews and of their claim to "totality" is that *they bring into effect a metaphysically grasped "rationalism" (cf. above) as the innermost power of their willing of power and reject all artificial "mysticism" and "mythology."* Descartes's rationalism is neither "French" nor foreign—but instead is Western, and the French aspect, if one indeed wants to know it, consists in its having brought into play a capacity to make knowable for the first time that interpretation of being. The knowable itself is neither French, nor German, nor Italian, nor British, nor American—on the other hand, it is indeed the *ground* of these nationalities!

{Index}

PONDERINGS IX

The Germans have even been torn away from their essential ground, one that has still not ever been discovered, let alone fathomed, and so they totter in the alien essence modernity foisted upon them. Therein lies the danger, namely, that they will fall victim to the exclusive dominance of their own distorted essence. Accordingly—need to think *ahead* into the other *beginning*—

But what about the *struggle* of those who think ahead so as to ground and found?

Being [*das Sein*] is beyng.

(Cf. ☐ gods, p. 45f.[1])

The Western care—only a few who are knowledgeable will surmise that the question of the truth of beyng is *the* Western care. No "thou" and no "I" count as particular cases of present-at-hand humans, and no "community" counts as a union of many humans—no mere separate people has, simply from its presence at hand, a claim to historical permanence.

Care is Western care—it draws us into the plight of the truth of beyng, for the concealed intimation of the vocation of the West to ground the space-time of the most noble and most abyssal gods is in danger of being received no longer into the fervor of creative hearts, ones in which a history of the gods can again arise in the sight of an awake humanity—instead of a historiology of blinded actions through which modern humanity totters up against a sheer self-instituted perishing.—

Where will the gods *then* summon beyng?

There where beyng has appropriated that clearing (Da-sein) in whose open realm it refuses itself, so that the refusal might once again effectuate the intrinsically vibrant event of a possible rejoinder to that which, through such self-encounter, is found in the essence of God and humanity.

---

1. {Martin Heidegger, *Besinnung,* GA66 (Frankfurt: Klostermann, 1997), p. 253f.}

1   *3*

If human goallessness has become complete (if only other purposes within beings are posited, and the means of actualization as well as the ways and the undertakings themselves become "the" purposes, and consequently their fulfillment ever more easily and definitively bestows the liberation of all claims, whereby the claims themselves seem ever more superficial and "closer to life"), then the human being is unwittingly and obliviously becoming the beneficiary of a great destruction presenting itself to him as a gigantic buildup. And why should this human being not feel himself to be well, and ever better, in his presumptuous ignorance, which he replaces with prudence and cleverness in exploiting the destruction? (Thus it is a destruction—perhaps one already not worthy of mention—when with the best intention Hölderlin's poetry is exploited for its proficiency of expression and thereby something of today is described. But what is decisive is not the misuse of Hölderlin, but instead the loss of every possibility of
2   surmising that this poet embodies a | decision of our history and perhaps demands decidedness in favor of renouncing all ink spilling in verse—until *his* words are liberated for the disposition of a joyful seriousness of a Da-sein.)

Why do we torment these well-intentioned historiological animals that in the historiology of their own advancements and gratifications become ever more content and jovial with questions that appear to them to be empty, eccentric, and snobbish? Out of the *animal rationale* has come the *historiological animal,* i.e., that living thing which pursues the conservation and enhancement of *"life"* and takes that for a "goal." But the pursuit happens "historiologically"—by way of calculating previous ideals and accomplishments (the "great past" as means of forming public opinion—) in the planned wishes and claims. The sovereignty of the historiological excludes the existence of any essential opposition; the calculation has overcome all admissions of anything which, as essential resistance, could make constant struggle a necessity with which the decisions might first comply and might replace the historiological animal into the history of Dasein. The more historiological the human being becomes, all the more bestial does the animal become, all the more exclusively does everything revolve
3   around | the conservation and breeding of life as life, and all the more improbable becomes the possibility of a downgoing. All comportment is appraised in terms of accomplishment, which is the expression of life, and life lives for the sake of life. In this way, the encirclement of historiology through the animal presses the historiological animal

down beneath the mere animal and altogether beneath all pure growth, indeed even beneath the "grown" rock, because here an essence spreads which, belonging to beyng but disloyal to it, sees the goal of its advancement in the abandonment of beings by being. But this applies above all where, in dependence on and in imitation of previous cultural "accomplishments," even something quite "respectable" is attained, because every decision is avoided and the manufacture of things that can be accounted "not bad" is held as more important than a renunciation stemming from genuine knowledge and from an originary power of reverence.

No one seems to grasp that we are confronting a decisive time whose anteroom must be filled by *essential abjurations*. No one seems to have an eye and a judgment for what is *not* done on the basis of a knowledge that thinks in advance, and no longer can be done on that basis, because it is producing only a concealing obstruction of the essential decision. | The half is justified by appealing to the necessity for something to happen; but no one surmises that this "half" only makes the need and the claims more composed and more secure and closes off the possibility that what is beginning a history is not the claim of *calculative* humanity on beings, but instead is the thrust of beyng on unguarded and unsupported humanity. In the space-time of this history, the gods arise—e.g., those that uncalculatively let the human being be steadfast in Da-*sein*, whereby the truth of beyng might announce the uniqueness of this extraordinary circumstance in which gods and humans could come to an encounter and could produce the moment wherein the *thatness* of beyng gathers itself against the blind inconsequentiality of nothingness.

This encounter *is* no possible goal and does not know any purposes. It essentially occurs as the abyss out of which all grounding draws its freedom. This freedom, whose ever incomparable uncalculability testifies to the essential occurrence of beyng, transposes the human being into the stillness of his most concealed dignity, from which comes to him not satisfaction and enjoyment, but quite to the contrary, that unsettling which raises him up against the intimation of the gods and into his affiliation with such encounter. | Only if the human being in advance and in uncanny inner convulsions endures the decision toward this history of beyng will he find the ground on which arises for him a source of necessary creativity. Within this creativity, every work preserves the truth of beyng in a being and through such preservation first lets beings *as* beings protrude into the open realm of the space-time of historical Da-sein and protects the moment of beyng as the highest possibility of this work. Out of such protection, beings first again find themselves on the way toward beings, and they thereby world on the basis of world and, as earth, survive their misuse as mere materials and forces.

4

Yet in order for this world of an ambiguous and variegated transition to exist and to remain luminous for the "tragedies" and sacrifices of the noiseless questioning, knowing, and deciding demanded by such a world, what is needed is a repose that thinks far in advance. Such repose withholds its knowledge and allows what is withheld to flow only into the disclosive questioning of the initially timid and yet de-
6   cisive distinctions and separations | the human being must traverse if he is to forsake the historiological animal and be able to prepare historical Dasein.

What we must *know* about this may be illustrated by an example, if indeed it can at all be termed "example."

How far do the horizons of our endeavors and arrangements in fact extend? Through three rubrics: *people, culture, Christianity.* "People"—is not a goal, but only the substructure of a way which never determines itself out of itself. "Culture" is the affirmation of the modern self-certainty of humanity in the machination of beings; not a goal and not a domain of possible decisions; still only an expedient for the assimilation to previous history. "Christianity"—a stopgap without any power of creativity, because it knows and tolerates no question-worthiness and seeks only compromise or at most consolations and vain promises. In no case do these horizons reach into the decisive domains, and yet the sovereignty of such horizons obstructs a sense and will for those domains and denies us any knowledge of them and keeps us in the compulsion of the calculation that still misinterprets itself.

7   Our thinking does not need to be "international" or even European; but it must indeed be Western and metaphysical if it is to fathom more originarily the ground of our history out of the essence of beyng, i.e., out of the "between" of the encounter of gods and humans. Incomparable is our care, as the care of Da-sein, wherein the truth of being is to strike roots. This care, in its holding sway, has extensions and proportions which are not at all touched by the superficial—although ever so rebellious and afflicting—confrontations with peoples, cultures, and worldviews—insofar as we take these as ultimate and do not surmise that they themselves already stand in the service of a beginning which is coming from afar. This beginning dislodges the human being into the need to come to terms with the very *goallessness* and *superficiality* of his most vital exertions and actions and to experi-

ence therein the first celebration of Da-sein. The unsettling attunes the celebration and makes us aware that beyng still awaits its grounding and that, out of the dialogue vibrating in beyng, the gods bring to language anew the essence of humanity.

People, culture, Christianity—in whichever of their variations and   8 combinations—are already things of the past, and because in them an originary relation to being and to its question-worthiness in the most manifold forms is in advance, i.e., at all times, closed off—indeed is never known and experienced—therefore people, culture, and Christianity possess no originary and essential power for the approaching decisions. Yet these three horizons now explicitly come up for discussion and pursuit, and *they* precisely cover over what is in truth merely their already severe horizonlessness, all of which indicates the *fact that* beyng is already driven within the Western forgetfulness of being and casts its still ungrasped signs into the domain of today's humanity and already brings up for decision this one single issue: whether now already the few will venture to surmise the signs and from these intimations will let flow (into the forthcoming questioning, knowing, and thus creating) another disposition and destiny—i.e., whether we, whether precisely the Germans, are strong enough to assume this highest and most hidden care, the care for the truth of beyng.

For we *"are"* kindred | to the Greeks not in that we take them as   9 models and guard them, perhaps especially and otherwise than did mere "humanism" and "classicism"—but rather in that we, like the Greeks, have to venture the first beginning of Western history and carry out the completely *other* beginning. And to carry this out we have to undertake a possibly very lengthy and downright "fantastic" preparation that will for a long time be misinterpreted and unrecognized. These preparatory *inner* decisions are called "inner" because they pertain to the concealedness of beyng and can therefore never be taken up in the manner of realizable plans and calculations regarding beings. These inner decisions (cf. Ponderings VIII and VII) must be thought in advance and said in advance by those who already seem to be striving for a sheer negation of everything hitherto and everything of today, as if they took nourishment from the most meager food of the lack of prospects of so-called cultural development and as if they grazed their fill on the "enjoyment" of the continued establishment of a "downfall"—which indeed presupposes the *calculation* of "ascents."

Furthermore, if we count on an obvious doctrine and an assignment to a blessed life, if we expect representations of objects, to which we can flee if necessary, and if we demand to be immediately saved

10   and to be spared every *essential* worry, then | Hölderlin and Nietzsche, each in his own way, leave us "unsatisfied"—so much so that we do not once manage to recognize what we need in order to grasp their intimating that speaks in advance.

5

More desolate and unfruitful than the crudest glorification of mere matter and of blind forces (also of the merely present-at-hand life-matter) is the small person's "idealism," which is noisy, horizonless, and unfit for decisions.

6

Can thinking also be an affair of "life and death"? Then into which domains must thinking venture forth?

7

Only the greatest equanimity permeating Da-sein can correspond to the unsettling, i.e., to that releasing of all beings into the concealedness of beyng, a releasing which arises out of the event.

8

What is now happening is only one of the many quiverings of the de-
11   cisionless essence of modernity. Two decades | after the world war, in spite of all the upheavals, the same blind frenzy, only apparently checked but not at all mastered, presses us into superficiality and fills the single foreground of a flat and loud horizon of the operations of modern humanity—all of which indicates that modernity cannot leap out of its rut and that, instead, the modern human being must carry out the ending of the modern age in one way or another as a purpose belonging to his own self. Already the transition to the other beginning must be prepared through knowledgeable motives moving in another decidedness.

9

The opposite of πόλεμος (i.e., the opposite of war and battle in the sense of the essential ground of their absence) is not lame peace, or the mere progressive advancement of culture, or the "moral" improvement of "society"; instead, what is originarily and completely other than πόλεμος is the decision between beyng and "beings."

πόλεμος — war — peace — decision

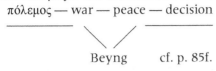

Beyng   cf. p. 85f.

10

Whoever does not know the decisions can also never know what war is, even if he has "partaken" in a war. | He knows only the horrors and   12
bitter shocks of what occurs therein, and he knows the impetuses for sacrifice and self-control within the unfolding encounters, but he never knows the ground of the truth, and the distorted ground of the fact that war and peace always lie on the *one* side (the side of beings) and never harbor the power of the essential occurrence of a truth *of* beyng.

11

As regards *essential thinking*, its impotence corresponds to its originariness, if "potency" means the capacity to dispose of the immediate accomplishment of something planned within things present-at-hand—for essential thinking eventuates in the projection of the truth of beyng. Yet the question remains: what *is* more fully, that capacity to accomplish and the included complete dependence on "beings" (in the sense of things already present-at-hand and guiding)—or beyng and the essential occurrence of its truth in the sense of the origin of other possibilities of decision? Essential thinking is by its very character inestimable and is not translatable into our ordinary pursuit of things, ever since the start of the sovereignty of τέχνη, which could become *technology* only through an essential transformation | of the practitio-   13
ner (τεχνίτης) and of the sphere in which τέχνη operates. This transformation of τέχνη into technology is, however, not something the machine effectuates; on the contrary, the *reverse* holds: the essential transformation into technology (setting forth as manufacture of objects for the subjectum) is what first conditions the discovery of the machine. The invention of the steam engine is only an occasion, not the reason, which allows the development of technology to proceed at a *tempo* that is also conditioned and carried out only *through* the very

ability of objectivity to be completely mastered—which also makes speed possible.

12

Credulity also belongs to the essence of a people—this is not a lack, but instead is a "condition" of unconditional action. The more thorough this credulity becomes and the more it can be dominated, and the more surely it underlies controllable institutions and dovetails with them, then all the more can it unfold into sheer *stupidity*. Credulity is an uncanny weapon, if it is simply kept opportunely and completely within its own desired limits. Historiology teaches that only *after* the guarantee of success can a ruler divulge to his "people" what 14   he *really* wanted. But for success to occur, the | people must be of the opinion that in carrying out the will of the ruler they are bringing into effect their own will and only that will. This disguising and feigning of the levels of will should not be deprecated from some sort of "moral" viewpoint. That is, unless one renounces reaching attainable purposes and unless this renunciation remains unnecessary because Da-sein is borne by a truth which creates other origins of ruling and knows no purposes and no "successes." But then "morality" is all the more impossible as a supplementary doctrine.

13

To "reign" ["*regieren*"] (from *rex*) means to be king: from being this, to act regally. We today understand "reigning" only as the established instituting of official administrative authority. One who can dominate and who seizes the opportunity to do so is not necessarily able to "reign." "Reigning" in the proper sense pertains to the nobility of silent being, which despises all noise and never falls to someone "ordinary."—

14

How does it happen that anyone who reviles and disparages is always wrong, even if the disparagement does correspond to the "facts"? 15   Wrong—| not in the sense of incorrectness or mere unjustifiability but on the contrary in the deeper sense according to which one who is wrong renounces the correct degree of noble comportment and dignity. (How is the "stirring up" of peoples to be grasped from this perspective?)

15

No one can appeal to *honor* [Ehre] if it has not in advance found its essence in being the protective shield of a *reverence* [Verehrung] in virtue of which everyone appealing to honor is summoned by necessities that never derive from already extant beings, but rather, as intimations of beyng, call him to an originary venture of truth: i.e., to the encounter of gods and humans. The domain of this encounter, which arises only with the encounter itself and at the same time vibrates right through it, is kept open only to *the seekers,* who are marked by the unrest of beyng and are dispossessed of beings everywhere, even if they must in the ordinary way pursue and use beings. Honor can never refer to something present-at-hand and thus also never to an "ideal." Yet where and when is reverence? But do the seekers have self-knowledge—or is everyone necessarily astray in his errancy and *for that reason* | exempt from all illusion?   16

16

If now a second world war should enter the human horizon, then it seems as if once again the *genuine decision* could not be calculated, for such a decision by no means concerns war versus peace, democracy versus authoritarianism, Bolshevism versus Christian culture, but rather: *meditation* and the search for the inceptual appropriation of beyng versus the *illusion* of the definitive anthropomorphizing of uprooted humanity. But the human being is perhaps so obsessed with the craving for a satisfying contentedness with his needs, and perhaps the "refined" massification of humans is inserted into a pleasurable state of knowing everything and being able to possess things, such that the human being of this epoch has become altogether incapable of decisions because of not needing any decision. Thus, in small and great matters, there now stands only one opinion versus another, one slogan versus another, whose sole evidentiary support is *the fact that* they are slogans. Nowhere do questioning individuals encounter one another so that, by reciprocally pointing one another into what is most question-worthy, they could open up the abyssal space of concealment, a space | tolerating no publicness but indeed making the seek-   17 ers into grounders of a world which is borne by the mystery of the earth and, through its holding sway and in strife with the earth, attains by way of strife the spatiotemporal field of the encounter of gods and humans. Yet perhaps now, and indeed in forms that are the most varied and the most oppositional and therefore are the *same* politically and culturally, that day is dawning in which the contentedness of humans in their pleasures (wherein integrity and violence go together harmoniously) will rise up to gigantic proportions.

17

The *claim* to appertain to the disclosive questioning of what is most question-worthy remains absent. And where this claim is lacking, the needs of the mere conservation of "life" become more and more pressing. As these needs veil their rebelliousness to a greater extent, and as "life" becomes more historiological and draws the "cultural" and "spiritual" assets into the domain of needs, so all the baser do the needs become—which is to say: the ordinary and more and more stimulated and calculable enjoyment becomes at the same time "more spiritual," inasmuch as the enjoyment incorporates the "spiritual" and "cultural" into its craving and so takes its right to everything as a demonstration of its justification and its "height." The craving of needs— the mania to stimulate | the needs and to satisfy them—produces a *claimlessness* which looks like healthy life and like the certainty of "instinct" but which nevertheless basically signifies the most uncanny blockage from beyng and does so precisely where, within this affirmation of life, there is a "struggle" over "ideals." It is important to know, however, that every life affirmation as an "attitude" and a "worldview" is the successor of a life denial—and this latter arises out of a refusal to let beings as such and as a whole vibrate in a basic disposition of seeking and venturing. The "affirmation of life" is always enthrallment in the present-at-hand and is testimony to the impotence of humans to allow their essence to arise out of decisions. Life affirmation, as recourse to a worldview, is then the appeal to what is given and posited by "*God*"—whereby the human being, in the extrinsicality of his "inwardness," "blinks"[2] at the name of "God" and does not ever think to come to terms with the presuppositions involved in such an appeal. Presuppositions which at once bring to light the groundlessness of this appeal or require assent to dogmas of "faith" once again preventing an "affirmation of life."

18

---

2. {Cf. Friedrich Nietzsche, *Also sprach Zarathustra: Ein Buch für Alle und Keinen, Werke*, vol. 6 (Leipzig: Naumann, 1904), p. 19: "'What is love? What is creation? What is desire? What is a star?'—thus asks the last human being and blinks."}

18

The *agreement* of the European peoples attains its overarching sense only by arising out of a decision in favor of the *question-worthiness* of the history of the West and thus in favor of a struggle for a more originary grounding of the truth of beyng; out of this grounding, a history might emerge once again. *Mere* agreement, on the level of an increasing indifference to all essential decisions, mere driving on to the comfort of compromise and to the guarantee of pleasure—this does indeed spare much that is dreadful and much grief and distress—but it still draws humans more and more and indeed more insidiously into an anthropomorphizing of themselves and of beings and presses humans into the scarcely still experienceable dullness of the a-historical dominance over everything.

The gods have become fugitive, because every path to a divinization has been closed off to them—indeed even for mere idols the anthropomorphized human being is too comfortable and too secure in the pursuit of all his needs and their satisfaction.

19

"Thunderous applause" is today still the weakest proof of approval.

20

If, with the increase in results, the contentedness as regards the essential sinks so much as no longer to be recognizable, then universal bliss and pleasure will seem to become the main state of affairs.

21

The—quantitative—increase of the people as an—essential—decrease in the possibility of the gods. But why still—ultimately there are still institutions for the ways of escape out of a possible flaming up of truth—why still gods? Why still an enduring of a possibility of decision regarding the gods, i.e., regarding the capability of the human being for the gods, i.e., regarding his unique "greatness," which is so essential that it is misinterpreted by the designation "greatness"?

22

What is stupidity? That communal situation in which the individuals persuade one another that the renunciation of every attempt at medi-

21   tation I is the gaining of an instinctual certainty, in consequence of
which those individuals are spared all the burdens and dangers of
what is question-worthy, mutually confirm their achievements as unprecedented results, and proclaim the flattening down to a claimless-
ness in knowledge of the essential as an advancement of "culture." An
individual can never be stupid in this sense.

23

To grasp beyng means to come to stand outside the world—i.e., outside
what is called "world," namely, representable and producible beings
as a whole. It does not concern beyng and its truth whether many—
quantitatively—surmise something of the fact that beyng is grasped
by, and itself appropriates, that which bears and determines the highest decisions.

24

Decisionlessness in the sense of standing outside the realm of decision regarding beyng or mere beings is the basic condition of the exclusive sovereignty of calculation.

22   ### 25

Every being that boasts it can stand on its own, in case such autonomy
is more than a sheer figure of speech, must not exploit its successes
as a replacement for being, especially not if it calculates these successes on the basis of the distance from the failures of other beings.
The standing on its own must always be appraised solely according to
self-instituted essential law. What can count as the measure thereby
is only the height and breadth in which what is self-standing decides
on its essential rank, in case decisions are at all still kept open to its
essence; for what is calculated according to successes, and from them
calculates being itself, mostly wallows in decisionlessness.

26

"*The German future*" and the human being as *the historiological animal*
(cf. above, p. 1ff.). What is that—the German future? Who could say,
since of course no one knows, what the coming time will bring the
Germans? Or does the term in question mean something other than

a mere later state? The mere further condition of the at hand, growing mass of people and of their cultural veneer—is that the future? No—that is the most present present, I complete futurelessness, which   23
in such a way and with this exclusivity can be pursued, and even attained, only by a historiological being, i.e., by one that investigates everything and calculates everything. This semblant future [*Zukunft*] does not allow anything to come *to* [zu-*kommen*] the Germans in the sense of that which would come to them by compelling them into the struggle over the question-worthiness of the most proper essential depth.

We do not "have" such a future on the basis of the prospect of a secure further existence—such a future is not at all something one could "have"—on the contrary, we must *be* it. But this will open itself to us only if the historiological animal is eradicated and if the will to its eradication holds sway in the will to the future. Yet how are we supposed to eradicate the historiological animal—modern humanity pressing on to its consummation—if we everywhere refuse to track it down and to recognize it in its ultimate transparency? How a future, if we do not want to know that it first and only becomes free in a struggle which is harder and longer than any horrible course of a modern world war, one arranged with all historiological—i.e., technological—shrewdness? Whence the I claim to a future, as long as the   24
mere conservation and increase of the present-at-hand remains the posited "goal"? How is that which could cast us into the question-worthiness of our essence supposed to come *up to us*—if we "*are*" *such* that we believe we can on our own attain the future, i.e., what is merely later, what still escapes us and is not yet incorporated? Where is the ground of this altogether Western-modern futurelessness—which, through the helplessness of planning (as a thinking in advance), ever more compellingly dissembles itself as a futurity? This thinking in advance does indeed not at all think out in front of itself by venturing out, through questioning, into another space of essential grounding— instead, it "thinks" only *back behind itself* by intending the unaltered form of the human being as the historiological animal and seeing his salvation in increase. *This* "thinking in advance" remains definitively distinct from that pre-thinking which by way of questioning exposes itself to the possibility of an essential origin and never calculates back behind itself, but instead precisely leaves "itself" (the past) behind.

Yet these departures must be endured first and often, until the I initial unsettling seizes some few of those who are futural and be-   25
stows on them their destiny. All gigantic plans, which definitively in-

stitute the historiological animal on the globe, are merely a very comprehensive—yet at the same time extremely shriveled—computational game, in the carrying out of which all complacent slaves and slaveholders are yoked together in the most varied forms and thereby carry on their exertions.

And yet all this is not a struggle—because everything is already decided through an evasion of decisions on account of an ignorance of them. The bedwarfing of humanity proceeds into the gigantic and is the last consequence of the "sovereignty" of the historiological animal. Yet for the futural ones to wrestle themselves loose, this extreme diminution of humanity must seem to be the greatest triumph—for only in that way does there open up the abyss dividing the future essence of humanity from the previous one.

What is the German future? That individuals of the Germans become futural, ones who—even if in each case only for moments—allow the thrust of beyng to come upon them, I who pre-think into this that is coming, who ever again ground for the earth a space of struggle over the decision regarding the gods, and who thereby lay the ground for a history. The futural ones will have to endure many a long period of solitude. They are in danger of abandoning knowledge *too soon,* in that they might leave it to an entanglement in a speed-thirsty calculation and assimilation in order to satisfy the—indeed "reasonable"—demand to do something for "one's epoch." They are in danger of diminishing too soon the unsettling that comes from the thrust of beyng, in order to make it at once "universally" accessible, since indeed nothing is *valid* any longer except what is stamped by public opinion. They are in danger, because they are questioners, of allowing their questioning to become something ordinary and a mere procedure rather than a momentary abyss that ever breaks open anew. The futural Germans will always and necessarily succumb to one of these dangers; i.e., the future—as German—will become a long struggle in which many will fall in silent reticence—I while the noise of planning and the roaring of the exploitation of the earth accompany the triumphal procession of the most diminutive of all human types.

And yet: the German future "will" not first "come to be"; it "is" already, ever since Hölderlin founded it—although this "is" possesses another truth, one closed to all correct and ever so correct representations and procedures. But this future cannot be snatched up as a "prospect" or something "desirable" or as an anticipated state—it "is"—inasmuch as and as long as the futural ones *are.*

27

Historiological (philological) science is slowly beginning to water down into platitudes Nietzsche's insights about Greek antiquity and to offer strict proofs of those insights after the fact, whereby such science, as in all similar cases, does not see that the *discovery* of proofs and grounds already presupposes the (historical) truth of that which is to be proved. But the "truth" of Nietzsche's interpretation of Greek antiquity is not a historiological one—on the contrary, it is a historical truth, specifically a truth of the end of the history of modernity, insofar as everything is interpreted in terms of "life" as will to power. Yet I out of the historical truth of that interpretation of the Greeks,   28 one does not merely fashion historiological correctness, but one now even believes that erudite comparisons of Greek antiquity with the German classical period (whereby endless discoveries are possible, if only one has the padded flesh to sit at one's desk long enough) will accomplish something for us ourselves and for the opened-up historical decision. Instead, historiological refinement is at most increased and "improved"; one knows a few things more and in different ways and thereby takes even further distance from the knowledge that something will be created for our future only if we place Greek antiquity into the highest opposition to us and recognize that we are excluded from it.

The pursuit of the popularizing of Nietzsche, Burckhardt, and even Hölderlin is now increasing to unbearable proportions, because it is proceeding much more cleverly and insidiously over and against the earlier classicisms. And yet a questioning is never encountered, for if such were at "work," then this magnification of "classicism" would never come about—a magnification that, despite its apparently greater depth, can lay claim only to a greater decisionlessness in relation to the older I "classical period." Basically even this Nietzschean-Burck-   29 hardtean-Georgian-Rilkean humanism, seasoned with folkish-racial [*völkisch-rassisch*] ingredients, is only an expedient of today's intelligentsia, allowing an *avoidance* of what Nietzsche and Burckhardt, each very differently, did not avoid, namely, the decision about the human being as the modern historiological animal, and it furthermore allows this avoidance to be concealed. Running parallel with this humanism is the renewal of Catholicism and the approaching of Protestantism to Catholicism under the slogan of a culturally fitting Christianity. And ultimately the political conditions of this humanism and of Catholicism will not remain unaffected, because "cultural politics" has become a political weapon. All this combines into a historiological brew with which the historiological human being slakes his thirst for "lived experience" and refinement or even becomes intoxicated at the idea of bearing culture.

How is all this possible? It is because humans evade the abandonment of all beings by being and have become clever enough to adorn 30   themselves with the entire past—it is because I the opportunity is readily available to amuse oneself historiologically with clever and "poetic" presentations of history provided by the already customary reportage in newspapers and on the radio. Not merely is there no more "time" available for the "sources" and for "reading" them, but "reading" itself does not want to be burdened with questioning and therefore corresponds to the classicist age when it can take its predilection for descriptions of journeys and countries, for comprehensive historiological presentations and "biographies," and unite these to lived experiences gained in the movie theater. Everywhere diversion and amusement—only no meditation. In case of need, one has one's "beliefs" and superstitions. And from this a German future is supposed to arise? The recording of all these phenomena admittedly does no more than scratch the surface of a process which indeed can be designated as the historicizing of the living creature, "human being," but is still not grasped precisely in its significance such that the forthcoming decisions could be sufficiently prepared.

To paint over a situation of modern humanity in these historiological ways is unreal, inconsequential, and without historical force. I 31   This situation presents itself only to a relentless meditation for which what is groundless and goalless, even if experienced only as essentially occurring in its distorted essence, remains more fully extant than all backward-calculating renewals of what, precisely in its unbroken pastness, still gathers together the unique power of historical being.

28

Meditation on concealed history is so difficult and rare today for two reasons: first, anxiety in face of the admission of goallessness (in face of the lack of such goals at which history must first break off and tumble over), and second, the acclimatization to a calculative procedure in everything, so that soon it will no longer be understood how anything lying beyond the calculable could still seriously be called a being. The two attitudes merge and at the same time appear in a form preventing us from seeking in them any sort of restraint or denial—;

this form of half-pretended, half-genuine, but certainly unweighty lack of seriousness which cannot disavow the uncanny influence of Americanism.

What can still be the reach of a thinking derived from such an attitude, and how is it supposed to consider a German future? Here there is only a passing by, and every attempt at a transformation is deceived about the metaphysically historical condition of humanity, since humanity had to proliferate in such an attitude and had to encompass its massiveness in such proliferation. 32

29

What can an epoch still accomplish, if it takes the avoidance of the self-instituted process of destruction as a gigantic success? How important is it to avoid a war, if at the same time the equipping for one is guaranteed to go on without any interruption? Once again—war is not the most horrible—more unsettling is the lack of a need for goals on the part of involuted historiological life.

But unsettling for whom? Not for those—the masses—who merely go along with the flow, but for those who are knowledgeable. Yet for them the unsettling is the abyssal disposition, on the far side of the ordinary horror and the usual pleasure; an originary thrust of beyng for which every joy remains too small and all sorrow too weak—to which we can be | faithful and offered up in a knowledgeable way only 33 if for essential moments we endure the incomparability of this basic disposition and provide beyng with the abode in which the passing by of the still fugitive and undecided gods—but gods nonetheless—intimates toward a unique recollection.—

30

If all dealings and plans, all pleasure and every contentment have got bogged down in the mere progression of secure expansion into the massive, and if the masses, driven to growth, require a determination of what "the" (their) "life" is, then no improving or raising of the "level" and also no introduction of well-established tradition or of previously esteemed assets can bring about a change. For it is immediately also the ambition of the masses to take possession of such things, i.e., to deprive these things of their historically effective power, which can always consist only in awakening a new question-worthiness of inexhaustible beyng in what is concealed and placing this question-worthiness in the path of humanity. To be sure—such improving and

rectifying of ill conditions, such conversions of the state of the masses
34   into order, | have their proximate uses and flow from well-meaning
sentiment, and yet—they amount only to an escape from the decisive
admission of goallessness, and goallessness has already become the
result of an incapacity for goals.

One will readily retort here with the counterquestion: how else
then is the massiveness of humanity to be subdued, how is the inundation in the ever better and thus increasingly definitive mediocrity
supposed to be averted? What is supposed to happen with humanity
instead? Answer: nothing else than what is happening—but we
should know that this gigantic labor, which yokes everyone and gives
enough to each, nevertheless remains only something altogether secondary and can never become the essential, namely, that apart from
this and without rejection or opposition, but even with a qualified affirmation of these activities, there is kindled *the struggle* by which the
ones involved in it first bring themselves to meditate on the circumstance that, without the assignment to the question-worthiness of
beyng, humanity is definitively denied a history. The kindling of this
struggle will require a *long* time and the *strength* to persevere in what
35   is inconspicuous, | indeed is conspicuously a nullity (calculated in re-
lation to those gigantic pursuits), in order to *know* (and not merely
"believe") out of a remote affiliation with beyng that a few will one
day sling the bridges leading over to the other beginning and, from
the wealth of such knowledge, will renounce hasty solutions, deliverances, and "truths." With these formations, individuals might perhaps only too gladly oppose their times. All of this is required by the
kindling of that struggle. But what is required must assert itself in
states of affairs, means, and procedures which nowhere cooperate
with it but also do not touch it at all.

Yet what is most essential and at the same time most rare, what is
necessary for the kindling of this struggle over the awakening of the
question-worthiness of beyng, is what we call the *courage for error*. The
reason is that the erroneous ways are fruitful only because in straying through spaces they come upon abysses, whereas mere correctness and the incorrectness it disposes of press the human being toward what he has already attained at that time and drive him away
from the essential domain. Nevertheless, always threatening is the
36   danger that the | sovereignty of the masses, entrenching itself ever
more surely into habit and use, will no longer tolerate what could
place such sovereignty in question. Therefore, the destiny of the West,
seen essentially, harbors a fourfold possibility:

Either the sovereignty of the masses, or the leveling down of Western political-cultural circumstances (democratic—authoritarian countries) to an equilibrium (i.e., to complete barrenness), or another beginning of history in the concealedness of essential individuals, or such a beginning as the grounding of a new people. The first two possibilities exhaust themselves in asserting and securing the priority of beings (above all, in the form of "life"); the other two open, and sacrifice themselves to, a leap into the question-worthiness of beyng and an enduring of the encounter between gods and humans.

31

The mere masses are not dangerous—at most, a brief outbreak of blindness and bewilderment. The masses are first essential as *led*, thoroughly organized masses. They do not thereby lose their massiveness and the force of mediate (and thus all the more uncanny) lawgiving—on the contrary, they first I come to themselves in the leaders and rul- 37 ers—these *are* the masses "rolled into a ball"—the masses as the ball which calculates its trajectory inasmuch as it itself is not what is thrown. In the massiveness of humanity, historiology first receives its bearing and the possibilities of full and rapid development.

32

Beyng—the forge of the glowing fire in whose darkness the creative-productive countergaze of humans and gods finds itself, so as to radiate in the guise of a being in the grounded preservation of its truth. But where are the sure blacksmiths who on such a forge hammer the truth of beyng into beings?

33

What is gigantic in the human masses is not their number, but instead is the way they bring to bear their decisionlessness as a power that gives the law and the measure, beyond what is ordinary and everyday in the communal life of humans and human groups. There is no exception to the claim of the masses, even where they, for purposes of their sovereignty and in *their* service, release the "individual" to his own proper task.

It is most of all and most frequently in epochs of the sovereignty of 38 the masses that the appeal to "personality" becomes loud. The sovereignty and the appeal correspond and have their common origin in the development of the human being into the "subjectum," wherein the predelineated form of the humans of such history unfolds into the historiological animal. To want to change something about this history—perhaps even through mere critique—is to mistake the bearing and essential power of a decisive, and therefore protracted, essential human form. But it is quite another thing to meditate ever anew on the apparently scattered and accidental fullness of the accomplished forms of this humanity as modern humanity and especially to see through the most oppositional forms in their one common root. Only in that way is modern history brought back to that simplicity with which alone this history can enter into the decision about the other beginning. In the most fugitive attention to what is most proximate of all contemporary processes, we must seek unwavering meditation on the most remote essential ground. To be sure, this takes from the undergoing of the preparation for the great decisions nothing of its 39   all-consuming | sharpness but rather holds it in the basic disposition of the unsettling presentiment which knows how decisively the intimations of beyng are already proceeding *toward* those who are futural. Indeed we are pursuing—strictly satisfying the claims of the *historiological* animal—mere genealogy and driving out immediately every trace of a great will to *surmise* what is most question-worthy. This surmising extends out the secretly transformative future to the human being and strengthens him for the leap into Da-sein.

34

Only an *inceptual* meditation can once again awaken the ancient presentiment of the humanity that is close to the gods and of the god who is drunk on beyng. And let this meditation at its start be as hard, barren, unreal, and tentative as the first inconspicuous and very shy trace of the early spring. Perseverance in the lengthy questioning involved in this meditation readies the human being for the courage to come to know the most worthy of all beings—beyng. But with the term "beyng," he says the truth in a *reticent* way and places *diffidence* over everything which may be acquired again as a being and unfolded in its most concealed possibilities.

40   ## 35

"Historiology" and recollection.—If now the historiological animal is ever eradicated and the reckoning with "life" according to "values" turns into something else, if in this way the past is no longer an outpost in

the calculation of the merely present and is itself a present, then recollection has triumphed. For recollection is not obsessed with the transitory past, grieving over it and torn away from it; instead, recollection guards what has been—again not as a recently saved "possession"—but rather in the sense that recollection *questions:* what then was what has been? In this questioning, what has been is refined into the simplicity of what is most essential; the possibility arises that out of what has been we might surmise what the future already once announced but had to pass by in the historiological animal, namely, that which—always calculating in advance—constantly comes too late for what has been. Questioning into what has been, however, is not wrapped up in fruitless rumination; this questioning is the carryover of what is already intimating into a concord of what is coming toward us. The fact that in the long history in which the gods become ever rarer and more godless, nevertheless beings as beings placed themselves over the human being and I bore him, and the fact that he   41
sought, even if more and more extrinsically and under compulsion and merely in reflection, to gain from beings something which not only beings could be—these facts show that in this history of humanity there already has been what as beyng waits for the originary founding and yet never strives to press itself in the place of beings— into the superficiality of everyday functioning and explaining. The questioning of what then has been in all the history of beings (and of their beingness) is not historiological, but rather is historical, specifically in the sense that this questioning helps the beginning of a history (what is proper to this history itself) to its space and its ground.

For a long time, and perhaps always, "recollection" was misinterpreted through historiology and burdened with the characterization that it merely looks backward, whereas "progress" and "life" are aimed forward. But what futurity is stronger and more decisive than the one which, in *essential recollection* (of the concealed beyng in the correctness of beings), has leaped over everything accidental and is not at all familiar with the *domain* of the back-and-forth vacillation between peevish denial of the present and an affirmation that overshouts itself? But can we and should we then attempt to take the complete inundation of all representation in historiological I explanation and   42
transfiguration and change it immediately into a recollection of the history of beyng? As if such recollection were merely a special sort of backward gaze.—No—here commences the long wait for the thrust of beyng, the superiority in relation to the veiled a-historicality of historiological results—the knowledge of how exclusively historiology pursues in each case only a *mirroring* in which the present and what *it* plans (the false appearance of a future) find themselves again and

confirm *themselves,* i.e., do *not* place themselves in question but, instead, justify "before history" the avoidance of question-worthiness, without clearly knowing what they are doing.

Yet *this* avoidance, as concealed as it may be and quite outshined by the light of the mirroring that spares nothing, harbors the secret relation to beyng—beyng as the ground of the decision about humanity—and is therefore, against its will and its "knowledge," a movement of essential history. Consequently, recollection cannot devalue even this avoidance but must rather assign it to the hidden destiny of the history of beyng and must experience therein the inexplicable concord of something futural. Through the suppression and fore-
43   closure of every attempt at recollection, historiology I *destroys the basic dispositions* from which the simplest effectivity in what is nearest at hand, as well as the ordering of things and the giving of hearts, arises in the long solitudes of those who are attuned.

36

The essence of historiology is best illustrated by the historiology of art (not only by this historiology as an established "science," but by everything attached to it and everything it might even unintentionally influence, such as ekphrastic literature and the administration of museums). And specifically this is not because the historiology of art is perhaps the earliest and purest development of "historiology" (in fact it is a late branch of "historiology"), but because here *"art"* is taken up into the domain of the objects of historiology, whereas art pertains to the originary grounds of *history.* Admittedly, as its name (τέχνη) indicates, art was already *very early* grasped "historiologically" in the sense of a procedural skill and then understood more and more (with the rise of notions of "culture") as accomplishment, expression, and creation, and was investigated historiologically according to all its conditions and influences. Today we stand before an either-or: the histori-
44   ological explanation and derivation I of the work or the "lived experience" of it. Yet this is likewise a mode of historiological calculation—except with the renunciation of explanatory cognitions, whose place is taken by nothing other than the lively "feelings" of contemporary opinion. That supposed either-or is none. Instead, the historiology of art has essentially co-caused the lived experience of art. In the historiology of art, fire and water are supposed to be mixed, but at most what results is an extinguishing of the last smoldering sparks of art (of the need and necessity of art and of its essential grounding) through the wateriness of historiological explanation.

37

Historiology and basic disposition.—Does historiology eradicate disposition only in the sense of the "disposition toward illusion"[3] which Nietzsche considers necessary for creativity and for the "constructive instinct"? In that way, "disposition" would merely be thought psychologically-biologically in the framework of the Nietzschean idea of "life," whose vitality he later grasped as will to power. Yet for us disposition is not the goading of feelings in a transfigurative semblance—but the exposure to the assignment to the truth of beyng, and this exposure cannot at all be attained through the mere discharge of a creative urge attributable biologically at any time to every human activity. | Disposition as *basic* disposition comes over the human being   45 as that event through which he is transposed into the differentiation of being and beings and is exposed to the decision between them. The basic disposition is especially rare and unique. And the long habit of psychological thinking will still keep us obstinately enough from the knowledge that might accord with the basic dispositions (astonishment—unsettling). Not because historiology disturbs "illusion" and immediacy—indeed these remain precisely conserved and fostered in "lived experience"—but because historiology in general clamps beings into explainability and thereby pretends to have grasped being as well (along with the remainder of what cannot be explained and is conceded to "lived experience"). In other words, it is because historiology extracts the human being from the plight of the differentiation between beings and being and holds out to him instead his needs and the results of cultural creation and thus entices him precisely into a "disposition toward illusion." *Thereby* historiology destroys the basic disposition. It is because historiology as such more and more has recourse to the animality of the human being as driving and creating and includes those traits in its explanatory schema. Since historiology definitively justifies the historiological animal in a historiological way and thus in the dominant horizon, | therefore it carries out a   46 complete blockading of humans from beyng qua the ground of the necessitation of every necessity that founds an essence.

The extent of such suppression into decisionlessness, however, comprehends only that knowledge which has grasped historiology itself in its entire essential domain and has also recognized *technology* as the

---

3. {Friedrich Nietzsche, "Vom Nutzen und Nachteil der Historie für das Leben," in *Die Geburt der Tragödie: Unzeitgemäße Betrachtungen, Werke*, vol. 1 (Leipzig: Kröner, 1917), p. 339.}

historiology of nature. Ordinary opinion is precisely here subject to an insidious delusion which sees "technology" as the most decisive opposite of historiology by juxtaposing them as a creative-inventive pressing forward versus a merely backward-glancing assemblage of what has already been found out and become "antiquated." Technology and historiology are *the same* (the metaphysical ground lies in the interpretation of ὄν as νοούμενον ["being as something thought"]. And as long as we do not recognize this sameness, we will know nothing of Western humanity; i.e., we will not overcome the anthropological view of the humanity of the human being and will not allow to come into history the knowledge of the human being as a knowledge incorporating a previous knowledge of the truth of beyng. Whence then that prominent semblance in which historiology and technology appear as extreme opposites?

47   Do both themselves, each in its own respective way, produce this semblance? Why? What is the *same*, which here bifurcates in seeming to be mutual exclusion? What if in this way the possibility of the plight of a basic disposition should be delayed as long and as securely as could be, inasmuch as historiology and technology partition between themselves the pursuit of beings and at the same time unwittingly exchange procedures, inasmuch as this partitioning of beings strengthens the semblance that now, outside of this, nothing more "is" and nothing more could be a being (unless precisely the human being himself, who as multitude and as race has instituted himself into the gigantic pursuit of both historiology and technology), and inasmuch as through this semblance of the sovereignty of beings (under the slogan of nearness to "reality" and to "life"), all being, at most still an obstructing smoke and a fading shadow, is driven out of all representation through an ultimate neglect and merely left to be treated by scholastic "ontologies"? But what if nevertheless, through this withdrawal from all publicness, beyng equipped itself for a most solitary thrust and already kindled a knowledge of the groundlessness of the

48   sovereignty of historiology and technology, I a knowledge which indeed never has need to get involved in an accidental and merely "romantic" aversion to "technological" progress? Should indeed the semblance of an oppositionality between historiology and technology guard this thrust of beyng from a premature and once again merely calculative grasp, inasmuch as technology (which is, however, indeed historiology itself) is assigned the role of creativity and production, so as to cut off at the root every other need according to origin and originariness, but also to leave undisturbed, though not deliberately, the preparation for another history?

Since historiology and technology apparently exclude each other, they can all the more exclusively pursue each for itself what is theirs and thereby nevertheless pursue the one same entrenchment of the abandonment of beings by being. Where both historiology and technology are yoked in such apparent oppositionality, they can unite to further that which once helped to ground human history essentially and which we call "art." Historiology provides well and quickly and in each case according to need all possible suggestions and exemplars for imitation; technology eases every sort of procedure as well as the delivery of the presentational means and the effective forms. The interplay of both, supported | by the increasing agility in the mastery of   49 every process, performance, and expression, secures an apparent superiority over all previous artistic activity. Yet everything is rootless and never tested according to need and necessity—but only calculated and given out as "lived experience." Such art, which would be raised up to these collections of its products, could never arrive where alone a beginning might still be possible: the domain of the decision about the essence and necessity of art out of the plight of beyng itself.

38

For the transition, the brightest light shines forth out of the recollection of what has been. The pre-thinking toward the other beginning does not lapse into a fanaticism for an empty future nor become overheated for mere progress.

39

Through *beyng*—as event—the gods woo the human being, and he burns out in beyng toward an appeal of the god. Meanwhile, the world stands open, and the earth reposes in the magic of its closure. And this *"meanwhile"* is the source of the moments of essential groundings of beings. Will this time become ripe once again?

40   50

The other beginning—in which history is grounded on the truth of beyng—is *older than the first*. Everything the other beginning brings into the open domain (and also refuses to grant) withdraws from measurement according to the usual standards. Humans find themselves in the strangeness of the strangest god, and everything is abyssal, such that all machination, without support and confirmation, falls to ruin.

41

The godlessness of the gods will persist through the anthropomorphizing of the human being in the distorted essence until beyng breaks
in between both. But who will endure this event and ground in it the
ground of a world which, well disposed to the earth, no longer wounds
it? Only what arises out of the enduring of this event retains in the
thoughtful person the necessity of a questioning. Those left over feel
content and justified in an acceptance that still offers here and there
a further pushing back and forth of scholarly issues.

42

That we allow ourselves goals, even though we perhaps do not once
meet the conditions on which the future essence of the human be-
51   ing I will be decided—indicates how little we know of the essence of
the human being and of his relation to the question-worthiness of
beyng. (The essence of goallessness thought in terms of the history of
beyng—cf. Ponderings X, p. 83ff.)

43

Originary ways are errant ways, and the venture of errancy carries
out the granting of the space sought by these ways. If they are originary, the ways must be *followed;* only ordinary ways can be traversed.
Every presentation of an originary way, if the presentation has any
right at all, again becomes a way and thereby renounces presentations and reports.

44

If the expulsion of the "science" (in very diverse forms) residing for a
century in philosophy (and in the representation of philosophy) succeeds without a refuge being offered to fanaticism at the same time,
then we could press on into the soberness of essential knowledge and
perceive something of the hidden course of the history of beyng. Yet
52   we are already too far removed from the space-time I of this history
for us to be sufficiently equipped to perceive such history immediately. Therefore, required first of all is a *recollection of the history* of
thinking, a history which, ever since its commencement, has been
obstructed by the historiology of philosophy. This historical recollection—in each case possible only through essential "works," never as
a pictorial total presentation—is always ambiguous in that it appar-

ently aims at a rebirth of what preceded or else at an intermediary continuation—whereas it in truth decisively seeks the other beginning. This beginning never wants to be the "new" but, instead, must be the oldest of the old and thus a fortiori requires historical recollection. But why does every attempt to awaken such recollection, and to make it constant, end at once in a historiological pursuit of historiology?

45

Christianity—the post-Greek West—has forfeited, just as did Greek antiquity, the possibility to ground an originary truth. On what then can a mere *anti*-Christianity still rely?

As a *counter*movement, it pursues the "affirmation of life" and is altogether shackled to that which it rejects. Thus that possibility of originariness is denied precisely to anti-Christianity in a *still more* decisive way than it is to everything which has already become "historiological." Even allowing for the confusion the term "affirmation of life" is supposed to cover over, this affirmation still leads to a twofold basic illusion. In consequence of this illusion, the "affirmation of life" has already become without fail that which it futilely hates as its mortal enemy; it has become a *renunciation*—indeed unwittingly or, better, witlessly—of beyng. This renunciation still essentially surpasses every *denial* of beings (i.e., every denial of "life" and of "reality"). The twofold "basic illusion" is the following:

1. The "affirmation of life"—the incitement of all the instincts that belong to life and that are familiar to *Christianity* (i.e., are denied by Christianity)—appears to itself in the semblance of drawing from the source of "life," indeed of being this "life" itself and thus something originary. The "affirmation of life" thereby takes itself already as a decision about truth—i.e., for it, about beings—and consequently is suspicious of all questioning. This indeed does no harm to questioning and could also never I impugn what is question-worthy. The "affirmation of life" does, however, become a mere flight into "life," so much so that it forbids itself to know who then values "life" and *who* demands what from "life" and who thereby first determines what is to be regarded as "the" life.

2. This affirmation of "life," an affirmation toward which all "powers" are striving, ones basically only negative and equal only to what is merely present-at-hand, does not simply exclude that which is worthy of question. It also has altogether no possibility of allowing a space-time for decisions, inasmuch as it could be given what it presumably wants—namely, the "enhancement" of life—only through

the hardship of long meditation. Yet this enhancement remains merely a quantitative and massive extension of the same, an ever more practical, ever more efficient, and ever more dubious diffusion of everything mediocre in all "life" that strives for what is average. Never attained here is any essential thrust by which all beings would be transposed into another origin. Affirmation *and* negation of life—in their respectively opposed way—remain bound to the priority of mere beings. They *each* surmise just as little the question-worthiness of
55   beyng, I so little that they are not even capable of turning their back on it. Thought in terms of the history of beyng, the odd weakness of the "affirmation of life" with respect to all beyng lies hidden (for those who know) precisely in the circumstance that the "festive"-noisy life-affirmation (which never surmises a motive for a "fest") is chained to an ignorant need to renounce beyng. But what if the noise of the full, modern, unconditioned affirming of life were a very conditioned and very unrecognizable echo of the clanging of those chains of the abandonment by being?

But where now the anti-Christian affirmation of life again becomes the object of a supposedly Christian countermovement, and where in such inescapable circulation, this affirmation at once places "life" and the "people" explicitly "ahead of God" with the greatest deliberateness and fastidiousness and from a full possession of truth, and just as cleverly makes its accounts with the "people ahead of God," there again the flight in face of question-worthiness is increasing, and the lack of originariness on the part of "life," apparently overcome, is now
56   made completely I definitive. Neither the affirmation of life nor its denial experiences even the least of the plight of both—the plight of a lack of a sense of plight—the most uncanny plight, because the most ambiguous and most radically veiled one.

46

If now again the long brown-black bands of freshly plowed fields rise up out of the last verdure of the meadows and spread themselves out against the autumnal sky—there perhaps comes to a standstill somewhere an hour in which beyng—futile yet for many human years—must shine out its illuminating power on the purblind obstinacy of beings.

47

Nietzsche's great delusion (cf. p. 67ff.)—is his belief that "consciousness" and "logic" could be replaced by appealing to the instincts. Nietzsche does not see that "instincts" (drives, etc.) as determinations of the human being stem from the same root as representations (παθήματα—νοήματα ["passions—thoughts"]). This means, however, that the essence of the human being can never I be changed unless   57 the root of his first Western definition (as *animal rationale*) is previously pulled up—i.e., unless the *question* of the originary possibilities of the essential determination of the human being is actually posed. The result of Nietzsche's anthropology is then also the dogmatic appeal to "the" "life" as "the" reality—pure and simple. As much as Nietzsche, right from the first, saw and captured the horizonal character of "life," so little did this notion of life lead him beyond the crude metaphysics of the present-at-hand.

Seen precisely, however, the reference to the instincts as the authentic principle of life is possible only within and on the basis of *consciousness*—i.e., on the basis of the *representational* presentification of the human being as something present-at-hand. The fact that Nietzsche makes the "body" and the bodying forth of life the basic reality includes on the one side the conditionally essential advancement into a domain (sensibility) which is / as a result of Platonism / neglected or else is simply related to cognition and perception. On the other side, however, Nietzsche thereby becomes definitively subject to a "biologism," one which is indeed quite reasonable for an epoch already alienated from all essential questions of thinking and which seems to be correct everywhere. Yet this "biologism" excludes every I possibility   58 leading to a *disclosive questioning* of beyng and to an establishing of the human *essence* in this relation to beyng. Everything belonging to the sphere of this decisive question is already taken up as unproblematic by its traditional assignment to "logic" (category and judgment) and by the biologistic incorporation of "logic" and "truth" into "life" in the sense of the representational consolidation of becoming, a consolidation necessary for "the" life. What makes Nietzsche's basic position a "metaphysical" one, and despite all the "inversion" arrests him in the past in an almost crude way, is not biologism as such. Instead, it is the uncritical assumption of the distinction between being and becoming (Parmenides—Heraclitus! scholastically flattened down) for the substructure of the determination of "the" life and for the interpretation of "the" life itself. Only if we think through these all-bearing relations, ones which seem merely to be names for the most general guiding notions and "ordering schemata," will the full fragility of this thinking show itself. The fragility was not first created by such thinking, but instead was taken over by it unexamined as something solid.

This now groundless metaphysics cannot be excused by appealing   59 to Nietzsche's other prominent "psychological" and "cultural-philosophical" insights. For all these are again for him and according to his intention only conduits to the essential determinations which, under the titles "will to power" and "eternal recurrence," make claim to an interpretation of "beings." Here opens up for Nietzsche, as for every essential thinker, that field of decision which for the most part remains inconsequential to the ordinary "cultural" application and utilization of "philosophy," is tolerated as sheer "speculation," and is disdained at the same time. In terms of the history of beyng, however, this field contains what is unique and essential to a philosophy, because decided there is the issue of whether a thinking is strong enough to stir up and transform the essential occurrence of beyng in the origination out of this field or whether the thinking shirks into the unproblematic and traditional, thereby withdraws from what is most question-worthy, and as an *interrogative* thinking, deprives itself of its most intrinsic and broadest vocation. The everyday "forming" and exploiting of "spiritual" assets will always | evaluate—i.e., historiologically calculate—in the direction of the usefulness of a philosophy and its "effectiveness" and "effective possibilities." But rarely and basically only from the side of thinkers is a philosophy grasped in its proper and unique character, grasped in its necessary limits, and thus never disparaged.

60

Since, for most people, anything not historiologically verifiable—i.e., basically, not graspable with the eyes and hands and nose—is also not disclosively thinkable in thought, therefore the history of thinking, as the dialogue of thinkers, and this dialogue as the history of beyng itself, remains concealed to public opinion and to ordinary representation. No facility, however great, in learning and cognition, in comparing and calculation, could substitute here for the essential (the ventures of thoughtful leaps and the knowledge of the intrinsic coherence of such ventures). On the contrary, here as everywhere the all too great and exclusive facility threatens to *exclude* the human being one day from everything essential and from meditation on his essence, because facility indeed ultimately also harbors the view that *it* is capable of all things. And at once this conviction—I also called "belief"—turns into the other one: only what this facility can accomplish *is* at all and has a right to count as a being.

61

As soon as humans come under the compelling sovereignty of this "natural" thinking, they lack all possibilities of the *essential* meditation which in each case signifies the convulsion and violation of an adopted position and also entails a decision in favor of the possibility and necessity of a transformation. Therefore, like every thinker before him, Nietzsche will be historiologically effective or else will be historiologically thwarted in his historiological effectivity—historically, however, like every essential thinker, Nietzsche does not need to "effectuate," because this thinking already *is*, in that it carries out the ending of metaphysics. The great delusions—which no thinker is spared—signify also here—as in the entire previous history of thought—the unavoidable confinement in the historiological tradition which always offers the nearest thing that is representationally seized for the elucidation of something quite other. Nietzsche's historiological-political effectivity—even abstracting from the concomitantly occurring misinterpretations and coarsenings—is not Nietzsche himself—i.e., not that l moment his thinking, as a clearing of the truth of beyng, gained through strife.   62

48

Ordinary notions and consequently all "science" suspect that *the thinking which is heedful of the history of beyng* amounts to an "idealism," one degrading and renouncing the properly "real" on the basis of some dreamed-up representations. Even if the thinking which is heedful of the history of beyng needs to see clearly that it can never make itself immediately "intelligible," yet it must not renounce the attempt to make its essence discernible even for common opinion. And here what comes first is the admission that indeed the ordinary notions and the traditional modes of appraisal, as well as the dominant interpretation of the "world" and of the "human being," remain relegated to their own currently actual and still futural ineluctability. No matter where or how often the thinking which is heedful of the history of beyng, as a disclosive questioning of the truth of beyng, sets itself off *against* metaphysical thinking and the Western notions grounded therein, this never happens through the calculative opinion that the traditional notions could be replaced by such thinking.

The two cannot at all be compared immediately; and what thereby   63
at first appears to be a repudiation and "critique" of the age is indeed only the platform for a leap to a meditation on that which is older than the blocked yet still essentially occurring ground of what is currently actual and also futural (the priority of beings over the truth of beyng). *Because* the thinking which is heedful of the history of beyng and only such thinking knows *how necessarily and uniquely* the priority of beings over being (as well as, founded therein, the succeeding priority of the human being as the center of the present-at-hand) is grounded in a peculiar history of beyng (disempowerment of φύσις as collapse of ἀλήθεια), therefore this thinking will in advance be protected from seeing in the present and future of modernity something accidental which in its essence could ever be touched by an equally accidental

opinion or critique or improvement. Quite to the contrary: the thinking which is heedful of the history of beyng recognizes the ground of the necessity of the imminent era and of the uncanny way that era follows consistently. This thinking knows such an era can be brought to its long ending only if the human being of this era is relieved of all
64   essential oppositions and decisions | and can live in the certainty of his own magnificence and enjoyment. How else could the human being of this era get over the "goallessness" of beings unless he constantly placed himself (in the form of an ideal of his own human figure) before himself as the goal that persists and is easily confirmed through the apparent eternity of "the" life?

The immensity of acumen and proficiency, of enterprise and institutional forms, must be set in motion so that the modern human being might maintain a space wherein *his* essence can breathe, a space that, in virtue of "historiology" in the literal sense, can also admit everything hitherto, according to need, and can provide the certainty of a rich possession out of which then the conviction of superiority arises at once. Nevertheless, the essential decision (cf. above, p. 6ff.) regarding the definitive a-historicality or grounding of history on the basis of the truth of beyng can occur only if that which is to be decided can itself unfold in its essential definitiveness (modernity) and essential originariness (at the beginning). What the thinking that is
65   heedful of the history of beyng does *not* | know, and on *its* course will always repel as essentially adverse, is all hasty improvement or reconstruction of a currently present time through planned—i.e., decisionless—goals and "cultural ideals." The history of beyng is the abyss over which beings—especially in their rampant machination—float without knowing it. How could the abyss ever hope for something from a disturbance of things that have become certain of themselves qua their own ground and therefore are impotent to surmise the abyss in its essential occurrence, in virtue of which they might originate the encounter of gods and humans and thereby originate the strife of world and earth? Seldom does anyone who is alien to it become at home in this history; and if this one is a human, then he can say only very little of this history out of which all beings arise and over and against which they renounce their origin, if with the help of historiology (i.e., with the help of explanation) beings have secured themselves against all question-worthiness. Only the *poetizing* and *thinking* of beyng can become constant in errancy, i.e., at home in this abyss
66   that is alien to past humans and also to future ones. Here awakens | a knowledge which knows itself equally remote from the human being and from the gods, yet indeed remote *from the latter* and thus in relation to the *abyssal nearness* of them. Here all familiarity and every con-

tentment have their limits—but so also do every conceitedness and all superiority. Here are eliminated all devious ways on which an ambitious currying of favor could apply itself to a lamentable "god" and could degrade the divinity of the gods to a matter of calculation.

The human being—existing on the basis of a steadfastness in Dasein—is a creature of remoteness; yet this "remoteness" must not be subjected to an "idealistic" Platonic-Christian misinterpretation and become an occasion of mere "yearnings." Here the remoteness stems from the abyssal nearness—from the knowledge that gods and humans do not interact as do extant things but, instead, arise *out of the essential occurrence of beyng*—in that they ground this occurrence through the indigence and the stewardship. The more originarily the human being is resolved toward his essence (to become a being that grounds the truth of *beyng* in Da-sein) and the more decisively he applies himself to his essence (something very different than adhering obstinately to oneself as subjectum), I then all the nearer (in the sense   67 of that nearness) is *for the present* the divinity of the gods. But then there also disappears every expectation of an ability even only to indicate beyng with the help of an immediate degrading precisely of beings. Only one thing is indispensable to the thinking that is heedful of the history of beyng—the recollection of the history of this thinking or, expressed more academically, the *properly understood* meditation on the guiding questions and basic positions of *metaphysical* thinking, for that is a thinking which, previously by itself, apart from the first beginning, bore the history of beyng, inasmuch as this history eventuated from thinking. In the current era, such recollection is the sole way to make intelligible to it that something unintelligible must first be grounded in knowledge if beings as a whole are to be exposed to a decision.

49

Nietzsche and the Determination of the Human Essence. (Cf. Ponderings X, p. 71ff.)

For Nietzsche, the human being is the "*still unidentified animal.*"[4] But with the specification as animal (ζῷον, *animal*[5]), the *essence* has already been identified. And inasmuch as precisely *this* identification is one with the definition which makes the human being the animal that apprehends I beings (ζῷον λόγον ἔχον, *animal rationale*), the animal is   68

---

4. {Friedrich Nietzsche, *Jenseits von Gut und Böse: Vorspiel einer Philosophie der Zukunft, Werke*, vol. 7 (Stuttgart: Kröner, 1921), p. 88.}

5. [Latin word *animal*.—Trans.]

also already identified. All that is needed is a sufficient interpretation of λόγος and of *ratio*[6] and of reason. The interpretation becomes insufficient as soon as *ratio* is grasped in the modern way as consciousness (self-consciousness); it remains insufficient even if the "instincts" and the "will" are added on. In other words, the basic Cartesian position is not overcome; instead, it is simply entrenched in the *corporeality* of this *animal rationale* and still further pressed down into a being of presence at hand (*subiectum*), as in fact happened through Nietzsche (cf. above, p. 56ff.). The identification of humans, the previous ones and those that have long been current, has occurred, specifically on the basis of metaphysics. But what is still outstanding is *that* interpretation of this identification in virtue of which a meditation on the human being could awaken and could lead him beyond his previous essence. This interpretation of the *animal rationale* must grasp in *ratio* that which constitutes the metaphysical essence of *ratio:* the relation to beings as such. Furthermore, it must recognize this relation as the one of explanatory representation—i.e., ἱστορεῖν in | the widest sense. (Cf. everything on "historiology.")

69

Then we see: the animal which is the human being is identified as the "historiological" animal—and the ultimate result of *this* identification is the human being as "superman," as the human being that *transcends* the previous one only insofar as he comes to terms with his previous essence—i.e., acknowledges "life," *animality* pure and simple, as the essentially determining ground in its entire bearing. The previous metaphysics has thereby already in advance settled the last possibility of its interpretation of the human being, as also the essence of the beginning strives to do—; the "superman" is the highest peak of the *anthropomorphizing* of the human being and therefore is an ending, not a beginning (cf. p. 12f.). The superman—the inversion of the "Platonic"-"Christian" human being—built back into the same determinations of beings, determinations which exhaust themselves in the general differentiation of being and becoming. If the already very long extant identification of the human being undergoes its hitherto missing interpretation, according to which the human being is now defined as the historiological animal, then it seems at first that an omission has merely been repaired, without the introduction of a consideration of the entire previous history of beings and certainly |

70

without a transition having been set into motion. But the term "historiological" is not simply interchangeable with "rational"—instead, it is supposed to indicate that the relation to beings as such remains

---

6. [Latin word *ratio* ("reason," "relation," "calculation") throughout this paragraph.—Trans.]

the explanatory investigation (whereby the modern unfolding of historiology is necessarily co-intended). In bringing up the relation to beings as such, however, the more originary relation to being is already recollected and at the same time thought in advance—the definition of the human being as the historiological animal thus places the human essence already within the transition out of metaphysics and into the thinking that is heedful of the history of beyng. *Transition* always means here the twofoldness of the *crossing* over to another beginning (thus the preparation for reaching something originary in a leap) and the crossing *over* what was hitherto, in the sense that the latter can no longer immediately—in its historiological tradition—determine the questioning.

50

"Historiology"—in case we do not think of it superficially and derivatively—is by no means the illness of the modern age but is rather the basis of its healing, if health means the undisturbed self-unfolding | course of a regulated process with the unimpaired utilization of all 71 available powers. "Historiology" is thereby thought in the essential sense, i.e., metaphysically, and not as the occupation of "historiologists" and certainly not as history. (Cf. p. 76ff.)

51

Would a *beginning of philosophy* have ever occurred if thinking had been able to appeal to the "results" of the "sciences"? But if the beginning is the essential and the highest, then there lies in the sort of unscientific beginning of philosophy the directive to get out of the way of science. Why did the opposite happen? Because thinking itself became unsure in its course and rigid in its questioning. The height of the independence from derived ways of cognition (even from the ways diverted by *thinking*) and from modes of explanation could not be held fast. Why not? Does the essence of beyng itself indeed never tolerate what later representations suggest as the constant progress of cognition? For there to be heights, must not dropping and plunging | ever 72 proliferate far about and secure themselves finally in the surveyability of what is shallow? It is not the incapacity of humans only for Essential thinking, but above all the dignity of beyng itself as what is to be thought, that demands what is Supremely towering and rare. Therefore a development of proficiency in thinking is of no use if beyng keeps itself unscalable and relegates to the priority of beings even the essential determination of humanity.

In the interim, however, thinking has become so completely alien from beyng that the requirement for philosophy to renounce science produces only the misunderstanding that philosophy is either arbitrary opinion or a belated, substantively unimportant, formal cleansing and sharpening of "concepts." Actions indeed change the *world*, and the greater the masses of humanity become, all the more must everything depend on the enhancement of the power to act so that the massiveness might constantly provide anew its appropriate domains of activity. But actions never ground a world, if indeed a l world assembles in itself the holding sway of beyng and only in virtue of this assemblage holds sway at all, be it merely so poorly that beings *as* such still remain experienceable in all actions and operations, rather than finally being incorporated, swallowed, and again repelled brutishly as mere concealed occasions for the conservation and enhancement of life in the course of a vital process and in the surrounding field of its expressions. Yet insofar as a world (which is "more" and essentially other than the mere sum of beings) qua the productive holding sway of beyng can be founded only in poetizing and grounded only in thinking, it can also be destroyed only through a breakdown of thinking and through an incapacity of poetizing. The breakdown and incapacity of both are already testified, however, where thinking and poetizing are simply admitted into the service of the sovereignty of beings.

The basic happening of modernity, that of the emergence of "*worldviews*," is the start of the destruction of the world within the historical domain of Western metaphysics. In the sphere of the sovereignty of modern humanity, an originary thinking is therefore necessarily l abandoned to unrecognizability, which, in terms of essential thinking, does not count as a lack and hindrance, but as abundance and safeguard. For all essential thinking needs the freedom to err, the long useless straying out of which only those who are destined to thinking and disposed to it "learn" what is most essential to themselves. The history of philosophy is indeed not the "history" of errors in the sense of a historiological series of one mistake after another; but the history of philosophy is indeed in itself an erring in which the errancy is experienced and in each case a fissure of the truth of beyng is surmised. Here we have for a long time not been proficient enough in travel to wander through this history without ending in the identification of what is false, or, which is of the same value, in empty praises of the philosophers. We can venture the decisive unscientificity of philosophy only if we are capable of wandering through the errant paths of the history of philosophy—i.e., only if we are radical questioners and only as such attempt to think. On this basis we might surmise a

little of the essence of the beginning of | thinking and survey some- 75
thing of what we must first think away from in order that we may disclosively think beyng; for this least of all occurs to ordinary opinion
and to its straightforward groping, namely, that there must be a thinking away from, one that does not disavow and destroy but instead creates paths on which those who question can direct their course. Such
thinking away from (formerly given the easily misinterpreted name
"dismantling" ["*Destruktion*"]) holds for the overcoming of the universally strong and at the same time unrecognizable priority of beings.

52

How many departures from the alleged basic positions must occur in
the *pre-thinking of the truth of beyng* until the welling up of an origin
(i.e., until the thrusts of beyng itself) can be experienced? The most
difficult departures are of course those from the positions of the initial questioning, themselves gained through struggle, whose burdens
of habituation can only rarely be shaken off by anyone. Nevertheless,
for those who know, already past are the times in which the way-
points of research had to be expressly presented and communicated.
The silent errancy alone holds good, until the right | to an essential 76
word has found its ground. The only futural "education" to "philosophy" is in the present age the one aiming at a grounded capacity
for silence, a capacity taking its measures from the highest standards.
(Cf. p. 113f.)

53

Everything "revolutionary" (as mere inversion) is necessarily still
overly "conservative" (caught up in the past and in the preservation
of things already verified) to ever offer an open path into the oldest
origin. The will to an origin nevertheless always retains—in its salient
unfolding—an inclination toward what is "revolutionary" and at the
same time toward what is "conservative." But the originary, issuing
from the essential occurrence of beyng, in truth never has a foothold
in verified things, because verification has already in advance posited
a standard the originary can no longer recognize as essential. Only
the originary, that which belongs to the necessity of beyng and is superior to all needs of beings, recognizes immediately that what is
"revolutionary" brandishes the mere semblance of originariness and
even can do so only as long | as it maintains a positive appraisal of it- 77
self through a negative appraisal of *what* it has inverted. Revolutions
are never radical; for what goes down to the root is that which out of

itself finds and grounds as its ground what is simple and essentially occurring. But revolutions are always the start of a consummation of that which gropingly first seeks its essential actualization. The peculiar modern character of revolutions indicates that modernity, because its essence has long been already decided, comes *to* itself only slowly and in growing proliferation of its possibilities of consummation and in turn develops these into a state of the *entire* planet—beyond the limits of individual peoples and continents. The slowness of this process avails itself of a concealment through the claim of speed and of the overcoming of distance. The age requires this concealment because otherwise the already decided abandonment of all beings by being would one day force itself upon the age and would threaten the running out to an end state. Therefore new revolutions are probable, but they do not indicate a remote sovereignty of what is originary and of the essential decisions assigned to what is originary; instead, they are signs that modernity is increasingly | certain of its essence (the force of historiology in this process). (Cf. above, p. 70f.)

78

54

Essential humans must leave to its claim that which commonly and usefully claims to set the inconspicuously public standard for everything, because they know the ineluctability of the distorted essence and never obtain the fire of their silent passion out of acclaimed results, but out of the concealed plight instead.

55

Not one of those who are acquainted with everything and rush at everything knows the moments in which stars plunge toward one another and worlds burn out. Such things happen noiselessly and without becoming the target of a notice sent to everyone.

56

Beethoven in effect says somewhere (Heiligenstädter Testament?) that he felt compelled, already at age twenty-eight, to become a philosopher and that that is exceptionally difficult for an artist.[7] But what if

---

7. {Ludwig van Beethoven, "Das Heiligenstädter Testament vom Oktober 1802" (Offenbach: Kumm, 1941), n.p.: "Already compelled in my twenty-eighth year to become a philosopher, it is not easy, and for the artist more difficult than for just anyone."}

someone already *is* a philosopher and must endure such Da-sein by way of steadfastness in the resolve to appertain to the truth of beyng without the capacity to become an artist | and without the endow-   79
ment of a captivating transport by means of the beings of a work, beings disposed and determined by beyng? Those who seek the spaces for what is ungrounded do not stand before works; instead, they proceed along ways.

57

If researchers and scientists believed that before they themselves even start to work their genuine discoveries have always already been carried out, then there would be no scientific advancement and no self-satisfied contentment with one's own importance. But the genuine discoveries have always already been carried out, because what is new, what brings sciences forward in their respective fields, does not properly consist in the explanation of beings, but in the adoption of another horizon of explainability. Science itself, however, never opens this horizon; instead, it is opened by contemplative thinking and by poetizing (in the literal sense of art). Because sciences can be nothing other than the subsequent pacing off and corresponding purveying of that horizon, they therefore always have a broad and long span as the opportunity for the display | of their activity. Subsequently and, so to   80
speak, on a reverse course to the one about which they can and might scarcely meditate, then even that horizon is represented, and there arises at times a startled surprise concerning this issue: into which depths of spirit would the sciences indeed be capable of advancing?

58

Even in a time of boundless talking and unrestrained writing, an unacknowledged distrust of the mere word may run high, and this mistrust itself may for a long time to come befall precisely the simple and essential word which harbors the demand for an inceptual meditation, and finally language may fade away into the inessentiality of idle talk and of very clever pen pushing—yet all words must once again resound inceptually and announce the resonating of beyng as grounded in its truth: for the word is the ground of language.

58a

Political action must not be measured with the yardstick of sentimentality or censoriousness. Nor can results | suffice as a justification after   81

the fact. In that way everything would remain in darkness. Whence does this action have its law? In some sort of use for the people, in the honor of the nation?—That requires a previous right "to be" in the sense of developable continuance—but where do beings (a people) to which we belong have the ground of their claim to be? Which way to be is conceived here, from what is it determined—how can it be determined, if meditation on the "to be" is suffocating and dying and declared superfluous by the appeal to "life"—whose "vitality" should be understood by anyone of healthy common sense. But who is to say what constitutes—not merely bodily—health here? Political action, which indeed is nothing in itself but is completely incorporated into the essence of modern humans and their history, finds *its* law only in relentless development toward the unrestrained pure calculation aimed at making the masses as a whole capable of motion—. All appeals to the conservation of the folkish [*völkisch*] substance and the like are necessary, but they always remain mere pretexts for the unrestricted sovereignty of the political. For what sort of goal would be
82   the mere conservation l of a "people" and its massiveness if "the" life were not seen precisely in the conservation and enhancement of the capacity to move? All "culture"—as cultural politics—is likewise seriously desired, but again only as adornment and a means of power—not as a possible basic form of humanness—a possibility already uprooted in virtue of the essence of so-called values.

59

What does not come under rules and merge into a plan has no reality. This modern preconception takes humans very far, so far that one day they forget to ask: whither? But we are moving forward, and ever greater masses share the view that we are moving forward; and finally there is on all sides a single haste and distrust and preparation and provision, and no one knows wherefore—but something is going on, and it seems this is "life." Indeed anyone knowledgeable should make no fuss about this distorted essence of beings and—should simply pass by.

83   60

One cannot predict, and does not need to predict, the form German thinking (in the sense of what once bore the name "philosophy") will take if this thinking arises out of a necessity. All analogies to the past are feeble and artificial. What alone matters is to experience the plight with regard to that necessity and to become strong for such experience. But the plight, if it must be the deepest one, which necessitates a beginning, has to arise out of what refuses itself in the downgoing of the previous philosophy as metaphysics: i.e., out of beyng. That at the edges of the abysses of nothingness an intimation might come to humans and that they might be able to encounter this intimation—is what is decisive. Hitherto, however, we have made nothingness merely an "object" and have reckoned that nothingness is of no significance and serves merely to name weakness and perplexity. Beyond this fleeing from an actual and lengthy experience of the plight (that beyng remains without a grounding of its truth), it is the habituation to the traditional forms of philosophy and to their communication that I claps our thinking in chains and lets us find satisfaction in the imita- 84 tions produced by mediocre and negligible adepts. Yet in such a situation—one propelling toward the essential decisions—a perspicuous endurance in the refused is more essential than floundering in illusionary formations which assist the flight from serious meditation.

61

Since a half-century ago, Nietzsche's work has come to its limit. Up to now the Germans still lack the possibility of preparing for preservation Nietzsche's fragmentary "masterpiece" in that form of future history which would implant all essential exertions of Nietzsche's thinking safely in German thought. Everything must still be expended in myopic and headstrong quarrel, in order to make visible at all the necessity of the *historical* task over and against a currently calculative pomposity of the smallest "dictators." I But perhaps the Germans 85 above all do not deserve that to them Nietzsche's thinking, in its significance for the history of beyng, should become a reality. Nevertheless, the few must seek what is most needful—to hold in reserve the future Nietzsche and the *last* thinking of metaphysics in the downgoing of metaphysics in the transitional form of that downgoing with regard to the "world." But irrelevant, i.e., unhistorical, aims and largely inconsequential motives push and pull everything onto byways, and so do personal vanities and public power struggles.—Even the exertion of individuals is today capable of nothing *immediately*; all of that is a false urge to activity, an urge that is supposed to match the prevailing bustle rather than pave the way for the complete otherness of the meditation which leads on toward the still undiscerned historical standpoint: this latter, however, is something pre-decided at the beginning of Western thinking, namely, the downgoing of thinking and questioning—which gives beings—reality—(for Nietzsche as modern thinker: "life")—the priority.

62

Days and nights of care regarding the destiny of the beyng of the
West—that seems to be found no longer | in any essential meditation.
People believe that if the threat of war is now dispelled the "world
war" would then have fulfilled its great destiny and the erection of
"culture" could start anew. That is well intentioned, but is thought
myopically, for it is historiological calculation within modern, national, folkish [völkisch], cultural-political horizons. All of this knows
nothing of the fact that the threat of war and arming to the extreme
for the sake of peace constitute merely a superficies of the machination of beings (the machination of historiology and of technology)—.
War and peace form an either-or which does not reach down into the
decisive domain: whether the human being can still venture essential being and its truth, so that he could encounter something self-re-
fused and most question-worthy which would determine him to a Da-
sein requiring higher bravery than does war and a deeper inwardness
than does all "peace" as mere accommodation to the purposes of a re-
assured career and of the undisturbed pursuit of the urge to dominate. (Cf. above, p. 11.)

63

For a long time, I resisted the insight dawning on me from my asking
the question of beyng, the insight that technology and historiology
are the same in a | metaphysical sense. For I still believed historiology
had struck deeper roots in history itself (cf. *Being and Time*[8]). But there
is no more avoiding this insight. The *sameness of historiology and technology* harbors the reason the human being, who pursues them and
has finally granted them priority, has become intolerable to the gods
and has been relegated to his distorted essence. This distorted essence
is now fully assisting beings to an exclusive ascendancy over the truth
of beyng. Yet in turn the sameness is grounded in the interpretation
of beingness as the constant presence which presents itself to and sur-
renders to representation and production (explanation and its clarity—
representational correctness as truth). This interpretation of beingness is the already co-decided downgoing in the first beginning of the
thinking of being as a beginning. Such downgoing is the start of the

---

8. {Martin Heidegger, *Sein und Zeit*, GA2 (Frankfurt: Klostermann, 1977), p.
518ff.}

history of philosophy with the still unrecognized tragedies of cognition in that history.

64

Humans, ones who by thoroughly questioning a long thought could carry out, in thinking, the deed of being without immediately writing a I book about it or making a worldview out of it, are dying out.   88
Moreover, for a much-planned era, people who have no usefulness are considered deviants. Where everything is valued only according to serviceability, offering, engagement, and deed, there is no Da-*sein*, that which—not without deeds and not poor in resolution—in advance and decisively brings beyng into the open domain and takes over a unique plight (the indigence of the gods) which could never be attained by all the neediness of all the needs.

65

What is more understandable than this: everything to be created is to be created for "the people" and is to belong to them? Therefore even those of our contemporaries who still retain a certain taste in the appraisal of what is precisely still possible (i.e., permissible) strive with their "works" to serve "the people." And that is not only to obtain a hearing for themselves; it is much rather because they find here what they always already sought for their need of effectiveness. As soon as this mode of thinking then underpins itself with a "philosophy of life," I its exclusive truth seems to be assured. From this arises a conception   89
of the life of the people, a conception that, rounded in itself, no longer needs any positing of goals and absolutely no disclosive questioning of them. This unneediness, which develops more quickly and more comprehensively into something self-evident, can no longer grasp the thought that purposes and reasons, tasks and goals, everywhere remain mere foregrounds, even if they roll up into themselves—foregrounds not of another ground further back but instead of the abyss [*Ab-grund*] in which eventuates the purposeless and goalless origination of the necessity of a plight of beyng. Where this abyss can no longer be known, what is lacking is the preparedness for the essential, which whenever it occurs requires the inceptuality of being and thus also the renunciation of beings and of their priority. Because this mode of thinking that is in service to a purpose has now, everywhere among peoples of "culture," become an explicit law, therefore it itself

testifies that beyng deserves the most hateful hatred, whereby the lowest realm of nihilism is first attained, provided this domain is grasped at once metaphysically and also in terms of the history of beyng.

90   66

Youth.—Do we have a young generation, and can we have such? No. Of course, in the biological sense young people and even younger ones are present-at-hand, and the supply is constantly replenished—but this is not "youth." On the other hand, nether does the popular saying hold without further ado: Youthfulness is possible at any "age of life," just as is senility.

Youth—those who are seeking and who at the same time perceive the essential placed into question and therein want to be tested; not mere escapism into the unproblematic.—A young generation is strong if it does not simply count on what is present-at-hand and if it also does not break under meditation or under the passion for what is obscure, and if it also becomes neither "aesthetic" nor apathetic.

The capacity for silence and yet without holding back the right word.

The young generation has its strength not only or primarily in muscles and voice, but instead in the power for *reverence*. In this power, however, there holds sway a proud overcoming of the currently won essential status.

Why and with what justification is "youth" a *historical* question? In the era of transition—since the essence of the human being as such must change—this question becomes necessary.

91   But it can never have the sense of a *psychological* self-staring.

67

Questioning—why is it almost impossible to keep questioning from *appearing* as mere doubt, hesitation, and mistrust? Because ordinary questioning does mostly stand in the service of these attitudes. But essential questioning—which is, and wherein is grounded, the truth of beyng—does not stand in service to something; instead, it is itself a sovereign basic disposition and pertains to the *originary knowledge* of the priority of beyng—and is the *restraint* of this knowledge, whereby such knowledge does not place itself over what is known—beyng—but rather always harbors a readiness to be assigned to beyng.

68

Ordinary opinion sees a downgoing wherever a falling and an ending show themselves, and it understands downgoing as the end of the ending. Or this opinion braces itself against the inevitability of such phenomena by means of a fabricated hopefulness from which it enumerates, and persuades itself of, all sorts of advancements. Seen essentially, such opinion hinders every knowledge of | history and above 92 all stands in the way of the basic recognition, one which admittedly must seem strange as long as we withdraw from historical meditation. This recognition opens up only one circumstance: that the lengthy history, now drawing toward its end, of the metaphysically grounded West is only the *pre*-history of a more originary history already posited in its first beginning, namely, the history of the essential occurrence of the Grounded truth of beyng as the appropriating eventuation of gods and humans on the basis of beyng. The liberation from the machination of beings through the transformation of the human being into *Da-sein*.

Previously and still now, as a consequence of the priority of beings, the human being as *animal rationale* could and can move only as it were in the concealed periphery of Da-sein, whereby to this human being "truth" and "beauty" became "ideals" and "values" and "purposes"—i.e., underwent an interpretation merely at the level of animals. The venture of the abyssal character of beyng and thus of the "true" inexhaustibility of the essential simplicity of beings was denied him and was replaced more and more by the furtherance and mere modification of what was already accomplished at the time. If we may for a moment (instead of thinking, as is necessary, out of | beyng and 93 back into it) consider history on the basis of humans and toward them, then the human being still ever (indeed now for the first time) stands before an unprecedented essential possibility: the leap into Da-sein. For Da-sein, the revering and preserving of beings become the great play, played out of the most intimate affiliation to the site of the decision regarding the nearness and remoteness of the gods. This that is unprecedented is nothing new in the sense of a mere alteration in the course of what has already become usual—instead, the opening up of the truth of beyng in Da-sein is that event of appropriation we still do not have the ears to hear or even to surmise.

No *"optimism"* ever attains the realm of the knowledge of this other beginning, for optimism always requires the counterattitude of "pessimism" in order to come into its own, since it, like pessimism, moves within a valuation of sheer beings left unquestioned in their *beyng*. The new young people will come to be only if they are struck *historically* by this other beginning and by the surmising of its future and become strong enough to listen to those who, leaping ahead into the

94   abyss I of beyng, make the transition to a time in which the continuation of the past into its new flowering might succeed, specifically in a way that without praise and publicity tacitly claims the most profound act is the one of poetizing and thinking. "Act" means here: to reach in a leap and to maintain the "there" which becomes the ground for every "where" and "when" in which—opening up the world on the reticent earth—the counterdirections of the divinity of the gods and of the humanity of humans are disclosively questioned. Those who stand intermediate in this "there"—summon the other generation for which *beyng* is *the* care.

69

The historiological human being—in case he can ever be surveyed—now encounters his most uncanny danger: that every essential plight of the groundlessness of still-forgotten beyng is definitively blocked in the success of the gigantic course of the proliferated machinations, without this danger as such ever being surmised and with everyone

95   instead seeing himself transposed into the I renewal of the peoples, a renewal compelled by this same historiological human being. This pressing forward of the historiological human being proceeds on its course with such uncanny sureness that he, in accord with the claims of the needs of reason for explanation, "prides himself on being able to ground his progress scientifically" through a doctrine of race and heredity—i.e., through a crude metaphysics of "life" which explains everything because it questions nothing, and which is clear to everyone because no one could admit that he—as a "living being"—would not know himself, and which immediately reinterprets everything "new" as something familiar insofar as this is indeed merely the "expression" of a life and of a people. But what will bring about a first meditation and a persistent listening in the midst of this blindness of "biological" thinking? Answer: the knowledge of the *relation* of humans to beings as such and as a whole—i.e., the questioning of the essential ground of this "relation," which can be called such only superficially, in a first indication. This knowledge and its transformative power, however, appear to remain impotent—indeed—never can they

96   "effectuate," but instead must I transform—i.e., create the essential ground for the effective possibilities.

70

If "thinkers" communicate their thoughts only after suffering, and questioning, a long plight of concealed beyng, then these thoughts must coalesce into the slight form of something simple; thence once again that which is rare of a discourse can arise, that which grounds history. But why does "plight" now always have only the distorted form of *"needs,"* whether of the "standing of the sciences," which poses the tasks, whether of literary dominance and the craving for validation, or whether of the contentment in the undisturbed further pursuit of the secured and the usual? Is all that merely the consequence of a gigantic indifference—or lying under it all is there a still ungraspable force of the entanglement of humans in their historiology?

71

Excessive demands are the source of the richness of temperament— and especially when they become intimations of something originary which requires of us a leap and unmasks calculation in its insufficiency.

72   97

What if "science," the more fundamentally it proceeds and the more comprehensively its teaching is utilized, must make *knowledge* ever more superfluous because in the arena of a settled "truth," good and very good cognitions are thoroughly satisfactory and "faith" in "science" (in the modern sense) is the undermining of meditative questioning? "Science" as the first champion of "dogmatism"—that is the intrinsic consequence of the modern claim of science to the mastery of beings in the sense of objectivities.

73

We hear now that the philosophers had earlier "gone wrong" in everything because they (supposedly) taught that the human being is simply an "individual" present-at-hand for himself. This "critique" of philosophy is so paltry that it cannot distress us at all. Such authoritative utterances are even pointless. How the "living space" of the Germans now takes in everything and must bear further. What will become of a people fobbed off with such groundless platitudes?

Is it enough that there are many who take no notice of them and flee into their own past?

98   74

Those who are entirely placid believe such "speeches" are inconsequential; that is the most facile way to protect one's own inconsequentialities from every disturbance. Certainly all "refutation" is ineffective here. But it does matter to know what for us moderns is the significance of *this increasing thirst for platitudes*—which processes bear these inconsequentialities and let them count as inconsequential.

75

A people is without relation to beyng if that people, together with its institutions and arrangements, cannot go down, such that out of the downgoing the beginning of an essentially creative poet might arise along with a thinker who disclosively questions beyng. But this does not mean the "individual" would take precedence over the "community," for those individuals are all the more sacrificed—; quite to the contrary, it means that the grounding of Da-sein—grounding as the site of the incursion and refusal of beyng and thus as the middle ground for gods and—humans—is the intrinsically and essentially occurring necessity on the basis of beyng—by way of a superiority of purpose. (Cf. p. 116.)

99   76

Why for a long time to come (calculated in human terms) will *beyng* leave beings to themselves—i.e., to the exhausting and deteriorating of a determinate beingness? Why this to such an extent and with such violence that beyng, like nothingness, is forgotten?

77

Being is never a "hinterworld" to beings—but rather is already the constantly overlooked foreground—as abyss [*Ab-grund*]. (Grounded: open in a transporting way.) Beings are also not an *epiphenomenon* of beyng—instead, beyng itself is beings—but beings as such—essentially occurring in the abyss—made fast for the most part in "grounds" which depend on not recognizing being, inasmuch as they turn being into the supreme being. "Idealism" comes "closer" to beyng—in the sense that it still in general allows beyng to count for something—; but thereby "idealism" is at the same time the deeper misunderstanding of the essence of beyng, because realism considers that everything "is" merely a "being," and so realism never summons up the height and power of a misunderstanding.

Beyng—only with difficulty will we overcome the Platonic way of thinking, which remains there even in its inversion—and yet—everything depends on it—especially when a thoughtless thinking proliferates and believes it can use "concepts" and "ideas" | simply as bio-   100 logical expedients.

78

The plight—that and how, in a grounding, beyng finds its own truth and the latter finds its essence. How is the plight precisely this—the essential occurrence of beyng? Because beyng is what is unique—what in each case grants place to beings as such, and because this uniqueness—as self-concealment in the proper essence of the abyss—is the most endangered of all, endangered by the semblance of being [*Sein*], the semblance all beings represent and proliferate. Without a trace of the truth (the Grounding clearing) of beyng, what is lacking is the Essentially founding bridge between gods and humans—beyng is the plight which reaches its peak when the lack of a sense of plight (the fact that that plight is not experienced and not surmised, indeed no longer can be surmised) as the abandonment of beings by beyng comes into sovereignty and this abandonment of beings is unwittingly falsified into the one finally reached nearness of "reality" itself—in the sense of intrinsically pressing and ongoing "life" as such.

To question the plight disclosively, to illuminate in thought what   101 is concealed in it—is the essence of philosophy—; thus not to make the plight some sort of human desire or need, some sort of urge to an occasion for removing a lack or satisfying it in a "worldview," but instead to see in beyng itself the plight and its ground and therefore not at all to take "plight" in the calculative sense of a mere predicament and difficulty. Plight—as the ground of what is necessary—possible and free—is to be thought primarily in terms of the basic disposition of astonished unsettling. The name apparently refers only to something "human"—and yet the very essence of humanity can exist only as a persistence of that plight, i.e., also as an evasion of the plight and a suppression precisely of its faintest and quietest intimations.

79

Historiology.—The correct calculation of the "advantage and disadvantage of historiology for life"[9] no longer suffices and is no longer a primordially decisive question, because indeed it is not historiology but "life" that is question-worthy; "life," again not with respect to its goal

102   but instead—instead with respect to itself: does it | constitute the essence of the human being and his essential ground, and can "life" in general be determined as *the* being [*Sein*] of beings? Are humans at all capable of asking this as a question, and are they equal to taking up what is most question-worthy? To direct one's steadfast and unique meditation onto this is to take the first path to the disclosive questioning of the plight and to dispel the lack of a sense of plight.

80

The plight—that and how beyng might ground its own truth—is the inner abyss of beyng itself, namely, that it bears in its essence the height of all heights, the depths of every depth, and the breadth of every breadth, and lets each being appear as something minor while yet itself remaining only the granting of a place for the time of the "between" for gods and humans. With the aims of placing himself in relation to beings on his own power, of compelling them into his dominion, of tearing away from them their last mysteries, and thus of venturing into the open realm from all sides, the individual of modern culture ever keeps on the watch for a shelter that secures him and

103   constantly occupies him: | the calculability and institutionalizing of everything is the protective covering he has already in advance thrown over everything. Never was the dread of what is essentially question-worthy so great as in the age of the human being avid for results, who already in advance delineates for himself the guiding lines of his historiology and calculates how he one day—i.e., in the forthcoming decades of the ultimate sovereignty of historiological humanity—will stand there in historiology. But those who are unable to affirm this era, even as they exploit its results, provide themselves with an assurance through the flight into religious belief with the appeal to what once was history, because it created that history. Everywhere—an avoidance and indeed even still a "struggle" among the avoiding ones themselves—everywhere—despite the great profusion of the most diverse sorts of "faith," a deeply concealed mistrust against

---

9. {Friedrich Nietzsche, "Vom Nutzen und Nachteil."}

the—ungrasped—definition of the historical human being, the definition—from which being [*Sein*] attunes the transformation of his essence toward ascending the height of his essential vocation—undertaking the stewardship of the truth of beyng.

That convolution of humanity into beings, in consequence of which   104
every horizon of possible and indeed essential questioning beyond
oneself is shriveled for humans to the point of complete disappearance, reaches its consummation when the human being as historiological animal retracts historiology into animality, places it under animality, and declares that the life urge as such is the basic reality. So proclaimed, the vitality of life is the death of every possibility for the human being to attain the truth of beyng even only as a question.

81

Nietzsche—did not understand that his inverting of Platonism, i.e., the postulation of "the" life as the exclusive basic reality, which also invalidates the distinction between the world here and the world beyond, had to work against his innermost intention directed toward the higher, thriving human beings (the great exemplars). For with that postulation, the massiveness of living things and of their life urge is justified in itself. Yet the recognition of this postulation as a ground and resistance for individuals is mere semblance, because the individuals I can know themselves immediately only as representatives of   105
"life" and thus *on behalf of* the masses and their welfare and fortune. To their own will, there remains only the echo of "life" and of its enhancement, and every "living being" will as such announce the claim to a right to live, and the increasing claim will enhance "life." In other words, the possible arena of a "self-surpassing" of life will become ever narrower, because this arena is already in essence—after the postulation of life—nothing other than an "illusion" necessary for life and itself only an appearance of life. It is an appearance that can disappear at any moment life itself becomes too burdensome for the living beings. Humans—as the historiological animals—will develop their own essence historiologically down "below" the animal by the fact that animality is explained (as life) in terms of the beingness of beings—i.e., the will to power is in itself necessarily recurrence of the same, specifically such that this recurrence itself becomes more and more historiological—i.e., technological—i.e., inconsequential. Therefore we now need "Nietzsche experts," who are cunning enough to veil under "catchwords" the genuine truth of this thinking in good time and to rescue the great thinkers for the "people." That means: to

106   bring the "people" before the great thinker in safety I and "prove" that
every domain of possible question-worthiness is nonexistent. That is
genuine "political science."

82

The convulsing of *metaphysics* (priority of beings over being, such that
being must become something accessory, i.e., an idea and an ideal),
whether as Platonism or its inversion, undermines the essential possibility of a "culture." All thinking in terms of "cultural" ideals and
"cultural" forms and certainly "cultural" programs is today still only
the rigidifying of the human being in the forgetting of being which
has already long been dominating him, as a *modern* consequence of the
abandonment of beings by being which installed itself in the Middle
Ages and in antiquity—*after* its great beginning. The forgetting of being appeared authoritatively, at the start of modernity, in the form of
"absolute certainty," thus in a form which feigned exactly the opposite, and in the subsequent centuries this illusion expanded into something self-evident. The forgetting of being is sealed in the primacy of
the understanding of the human being as *subiectum*.

107   ### 83

The ordinary concept of *belief:* persuading oneself that one is satiated
in one's (in any case) weak claims to an interrogative meditation on
beings and on the relation to them; such satiety takes the blind for
the genuine seers. The intrinsic precaution of this sort of belief entails a constant proclamation that belief is something very difficult,
whereas it is—the easiest.

84

"*Science*" as the "ideal" of cognition is an ambiguous term. Science can
mean: mere acquaintanceship and explanation are still *not* cognition
[*Erkenntnis*]—the latter commences only in essential—interrogative—
decisive *knowledge* [Wissen]. "Scientificity" ["*Wissenschaftlichkeit*"] is
thus only a title for that attitude which has left behind all calculative
"science" as "positive research," but a title expressing merely a desper-
ateness, since "science" in the interim has received that other meaning according to which the essential is not *knowledge*, in the sense of
the projection of the essential ground of beings (as the venture of the
truth of beyng), but instead is the dismissal of such knowledge in

favor of *scientia* ["knowledge"] in the sense of science,[10] the explanatory-dominating calculation of what is in every case Objectively useful and important.

The ambiguity and the arbitrary sense of such terms (faith, knowledge, science, culture, etc.) do not represent mere oscillation within an intrinsically grounded field of meaning—(inasmuch as all language originally possesses this variability of meaning as part of its essential power and cannot be a semiotic system and certainly not a "standardized" one)—but instead indicate an uprooting of the truth of beyng—in case a rootedness in beyng itself ever did exist. The consequence of the fact that "language" and "thinking," "concept" and representation, have been degraded and externalized psychologically-biologically into means for the instituting of the mastery of life. Not that one is unable to make up one's mind about essential goals and their grounded precept, but that in general the experiential gaze upon beings is confusing and this confusion claims to pose no danger, since immediate usefulness justifies everything, while "damages" and "mistakes" as such do not count.

85

How is it that since the nineteenth century (second half), "life" has achieved the rank of *the* all-encompassing reality—? | Once through Schopenhauerian philosophy—despite its Platonism; then through Nietzsche's inversion of Platonism; above all, however, through the Impotent pretension of all "idealisms" (theory of value), i.e., through the self-evidence and comprehensibility of all "positivisms" for the rising masses—; and finally through the sovereignty of "lived experience" in place of encounter and meditation. The apotheosizing of life in the life of the peoples and races is at the same time the consequence of *nationalisms* and of modern culture. *Egoism*—which is not restricted, indeed least of all, to the individual "I"—has instead its great possibilities only in the "I" which is the subject of a community. The obvious appeal to "life" as "the" natural being and the only real one and as what lends all things their space and light has become so clear that it already no longer offers any definite foothold for meditation, but has instead found its highest certainty in hackneyed slogans.

---

10. [English word in the text.—Trans.]

86

The times German thinkers need to become understood—*in the essential unintelligibility of these thinkers to common understanding*—are always
110   lengthy times—indeed they are perhaps now becoming | unforseeably long. But what if meditation on these "facts" were a not yet overcome remainder of historiological calculation? Those "times" are inconsequential, because they are still taken in terms of the succession postulated in "time reckoning." We must keep in mind that poetizing and thinking already enclose within themselves their own times and that these times cannot ever be appraised or even only encountered according to the duration of effectiveness or according to the temporal points heeded. Even here, historiology thrusts itself between the times of calculation and the times of history. Times of history arise in each case only out of the clearing of beyng and are themselves only the way this clearing disposes of its field. Today's "time" is already and indeed necessarily *a-historical*—because the truth remains barred to beyng and humans are indeed relegated to the instituting and proclaiming of gigantic machinations, while nowhere are the spaces of essential decisions and the leap into those spaces deemed of any worth. "Cultural" politics and in general all "thinking" in "cultural" terms (cf. p.
111   106) now constitute the form in which | humans supposedly are making "history" but in truth are promoting a-historicality in the form of the unconditional sovereignty of historiology.

87

The question of *being* is the question that encounters the essence of truth and experiences truth as belonging to beyng itself. The question of being therefore knows itself as the disclosive questioning of what is unique, of what tolerates no supports and must remain without protection and whose essence is *plight*, on that side and this side of lack and excess. Being is the plight, one which the gods require for their essential occurrence and one which at the same time compels the transformation of the human essence into what grounds the truth of beyng. The plight, as the ground of this requirement and this compulsion at once, is (if ever thinkable as privation) always only that which "lacks" what is derived and grounded, explained and dominated, for in a countermove to the appropriating eventuation, it points to the gods in their essence and casts the human being into Da-sein, in order to compel the gods and humans—in such separation and the broadest casting asunder—into an originary and reciprocal gaze at one another.

What so uniquely compels must in itself be the supreme plight   112
which in human nomenclature could also be called "blessedness"
["*Seligkeit*"] if endless temptation to the crudest misinterpretations did
not lurk behind this term which immediately calls up to all opinion
the notion of an "ideal." Therefore this opinion also admittedly thinks
of something unblessed and wretched in the word "plight"—i.e., it
calculates according to an "ideal" and on the basis of the state of feeling coordinated with it. But "plight" is here the word of beyng itself
and of its essential occurrence. And in correspondence "care" is not
the plaintive worry over the troubles of "life"—instead, it is the name
of a first faint resonance of beyng in the essence, and as the essence,
of Dasein. As long as we indeed think "metaphysically"-historiologi-
cally, compare opinions, calculate standpoints, and thereby still have
our "lived experiences" of things in terms of "worldview," we will not
surmise the originary domain out of which, in asking the question of
beyng, "the inceptually beginning *plight* is disclosively questioned"
and "care" is brought into knowledge.—As soon as what counts is to
lead, on any path whatever of *immediate* agreement, into the domain
of the thinking that is heedful of the history of beyng, I it may be ad-   113
visable to keep silent about "plight" and "care." Seen in this regard,
Being and Time is too immediately hasty (apart from other "defects"),
since the contemporary human being still all too readily "thinks" of
everything essential and *abyssal* in terms of something detrimental to
his comfortable pleasure and his certainty of success, something casting a shadow over these. In short, he calculates on the basis of *beings*
and only with beings—; *of what avail to him then is the excessive demand
of beyng*—how is he even supposed to surmise that this demand encloses the fullness of the simplicity of everything inceptual? How is
he / coming from *there* (from the pursuit of beings) / supposed to know
that the plight as abyss is freedom itself—as the inceptual jubilation
in which gods and humans, out of the remotest remoteness of their
surmised proper essence, rush *toward* each other and nevertheless, out
of the strange nobility of their proper essence, abide in the distance of
intimacy?

The *question* of being is not the beginning itself—rather, it is the
tolling of a breakthrough to a preparedness for what is without protection and without support, wherein alone the thrust of the plight
finds its appropriate spatiotemporal field. Within the horizon of the
historiological animal, we are of course constantly subject to the
danger (instead of tolling again and again, i.e., instead of remaining
with the I simple meditation and preparation of that preparedness) of   114
prolonging an (at least apparently) erudite discussion which perhaps

sets over the "human being" new or old "concepts" and delivers further material to the activity of pen pushing. But that "tolling" is the chiming of the stillness of meditation (cf. p. 75f.), and a proper knowledge is required to carry it out: the more originary the questioning, all the more reticent remains the discourse; the more rare the latter, all the more necessary the reference to the accomplished—but not past—and only futural beginnings (the first beginning of Western thinking; Hölderlin's completely other beginning; the sign of a transition in Nietzsche's thinking, despite the peculiar reversion into the entirely precedent and indeed past metaphysics—precisely through the "inversion" and "revaluation"). The more restrained this reference, all the more decisive the enduring in the transition and the overcoming of the semblance of an already arisen beginning.

88

Historiology by essence delays the decisions and avoids the domains |
115   of decision. If therefore historiology possesses the essence of the human being (as the historiological animal), then historiology makes needful a long elapsing for the "history" of this human being. Such elapsing appears as the gigantic future and incorporates all "constructive" powers—what is constructed is a gigantic work of the final destruction of every possible bridge into the plight of beyng. But all this in the horizon of the satisfied experience that peoples are grasped everywhere in ascent and that the "world" is changing. But the change consists only in the removal of the still extant veilings of the already decided essence of the "world"—an essence in which the machination of beings has the priority and requires of humans the "lived experience" of life, whereby the machination must now proceed into the glaring brightness of what is common and public.

89

Art—is to be justified *inceptually,* futurally, and only on the basis of the "work" insofar as the work sets the *truth* (of beyng) into a being and brings beings to themselves (as preservers of beyng) in such a way that beyng might eventuate as the event of appropriation. The work therefore not as *performance,* and performance not as the "production"
116   and execution of an "act of life"—all this belongs to the | past history of metaphysics. Nietzsche did not transcend an interpretation of art and of the artist in terms of a metaphysics of life. On the other hand, the intrinsically facile emphasis on the "work" as "work" does not

mean anything unless we disclosively question the essence of the
work and especially the essence of poetry, as such an essence is conceived in terms of the history of beyng, and unless this questioning
beings about a transformation of humanity.

90

Beyng, grasped as plight [*Not*], does not mean something which is
necessary [*not-tut*]—for example, in the idealistic sense of a necessary
condition for the grasp of beings as objects. Beyng "is" and only beyng
originarily "is"—it is not "necessary"—but, instead *necessitates* [nötigt];
beyng does not correspond to some sort of "needing"—but is rather
the abyss of all essential dispositions which, badly disposed, flee into
the mistaken form of mere needs and as such claim the human being.

91

Nietzsche—a decisive overcoming of Nietzsche (not a "refutation" of
him, which is always unphilosophical) can never be carried out im-
mediately; it consists rather in the convulsing (undermining) | of   117
Western metaphysics as such; thereby the postulation of "life" as *the*
being becomes groundless—because "beings" altogether lose their priority. Concurring with the overcoming of this postulation of "life" are
the characters supposed to constitute the beingness of "life," namely,
will to power and that which fulfills the mode of being of "life,"
namely, eternal recurrence. The overcoming of metaphysics is the convulsion of Platonism—i.e., the convulsion of Platonic philosophy and
of its history, the convulsion of every inverting of Platonism, and ultimately the elimination of every domain of such an inverting and of
the postulating of the ἰδέα as beingness. Any other confrontation with
Nietzsche is uncreative and superficial and mere shadowboxing. In
particular, every confrontation of Christianity—insofar as the latter
is still actual—with Nietzsche is a bad joke, since here indeed a crude
Platonism merely stands over and against its counterpart.

Why is Nietzsche, through his battle against the contemporary biology (Darwinism—struggle for survival—selection) driven ever
more decisively into his metaphysics of life? Is he so driven—or does
he not precisely therefore take up that battle because he has already,
through Schopenhauer and Goethe and romanticism, set foot in a |
metaphysics of "life," i.e., in such an interpretation of beings as a   118
whole, an interpretation in which and for which "life" constitutes *the*
basic reality? Decisive for Nietzschean metaphysics is the inversion of

Platonism (primarily Schopenhauer's) and thus the incorporation of the nonsensuous (the spiritual—genius and its works) *into* life itself. Yet this inverting includes an ever more decisive grounding of everything in "life" *as such,* insofar as the latter is not mere desire and urge but instead is *creation* and *increase* and thus also makes any positing of a goal something supplementary. History is only a form of "life"—i.e., a form of *physis* in the literal sense. Life—as pure creative self-transcendence—is to be brought into enhanced life. Will to power. Essential what cannot be carried off and everything incorporated into its atmosphere; *horizon*—but precisely in the literal sense as enclosing—delimiting—/ not the opening-up displacement into beyng / indeed such that on this basis is determined first and foremost the essence of the human being and the limit of everything that is merely alive. The legitimate "anxiety" in the face of any relapse into Platonism and the mere *half*-thought of Platonism (without a surmising of the question of being) drove I Nietzsche ever more exclusively into a sheer glorification of life—as enhancement of power—; i.e., they drove him away from every question of whether the human being in his essence is not to be determined *still more* originarily on the basis of a transported and open exposedness to being—as event—whereby at the same time and with the same originariness every possibility of a Platonism is destroyed and so is every anthropological metaphysics of "life"—indeed so is metaphysics in general and thus the pretext to "refute" Nietzsche's metaphysics in either a Christian or political way, such as through a return to a hazy Wagnerism.

119

In accord with the historiological tradition and in connection with the Leibnizian doctrine of perspective (*point de vue*), Nietzsche's concept of "horizon" always has the sense of limitation and of restriction and thus of security for "*life*." (*Being and Time,* however, understands "horizon" as outlook—as the open and free domain of transporting—as the affiliation to being itself—understanding of being—but that is not an "idealism"—which forgets and devalues "life"—but is instead a completely other beginning of the determination of the human being on the basis of Da-sein. All this lies *ahead* of every anthropological-biological postulation and is directed exclusively I to the question of being as the disclosive questioning of the truth of beyng.) In accord with his way of thinking, Nietzsche demands the pure self-developing "action" of self-enhancing "life" itself; nevertheless, he is thoroughly reactive as regards the decisive—the postulation and interpretation of "the" life. Nietzsche thinks on the basis of an opposition to Schopenhauer (life as mere desire) and Darwin (life as mere struggle for survival), on the basis of an opposition to Hegel and Hegelianism (history as actuality of reason—the goals and purposes of reason), and

120

on the basis of an opposition to Plato (postulation of the sensuous—"life"—as μὴ ὄν ["nonbeing"]).

All the oppositions flow into the one of a pure affirmation of life as such, life which is oblivious of itself and of goals. But do not the oppositions derive from this more originary affirmation? Certainly. Yet this one does not need to unfold into an affirmation of beings in that reactive way. Why does the affirmation of life *as* an affirmation of beings not become the affirmative question of beings as such? Why does Nietzsche remain *within* metaphysics? Why does he not disclosively ask the question of the distinction between beings and being, the question wherein all metaphysics I is rooted first and foremost, in such   121
a way that metaphysics gives the priority to beings (even Plato—the εἶναι as οὐσία is the ὄντως ὄν ["to be in the mode of a present-at-hand thing is the most beingly being"])? Why does Nietzsche again think the whole of metaphysics on the basis of the inversion of its predominant configuration? It is because he has to be the end of metaphysics. How can we know that? Through the basic experience of more originary decisions in the beginning itself. But such experience comes under the intimation of beyng. As meditation in the inceptual, this experience must renounce accepting any subsequent forms and ways and must seek its own inexhaustibility in the impulse to the disclosive questioning of beyng.

Nietzsche is the last, greatest, crudest, and thus most dangerous obstruction and retardation of the inceptual question of being—(not the question of beings—which he *also* calls "being," in accord with the times). Therefore he is the end—which means *the start of a lengthy elapsing,* in which everything is mixed together and only what is useful—appropriate for some use—is differentiated. With Nietzsche, the decisive portion of modernity commences. (Cf. p. 67ff.)

The measures of thoughtful judgment, which is always a determinate—detached—revering of something ever unique, can be taken, even in the case of Nietzsche, only out of what is unique itself. I   122
Thoughtful reverence derives from the innermost necessity to acknowledge—affirm—the essential, and this has nothing to do with acquiescence, nor a fortiori with agreement. The positions taken toward the essential thinkers are seldom thoughtful—instead, they are mostly "scientific" (ones that calculate according to "correctness" and "falsity") or "ideological" (ones that evaluate according to basic intuitions, without recourse to a more originary questioning) or "artistic" (ones that appraise according to literary, architectural, or sculptural taste). All three interpenetrate, and this tangle confuses thinking and shifts the proper history of thought and also its unbroken futurity outside the simple relation of originary reverence.

92

Meditation—the courage to track down one's own presuppositions and their rationale and to interrogate the goal positings with regard to their necessity. Today every attempt at "meditation" ends quickly in a "psychological"-"characterological"-biological-typological dissection, i.e., in a barren and facile retracing of beings and of "life" to the kind of "lived experience" and to the impulses and needs of such experience.

123   It might seem strange that meditation could question out toward something completely other, toward being and its truth and toward the ground or groundlessness of this truth—such that meditation as self-meditation has nothing to do with an expert's opinion on the backgrounds of lived experience; the form of this dissection has remained, even after Jewish "psychoanalysis" was used as a pretext for it. This form must remain, as long as we do not abandon the view of ourselves as persons of lived experience. Until then, however, meditation in the thoughtful sense will be impossible.

93

Why does beyng persist in impotence over and against beings? Because the human being has been unfastened from beyng and has opened to what is objective and conditional the last gates of his public distorted essence and finds his satisfaction in this admission of "beings." Is that due to the arbitrariness and egotism of the distorted essence of the *human being,* or is this arbitrariness, disguised in gigantic accomplishments, only the stimulating semblance concealing a compulsion of beyng, a compulsion which constrains the human being

124   (as the still undecided steward of the | truth of beyng) into the decision, inasmuch as it releases him into that unfastened condition? What does it mean that *beyng no longer poses excessive demands on beings,* in that beyng relegates "temperament" as mere "soul" to the "lived experiences" of "life" instead of throwing "temperament" into the essential possibility of Da-sein (Da-sein as the ground of the changed human being)?

It is the "thrownness" of the human being into Da-sein already the anticipation of a thinking that leaps ahead and that the human being as historiological animal can follow no more, because he has long since falsified his fear of beyng and of its question-worthiness into a "heroic realism"?[11] If the human *essence* decreases itself, i.e., falls into

---

11. {Ernst Jünger, *Der Arbeiter: Herrschaft und Gestalt.* (Hamburg: Hanseatische Verlagsanstalt, 1932), p. 34.}

the distorted essence of the unfastening from beyng, then what increases is the arrogance of the "real" human being, the one "standing with both feet in reality." Why should his successes not persuade him that there are no accidents and that everything is merely a matter of "will"? But what if beyng were the accident for every being, because beyng is what alone is necessary—the plight itself?

94   125

One may now, as it is time for maintaining what is up to date, forcefully and with all the expenditure of "literature" and the opinions about it, "overcome" the "philosophy of existence" through a joyous "refutation." Yet this entire pretense does not in the least surmise the question and the inner and uniquely thoughtful claim in *Being and Time,* but instead merely obstructs it—perhaps even this has its good points—the claim, namely, that still for a long time to come the genuine question will remain protected against the importunity of the increasingly noisy impotence of thinking. A precondition here, however, is that this impotence feel hale in its own magnificence.—

Meanwhile, the mystery of the essential thinkers of Western metaphysics is becoming more and more mysterious, since every essential thinker, on the basis of his origination, has already been withdrawn from all possible refutation.

What does Heraclitus say? κύνες γὰρ καὶ βαΰζουσιν ὦν ἂν μὴ γινώσκωσι.[12]

"For so do *dogs* bark at those they do not know."

Supplements

1

What is most common is the universal and its universalization.

It—from the incapacity to experience the ever-incomparably unique in the same and to maintain it in its mystery—in gratitude for this!

---

12. {Heraclitus B97, in *Die Fragmente der Vorsokratiker: Griechisch und deutsch von Hermann Diels,* ed. Hermann Diels and Walther Kranz (Berlin: Weidmann, 1922).}

2

A recent graduate from a secondary school said about my Hölderlin lecture[13] in Munich: "How he did not at all touch upon the poem! How he created a background on which the poem became visible of itself. This is art, this making visible."

3

To shine forth:
   To turn to the light
   To receive what shelters
   To pertain to the event.

———

To shine forth—but not to gleam.

4

"And to sympathize with the . . ."

". . . instead, life, buzzing hot even from
                              shadow echo
As in a focal point
Gathered. Golden desert.
                    II, 249[14]

      and lost love."

5

πρώτιστον μὲν Ἔρωτα θεῶν μητίσατο πάντων.
Parmenides frag. 13
["But Eros was devised as the first of all the gods."]
          (σελήνη)
νυκτιφαὲς περὶ γαῖαν ἀλώμενον ἀλλότριον φῶς . . .
["(The moon) nightly shining, wandering around the earth, borrowed light . . ."]
αἰεὶ παπταίνουσα πρὸς αὐγὰς ἠελίοιο frag. 14, 15

———

13. {Martin Heidegger, "Hölderlins Erde und Himmel," in *Erläuterungen zu Hölderlins Dichtung*, GA4 (Frankfurt: Klostermann, 1981), pp. 152–181.}

14. {Friedrich Hölderlin, *Gedichte nach 1800, Stuttgarter Ausgabe*, vol. 2.1 (Stuttgart: Kohlhammer, 1951).}

["Always peering toward the rays of the sun."]
γαῖα   ὑδατόριζον frag. 15a
["Earth   water-rooted"][15]

6

Wittgenstein—/
    in a lecture in Vienna:
    "The absolute is the proposition."—
    i.e., the *assertion*.[16]

7

Michel, Wilhelm
    Hölderlin's translation of a divine name (Persephone = light)
    Kunstwart. Jahrgang 41, 2. 1928
    pp: 59–61

Hölderlin: Translation of *Antigone*, v. 922ff. (Strophe A):
    "O tomb! O bridal bed! subterranean
    Lodging, ever awake! There will I journey
    To my own ones, most of whom,
    Having gone among the dead,
    Were greeted by a light
    Angrily-compassionately."[17]
Eleusinian Mysteries
    "After purification, the mystic descended into the underworld, just
as happens after death. He went through narrow passages in the dark,
until he reached a space where a couch was situated, symbolizing the
mystic marriage with Persephone, who received him there. And then
a strong brightness appeared to him, illuminating his further way.
Persephone is thus in this rite entirely and plainly the light principle
of the underworld. At the moment she greets the wanderer in the
underworld, a new strong light radiates on him, a counter-sun which
expels the terror of death's night."

—

15. {Parmenides, *Die Fragmente der Vorsokratiker*.}

16. {Neither the "lecture," nor the quotation, nor Heidegger's source is known.}

17. {Friedrich Hölderlin, *Übersetzungen*, *Stuttgarter Ausgabe*, vol. 5 (Stuttgart: Kohlhammer, 1952), p. 242.}

"In this way, the rendering of the name Persephone as 'light' receives a deep and impressive meaning. The myth is here made 'more demonstrable' in that Hölderlin lets flash up in it the deepest thought of the old mysteries and of his own religion as well and mixes into a dreary, sepulchral name a mystery of joy. Persephone, who, murky in black, rules over a clotted world of dust and shadow, was offensive to glowing life therein, and she was doubly offensive precisely on the lips of this Antigone, whose animating love has already ventured forth so far into the realm of shadows. Thus death becomes a 'continuance' and passageway, and Persephone the goddess of the counter-sun. The word 'light' used for the queen of the underworld tears away the deceptive appearance of end and petrification and arches over death a flowing heaven of eternal life."

8

αὐδάω
   say—name—call—
σύμμαχος
   ally (of the gods)

9

The traditional congealed opinion
   beings "are" being
          |
   come to presence as
             and
          carry out
             but
   being "is"—beings
      eventuates   (the thing)
   (But this not in the Platonic sense.)

10

"not into the maelstrom of thinking"
—

the proper domain of experience
   without thinking—without silent monologue—and musing.
   /
   Hölderlin:
   "They gladly pick the grape, yet they deride

Thee, misshapen vine! that thou
capriciously and wildly stray about the soil."[18]

Think *thou*—since thou dost not (subjectively) claim them as thine
own—I consider!

"On the procedure of the poetic spirit"!
III, 277–309[19] | "Language"
In *thinking*

11

Relevance
  insight
  illumination
  how without ἀλήθεια!?

12

All that matters is whether one notices, feels, that the clumsy book of
P. H.[20] is remunerated malice and thus mendacious especially where
the author seems to hand out praises—or whether one, instead of
choosing in the matter of H., thinks through, thinks over, the matter
H. is endeavoring to think. Everything else is a misunderstanding of
the uncanny power of public opinion and of the vindictiveness ruling over it.

13

Death
  Hölderlin: *Hyperion* Book I. The three last missives
             Book II. The third missive.

---

18. {Friedrich Hölderlin, "Gesang des Deutschen," in *Sämtliche Werke*, vol. 4
(Berlin: Propyläen, 1923), p. 129.}

19. {Friedrich Hölderlin, "Über der Verfahrungsweise des poetischen Geistes,"
in *Sämtliche Werke*, vol. 3 (Berlin: Propyläen, 1923).}

20. {Paul Hühnerfeld, *In Sachen Heidegger* [On this matter of Heidegger], *Ver-
such über ein deutsches Genie* (Hamburg: Hoffmann und Campe, 1959).}

14

"In the end, when one is no longer scattered and occupied with particulars, with what is current, with happiness and unhappiness, when everything is already decided, does not the beginning always show itself as emphatically there, including everything that had to be forgotten so that one could go on, everything that inundates a human life with overfulness? And does not the beginning always show itself as what most properly is, as the indestructible, as the core?"[21]

Rahel Varnhagen   H. A.
p. 160f.

15

Thinking is—the passion for what is useless. The latter mostly counts as of no use. Therefore it is not used. Insofar as everything is geared to usefulness and accomplishment, thinking is passed over. *One* corresponds even in this way to thinking—but only in the adverse sense.

16

The three H's: Heraclitus, Hegel, Hölderlin.
    Event: not understandable—to the understanding
            not reasonable—for the faculty of reason—
    Looking out in accord with the corresponding thinking—the (*ambiguously*) restrained (*in a preserving way*) renunciation.

17

"The natural language"—
    natural = ordinary-everyday—i.e., *common*—habitual.
    Out of what habituation?—in the tradition, and whence the latter determined?
    (natural and *nature* of the matter at issue; "essence"—natural language essential language!)
    (What can this mean?)

---

21. {Hannah Arendt, *Rahel Varnhagen: Lebensgeschichte einer deutschen Jüdin aus der Romantik* (Munich: Piper, 1959).}

18

Anyone who has never thought through Books Γ IV Z VII Θ IX of Aristotle's *Metaphysics* in the original language, anyone who has never thoughtfully traversed Hegel's *Logik*, will never be able to grasp—what it means—to think beings as beings.

Yet the concern is not with learned historiological cognitions of past philosophy—instead, what counts is the consummated language of present ages in their world history.

19

If we early on may preserve something surmised, something scarcely intuited in long searching, preserve it unwittingly in the demeanor of the *single* jointing play played together—and in such preservation tend to that which endures and out of it become ones who remain steadfast.

{Index}

Artwork [*Kunst-werk*]: 115f.

Beginning [*Anfang*]: 39, 50, 71ff., 91f., 126 [*sic*].
Beyng [*Seyn*]: a, 21, 37, 49, 95, *100, 102*, 111ff., 123f.

Culture [*Kultur*]: 106

Da-sein: 92, 98
Decision [*Entscheidung*]: 7ff., 64f.
Disposition [*Stimmung*]: 44f.

Future [*Zukunft*]: 22ff.

Go.{ds} [*Gö.{tter}*]: 4
Greek antiquity [*Griechentum*]: 27

Historiology [*Historie*]: 2f., 37, *40ff.,* 45, 64f., 70f., 86f., 96, 101, 109ff., 114f.
Historiology of art [*Kunsthistorie*]: 43ff.
History [*Geschichte*]: 6ff.
Hölderlin: 1ff., 27
Human being [*Mensch*]: 1ff., 66ff., 97f., 104

Language [*Sprache*]: 80
"Life" ["*Leben*"]: 52ff., 94f., *104*, 108f.

Meditation [*Besinnung*]: 33ff., 122f.
Metaphysics [*Metaphysik*]: 116

Modernity [*Neuzeit*]: 102f., 106, 121

Nietzsche: 56ff., 67ff., 84f., 104, *116ff.*
Nothingness [*Nichts*]: 83

Pe.{ople} [*Vo.{lk}*]: 13
Philosophy [*Philosophie*]: 51, 71, 75f., 78, 83f., *99, 100,* 121
Plight [*Not*]: 100, 102, 111f., 116, 124, (cf. [Ponderings] X)

Questioning [*Fragen*]: 91

Recollection [*Erinnerung*]: 40ff., 67
Reverence [*Verehrung*]: 15
"Revolution" ["*Revolution*"]: 76f.

Science [*Wissenschaft*]: 79, 97, 107

Technology [*Technik*]: 12ff., 46f., 86f.
Thinking that is heedful of the history of Beyng [*Denken seynsgeschichtlich*]: 62, 87
Transition [*Übergang*]: 70

Ways [*Wege*]: 51
West [*Abendland*]: 89f.
World [*Welt*]: 72f.

Youth [*Jugend*]: 90f., 93

PONDERINGS X

a These "Ponderings" and all the previous ones are not "aphorisms" in the sense of "adages"; instead, they are inconspicuous advance outposts—and rearguard positions—within the whole of an attempt at a still ineffable meditation toward the conquest of a *way* for the newly inceptual questioning which is called, in distinction from metaphysical thinking, the thinking of the *history of beyng*. Not decisive is *what* is represented and compiled into a representational edifice, but only *how* the questioning takes place and the fact that being is questioned at all. Equally great in such questioning must be the reverence toward essential thinkers and the renunciation of any sort of imitation. Of such reverence and renunciation the staunchly ongoing "philosophical" literature needs to know nothing, for this literature can secure a market for itself only on the distorted ground of something contrary to its own timeliness.

In proportion to the unique political results, the concealedness of the plight with respect to the history of beyng grows, and the strangeness of essential meditation increases. Can a people accomplish both at once or even only in succession? No. But both are to be ventured, each in the decisiveness of its salient opposition to the other; for *history* is neither that which historiology brings forward as an object nor that which the present time offers to "lived experience"—history is the trace of the truth (and thus likewise the trace of the *errancy*) of beyng.

Beings in the whole of their Western objectification constitute a heavy, long-since-closed door, from which in the meantime even the space has been lost into which the door is supposed to lead. This door must be taken off its hinges and forced open, so that nothingness might appear as the first genuine shadow of beyng. Who will take beings off the hinges of their extreme anthropomorphizing? Who will venture to know that this alone is necessary?

Who will surmise that such knowledge and its preservation can imprint on another age the law of the structure of its groundings and also surmise that an originary questioning is genuine mastery and not the deprivation of the answers which ever and again draw the human being away from the struggle over his essence? Yet this essence is precisely that struggle of the interrogative grounding of the truth of beyng.

Of what avail is conceptual clarity, if it cannot arise out of the clarification of what is obscure, and if the obscure again remains only the unclear in the sense of the confusion of something superficial and is not the unfathomability of an abyss, and if this abyss does not essentially occur as *beyng* itself but presents only the semblance of something unclarified in the form of something not yet researched in the domain of beings? Of what avail is thinking, if it does not become the venture of that excessive demand posed by beyng itself? But how does such a demand create its space-time? Or is space-time the still-not-grounded opening up of that open realm which springs forth in the demand?

4

Only in dialogue should one cross swords with the history of think-ing in order then to *say something about history,* and thus one must be a thinker oneself, originating in that very history. The interrogative ap-peals of the thinkers are the unheard echo of the excessive demands placed on thinkers by disclosively questioned being, such that those 2 appeals do not break the silence of the openness of being, I but quite to the contrary, in penetrating through, create silence for this open-ness and preserve the essential occurrence of the abyss out of which all grounding speech and denomination can speak and language can emerge. Otherwise, and long since in the habituation of historiologi-cal everydayness, language appears as the mere use and consumption of words. Language then counts as the covering with which all beings are shrouded and out of which a patch is snipped for each thing since the need for designation depends on such a patch.

Why this uncanny perversion, such that what in itself forms the cleft of the abyss of beyng becomes the neglected uniformity of a sub-sequent (and thus in everydayness always the first) leveling down of beings and guides all purported meditation on the essence of lan-guage, even when, in place of the grammar of propositional logic, an accommodating "hermeneutics," an "aesthetics" of expressive feeling, a psychology of linguistic melody, and even metaphysics have stepped forth? The perversion is not a perversity; instead, it is the suppression of what is originary in beings which drive toward the abandonment by being and no longer contain anything originary.

3 This suppression, seen inceptually, is the guarding I and preserv-ing of the origin for the essential decisions between the grounding of a truth of beyng and the priority of beings. The alienation of the es-sence of language makes possible an infinite increase in literature and speech (in the guise of pen pushing and idle talk), such that one day the historically decisive poetry and the preparatory thoughtful dis-course will remain behind as things entirely strange and so will pro-vide a first intimation into what not only is unmastered out of the machination of beings but also can no longer be repudiated. In the face of the strangeness of what is utterly strange, even rejection gives way and takes recourse to its usual things. The ways of the origin are—historiologically calculated—on the basis of beings—always roundabout ways. That is to say, those who reflect back to the ground-ing of the truth of being must surmise the roundabout way in the pre-dominance of beings and—must learn to tolerate it. They must not avoid this predominance, but instead need to venture the least thing

in order to break under that predominance on the way of thinking and poetizing. Therefore even language and speech cannot be "improved" immediately. Here—in accord with the incomparability of the origin—only steep plunges are ever possible, or summits.

These are not two separate things—but—often long unrecog- 4
nized—the same. Indeed the plunges are therefore still not the adverse and smallness of decline; they are more essential and must never be thought in terms of mere insufficiency. The fact that language expands so predominantly in its distorted essence (i.e., in its use) can indicate how secludedly the abyss of beyng has engulfed the origin.

5

We must acknowledge that the human being no longer wants or can want an originary decision between the grounding of a truth of beyng and the raising up of the machination of beings to a definitive predominance, because he has already, by avoiding the decision, "decided" in favor of the priority of beings. Within beings he finds everything he needs, since in fact his "needs" have long since been provoked and driven by the priority of machination. We must acknowledge that the "needs" suffocate every possibility of knowing the plight of beyng and that historically a state of affairs is arising and becoming the inversion I of that time which saw the beginning of the first truth of 5
beyng. The machination of beings (i.e., the sovereignty of beingness as machination, which compels toward "lived experience" and requires "life" as the "goal" and basic reality) can admittedly never extinguish beyng. It is just that the solitude of beyng becomes greater, the inner illumination of this solitude more unique and purer, and the possibility of the gods and humans gazing at one another more unthinkable.

In this turning back, beyng first acquires its uniqueness. And only in the high arc of a rare knowledge can a Da-sein of the human being still at times radiate in its fire. But no longer does the smoke as a sign of this fire penetrate into the sequestered infinity of the public needs of the human being, who with increasing cleverness orders his goallessness toward gigantic tasks and rolls out all his powers toward their accomplishment. In the meantime, there still remain those who question—; but is this concealed history of self-refusal of beyng a loss? By no means—quite to the contrary; the opinion that beyng would ever let itself take the place of beings, as it were, or ever only be cultivated as an "ideal," would be a I reversion to metaphysics—a meta- 6
physics that bears much further a derangement of the truth of being.

But the habituation in metaphysical "thinking" is so obstinate that we—rather than grasp essentially the originary concealedness and rarity of being—falsely turn them ever again into the unattainability of an ideal, whereas they constitute the essential occurrence of genuine history.

6

No one knows the grounding word that casts into beings the convulsion through whose intermediate grounds beyng is lit up. Or is such a word cut off by the compulsion into beings? Perhaps beings in the progressive preparation offer something more agreeable; the wholesomeness of life is rising—what would then be the purpose of beyng?

But beyng denies you such a question; so uniquely is it only itself: *the origin* [Ur-sprung] (in the sense of what allows an origination [*Ent-springen*] of the encounter of gods and humans with respect to their history-grounding essence) of *the leap* [Sprung].

7

What first originates out of beyng is nothingness—nothingness is "contemporaneous" with beyng and yet originates only out of the essence of beyng. Least of all do we grasp this that is most uncanny—the affiliation of nothingness to beyng.

But only on that basis does the human being experience the uniqueness of beyng and the contingency of all beings; only thence does he measure the uncanniness of the abandonment of beings by being—namely, that this abandonment can, in the semblance of the highest reality, lie over humans and all their productions. What does it then signify if for a people "geography" steps into the place of thoughtful questioning (i.e., into the place of philosophy)?

8

The essence of metaphysics: the being of beings transferred into a highest being—which is either the nonsensuously supersensible—or the sensuous that degrades the supersensible into a mere expression of the sensuous and into an expedient—while the metaphysics of the supersensory devalues the sensuous. (Essential: 1. the *"over and beyond to a being"*—the direction of the μετά reciprocal; 2. the genuine being equated with being itself; 3. the priority of beings as such.) (Cf. p. 55ff. and p. *99*.)

9

"Barbarity" is a prerogative of cultured peoples.

10

If amid a people there can be found several hundred "poets" and a few thousand "artists," then we can assume that from this people the power (i.e., the essential decision) for poetry and art must have withdrawn—but that is so because this people has raised the abandonment of beings by being to the supreme purpose of "life." Among those many (poets and artists) are certainly some whose "works" embody good "skill" and are borne by seriousness, such that these "works" bring consolation to many, offer pleasure, and even give support.

But—it is not enough—these are ones who branch out from a "cultural" tradition but are not ones who ground or who "begin" out of the most originary plight.

11

Stefan George and Rilke deserve esteem, but they should never be employed as aids to the interpretation of *Hölderlin*, for they are nowhere equal to or even close to his historical destiny and cannot at all be compared to him.

12

Only the most originary meditation can rescue us—*into* the plight. For the current "fortune" an escape is always already | found, even if this is only contentedness and the foregoing of excessive demands. Rescuers from the "plight"—certainly—but rescuers *into* the plight? Who are they? Those who venture into the unpaved and unformed domain of the opening up of the plight which compels in that it places on humans the excessive demand of freedom—to bear the abyss. This plight is beyng itself. (The plight "of" beyng is not a plight in which beyng is "involved" but, rather, one which it *is*.) (Cf. Ponderings IX.)

13

Does *refinement*—(i.e., originary—configurative—restriction to the essence that is first attainable in this way) arise when the refinement of the "refined ones" is made accessible in the corresponding forms to

those who were previously "unrefined"? Or thereby is not unrefinement first made into a communal "lived experience"? Will not every need to meditate on refinement be eradicated here? Why are we so far deflected from what was sought and projected as *refinement* in the age of German Idealism? Why was even that already no longer anything originary, but instead only the German attempt to master modernity in it and for it? On what ground does "refinement" belong to-
10   gether with "culture" I as the destiny of modern humanity? Why does there lie in both—precisely when they are essentially thought and willed—a suppression of the originary decisions? It is because the modern essence of the human being is already prefigured in his determination as the historiological-technological animal, whereby the avoidance of the excessive demand of the plight of beyng is already decided.

14

The thinker—is the person who projects a question that ventures the truth of beyng, without a possible support from a response, in the midst of the onrolling curiosity of those who are always unquestioning, *in such a way* that the question remains standing in itself as a salient abyss in the midst of what is well calculated, cleverly upheld, and presumably indigenous.

15

The characterization of stone, animal, and human being by way of the kind of world-relation (cf. Lecture course 1929–1930[1]) is to be maintained in its interrogative approach and yet is insufficient. The difficulty lies in the determination of the animal as "world poor"— despite the reservations and restrictions noted with regard to the concept of "poor." The proper characters are not: worldless, world poor, world forming. Instead, the more appropriate versions of the domains in question are: *fieldless and worldless, / field-dazed—worldless, / and world*
11   *forming—earth disclosing.* Thereby I the characterization of the "stone" as fieldless and worldless requires at the same time and above all a proper "positive" determination. But how is that to be had? Indeed from the "earth"—but then entirely on the basis of the "world."

---

1. {Martin Heidegger, *Die Grundbegriffe der Metaphysik: Welt-Endlichkeit-Einsamkeit,* GA29–30 (Frankfurt: Klostermann, 1983), p. 261ff.}

16

Greatness—we always take it to be what is biggest and seldom consider its essence. Two basically different "kinds" of greatness are to
be distinguished: the one that always needs the small, the opposite,
to prove itself and find itself confirmed, and the one that receives
this name only as something supererogatory, because as grounded
in itself it silently returns to the concealed beginning, does not need
proofs, and dispenses with devotees, since it manifests itself—only to
those who know—as a grounding of the truth of beyng.—If what is
small becomes ever smaller, then ultimately smallness, merely provided it is sufficiently violent and vain, must one day appear as gi-
gantically great.

17

Who still surmises the pitifulness in the fact that cultural Christianity
now supplies itself with a "collectedness" and a "renewal" on the basis
of political antagonism—i.e., on the basis of the procedure by which
this Christianity is shown immediately in its | previous cultural-po-   12
litical claim and thus mediately as faith within its limits, and that it
itself asserts its politically-culturally driven claims under the pretext
of saving the "faith"? Nothing easier and more comfortable than to be
a "Christian" today and behave like a protector of the Christian West.
Yet these supposedly spiritual and elevated attitudes do not decide
anything—and that is the reason "decision" has become a catchword
precisely here. What could be the point of a decision where the possibility of a *question*—an actually and freely posed question—is disavowed and this disavowal is made the terminus of a "decision" and
obscuration is brought into play under the mask of the saving of the
"spirit" and of "culture" in all forms? Why is "Christianity" relieved
so crudely and comprehensively of its dark dealings?
    It is because everything of today—as modern—moves on its own
soil and in its own forms and does so most obstinately when it is a
mere inversion; it is in the *modern* history of the West that Christianity
has found its possibility to be effective qua "politics" and thereby to
entrench itself in the essence of the age. | Supposedly this is the power   13
and testimony of faith and is the working of the Christian God,
whereby the "truth" of Christian doctrine is confirmed. In essence,
however, all this is merely a consequence of the abandonment of beings by being, which conditions a constant diminution of the human
essence as subjectum. One is then indeed not Christian, but one "remains" "religious" and at any given moment "invokes" the "Almighty."

Or one is "Christian" and must deny "the world" and "force" but does one's duty in the service of "culture." Each one is each thing, and all are basically "nothing" and yet are real, in that each person is "effective"—and all the helps of cultural pursuits (art—"religion"—"science" and so on) are ever refilled with changing matter.

Yet all this is merely a weak reflection of a hidden process—that of the genuine history of beyng, about which the human being can never give reports, because he is directed by it. Nevertheless, a sign: the aversion to essential meditation gives rise, in the midst of the universal lack of questioning, to the superior play of sham powers which find their rootedness only in "life" itself. The same aversion, which does not need to be expressly uttered in such a form, brings everything into
14   a decisionlessness in I whose space the apparently greatest opponents battle and yet concern themselves only with the same thing: the definitive entrenchment of the abandonment of beings by beyng. Both opponents press the modern human being into the domain of his Christian and political machinations, make him insensitive to what is question-worthy, and provide him with every sort of comfort useful for the continuation of the already long-extant "progress." Thus the human being constantly and readily adheres to what is undecidable—because in its distorted essence the same—rather than venturing to surmise that in the renunciation of all crutches and expedients within "beings," there lies no mere relinquishment, but instead the preparedness for the excessive demand of beyng.

18

The peremptory development of the *historiological* human being, i.e., the previous human being as the historiological animal, signifies the elevation of his essence to something self-evident. But his essence is the productive representation of beings in their objectivity. The ultimate consequence of the sovereignty of the historiological human being announces itself when he starts to produce his own present time as already "historiological," which means: when he starts to prepare his present time as history and, by calculating in advance, to direct its
15   insertion into remembrance and into I tradition. The consequence of this sovereignty of "historiology" over the historiological animal then brings about a complete annihilation of the possibility of a struggle regarding the originary, and the golden age of the untrammeled prerogative of sound common sense commences its "eternity." The historiological animal (having become certain of its historiological magnificence and thus now for the first time consummating Descartes's *ego cogito—ergo sum* ["I am thinking—therefore I am"]) does not need

to bear, or even only remember, what has departed into its most proper *historical* space of uniqueness. All forerunners can now be effaced, because forerunning in any case signifies only that which perhaps still obtrudes on the consummation of those who no longer have come along, obtrudes as a delusional formation. At once the so-called Germans will trample Hölderlin's work, because indeed what this supposedly romantic classicist merely yearned for has arrived long ago. The unfortunate one is denied the possibility of going along [*mitgehen*]; therefore he must perish [*"eingehen"*]. That is the law of the steps of progress in the age of the commencing a-historicality. Happy is the one who, thanks to his certainty of instinct, surmises nothing of his abjectness through the beyng that refuses itself to him.

19

16

The incomparability of the situation of thinking *after* the ending of Western metaphysics does not consist only in the question now to be asked (the question about the truth of beyng and about Da-sein) but also includes the kind of compelled discourse in the age of the modern disempowerment of the simple word. The "stance" of the thinker is such a strange one because now nothing more is given to "investigate" and because no necessity exists to gather together into "systems" things found and familiar. The sign of this is precisely the massive proliferation of "popular philosophical" and "popular theological" "systems" which all report back, merely in a different order and with different completeness, that which is decisionless and similarly unessential. *Before* all building, there must come the long passageway on which Western humans do not already within an assigned space seek the place whence the humans thrown into Da-sein depart on the way to the experience of the decision demanded of them. We are seeking first, without space, the "space" which can grant us that place in which guise beyng itself is surmisable, such that it throws itself among beings, whereby it is decided who should approach whom so that the human being might primarily experience the encounter of a self-refusal as the highest demand and might learn to think this encounter in a disclosive way.

20

17

Is it grounded in the uniqueness of beyng and in the rareness of a grounding of its truth, that as soon as beyng comes to "history" (in metaphysics) there arises the inappropriate hope to secure being just like "beings" in the sense of something objective and "given"? Or does this expectation arise only out of the importunity of the historiological animal, the one that has incurred the loss of every power to revere and every power to preserve legacies as essential demands of the origin? Must not beyng, in accord with its essential occurrence, come into its truth ever more seldom and then only to those who are ever unique? Must not history—seen from the publicness of historiology—become ever more concealed? // That seems to be flight from "reality" and should tranquilly seem so. Yet here *"is"* something else—which can be invoked only by its semblables.

21

Rather than lament the decline of culture (whence then?), rather than seek an expedient in a sham renewal of "cultural Christianity" (whither then?—into comfort and happiness?), rather than take the
18   present for "eternity" itself, only one thing is | necessary: to grasp those processes which are now drawing modernity *toward* its essential consummation. But already required thereby is to perform, on the basis of the projection that gazes forward, another sort of "seeing" than the one historiological calculation is capable of. The processes arise from the struggle of beyng with beings, and this struggle is displaced first of all into the realm within which the destruction of every concord of a truth of beyng is carried out: in the realm of the sovereignty of the "subject" striving for his historiological animality. Animality is in itself sequestration[2] against beyng; "historiology" attempts to replace this [i.e., the sequestration] through the production of "beings" without engaging in beyng and in meditation. That deepest, unendured, and never-surmised ambivalence hinders every venture into the oppositions involved in the genuine struggle. And this constant hindrance takes the form of the claim of the masses to "life" and "culture." This is nothing "political" and nothing "sociological"—instead, it is the might of animality (not as so-called sensibility) in virtue of its essential abandonment by being, which nonetheless is in-
19   stalled as the bearer | of humanity.

22

Mildness can harbor great strength, and hardness is often only a facade to cover weakness.

---

2. [Reading *Abriegelung* for *Abwiegelung*, "appeasement."—Trans.]

23

"Greatness," in the age of the complete historiological animal, must sink to the level of an everyday market commodity anyone can claim to recognize. Previously, greatness signified a reaching back into the constraints of a beginning. To want to *strive* for "greatness" is a dwarf-ish commencement. Meditation on greatness can now only have the sense of knowing that we are ever further removed from a preparation for its origination.

24

Language—only if speech has acquired the highest univocity of the word does it become strong for the hidden play of its essential multi-vocity (as withdrawn from all "logic"), of which poets and thinkers alone are capable, in their own respective modes and their own directions of sovereignty. Starting with the most proximate | verbal   20
usage, the ascending levels of the essential occurrence of the word are these: *the word designates, the word signifies, the word says, the word is*. The latter means: the word belongs to the essential occurrence of beyng itself and in that way consummates the highest fidelity to its own unique essence. But because it does this so incomparably, the levels of decline and the fall of the distorted essence are so measureless, and in accord with such proliferation they are violent enough to cover over the essence entirely and for long ages. That is why meditation on language in "linguistic philosophy" has gone astray, instead of pressing on to a rescuing of the word. The first "act" of this rescue consists in the capacity for silence, and the second in learning to hear the rare dialogue, while the third undertakes a reference to an essential word. Now, however, every endeavor so directed makes its way into the sphere of what is already written and said. And even if it raised itself out of this sphere, it would yet remain in the trammels of the usual distorted essence of language and would count, at most, as an exception. What gets stamped | in this way is already deprived of the possi-   21
bility of its genuine "effectiveness": namely, to be transformed into another basic relation to language, over and against which the supposed exception remains precisely only a preliminary groping.

25

As *subiectum*, the historiological animal is related to "itself," but in such a way that it more and more transfers its essence back into something already present-at-hand, animality—"life"—and explains "historio-

logical" comportment itself as an "organ" and "function" of life. This final step brings subjectivity to exclusive sovereignty, so that everything "egoic" and "individualizing" appears as an aberration, while the greatest violence and every fanaticism take their "good conscience" from their affiliation with the *subiectum*, the "stream of life" which flows under and through all individuation. The repudiation of the originary selfhood, on the pretext that it is egoity, does not derive from an affirmation of "community"—instead, this affirmation is itself the consequence and the last expedient of the transference of the human essence into the subjectivity of something present-at-hand—
22 which I reveals itself most basically as "life" and massiveness and justifies itself by drawing everything into itself and acknowledging no other domain whose reality would not be seen from the self-evident facts, with the result that even such a domain is an "expression" precisely of this life.

26

Hölderlin's poem, "In lovely blueness is blooming . . . ,"[3] contains in its first seventeen verses my childhood around the church tower of my Swabian homeland: the bells and the stairs to the belfry; the clockwork with its eerie weights, each of which had its own essence, when among them in the half-light of the tower the pendulum took its measured and incessant course; the sweeping view—daily—from the tower over broad land and its forests, the day and night tone of every bell—the first great gathering of my small world onto the height and essentiality of something abyssally holding sway—the old towers of the nearby castle and the mighty lindens of its spacious garden—protected an early thinking, one that did not know its whither but was
23 aware of the decidedness toward decisions I and of the ineluctable progression into the unrest of what is abyssal, a progression that gathered itself to its constancy in a single question that had to question disclosively that which is most question-worthy (the truth of beyng).

27

Philosophy displaces no one onto new mountains and peaks—but it does fathom abysses out of which what protrudes becomes visible for the first time, while the bridging over and traversing of the abysses become necessary. The fathomers of the abysses do themselves stem

---

3. {Friedrich Hölderlin, *Dichtungen—Jugendarbeiten—Dokumente, Sämtliche Werke*, vol. 6 (Berlin: Propyläen, 1923), p. 24ff.}

from high mountains—ones lit up by their own sun—; said conceptually: beyng could never be explained on the basis of beings, and beings are also never the "effect" of beyng. Unexplainable and ineffective is beyng—knowledge of that pertains to the beginning of thinking. But such knowledge signifies the opening of the *uncanniness* of beyng qua a determination of its truth—; whereby this uncanniness has nothing to do with the usual one encountered within beings.

28

The decisions about the *essence of the human being*—in which essential grounding he is to become steadfast in the future—no longer reside in the domain I of the metaphysical distinctions of body, soul, and   24
spirit; whether one of these should have priority over the others, or how their unity might be configured—; the decisions open up something more originary: whether the essence of the human being decisively unfolds or not *on the basis of the relation to being;* whether this relation (as ontological understanding—i.e., what is indicated in *Being and Time* as the projection of the truth of being) manifests its abyssal character and holds the human being in meditation on that character or not. Whether Da-sein as the future point of departure of another history is grounded or not; whether the human being breaks his subjectivity or definitively entrenches it; whether the question of the human being is asked only as and out of the question of beyng or everything again falls back into anthropological self-appraisal.

Accordingly, as long as we speak only of "decisions" by and about the human being, decisions which occur within the traditional "essence" (*animal rationale*) that is more and more falling into the distorted essence, then the word "decision" is not a word but a figure of speech merely covering over the fact that one wants to go *back* into what is already decided and held as long-since decided—whether this be Christianity and thus the I salvation of the immortal individual   25
soul for a heaven beyond, or whether it be something already decided with the *animal rationale* but not yet brought to its end, namely, the immersion of the human essence into the "stream of life" as such and into what is most graspable of it, blood, and the concomitantly given unleashing of *ratio*[4] as pure calculation and planning—yet could not a "struggle" over these decisions in what has long been decided bring to the fore the truth that within the sphere of the sovereignty of Western metaphysics no genuine decisions are possible any longer—in other words, is there still possible a digression of the human being

---

4. [Latin word.—Trans.]

onto a more originary ground assigning him to the plight of beyng? It could be—but just as possible is that this "struggle" might definitively suppress that truth, without the loss—as such—surmised by the humans who endure the struggle. Is that truth thereby eliminated? In no way. But it is deferred to the time when beyng casts its most proper, longest, and widest shadow (namely, nothingness) over the all too correct correctness of those who are decisionless and over their all too advanced results and shows their artificial super-brilliance and cleverness as the devastation of the yet remaining beings.

26   This overshadowing of beings by nothingness—the latter is separated by an abyss from the common understanding of it—is first and properly seen only by those whose essential gaze is already struck by the most remote shining of beyng. But this shining now no longer guarantees only the presence of beings, insofar as they have in general emerged as such—but now beyng essentially occurs as the ungrounded "between" for the self-encountering essential disclosures of the gods and humans. Beyng is liberated from the danger of adherence to beings and is sent back into its most proper plight, from which it compels to the essential disclosure; out of the event of this disclosure, the space-time for beings first arises.

The liberation of the human being from "historiology" in the metaphysical sense happens not through some sort of calculation of its advantage or disadvantage *for "life,"* but through an overcoming of all metaphysics. This overcoming eliminates every possibility that beings might thrust themselves forward immediately—in whatever form, such as that of "life"—and "assert" themselves as the domain, measure, and source of needs, claims, and goals.

27   *29*

The *historiological animal* must finally arrive at the calculation and justification of its animality and of the needs and instincts of that animality and thus at a reciprocal interpenetration of historiology-technology with animality. The human being thereby becomes more and more accustomed to taking his goals from the acts of possessing and satisfying. Nonpossession appears to him as a lack, and everything requiring renunciation or even postulating the relation to the renounced as an essential ground of the human being must seem to him reprehensible and a denial of "the" (i.e., *his*) life. Yearning (even the not sentimental one for the *disclosive questioning* of what is most questionworthy) appears as weakness or as blindness, over and against the already acquired possession. A simple decidedness in favor of what refuses itself is something the historiological animal cannot appraise as that which alone seems to him worthy of possession—i.e., as *power*. The *historiological animal* does not know the essence of power—because this animal—in subjection to metaphysics—understands power as a being (present-at-hand force)—rather than as the preservation of beyng itself, and that preservation can overthrow nothing, because it is itself the field of all thrownness.

We are determining the human being not as the "historiological" human being, but as the *historiological animal*. The historiological human being is the one prevented by historiology from becoming attentive to the essence of historiology and from admitting the assignment of historiology to animality as essential ground.   28

30

What delays, if not indeed destroys, the essential decisions (the transitions into a historical beginning) is today's universally increasing "refined" Christianity which is not hesitant to appropriate even un-Christian and anti-Christian impulses, formulas, and timely figures of speech and with this insidious concoction produces a supposed testimony to the "truth" of Christian faith for those who are mediocre and famished. One never becomes rude and always remains sly; one avoids all tastelessness and is always ready to "affirm" at the right time whatever is in season. One is "open" to everything great, precisely so as to eliminate and not let appear (perhaps unwittingly) the basic condition of all greatness: namely, the passage through essential decisions.

The danger of Christianity consists not in its beliefs and in its proffered "truth," but rather in the ambiguity of its affirmation of this world and its hope in a beyond. This ambiguity is tacitly raised to a principle, and one or the other side is preferred according to circumstances. The playing with this ambiguity, in which one can be everything to both halves, leaves no room for a disclosive questioning of that which the historiological animal in the time of metaphysical history has always kept aloof from as the most self-evident, namely, the question-worthiness of beyng.   29

31

If there are signs that modernity is now elapsing in a lengthy end state, one that does not exclude "progress," then these signs consist in the process of the flight of all yet "refined" and "devout" "powers" into Christianity, if indeed not into the "Churches." The genuine renunciation of the will to the beginning is not the much-feared "barbarity" but instead is this "rescuing" of the "highest cultural values."

32

Why do the Germans grasp with so much difficulty and so slowly that they lack the *chaos* they would need to arrive at their essence and that "chaos" is not confusion and blind | ferment but is rather the yawning of that abyss which compels a grounding? Why do the Germans ever again allow themselves to be led astray (through "cultural politics" on the one hand and "cultural deliverances" on the other) into "mandates" which are not in fact such but instead are palmed-off goals of modern history, in the pursuit of which no one and nothing can stay behind? Why do the Germans grow more and more into the "void" of what is usual and easily attained, and why not into the darkness of their roots—of their poetizing and thinking, i.e., of a grounding into the ungrounded? It is because these things require a *passion for the plight* and a disclosive questioning of what is most question-worthy.

Indeed we readily fall into error here insofar as we believe the beginning would have to set in, as it were, at an appointed hour and simultaneously everything previous to it would be repudiated and overcome. Such an idea could perhaps be justified if the beginning began with a particular being and its establishment. But the beginning is in fact an origination of the truth of beyng and will therefore not only tolerate but will even demand previous beings in their still | extant sovereignty. Thus even the flight into what previously was and the pressing on toward progress can placidly pursue what they want—the beginning is not thereby affected—although the transition into the preparation for its grounding in beings can be delayed and even destroyed.

The historiology of beings can cover over the history of beyng and keep that history far from the purview of humans—but it can never affect the act of beginning as such. On the other hand, the beginning can be prevented, on the basis of its history, from transforming historiology; the possibility exists that historiology might seize upon the intimations of the beginning (intimations that are not understood, i.e., not grasped in their truth) and might reckon up all things according to its own developments and valuations, i.e., immediately transform everything into something past which has been overcome—(the beginning as the "primitive"). With respect to the history of beyng, all meditation on the currently notable age has the one single goal of keeping the incomparability of the beginning and of its plight from getting mixed up with the age, and not what might readily be thought, deriving the decisions of the beginning from the needs of the age.

30

31

For a beginning arises only in an inceptual struggle with a begin-   32
ning—and in case the beginning must be the first, its origin is the
struggle over the act of beginning as such; i.e., its origin is the first poetic-thoughtful awakening to being, and this awakening, in accord
with this first beginning, becomes precisely the apprehension of beings as such. But now because beings have thrust themselves into a
priority that was strengthened in metaphysics, i.e., became self-evident, the history of the first beginning altogether relegated the inceptual to forgottenness, so that the act of beginning is currently as alien
as it was previously in the first beginning. Insofar as the question of
being, as the question of the truth of beyng, *is asked* and is no longer
eradicated—but at most forgotten—the other beginning has then
found itself—although it is at first unprotected against the pressing
offshoots of metaphysics. Consequently, the other beginning is *either*
misinterpreted in terms of "epistemology"—as if at issue were only
the question of the conditions of the possibility of ontological understanding. This interpretation, kept within its limits (cf. Kantbook[5]),
can contain a mediate reference to the originariness of the question,
although it is more readily mistaken as an adoption of transcendental   33
philosophy, even if "transcendence," as transformed, is taken back up
into Da-sein. Every historiological comparison contains as many ab-
errations as references—but in truth is never equal to what it is supposed to accomplish, namely, historical transformation. *Or,* on the
other hand, the beginning (out of the question of the truth of beyng)
is misinterpreted in terms of the "philosophy of existence"—insofar
as this question encloses the grounding of Da-sein and the transformation of the previous essence of the human being; but this suggests
itself more readily as a kind of "ethics" and "muster," especially if, as
in *Being and Time,* the concept of "existence" is still employed. Yet neither the appeal to "transcendence" nor the invocation of "existence"
was to be renounced when in general some sort of bridge of understanding (not mere agreement) was to be slung and especially when
the genuine seeking wanted to maintain a steady course—such a
course must always hold out the possibility of self-clarification in the
overcoming and twisting free. The danger of stagnation is unavoidable, and an inceptual configuration impossible out of what is seen in
advance at the start.

Of course, what is also denied the moment the essential occurrence   34
of the truth of beyng (as the clearing, grounded in Da-sein, of the self-

---

5. {Martin Heidegger, *Kant und das Problem der Metaphysik,* GA3 (Frankfurt:
Klostermann, 1991).}

refusing event of appropriation) comes to be experienced is any possibility of attempting a configuration in the forms of the previous communication and presentation, because these forms, as thoroughly
"metaphysical," either "exhibit" or "invoke"—i.e., lose themselves
in—the "transcendental conditions" or in "existence," whereas the essential occurrence of beyng itself is supposed to come into the *open domain* of a knowledge which is at once useless and goalless—since this
domain is the abyss pertaining to beyng and tolerating no compulsion. Quite to the contrary, the abyss demands the grounding of the
respectively different affiliation of the gods and humans to itself.

33

"Heroism" is alien to heroes, for it would indeed encapsulate them in
an ontological mode lying over their essence as a fixed ideal—whereas
their being opens itself to something unique and abyssal and in face
of these riches becomes simple and ever more reticent and inaccessible to every platitude of praise and oratory. Only to heroes is a hero
35   an insoluble | mystery; the others understand everything and drag
everything into the publicness of what is historiological.

34

Historiology—taken *metaphysically*—i.e., as belonging intrinsically to
metaphysics—is *one* single immuring of every space-time for an accord of the self-refusal of beyng. The calculation of the advantage
and disadvantage of "historiology" (in the stricter sense of the relation to the past) for "life" does not at all pose the decisive question of
the relation of the historiological objectification of beings as such to
the truth of beyng, and thus no originary position toward "historiology" is thereby attained.

35

Why does the young Nietzsche already name the folklorist Riehl, who
in the meantime became the "classic" of the future configuration of
the human sciences, an—**"old maid"**?[6] Perhaps because Nietzsche

---

6. {Friedrich Nietzsche, *Jenseits von Gut und Böse,: Vorspiel einer Philosophie der
Zukunft, Werke*, vol. 7 (Stuttgart: Kröner, 1921), p. 148. There Nietzsche speaks of
the "scholar" as an "old maid." A passage referring in this sense to Wilhelm Hein-
rich Riehl (1823–1897) could not be found.}

thinks in opposition to "the people "? No—on the contrary, because he knows and insists that our concept of the people cannot be sufficiently essential and high and must not be drawn from the banality and good-natured character of folkloric "research." Who would want even today to speak against the innocent, | neat, and perhaps indeed   36
useful pursuits of "folklore" as the basic human science, i.e., the basic science of the "spirit," and begrudge researchers (at a loss for objects of this science) of an erstwhile "philosophical" faculty the prospect of an inexhaustible field of new and remunerative investigations into a distorted essence? This may all remain so and may at the same time be joined to ethnological questions—and develop into typologies and the like and in that way serve the "people" and produce a new flowering of a finally attained science that is "close to the people"—enough if at one place or another an essential human being can still meditate on the fact that *thereby* nothing is decided about the essence of the people, because the will and basic disposition toward meditation on the essence of the Germans have been suppressed—through the preconception that such is out of the question. But—the aim of showing that Folkish [*Völkisch*] being is the goal for a people—is that then an aim at all and not rather its destruction? And what then is the significance of the subsequent scientific concern over the already decided and unproblematic concept of the people? The maiden-aunt quality of this well-intentioned pursuit, in which | even the unavoidable ca-   37
reerists find their place, is, if anything, surpassed by its conventionality, which provokes a placid smile at every attempt to meditate. But the decision is this:

For a volition aimed at the Populist [*Volkhaft*] being of humans—assuming this is indeed a matter of "will"—can "the people" ever be the goal, the domain, the object of concern, the object of lore and research, and be this in an exclusive sense? For a people to "become" a "people," must not this people first *be* itself in *essence,* and for it to belong to this being, must not a way get paved on which for the first time a people, through its reticent heroes, might attain for itself by struggle its affiliation to beyng as what is most question-worthy for that people? What if the merely straightforward—folkish [*völkisch*]—volition were simply the last offshoot of that modern humanity which, in accord with the postulation of the human being as the subjectum, forecloses all meditation on, and every leap into, the interrogative affiliation with beyng? What if that which, *prior* to the excessive demand of an intimation and word, must be drawn out of beyng and inserted into its essence, namely, the people of the Germans—makes itself into a "myth" in what | is first to be attained through the truth of beyng and   38 thereby transformed—without the facile and "refined" escape into Christianity? What is fatal here is not some particular doctrine, but instead the *mode* of "thinking," a mode which is nothing other than (calculated into the gigantism of the body of the people) the *cogito ergo sum* of Descartes in the form, *ego non cogito, ergo sum* ["I am *not* thinking, therefore I am"]; because subjectivity as populist [*volkhaft*] has become gigantic, it creates the sham impression of pure objectivity, an impression in fact belonging to it but at the same time strengthening the preconception that in such a way all beings would be encompassed and determined—which finds expression in the adoption of the metaphysical doctrines of wholeness with their different varieties. This "mode of thinking" debars all meditation on *the exposedness to the self-refusal of beyng*—because it believes beings themselves are preserved in the possession of the highest certainty. This mode of thinking can change only if once again there are questioners who do not proclaim "truths" but instead testify to the question-worthiness of beyng itself. Yet all of this is not a matter simply of a—our—individual "people"—but rather constitutes *the* | question of Western history itself, the question to which we can be equal only on the basis of an assignment to what is *inceptual,* the question whose mastery is assisted not by any renewal of the past or by any refined wallowing in all the beautiful possessions of bygone "cultures," but only by the long, persistent questioning that does not shun that which refuses itself, the questioning of where and how the modern human being arrives at an essential transformation that snatches him from anthropomorphization and makes him mature for the abysses of beyng.

39

The issue is not that the people might become an idol or that the people might be delivered over to the dead God of Christianity—i.e., to his "Churches." On the contrary, the issue is whether, out of the people, there might come forth those futural individuals who first establish a preparedness for the decision between the gods and humans (a preparedness that would constitute the basic disposition leading into the history of the Germans), on the basis of knowing that the history of *beyng* (beyng as the spatiotemporal field of this decision) happens simply, rarely, and in long silence, on that side of happiness and unhappiness and on this side of advantage and disadvantage. The most proximate decision: which Western people is capable of developing and above all enduring *a completely other mode of thinking on the basis of beyng,* over and against all metaphysics and myth, and has this capability by preconfiguring it | in itself, i.e., in its precursors.

40

In the interim, the "people" must be satisfied, as before, with the modifications of the past, i.e., must constantly be confirmed in its unproblematic needs, for "the people" as a whole is incapable of "think-ing" and therefore cannot ever transform a mode of thought, but can always only entrench and use up a mode that has already burst forth, within the domains of which the people can provide itself with its "happiness"—seen from here, the education of the people into the his-torical animal has in large part a "historiological" necessity. The fact that "life" mostly does not bother about these decisions, that it, unaf-fected by them, everywhere still bestows its charm and its radiance, and in due course retracts them and just as often restores the burden and worry, revels in victories, bears up with defeats, secures a little happiness, averts unhappiness, and sees the brave and the cowardly—the fact that everything remains as it "is" and as it at all times seems to be—these circumstances do not speak *against* the decisions between beings and beyng or against the history of those who are excluded on account of it. On the contrary, such circumstances are merely the clearest witnesses *for* the uniqueness | of beyng, beyng which cedes   41 its preservation to the "life" of the historiological human being only in the mode of *the forgottenness of being.* This forgottenness is so origi-nary that it can never forget itself, not because it constantly remem-bers the forgottenness, but because it has fallen out of all *retention* in such a way that retention can never fall to it—; for even where it rec-ollects being, in such ἀνάμνησις ["recollection"] it turns being itself into an ὄν ["individual being"]—so strictly is the human person, as soon as he has become an "animal," i.e., a "soul" (ψυχή), prepared for and delivered over to *beings* and only to them. Christianity has an easy task with this person, and an even easier task with him has the his-toriological-technological instituting of humanity as "culture"—and as "affirmation" of "life."

36

Of what avail is all progress, all invention, all historiologically bound-less mixing and reworking of all cultural productions into ever other and "new" offshoots; of what avail is the massive frenzy of humans and even the subduing of the human masses into forms that operate reliably; of what avail is all arming and breeding—if the human be-ing is no longer granted any god | and if the human being forgets more   42 and more profoundly that the history of his Western culture consists in the fact that no more gods are granted to him? It is not as if he could "fabricate" them—; for the gods to be granted, something more is re-quired: the originariness of the affiliation to being, such that being it-self (not the fabricating human being) necessitates gods in their essence and indicates a turning toward the human being, who is not to be relieved of the gods, but the reverse—is to strike up against them in his concealed essence.

The historiological human being still has little capacity for knowledge, so little that to him the realization once suffered by Hölderlin and attained by Nietzsche in his own way (two millennia and not a single god[7]) cannot become a matter of knowledge and he can find nothing in it, except for an exaggerated and merely negative observation, over which it does not "pay" to tarry for a long time and certainly not *incessantly*. If a meditation happened here, then an hour would have to arrive in which this apparent observation changed into the

43   question of who then is a god. But this | question is not a "theological" one—on the contrary, it is at most the bane of all "theologies," that know themselves best secured in the domain of the machination of beings, i.e., in the sphere of the historiological animal.

Who is the—a god? What denominative power can the human being still impart to this name? Does he invoke this name only as a vague expedient on the occasion of fortuitous needs and gratifications—in the latter case for confirmation and explanation, in the former for deliverance and consolation?—Does the human being believe he can have a "lived experience" of the gods *most immediately* when he troubles them over his "lived experiences"—and directly relates the gods to himself and thus himself to them—? When will he grasp that the gods are separated from him by the long bridge of beyng and remain referred to their own essence—? The historiological animal will never grasp this and will always strive in some form or other to include his "God" as a "factor" in calculating his fortunes and misfortunes, his successes and defeats. Therefore even the "historiological" human being will be able to demonstrate easily and convincingly that

44   that remark by Nietzsche and the Da-sein of Hölderlin are | errors, since indeed other Great men, especially Goethe, had very well "experienced" what is "divine," and since anyone may now find opportunities enough for such "lived experiences."

An interrogative dialogue with the historiological animal regarding that question will not be possible, since this historiological animal is indeed at the same time the ideal form of the "theologian"—and where are the gods "sublated" better than in theology?

God has as little in common with "religiosity" and "theology" as has philosophy (the thinking of beyng) with "culture."

---

7. {Friedrich Nietzsche, *Der Fall Wagner, Götzen-Dämmerung, Nietzsche contra Wagner, Umwerthung aller Werte I (Antichrist), Dichtungen, Werke*, vol. 8 (Stuttgart: Kröner, 1919), p. 235f.: "Nearly two millennia and not a single new god!"}

37

If we bypass all provisional works in the history of thinking, the intricacies of "science," the supplementary additions and developments, the contingency of contemporary communication, and the unavoidable historical origination, and if we direct our gaze only toward the place something essential is thought, i.e., questioned, then this history is a temporary flaring up of an illumination cast over the truth of being and over the being of truth—primarily in the form of an interpretation of beings as such.—I Illuminations creating a clearing   45
which appears to be almost groundless and again threatens to collapse under the pressure of self-evident beings in their convergence—clearings in the midst of beings—expressed in a few felicitous dicta and propositions—the remainder, however, is for the historiologists and psychologists. Why do those clearings remain as *remote* as they are rare in opening up? They are the concealed bridges on which the gods and the human being encounter one another and, as turned *toward* one another in the indigence of beyng, burst *forth* into the development of *their* essence; the encounter in the clearing (which is beyng itself) traverses the abyssal character of beyng and preserves beyng in its richest solitude. But here is the origin of beings—i.e., of the fact that the world opens up and the earth is closed and each thing comes to stand in the clearing—provided the human being is able, as that encountering one, to *be* the "there" and from the spatiotemporal field of this "there" to see the structure of beings and to become the steward of the clearing which remains as long as it refuses itself, i.e., as long as its abyss compels into the plight of the grounding I and denies   46
to the human being, *as* the one assigned to beyng, every comfort in his own fabrications and thus bestows on him the height of his essence which finds itself in its beginning as it is appropriated by beyng itself. This concealed and authentic history does not happen, however, in a realm beyond and apart—but rather in and as the clearing of beings which always remains, to all who are turned toward beings, something invisible and nonexistent.

38

The thinking that is heedful of the history of being is inceptual inasmuch as it prepares a beginning by thinking disclosively of beginnings alone. But "beginnings" are not here historiologically "exhibited" and certainly not explained—no beginning admits of that—; calculated historiologically, every beginning is a pure "fabrication"—but the apparent arbitrariness of the disclosive thinking changes at once into

the unique and authentic necessity deriving from the plight of being. The disclosive thinking directed at the first beginning—at the saying of being as φύσις—is not a belated attempt to transfer oneself "historiologically" into something earlier; on the contrary, it occurs as this beginning itself, which indeed does not simply pass over (and certainly not constantly submerge in the past) everything following after
47   it as start | and advancement, but instead inserts itself ever more decisively and unavoidably into the future decision of thinking as the disclosive questioning of beyng. The beginning of the truth of beyng—the fact that beyng would be grounded in its own open domain—can be thought only in the history of beyng—; the imperishability of beyng within and for this history consists, however, in its unavoidability. The more essential the beginning becomes and the more necessary is ever again another beginning, all the more inceptual becomes the first—all the more invincibly does its uniqueness emerge and all the more purely shine forth.

And everything here says only the one thing: being cannot be explained through beings—nowhere does it "have" an origin, since it itself is the *origin*, the *primal leap*, which must submit inceptually and at the earliest to the predominance of the beings arisen from it, because it lets all of them sink into nullity once they have been entrenched in the abandonment by being. Nonetheless, beings arise from beyng in such way that by *not entering* into its abyss they remain in a
48   mere presence and in the constancy of what is | present-at-hand. The arising is not a derivation from something or other, and therefore neither can beings be explained through being. The origin, the primal leap, is rather the inceptual fissure—the clearing which comes into things that were previously closed and undivided and in itself essentially occurs as this open domain—(ἀλήθεια). The origin is neither the cause of the arising nor the supreme condition of a judgmentally transcendental positing in the sense, e.g., of Fichte's absolute idealism—the origin cannot be thought *metaphysically*, because indeed metaphysics (i.e., its prevalent and as such already forgotten truth of being itself) is already something originated.

The origin can be originated only in the sense of a self-beginning disclosive thinking. The origin as the beginning fissure (clearing) is disclosively thought in the origin as the pure originating which cannot creep up to a beginning step by step under the guideline of the cause-effect relation. In the thinking that is heedful of the history of beyng, the notion of origin is ambiguous—according to the respective
49   task, the expression has the one meaning, without forgetting | the other, even if not explicitly naming it. The origin is inceptual, is the

beginning, not inasmuch as something else follows after it, but inasmuch as the *clearing* is that attack on what is closed and undecided which shifts this into the abyss and so into the plight of grounding. Yet the closed and undecided "is" not even nothingness—and lies instead on this side of nothingness. Calculatively thought, nothingness is "more" than that, because nothingness already requires beyng. But "beginning" and "origin" never allow of "definition," because the thinking that is heedful of the history of beyng knows from the first their abyssal character; the univocity of the expression of such thinking consists in the steadfastness of the questioning that does not deny the bifurcation of beyng but, instead, appertains to the wealth of beyng. This wealth always unveils itself to the genuine thinking aimed at what cannot be grounded in that which is simple. Yet such unveiling first and only lets the self-refusal come into its proper clearing.

If origins are so rare in the history of beyng, how rare would they then be within the brief history of an individual thinker? Perhaps the latter history is often then I only a constant approach run which never   50
comes to the take-off point for the leap but all the more easily comes into the danger of taking the approach run for the leap itself and maintaining that what is experienced in that run is the essential and calculating it into the historiology of previous thinking. So that this basic delusion might never become too powerful, futural thinking must ever again go past mere beings (the objects of the historiological animal) and traverse them by questioning into them, though to be sure without ever expecting the origin from them. Only that which we enter into can become something we can truly go past—in order to initiate the leap.

The origin, the primal leap, as the inceptual fissure of the clearing for the encounter of gods and humans, can also be thought in the sense that it allows this encounter to arise, although of course not in the manner of a *cause*. Instead, the clearing, in which the encounter first finds its abode and course, is the origin, and what originates from it is then precisely that which takes up the plight of the clearing and remains as a leap—in other words, encloses the appropriation in the perseverance of I its own essence.—   51

They call this "word philosophy" as mere playing with the meaning of words and do not surmise that this alleged insult could already be a token of great esteem—; if they surmised even only a little of the word and of its affiliation to beyng, since beyng itself and only it— that clearing—is *word;* and only because the human being *can* ground therein his most inceptual essence, namely, the attaining of the stewardship of the truth of beyng, and because his essence is distinguished, i.e., delimited, by the relation to beyng, therefore he can take the word and "have" "language" (discourse)—(λόγον ἔχειν). But the word does not first become word through utterance—on the contrary, it is the reverse—the human being can take beyng only in the word, because beyng is in itself word—. But what does "word" mean here? The sounding of the word is already an echo of that *leap*—the word is in essence the *fissure* of the clearing, i.e.,—the silent ringing out of the rending of that fissure of the clearing—, whose open realm first grounds all "signifying" and allows the spoken word, as genuine, in each case to open up beyng. That "leap" of the origin, i.e., the leap of the primal leap—beyng as appropriating event—is the silence itself out of which alone a sounding is able I to come and in which a sounding is able to remain. That fissure is the primal word itself; only the anthropomorphizing of the human being into the historiological animal believes it can explain the word (according to meaning and sound) phonetically-physiologically and psychologically as something "spiritual" and "sensuous."

The thinking of beyng that is heedful of the history of beyng does not extract a meaning out of snatched-up vocables, in order to proffer this meaning as the "thing itself"; instead, it takes beyng itself in the word and ventures, out of the origin, to win back for the word its homeland. But does not everything verbal always mean some being or other?—Certainly—and nevertheless this is superficial and illusionary due to the long and essential misunderstanding of the word as language and due to the consequent misinterpretation of language through "grammar," aesthetics, and theology—(i.e., in brief: through the *metaphysical* misinterpretation). For the essence of the word is the truth of beyng and is not the belonging of the word to a *language,* one determined on the basis of the experience of the speaking animal. And this determination remains prescriptive even where λόγος is conceived as gathering and unifying—in the sense of the addressing of something as something—and the relation to being remains concealed and, moreover, so does the fact that being itself is the primal word. To take beyng in the word means to say beyng itself as word; I this saying as Da-sein is the essential occurrence of the truth of beyng and thus is beyng itself in its appropriating eventuation. Language is the pronouncement of the word and is grounded in the word; it is not the case that words first arise through language.

Yet what is alone ineffable is that which is to be said, to be instituted in poetizing, to be disclosively thought in thinking—beyng is self-refusal and is ineffable in the word qua word. But language as pronouncement of the word (i.e., pronouncement of beyng) speaks

out of the relation to *beings,* which are already encountered through the unspoken word as such—; and all the "vocables" of language which do not immediately mean beings then signify a relation between beings—drawn out things—abstract things. Through language, words become vocables. The essence of the word lies in the silence of the leap, the silence which, broken in speech, is transformed into the interpretation of an inceptual naming, into the word as a possible possession of language. But because the word says, and is, beyng, it intrinsically bears the structure of beyng itself, a structure previously covered over by language (and by the opinions that think concomitantly with it) and expressed in "categories," in accord with the predominance of metaphysics. (The attempt to distinguish between "categories" and I "existentialia" in *Being and Time* does not go far enough.   54
For a thinking which is heedful of the history of being, the categories fall completely within the sphere of metaphysics, and such thinking is over and done with metaphysics. The "existentialia" are indeed related to Da-sein and thus exclusively to the question of the truth of beyng. Nevertheless, they are not thought originarily enough out of the essential occurrence of beyng, and so it seems they are supposed to take over the place and role of categories of Da-sein. And precisely that is *not* intended, but the affiliation of the existentialia to the truth of being is scarcely visible, because everything is still arranged too much on the basis of the tradition and in an attempt to overcome it at the same time.)

The basic experience of the thinking that is heedful of the history of beyng is now intensifying: for the discourse enjoined upon this thinking, the previous language is impotent, whereby the "previous language" refers to the developed, already long ago pre-coined conceptual discourse of Western thinking. But at the same time every word of *our* language (the *other* thoughtful language after the first one of the Greeks) arises out of the disclosive thinking of beyng, into its clearing, and toward its originary power of denomination. The ground of this is simple: the thinking "of" beyng must with its first steps be in bondage to the essence of the word, I since such thinking disclo-   55
sively thinks the origin as event of appropriation and becomes steadfast in the truth of this origin, while in the sphere of such beings another history commences. For, now what is questioned is no longer merely the beingness of otherwise and in advance acknowledged and pregiven beings and their objectivity; on the contrary, placed into question are beings themselves and the truth in which they are pregiven and above all *the fact that* they are pregiven as protrusive—placed into question in the sense of the history of beyng, and that sense re-

quires a transition into an age of beyng, entirely foreign to the metaphysical age.—

39

The modern *form of metaphysics* attains its consummate development
in Hegel and in Nietzsche (apparently opposed, they are the same).
Grasped universally, "life" as the unconditioned (the absolute spirit—
the all-encompassing life incarnate [*das leibende Allleben*]) should become the "origin" for all beings, which are established in the main
configurations of culture (religion—art—morality). Thereby either
life, as absolute thinking, is the condition of the possibility of the absolute objectivity of beings as things that have become fixed and crave
permanence—or "life" requires only fixed things (qua beings) in
56   order I to overcome itself in each case in its growing beyond itself and
turning back into itself—similar to the fixed levels and steps on which
life stands in "coming to be" and passing away in order at once to destroy them again, i.e., to demolish every objectivity and to start the
flow of pure life. Hegel is the modern absolutely subjective-objective
Platonism which has imbibed Christian dogmatics; Nietzsche is the
inversion of *this* Platonism under the exclusion, or inversion, of everything Christian. Both, in their oppositional affiliation, constitute the
consummation of Western metaphysics.

The oppositionality, however, results from two circumstances: *on
the one hand,* the fact that both—despite their apparent and at the same
time respectively different ways of overcoming Descartes—are
grounded on the *subiectum,* except that they grasp it as *absolute* life; to
this corresponds the postulation of beings as the fixed and settled objects of representation, these objects taken up in the sense of the entire domain of history and nature in their natural-historical and his-
toriological-natural becoming. *On the other hand,* the possible inversion
of Platonism ushers in the second oppositionality. This inversion is almost compelled negatively by Hegel's basic position and is proximally I
57   prepared by the sovereignty of positivism. The philosophies of both
Hegel and Nietzsche are metaphysics, because beings are postulated
in their beingness in light of *thinking* as the guideline for the determination of the "is."—For Hegel, what counts is absolute thinking, which
forms the three intrinsically echeloned basic possibilities of the subject-object relation as a relation to itself and thus as a relation beyond
itself into the whole of the previous relations to the basic structure of
thinkability and thoughtful determination. For Nietzsche, the beingness of beings is likewise related to "judgment," but this latter is not,

as a simple assertion of immediate thinking, sublated into the mediation of absolute thought but instead is taken back into the stream of life as a necessity of life on account of its mere serviceability and so is indeed likewise made something unconditioned.

The question of the truth of beyng—thus here the question of whether the essence of beyng can be determined on the basis of thinking as recollection or whether this interpretation is only an already belated and very superficial characterization of the ἰδέα and οὐσία— is not asked, because it lies outside of the interrogative possibilities of metaphysical thinking and its intention, namely, to understand "beings" in terms of "life" (becoming) and to rescue becoming itself as the basic reality and thereby to calculate and dominate, by way of representation and production, the totality of | what can be thought and   58 experienced. The genuine "beings" (as life) are equated with "being" itself (as life), and thereby the priority of beings is confirmed and indeed in that coinage which was grounded in the first beginning by Heraclitus and Parmenides and consequently in a very different way than everything "Platonic." (Cf. above, p. 7.)

This pondering over the modern consummation of Western metaphysics would not be one, i.e., would lack meditative decision as a determining ground, if it were taken only as a historiological "typology" of two "figures" of metaphysics and as setting down and thus setting aside the past, be it for the sake of examination and erudite research, be it for the sake of a supposedly exemplary synchronic view. Instead, here the consummation of modern metaphysics is experienced as the *history* already prevailing far in advance over us and under us. The reality of this history has still hardly come into play, although it has intruded in a way characteristic of the sovereignty of the modern age— since, in other words, that which today in the current decades of the twentieth century asserts itself, in manifold variations and malformations, as "beings," "life," and | "reality" is a tangled mixture of Hege-   59 lian and Nietzschean metaphysics.

That does not refer to the erudite renewals of Hegel's philosophy which only come *after* this process or to the imitations of Nietzsche's thoughts and positions—on the contrary, precisely the common, everyday, public representation and evaluation of beings is borne— without needing to know it explicitly—by that consummation of metaphysics. The concealed historical power of the deep-seated affiliation between Hegel and Nietzsche derives from Leibniz's metaphysics— admittedly in the form of the crude and wide-meshed vulgarization which has been its lot since Herder and Goethe. The consummation of Western metaphysics is therefore a thoroughly German necessity in which Descartes, as well as the Platonism and Aristotelianism of the West, and thus also the spiritual realms of the Middle Ages and of the cultural Christianity of modernity, are amalgamated into a last stroke of metaphysical thinking.

What today is *real*—whether seen in terms of politics and "worldview" or in terms of "cultural historiology" or Christian denominations—has its ground in this one reality of modern German metaphysics. Our reality does not consist in the palpable presence of | 60 motor vehicles and airplanes and not in the organizations of the body of the people—instead, what is closest and most effective and thus *not* palpable is the interpretation of beings in the horizon of modern metaphysics. This interpretation is consummated in the sovereignty of being [*Sein*] in such a way that this being, as machination, withdraws into forgottenness in favor of the beings it prevails over, which are then taken as the "real" and effective; cf. Hegel's basic concept: being as *reality* [*Sein als* Wirklichkeit]! Because the metaphysical reality has now become quite unrecognizable, although it bears everything and provides all perspectives and measures and thus is least experienceable, therefore in the current age "closeness to reality" has become an explicit demand and an object of planning and of activity. The public human being, mad for lived experience and close to reality, least of all sees what is genuinely real, i.e., effective, what indeed thoroughly bears him and directs his steps. It would also be mistaken for this human being to want to calculate historiologically an influence of Hegel's or Nietzsche's philosophy on the present age. Meditation on the historical consummation of Western metaphysics and on the first ending of the West is a plight and a necessity only for those who are transitional—who today must ineluctably be those that are crossed over because they themselves are the transition and no longer "keep pace" with the time—not because they | limp behind it but because they are 61 thrown in advance of it, not as ones who ground and herald, but rather as ones who prepare and question.

They first create the space-time within which the history of the ending of modernity, a history borne by metaphysics, is brought before the *decision:* whether the abandonment of beings by being, carried to an extreme in modernity, will degrade the human being in mere anthropomorphizing and assure him an endless duration there, or whether being will become the plight, in which guise it might essentially occur in its concealment and whether this plight will bestow the freedom of an inceptual grounding of beings in the simplicity of their essence. Only from recognizing this decision can metaphysics be placed historically into knowledge and its consummation be experienced as the effective reality of today's modernity.

40

Modern science and the university. (Concerning the lecture on the ground-ing of the modern world-picture through metaphysics[8]). One now fears the transition of the university into a trade school, i.e., into a collection of such schools. At bottom, however, one is only afraid of seeing | what—in essence—already *is*. One sees in this transition a   62 lowering of the dignity of the university; i.e., one presumes to at-tribute to the university a dignity it hardly ever had. Yet this very late enthusiasm for the *high* vocation of the university is only the last off-shoot of the endeavors to uphold the previous "spiritual" and "refined" pursuit of culture. In truth, everything here undertaken rests on a lack of clear thinking. One believes thereby that the university is slip-ping down into a mere trade school, that it is dissolving into a research institution which cuts itself off from "theory" and from "theoretical" activity. Yet it is not the exclusion of theory but precisely the "align-ment" of theory to usefulness that conditions and justifies the exis-tence of the trade school. The preservation of the unity of research and theory does not signify any protection from a "sinking down" into a trade school; on the contrary, the unity of research with theory merely accelerates the sinking, even if the research receives the same goal of the calculation, exploitation, and ordering of beings as does the theory. The decisive question is therefore not at all whether the unity of research and theory is canceled or | preserved; the question   63 is rather whence this unity is determined and wherein it is grounded: either in an originary—venturesome—questioning or in subservience to a demand for usefulness, even if on behalf of "the people" in some sort of clever camouflage. But because that questioning must al-together turn *against* the modern essence of science and thus no longer has a place, or is possible, within that essence, therefore the clear de-cision *in favor of* the essence of modern science—in favor of its research character—is superior to all half-measures which still attempt to make the university an institution of "spiritual" education in the previous style, with the incorporation of the necessary up-to-date modifica-tions. For the research character of science does not exclude a corre-sponding "theory"; on the contrary, that character will ever more clearly establish the limits of what is worth knowing and what super-fluous, since indeed research is able to see and determine, most prox-imally and most broadly, the goal of usefulness. The fact that within research, some is pursued which is "pure," i.e., which does *not* imme-

---

8. {Martin Heidegger, "Die Zeit des Weltbildes," in *Holzwege*, GA 5 (Frankfurt: Klostermann, 1977), pp. 75–113.}

diately and palpably apply to a predetermined use, does not prove the least for a freedom of questioning on the basis of the plight of medi-tation and thus for the possibility of a change in the guiding relations 64   to beings themselves. In truth, I the unity of research and theory is determined neither from the one nor from the other, but rather from the kind of relation to beings as such and from the interpretation of them, i.e., at the same time from the relation to the essence of truth and to the grounding of that essence.

Because meditation cannot venture forth into *these* domains, since meditation must altogether become more and more alien to the age, therefore all attempts to "rescue" and "renew" the university remain mere figures of speech and sheer twaddle. This does of course not pre-vent the sciences from progressing all the while to new discoveries and the forms of instruction from changing, although that proves nothing *for* the university but merely testifies to the long since decided deter-mination of the essence of the modern sciences, which are more than ever compelled by the *apparently* "irrational" powers into their ser-vice. Tomorrow's university—seen in its essence and not appraised ac-cording to its public appearance as service to the people—will there-fore become ever more necessarily the university of the day before yesterday—it will not be able to extract itself from the process of the consummation of modernity. But in each case the scholars affiliated with it will be able to secure their appropriate comfort and their in-sulation from actual questioning all the more "securely," the greater the esteem on the part of "the people."

65   *41*

The mystery of language: we understand a "result" ["*Erfolg*"] as the ef-fect that *follows* [folgt] upon a cause; but is not the result now what *precedes* that which is supposed to count as "true"? A result is not so much something effectuated as it is the first properly backward effec-tuation, insofar as the result extinguishes all other possibilities, ones which then would have the result of being able to deny the claim to be what is true. The esteeming of results is only the last consequence of the sovereignty of the human being as the historiological animal. This esteeming not only beatifies progress as such but above all brings into play a repercussion on the past by which all history is completely surrendered to historiology. This means the human being drives him-self and his essence more and more into an anthropomorphizing, be-cause now even the "beings" of the past are completely determined from the horizon of planning and using, and the human being is se-questered from all beyng. His omniscience and his calculations become boundless ignorance. Perhaps the modern human being thereby finds the means to become the inventor of "happiness"[9]—he, *the one pursued by results*—and utterly inconsequential and thus infatuated with his "eternities."

A result, not simply used as testimony to what is "true," but having itself become the "true," does not effectuate immediately forward on behalf of further progress—its genuine and essentially still unheeded effectivity is backward, in the sense of a determinate historiological stamp impressed on past history—; only this stamp—drawn through the backward-painting that colors over on the basis of the result—has an "effect" on the structure and planning of the further "results"—; an essentially historical grasp shows that the humanity entangled in *results* and in their calculation and production twists history into a constant and increasing backward motion and indeed one extending behind the obviousness of the progress which everyone can see and which is all that is seen. Both—that regress and this progress—belong together. "Regress"—means here, however, not a cultural-political evaluation in the sense of the decline found everywhere and always—instead, it refers to a preeminent form of the movement of history, a form pursued and brought about by the ascendancy of "historiology" in the essential sense of modern humanity. This backward effectivity erects the genuine barrier to all meditation I on the beginnings, because indeed what happened is seen only in the horizon of results and precisely *not* out of the origin in the sense of the preservation of possibilities pregnant with decisions.

The modern human being twists himself into a contortion of his supposed essence; and this contortion is his "true" essence, inasmuch as it compels him inevitably to a postulation of animality as the genuine force of his "life" and restricts him to the striving for "power" and "beauty" (i.e., excitation of pleasure—Wagnerian music as symbol) as the unique and supreme "goals."

The calculation of the past on the basis of results has as its necessary parallel the explanation of consequences and results on the basis of heredity. The fundamental form of this interpretation of humans and of beings as a whole does not stem from individual political "worldviews" but, instead, has its historical-effective (not historiological) source in Hegel's metaphysics (cf. p. 55ff.)—i.e., in the one mode of the consummation of Western thinking. The desire to battle politically against political worldviews, indeed the desire to burden them

66

67

---

9. {Friedrich Nietzsche, *Also sprach Zarathustra, Werke,* vol. 6 (Stuttgart: Kröner, 1919), p. 20: "We have invented happiness—say the last humans, and then they blink."}

with accidental and isolated misgivings, means to misunderstand that in them something is happening of which they themselves are not the master and of which they are only the driven and shackled exporters.

68   This something is I the abandonment by being, an abandonment relegated to beings by beyng itself; in other words, it is the concealed refusal of the beginning and of the site of the originary decisions.

Therefore, meditation would never think to take seriously the everyday, myopic objections against those political movements—as little as meditation can accept their accompanying "fanatical" affirmation {?} as evidence of their *essential* truth. The thinking person, the one struggling over the essence of the Germans, can never think "greatly" enough of those movements, in the sense of the "magnitude" these "worldviews," in accord with their historical destiny, set up as a measure. The "result," as the true itself, harbors a mystery of language, and language at times, but in each case in essential domains, harbors (in the opposite of what it says) that which *is*. In this way, language manifests itself, to those who know, as beyng itself, which bears and thoroughly rules humans in their essence, insofar as within the arena of the decision regarding the affiliation to being, beyng either repels humans and lets them fall away from the assignment to being or on the contrary intimates to them the rarity of a grounding of the truth of beyng.

69   *42*

It is critical, in both a good and bad sense, for a person to enter the domain of what is "great," especially if that person is small; therefore, it *can* be beneficial if everything is aimed at keeping the human being away from that domain. "Greatness" here refers to a current *decision* for or against being, whereby is decided an abandonment of beings by being or an originariness of beings. The decision is what is great—i.e., what protrudes through all relations toward beings. The human being is disquieted—i.e., dominated—by "greatness," not because he is for the most part "small," greedy for fame, avid for prestige, and hungry for success—but because "great" and "small" are only the seemingly Calculative names for his proper essence, in each case borne by a decision—the relation to being—the steadfastness and the lostness in the truth and untruth of beyng—the assignment to beyng. But if such is ever experienced—which has not yet happened—in all decisiveness and made the ground (which is an abyss) of the entire determination of the human being, then which historical "meaning" (historical in the sense of providing a ground for history) bears in itself the question of being, and how superficial is all thinking about "great-ness" and troubling oneself over it?

43

With necessary regard paid to the fact that the human being is essen-tial here, not on his own account, but "for the sake" of beyng and on behalf of beyng, then the *transitions* and *entryways* to be built out of metaphysics toward the question of being as the Interrogative ground-ing of the truth of beyng must involve asking:
Is the human being a microcosmos,
or is the "world" (cosmos) a macroanthropos,
or are both valid,
or neither?
Whence is this to be decided?
Is it at all decidable?
If not, why not? (How and how far not, and why not?)
Whence and how are anthropos and cosmos determined thereby?
(ζῷον λόγον ἔχον ["animal possessing discourse"] and φύσις.)
Whence—on which path of projection—are we questioning here?
In view of the fact that the human being questions beyng and *on his own* determines its "essence," is it *then* not an anthropomorphiz-ing of being and thus of all beings if the human being himself *in* this questioning (precisely in advance and always more originarily) deter-mines *his* essence on the basis of beyng and does not already make himself, as something decided, into a subject in the anthropomor-phizing and into a "living being" | in the animalizing? But how does   71
this questioning proceed?

44

The human being—let us now consider that the Western human be-ing has been defined for two thousand years as *animal* (*animal ratio-nale*). And if Nietzsche believes the human being is the "still uniden-tified *animal*"—(*Beyond Good and Evil*, no. 62)—then he is taking over precisely the basic identification—but at the same time is overlooking the fact that the identification he thinks is lacking has already been carried out and is merely invisible—even to Nietzsche—as long as one adheres to the formula, *animal rationale*, without seeing that "*ratio*"[10] has been determined as *subiectum*, which is precisely an affirmation

---

10. [Latin word.—Trans.]

of animality. (Cf. Ponderings IX, p. 67ff.) The animal is so definitively identified that precisely the identification of the human being as the (in the essential sense) *historiological* animal includes and unfolds the utter preservation of animality and thus impedes an originary questioning into the human essence. The identification of the animal, "human being," consists precisely in the fact that the human being, who was already determined centuries ago (Descartes), is not able or willing to do otherwise than define himself as animal and hold himself to be thus defined. Nietzsche, even Nietzsche, is accordingly the last witness for this characterization of "the" (modern) human being.

72   Then could the definition of the human being as *animal rationale*—the definition on which even the entire *Christian* doctrine of the human being rests—be an error and for more than two millennia drive humans about in errancy? But what do two millennia signify for an error in such an essential question—especially if an error is something more essential than mere "incorrectness," something abyssal over and against the superficiality of a mere "mistake"? Such that an error of this kind may yet bestow on humans their history—because the claim of humans to truth—because the right to the preservation of the essence of truth—is not decided. *If* therefore in the delimitation of the human being as ζῷον, as *animal*,[11] animal, an error is supposed to hold sway—we are here only *asking*—then there would exist the possibility, indeed perhaps even the neediness of necessity, to define the human essence more originarily—thus not primarily and generically as animal, but then also not primarily as body and so also not as soul and thus also not as spirit and "heart" and a fortiori not as a mixed formation of body, soul, and spirit.

        Perhaps that epoch of the world is not so distant, since the human
73 being identified long ago—the rational animal—I is perishing on his rationality and at the same time on his animality—and is doing so in the most insidious form—namely, by his taking this essential characterization as rational animal to be the eternal and inalienable truth and by definitively taking up this abode therein. For in this way he destroys every possibility he has to convey his proper essence out into the transformative danger of undisclosed essential developments. Instead, he secures for himself an ever more steadfast duration, one which above all denies him what is greatest, since that is granted only to one who is great—namely, the downgoing. For only what is great possesses the height needed to plunge into a depth. The depth of the plunge manifests the range of the power for reverence which is borne

---

11. [Latin word.—Trans.]

by the great in itself for—beyng. The small remains on the flat road-way of broad streets.

Are we giving sufficient consideration to the fact that the human being is still always defined as animal?

For how long yet will we be led to believe the greatness of the Greeks would consist in their becoming and remaining the occasion for a "classical age" and its "classicisms"? When will we grasp the essence of the Greeks in the uniqueness of their very steep downgoing? This, however, because the Greeks, as inceptual ones, ventured the assignment of humans to being, whereas those who came afterward built their edifices only on what was left over and was without any risk.

As long as the essence of human being remains pre-defined by an-   74
imality (*animalitas*), only one question can be asked: *what* is the human being? Never possible is the question: *who* is the human being? For this who-question, as a question, is already the originarily other and unique answer to the question of the human being—this questioning itself assigns the human being to his essence as steadfastness in the truth of beyng. It is that question about the human being which does not merely question him regarding his cause and the like, and indeed questions him not for his own sake but, instead, for the sake of beyng, because beyng displaces us into an encounter with the human being as the one who grounds truth. Only this question overcomes the modern *anthropological* definition of the human being and along with that definition all previous Christian Hellenistic—Jewish and Socratic-Platonic anthropology.

45

Even "solitude" is discussed in series of lectures at public conferences explicitly organized around that theme, and the discussions are presumably very clever and perhaps contain very much that is "correct." Yet where does anyone surmise the dreadfulness that *is* behind this (along with much else) otherwise Inconsequential occurrence?

46   75

"Culture"—as something undertaken and instituted, presupposes the anthropomorphizing of the human being. Nietzsche's thoughts about culture, despite his concept of culture, betray the retrograde, modern essence of his thinking. The only people that had *no* "culture," because they had no need of it inasmuch as they still stood in being [*Sein*], were the Greeks of the sixth century BC.—But now everything is dripping with "culture."

The hitherto "highest" level attained in the modern definition of the essence: the human being as the animal pursuing cultural politics.

The "proud" grounding of a worldview on the "conclusions" of "the" science is the most vulgar comedy, one that started to play out at large in the second half of the nineteenth century. Nietzsche's thoughts about culture show he never overcame *Wagnerism,* despite all his later resistance against it. If a people is devoted to the "fostering," i.e., "cultivation," of "culture," then this people has already withdrawn from the danger and venture of essential decisions. The cultivation of culture corresponds to the sovereignty of the self-absorbed "subjectum"—this cultivation, with increasing cleverness and a cor-
76   responding exploitation of "creative personalities" from | previous history, might accomplish much that is "good" and is "tastefully" unobjectionable, and individuals who had been forced to do their daily work well or ill in a delimited domain will now find the opportunity to devote themselves to "great" "cultural missions." "Cultural politics" is now becoming a global epidemic and besides—the French have invented this remarkable formation, and only later did we recognize the utility of this "political" tool. Is it, however, therefore any less that which it remains, the "historiological"-technological "instrument" of the Latin-Romance—modern spirit—un-German to the core?

One now occasionally adds to the dubious finery of machinations by dragging in Nietzsche as the supposed star witness for the "cultural politics" that is to serve "the people." But one does not mention, or—said by way of "excuse"—one does not know, that "culture" has only the one purpose of bringing forth the "highest exemplars" of creative humanity—i.e., "the" people has to serve the great "individuals" and only them, and not the reverse. But to fulfill this purpose it may be
77   good if "the" people | believes and persuades itself that "it" is itself the purpose of all beings. Even the fulfillment of this purpose leaves room enough for the "cultural-political" apostles and emissaries to gratify their vanity and be held up to "the" "people" in "sight and sound" day in and day out. The word is now whispered about, like a great secret, that a "cultural agreement" between "Rome" and Germany[12] is in preparation as the (naturally) greatest and entirely unprecedented[13]

---

12. {The German-Italian cultural agreement of November 23, 1938 primarily regulated student exchange programs, book shows, and language classes (foreign language positions) in secondary schools and universities.}

13. [Reading *bisher nie dagewesene* for *bisher dagewesene,* "already extant."—Trans.]

"cultural" "happening." Does anyone know that Nietzsche calls Rome the "most indecent place on earth"[14] for the poet of *Zarathustra*— whereby Nietzsche refers not *merely* to "Christian" Rome but to everything signifying a despotism of opinion and a mishmash?

Yet even Nietzsche "thinks" as an artist, i.e., here, in an aesthetic-Wagnerian-Schopenhauerian way, when he postulates "genius" as the goal of humanity. Nietzsche remains held fast in the enclosure of biological metaphysics, and therefore one can with equal justification on the ground of this metaphysics, even in its inversion, postulate "the people" as the purpose of itself—both are the "same"—and only thereby do we attain the realm from which the *merely at first* and superficially taken cultural pursuit | constantly and uniquely receives   78 its grounding and, unwittingly, its genuine impetus: the sovereignty of modern metaphysics in its final form as the anthropomorphizing of the human being. All cultural politics and all cultivation of culture are slaves of this that is hidden to them, namely, the sovereignty of the *subiectum* (the sovereignty of the human being as the historiological animal).

By essence, this sovereignty of the "subject" means that what is sovereign can foist onto its servants without danger, indeed to its own advantage, the opinion that they themselves, the slaves of the abandonment of beings by being, are the "masters" and the inaugurators of a "new" and unprecedented (which is indeed the case) "world-culture."

Yet if "culture" has become a justified "instrument" of "politics," then the point must finally be reached whereby people reciprocally deceive one another with the help of "cultural" pacts and agreements— and conceal their own respective desire for power and their own intentions—a process only naive individuals could note with "moral" indignation; in truth it is the necessary consequence of something that has *already existed* for a long time.

46a   79

Every dogmatism, whether ecclesial-political or civil-political, necessarily maintains that any thinking or acting that apparently or actually deviates from the dogma is an acquiescence to something *inimical* to that dogma—whether the enemies are the pagans and the Godless or the Jews and communists. In this way of thinking lies a peculiar strength—not the strength of thinking—but that of the enforcement of the promulgated dogma.

---

14. {Friedrich Nietzsche, *Ecce homo: Der Wille zur Macht; Erstes und zweites Buch*, *Werke*, vol. 15 (Leipzig: Kröner, 1911), p. 91.}

47

Why are many persons—perhaps even already the entire still extant Protestantism—now turning to the Catholic Church? It is from fear of—Catholicism. Political Catholicism has been replaced by a "Catholic" politics; the essence of what is "Catholic" lies neither in Christianity nor in the ecclesial as such—instead, καθόλον ["catholic"] means—prevailing over the whole—it means the "*total*." The Catholic "Church" is deceived if it believes that those flocking to it are driven by "*religious*" needs, and National Socialism should not wonder at having to become the pacesetter of this flocking. In that way the domains of the forthcoming decisions are merely concealed again—but what 80 is "Catholic" was never, especially not in the "Christian" | Middle Ages, the origin of a configurative struggle with regard to being—such an origin always lies hidden in the solitude of a few who remain nameless.

What is "Catholic" acquired its genuine form for the first time in *Jesuitism;* here is the Western model for all unconditional obedience, the elimination of all self-will—the decisiveness of "organization," the sovereignty of propaganda, the justification of oneself through the disparagement of the enemy, and the model for the exploitation of all means of "knowledge" and skill, for falsely changing these to one's own discovery, for the historiological revision of history, for the glorification of volition and of the orderliness of what is soldierly within Catholicism, for the basic comportment of the counter to . . . (Counter-Reformation). "Catholicism" in this essential sense is in its historical provenance Roman—Spanish—; utterly un-Nordic and completely un-German.

48

To appropriate "culture" qua means of power and thereby assert oneself and allege a superiority—this is in its ground a *Jewish* comportment. What follows for *cultural politics* as such?

81
49

The dangerousness of a "spiritual" struggle resides not in the possibility of defeat and annihilation, but in the certainty of an unavoidable dependence on the opponent, in the *taking over* of *his* essence and distorted essence. "Struggle" is not at once evidence of originariness, and victory in such a struggle is not at all proof of "truth," because indeed perhaps precisely that which is struggled against, instead of giving way, entrenches itself in a hidden and unassailable form.

50

Schopenhauer's boundless superficiality became a doom for *Nietzsche*. Even if he later inverted Schopenhauer, Nietzsche could never overcome him. Nietzsche became the great and bold inverter; and such inversion brings to light much that is startling, that constantly turns against common opinion—but it remains an inversion, a *turning around*—even if carried through as decisively as in Nietzsche—but is never a *turning toward* the origin.

Yet why can we not simply leap over this inversion? Because in it what was inverted | remains all the more preserved—because no interrogative confrontation whatever has yet commenced.   82

51

Every *beginning* is by essence without effect; effects and consequences are inappropriate to it. Every beginning must, by turning back into itself, become more inceptual if it is to remain a beginning and preserve itself. The beginning, as the beginning of beyng (of beyng as beginning), is the origin, the primal leap, the torn-open fissure in whose abyssal (but as such still concealed) clearing beings can first "be" as coming to presence—can be taken up by the clearing. The beginning is all the more inceptual and thus ever *nearer* to its own concealed essence the more decisively it is a going to the ground, which ground is the abyss and as such is the plight of grounding—*beyng as origin is the appropriation of the human being in an assignment to the truth of being*—the determination to the basic dispositions of one who grounds. But in advance—i.e., after the history of the first beginning—the beginning which withdrew itself in favor of the commencement which followed it—the human being must *first* become the *steward* of the truth of beyng—this is the other beginning.

52   83

The modern age, which is now starting to enter the decisive "phase" of its consummation, posits humanity as the "goal" for the human being. Insofar as the modern human being is certain of himself as the center of "life," he needs no further "goals."

Modernity is therefore the age that utterly needs no goals, not simply the age of sheer goallessness—; in such an age, everything is then calculated according to "purposes" and "uses," inasmuch as *purposes* are nothing other than salient affirmations of the unneediness for goals. Should this age ever have to be overcome, then the task assigned to humans cannot consist in establishing—or even only seeking—"goals" "over and against" the unneediness for them—instead, the first step is meditation on whether the human being can himself be a goal and whether he is supposed to "have" "goals," and whether and under what conditions he requires "goals," and why he ultimately disposes of this "requirement" in the form of the unneediness for goals. But "goal" here does not mean the aim (purpose) of human activity; instead, it signifies that *toward* which such an aim proceeds. 84 The unneediness | for goals then signifies that the human being does not require any arena in which he would have to protrude as the purpose of himself, since indeed everything that "is" presents only an "expression" of his "life."

The decisive meditation does not consist in first distinguishing that *toward which* the human being is supposed to proceed; instead, it is a matter of questioning what the human being, as one who proceeds toward, is supposed to be—whence then the very essence of the human being is determined, whether his determination *arises out of an assignment,* and whether that to which he is assigned can ever be grasped as a "goal" or is not thereby misinterpreted. The question is whether the human being, as assigned, proceeds *toward* something which in accord with this assignment can precisely not be a "goal" for him—such that the proceeding toward would find its essence in becoming a renunciation and a self-withholding, which signifies not a "loss" of essence, nor a "gain," but pure steadfastness in the essence itself, namely, to be the steward of the preservation of the truth of beyng as self-refusal (event—origin) through the grounding of Dasein. If Da-sein essentially occurs "through" the human being *for the* 85 *sake of* | "beyng"—then this is not a "goal"—at which the human being is at some time supposed to "arrive"—but is that which, as self-refusal, is the clearing wherein humans and gods encounter one another. This encounter is the history of their own respective essential grounding.

In the unneediness for goals, which in fact takes its life from having overcome the setting of goals, there is carried out a further removal from the true human *goallessness.* This name does not designate a lack and doom; instead, it contains an intimation into the essential depth of the human being, a depth he will attain only if being itself appropriates him again in another beginning of its history. Then

would goallessness therefore be the "goal" of humans? This captious formula withdraws precisely to where such formulas always readily entice, namely, away from the genuine thinking of what is to be thought. Goallessness can never be the goal, if it is supposed to be grounded as the essence of the human being; for this grounding no longer issues from the setting of a goal, but from the preparedness for a necessitation of the plight which is beyng itself, and beyng casts itself, as the event of appropriation, between the humans and the gods and so refuses | ever to be taken as an attainable being or even an un-   86
attainable one.

The age of complete goallessness[15] (unneediness for goals) can indeed be understood as such since a tacit aversion to any setting of a goal prevails. Yet this understanding—should it remain heedful of the history of beyng—on the basis of the essence of beyng—must not assume a "goal" would actually have to be sought and posited and the need for goals awakened. In fact a goal would precisely not be needed, since of course in unity with the emerging unneediness for goals, the countermovement is also already asserting itself in the form of a positing of goals, even if this positing is only a reestablishment of previous goals (in the sense of Christianity or of the previous Christian "culture" of the West). The need for goals thus impedes the transition to meditation at least as much as does the unneediness for goals. Yet if the thinking and discourse that are heedful of the history of beyng cannot always avoid speaking of "goals," and if it is said, for instance, that the grounding of the truth of beyng is the "goal"—then "goal," in the context of this thinking, means | only that toward which the   87
human being is proceeding and which precisely casts him back, since as beyng it is not the "highest," but is even higher than everything highest (i.e., goal and final goal), insofar as it assigns the human being to the abyss of the clearing, and beyng essentially occurs as this clearing.

Yet the unneediness for goals secures and strengthens itself as well as its sovereignty in the increasing palpability of its purposes and thus in the self-evident significance of the means. And if apparently the means are only in service to the purpose, and the latter justifies the former, then basically the purpose is the hidden slave of the means, which in turn is the idol of the purpose. The "means," however, are the now accessible beings themselves—the "real," things that are effective and, in virtue of their results, prove to be what is true. The "purposes" are only *pretexts* for the means—the purposes claim to be the center of beings, whose beingness has for a long time been deter-

---

15. [Reading *Ziellosigkeit* for *Fraglosigkeit*, "questionlessness."—Trans.]

mined as "reality," and beings have served as masks in which the apparent forcefulness of being "works itself out." (Cf. Beyng and force.[16])

Nietzsche established the goallessness "of life" (i.e., its unneediness for goals) through an absolute postulation of life as the basic reality; he does not question Da-sein's goallessness, which is grounded in the essence of beyng qua | event of appropriation and thus qua Self-refusing clearing. Nietzsche's goallessness "of life" is only the inversion of the Platonism which posits being in the sense of the "idea" as prototype and "goal." That means: like no other of his time, Nietzsche strives to set up once again a "goal" beyond the human being, and this "goal" is the superman—that the current human being might go beyond to the superman, who has his truth in the highest flourishing of streaming life as such. But what is decisive about this setting of a goal resides not in its "content," but rather in the fact that it, precisely *as* a setting of a goal, remains metaphysics and does not know or venture an originary questioning into beyng.

53

The basic experience in the dialogue with the "thinkers": the more essentially a thinking (within the history of metaphysics) attempts to think being (qua the beingness of beings and on the basis of beings), in that it compels the whole of beings into the objectivity of an unconditioned thinking (i.e., self-representing representation), then all the more decisively does being refuse its appropriate truth and even the question of that truth. Yet this does not indicate a mere mistake and a | lack; instead, there lies precisely here, for those who are thinking, an intimation of the essence of essential thinking, which cannot be calculated according to "correctness" and "incorrectness": the more decisively thinking thinks being, all the richer becomes that which in such thinking is still unthought and is first to be thought. The immediately asserted is not the genuinely said and disclosively questioned.

Who could ever think that which is inexhaustible of a thinking? Yet this is not meant *historiologically,* inasmuch as a thinker who has entered into history always gives rise to a new interpretation, one which is in each case kept open to a subsequent present time—but historically, in the sense of the history of beyng itself—and beyng in such self-refusal holds open the Simple uniqueness of its essence for those to whom beyng remains the most question-worthy.

---

16. {Martin Heidegger, *Besinnung,* GA66 (Frankfurt: Klostermann, 1997), pp. 185–196.}

54

By what do you recognize a thinker? By the fact that it never occurs to him to refute another thinker, to calculate up what is incorrect about the other's thinking, in the belief of being able eventually to calculate out what is correct "in itself." A thinker replies to thinkers, i.e., requites their affiliation, only insofar as he grounds an | originary   90 question of being and knows that this grounding cannot be convulsed by "refutations," since it is never even reached by such calculation in terms of correctness and incorrectness.

In epochs when the human being becomes the historiological animal, he requires historiological literature which calculates up the historiology of the history of thinking into an apparently "new" and in fact "unprecedented" blossoming of "philosophy." A sense of proportion is then completely missing: Heraclitus's thought is essentially there, despite all that has been lost, in twenty pages of a brief text; the seven to eight thousand pages of a philosophical pedant are thoroughly inconsequential and merely constitute an entry in an index of "new publications." What does such a disappearance of proportion signify? It signifies the uprooting of the *historical* essence of humanity, in accord with which this essence must fall victim to historiology or else can become the task of grounding the truth of beyng. Thinkers are thinkers "of" beyng, or else the name "thinker" refers to a play-actor on the public stage of historiology. Essential thinkers can testify to themselves | only through their mode of being, and above all   91 through their mode of nonbeing—namely, as *thinkers* of beyng—(not the way the historiological citizen calculates this, namely, through the mode in which the thinkers "actualize" their alleged "worldview" in so-called praxis, i.e., in adapting to what is "ordinary").

Seldom do people know who is a thinker, and even more seldom who is a *poet*. And common opinion says that if a poet names the gods, then this poet "is" a "priest" or is behaving like one. To be a poet has as little to do with the "priesthood" as to be a thinker has to do with the "research" of the "sciences," or "art" with "aesthetics."

How abyssally separated is Hölderlin from all "priesthood" and from the least claim to be a "priest"—precisely *because* he poetically (by founding being) names the gods? The attempt to claim Hölderlin for "Christianity" or for any other "religion" strengthens the notion of the "priesthood" of the poet and so obstructs all paths to the standpoint from which Hölderlin's saying and recognizing of the gods can be heard.

"Priests" can never found being; they at most tend, uphold, and   92 preserve beings. The mishmash of today's notions, completely ravaged by "Wagnerism," can no longer see anything of the simple clarity in which the crests and peaks of poetizing and thinking gaze at one other out of an essentially different discourse.

55

The human being? A creature of possible steadfastness in the truth of beyng.—

The word—the First and Highest projection of beyng itself in the appropriation of the human *essence* toward its encounter with the indigence of the gods. The word arises out of the origin, the primal leap—thus out of beyng itself, and the human being is only the one who seizes the word, which *he* then to all appearances pronounces purely out of "himself" (as *animal rationale*) in order thereby to demonstrate that he is speaking (or else he does not seize the word and becomes mistaken about himself).

The human being—a creature who can enter into the projective circle of the "word" and to whom there stands open the misuse of what is projected, and in unity with that, the mistaking | of his most proper essence (in his vocation to an affiliation with the truth of beyng).

93

56

Culture—understood as a unitary-unifying fostering of the unity of the faculties and aptitudes of a "people"—is ordained in advance merely to be a means. But inasmuch as at the same time the humanity of humans makes itself the *goal* (and, in consequence, so does the people), the means must necessarily become the goal—indeed, even further, both must intermix in their essence, such that culture becomes at once the means and the expression of the people—goal and way in one; culture loses necessity and grounding—but thereby becomes pursued all the more loudly.

The prevalence of the cultivation of culture, just like, in general, the Explicit mediocrity of culture and thus the "idea" of culture, is a *consequence* of metaphysics, insofar as metaphysics led the anthropomorphizing of the human being up beyond the interpretation of beingness as objectivity for production and representation and entrenched the forgottenness of being, such that the fostering of beings was in any case granted exclusive rights. Coming to this metaphysical predetermination of the priority of "culture" as such and | still coming to it are the pressing forth of the massiveness of humans and the exigency of its being subdued and led—and all this again in a "world"

94

for which the gigantic had to become the paradigm of what is great. Nevertheless, the gigantic allows the appropriate summoning of all means in order to maintain at least the semblance of an extant *culture*. But this is necessary for the world-era of *modernity*, since it offers the last remainder of a form of unity and of cohesion, whereas the unneediness for goals dominates everything and there are no longer grounds out of which an origin could come forth—since everything is mere effectivity and proves itself as effectivity in its results.

A great inundation of the "earth" by this modern culture has set in—the human being creates for himself, in the anthropormorphizing, his own form of unneediness which tears down all bridges (if indeed there still are any) leading to an originary plight and keeps the frenzy in the decisionlessness for the "good fortune" of decisiveness. Therefore, it is a mistake in this age to try and raise humans above themselves—unless in advance beyng itself once again holds the human being worthy of an assignment I to itself.   95

But at *this* moment of the history of beyng is there any recourse for humans? Any preparation? Or is something quite different happening already, something we cannot see with all our historiological acuity, something withdrawn even from historical meditation? Is the uniqueness of beyng choosing for the abode of its history only the most solitary site—or has it always so chosen? Who could know that?

Then are there still future humans of the last god—after a long interruption in the human capacity for gods? Then would culture—itself still as mere semblance and as object of a semblant pursuit—always be the remainder of an attempt, without knowledge of the history of beyng, to rescue a few individuals over to a future in which once again the human being and the god might meet for the last struggle over their essence? For the *last* struggle—whose *"when"* we do not know. But we do surmise its *"that"* from a knowledge of beyng, which, on the basis of its uniqueness, must for once testify even to this uniqueness in a supreme *transiency, after* which even and precisely *nothingness* does of course no longer find any arena for its essential occurrence.

Only out of the horizon of this thinking in advance into the uniqueness I of beyng can the utter superficiality of all "culture" be recognized.   96

57

What is *historiologically durable* supports itself on the claims of the common opinion of the historiological animal that "thinks" superficially and makes the current the measure of the permanent. Therefore the properly durable in *historiological* history (the history objectivated in terms of historiology) is anecdote, legend, propaganda—in short, *semblance* (which of course is precisely *not* recognized *as* such). The attempt by historiological science to secure the "objective" truth over and against this semblance is merely the converse acknowledgment of that semblance and takes the form of the will to rescue something lasting out of history for future ages—something—as it "actually" was—; here all knowledge of being is absent, for beyng can precisely *not* be encountered on the path of a seeking for what is permanent.

Even Nietzsche, with his three types of historiology, is caught in the historical as the historiological which is in each case determined as such and such. But "history" is primarily to be thought as the struggle against the threatening by beyng | in the form of its self-refusal—, provoking the human being into the pursuit of beings and delivering him over to historiology. Historiology arises out of an ignorance of history and an inconstancy in it, i.e., out of the abandonment of beings by being, which, as the forgottenness of being, holds the human being spellbound.

58

"*Standpoint.*"—The thinking that is heedful of the history of beyng neither "has" a standpoint nor is free of standpoints—if standpoint is supposed to mean that from which beings are viewed and from which a regard is taken toward beingness. The standpoint of all metaphysics (and only metaphysics requires a standpoint) is constantly an outlook toward beings as such—whether beings are thought "idealistically" or "realistically," whether the outlook is delimited by the present-at-hand human being or by the absolute subjectivity of spirit. The alleged absence of a standpoint is merely the incapacity—or perhaps only the unwillingness—to see the already occupied standpoint— the closing of the eyes in front of the basic relations of the thinking of beingness, a flight that persuades itself it is the overcoming of all destructive "reflexivity."

The thinking that is heedful of the history of beyng does not think on the basis of an outlook on beings, which then for its part is incorporated into | beings or is simply forgotten—; instead, this thinking disclosively thinks the truth of beyng—and in that way first and constantly endures the steadfastness in the clearing. Without a support in beings and without fleeing into beingness, the clearing expands and thus does not become an object. Instead, it opens itself to the abyss—i.e., it clears the abyss, and so the clearing essentially occurs as itself and manifests the self-refusal (beyng) prevailing in it. The enduring of the steadfastness is the grounding of Da-sein. And the initially pursued talk of the *"metaphysics of Da-sein"* (Kantbook)[17] is merely supposed to indicate that the intention and the task concern not epistemology and anthropology, but only the question of being, and that for this questioning Da-sein is endured as the first basic domain to be opened up.

An initial agreement concerning what is wholly other can be achieved only through an assimilation of the past—whereby to be sure the danger is increased that what is genuinely and uniquely questioned will become lost through the facile calculation of the past, especially if the interpretation attributes to the past a more originary "dimension" (Kant and his doctrine of transcendental imagination). Nevertheless, thereby a standpoint, i.e., | the assimilation of an earlier one, is made fast, and people naturally believe they already know this standpoint, simply because it preceded them. The thinking that questions on the path of the originary question of beyng is relegated to "metaphysics"—and why not, since it does call itself "metaphysics." But "metaphysics" is here, in the transitional thinking that is heedful of the history of beyng, necessarily ambiguous, which means: the title is so broadly used and at the same time so essentially, that it designates contemplative thinking in general as the thinking of being.

Metaphysics then means the asking of the question of being, whereby intended at the same time is the previous and *properly* "metaphysical" thinking in the sense of the thinking of the beingness of beings on the basis of *beings* (cf. above, p. 7)—but also includes the thinking that is heedful of the history of beyng, which disclosively thinks beyng on the basis of the *grounding* of the truth of beyng as Da-sein. Indeed Da-sein is not the truth of beyng but, instead, is the grounding that belongs to beyng. In the *transition* from the first beginning and its history to the other beginning and its preparation, all thinking of being, the more decisively it presses on to clarity, becomes all the more *ambiguous,* if indeed it has transcended this in order to place itself at rest in a standpoint, no matter whether it itself is the standpoint of the freedom from standpoints.

This *ambiguity* is not a lack of decisiveness; instead, it is the unavoidable consequence of decisiveness—and therefore the thinking that is heedful of the history of beyng requires an "inner" freedom which can be grounded neither through "morals" nor through "worldview" but is determined only through the essential occurrence of beyng itself, insofar as beyng, qua self-refusal, lets the enduring of the steadfastness in Da-sein, and thus Da-sein itself, become the plight.

99

100

---

17. {*Kant und das Problem der Metaphysik,* p. 218ff.}

59

"Decision"—is what they now call the flight into something long since decided—which, as cultural Christianity, has finally demonstrated its absurdity in the course of the first world war. One speaks of "decision" and *in advance* renounces all *questioning* and also all experience of the necessity of essential questioning—; one reels off the old Christian-Catholic apologetics in modern-Protestant form against a "paganism" which lacks *everything* even only to be such—i.e., it lacks the gods and the power to create gods. One puts on—presumably with the greatest "subjective" honesty—a "literary" drama, and all the "reviewers" of
101   all the "newspapers" and "magazines" are | eager not to neglect the idle talk about "Western decision."

Yet ultimately this prattle about "decision," grounded in a complete lack of questioning of everything that is first *to be questioned* and only then brought up for decision, is merely the echo of the *equally* superficial "National Socialist philosophy," which, with help of embellished figures of speech and slogans, pretends to have overcome "Christianity" and allegedly poses "decisions," after it has beforehand offered up a "sacrifice of thinking" in comparison to which the "thinking" of a Catholic curate could be called "freethinking."

Where have the Germans arrived? Or have they only always still remained where they always already were and where ultimately Hölderlin found them and Nietzsche still came across them? To be sure, Nietzsche previously only realized that they accustomed themselves to a "pride" to stand in "life" wherein they—despite their "exceptions"—constantly have stood. But perhaps the essence of the Germans—and perhaps whatever they are "capable" of comes to light through the "Americanism" they practice *even more* radically and the
102   "Romanism" | they carry out *even more* "tirelessly"—*is* that they are called the "people" of thinkers and poets only because as a "people" they do *not* want this thinking and poetizing, i.e., are not prepared to seek their ground in such danger—but always still and more and more unwittingly—glorify and imitate what is "foreign." Indeed who would then say that a *"people"* must and could be that which prepares on behalf of beyng the site of its truth?—

Are we not thinking of human beings still only in terms of *animality* when we "think" of them as a "people"? Is not indeed this view, despite its unassailable "correctness," the gigantically instituted decline from the inceptual Western characterization of the human being in terms of an affiliation to beyng—such that the Western decision never occurs where only an a fortiori decisionlessness *within* the already decided, i.e., Hellenistic-Jewish, "world" has arrogated the sovereignty—; so that the decision can never be one between Christianity and "paganism," because both already secure their continued existence out of the impotence I for decisions in general.—				103

The decision, however, is this: whether the human being of the West gives himself over to beings as objects, or whether he attains beyng as abyss and from this attains the plight of a grounding of his essence out of the assignment to being. Because such did occur in a first beginning with the Greeks—because they ventured to determine themselves on the basis of being, then that brief and unique history had to be possible as long as this venture was risked. All "blood," all "race," all "ethnicity" is otiose and a dead end if it does not already live within a venture of being and, as venturing, set itself free for the lightning flash which strikes it where its dullness must break asunder in order to grant a place for the truth of beyng, within which place beyng can first be set into a work of beings.

60

Many things of many sorts are possible, but still "more"—i.e., the essential—remains *impossible:* that a human, ensnared in beings, could ever of himself assign himself to beyng in its essential truth.

### 61				104

The genuine discipline (i.e., self-control in what is essential) of contemplative thinking can never be established immediately—it rests in what is unsaid. And the latter can hardly be assessed by anyone, because we seldom grasp what is said—i.e., know it on the basis of its being said.

62

We have "adages" enough and even "paradigms" for every domain of activity—and today all this can be conveyed easily, quickly, and even tastefully. And yet—such possessions are not capable of anything, as long as the human being, in service only to beings, turns his back on beyng, so to speak, and finds no motive to risk his own *essence* in the struggle over the essence of beyng and thereby perhaps surmise "only" the Godlessness of beings and in such surmising enter a historical space of beyng, out of which the storm of the question of the abandonment of beings by being and of the question of the ground of that abandonment might strike up against him. These are happenings to which the metaphysically determined human being is still blind and

apathetic—but which nevertheless suffice to create another world, |
105   even if only the one in which the human being has become essential
enough to ask disclosively and truly what is quite preliminary:
whether the human being could not be destined to the stewardship
of the truth of beyng, if indeed the unsettling in the face of the self-
refusal of beyng thoroughly penetrates him and takes from him his
self-certainty and also any flight into a hasty faith. How could it not
actually happen at such a "time" that the history of Western human
beings in its semblance as a formation of historiology implode upon
itself and the centuries shrink into a short span filled only by the free
fall of humans out of the scarcely grasped truth of beyng into the increasing machination of beings? The upshot would be the occurrence
everywhere of only an imitation and modification of that which is
posited with and after this freefall.—"Adage"—without a disclosive
thinking of beyng—is night without the day.

The human being never comes to himself (to his essence) by representing himself (to himself)—in representation [*Vor-stellen*], he
"places" ["*stellt*"] himself only where he already stands—the coming
to oneself is a coming forth out of that wherein the human being be-
106   longs | in the ground of his essence—out of beyng. "Self"-consider-
ation therefore never brings the human being into a coming to himself. But what about *activity*? Not even that—if it remains merely a
process within the calculability of the goals, ways, and means of an
epoch. Here—through activity—much can be brought into motion
and be "overturned," and yet this can remain merely a renewed entrenchment of the human being in his previous distorted essence. But
that coming forth out of the essential affiliation to beyng—how is it
supposed to happen—if the human being has not—in poetizing—in
thinking—cast himself out already into this affiliation by way of a
projection in which he himself is the projected—i.e., in which he is
appropriated by being qua event?

The fact that the human being (i.e., humanity), with all the agreement about himself and about his self-evident character, moves
rather in an alienation and takes his needs, insofar as they merely
make themselves felt and assert themselves, as already proven and
genuine—this fact can, despite all the overturning, remain that which
abides.

The danger for philosophy—i.e., the endangering of a grasp of what
and how philosophy thinks—does not come from the place where
107   philosophy is disdained as superfluous | or is still tolerated merely as
an ornament of culture; it comes instead from those who pursue a
"spiritual interest" and so delve into philosophical works but—are un-
willing to question and so avoid every decision, especially one re-

garding the utter question-worthiness of that which must be thought in philosophy. "Philosophy"—often along with much spiritual "culture"—is fostered as a spiritual occupation to deck out "cultural" endeavors and is also frequently used for the conceptual clarification and conceptual sharpening of those endeavors or for building a facade in front of Christian beliefs. And so philosophy is very thoroughly suffocated in its essence.

63

Pascal. For some time, Pascal's world of thought has been finding even among us its serious reverers and also its scholars of preeminent spiritual taste. So now slowly and in increasing breadth the first great *modern* "Christian←→thinker" is coming into the light of historiology and thus is coming to conscious historiological reckoning for the urgencies and predicaments (but not for the essential *plight*) of the present time. Yet if already the essence of a "Christian←→thinker" bears an originary brittleness, not to say mendacity (mendacity is not meant *here* in a "moral" sense as "subjective" untruthfulness but refers instead to an essential distortion, and thus concealment, of one's own essence), then with what irreconcilable | "oppositions" must a modern "Christian—thinker" first find his way about, especially if, as happens in Pascal, "thinking" and believing are developed so decisively (within the limits of the possibility of the traditions of each) against each other and yet are "proved" again as necessary *to* each other? | 108

For Pascal is indeed not a "Christian" thinker the way the entirety of modern metaphysics from Descartes to Hegel (and even Nietzsche!) is still determined by Christianity (human being as "subjectum," world as "cosmos," "God" as ground and cause of everything). Pascal is Christian as a believer whose capacity for faith and whose summons to faith far surpass all average believers and institutional Christians. And he thinks, as *this* Christian, the then already modern Western thinking in a *form* that is not inferior to the greatest ones. But he also thinks this thinking only *for the sake* of faith. Pascal created the basic form of *modern* Christian apologetics, although the Churches have long since not sufficiently grasped and utilized this form. But in the meantime dawn seems to be breaking. People are starting to surmise and may even say that here a—indeed *the*—possibility is demonstrated for Christianity to stand *within* modernity, with the means of the thinking of modernity, and yet at the same time stand *opposed* to modernity: | to hold fast to the "truth" of Christian faith as a basic standard, to count equally in modernity as a fellow modern, and to participate in and utilize all the advancements of modernity. | 109

The fact that Pascal created the basic form of the possible modernity of cultural Christianity (a form misunderstood for centuries and
suppressed by the Counter-Reformation of the Jesuits) is the operative, though not authentically grasped, motive for the currently commencing discovery of his work and for the utilization of his kind of
thinking and way of believing on behalf of the modern vindication of
Christianity and of its still extant Catholic and Protestant Churches.
Jesuits and Protestants find themselves therefore on this "new"—
for both, equally "modern"—ground—in truth, they are driven together by a common opposition against a sheer un-Christian outlook
which replaces the creator God with the political race—the danger
of their opponent consists in the fact that even this opponent thinks
in a Christian, and specifically "Catholic" way, merely in reverse—
on account of which, Protestantism now places itself behind Catholicism (cf. p. 79).—

To be sure, Pascal never overcomes Descartes, but instead justifies
Descartes from the point of view of faith and conversely justifies faith
to modernity: the "logic of the heart"[18] permits the affirmation of the
"*lived experience*" that is essential for modern humanity (as "subject")
and allows it specifically in unity with the affirmation of the | "mathe-
matical" and thus with "technology" in the metaphysical sense, and
both of these out of and in faith in Jesus Christ. The Pascalian "orders" are consequently the most profound *rescuing* of Cartesianism
through Christianity and accordingly the most insidious affirmation
of modernity through cultural Christianity *and therefore,* above all, the
most decisive avoidance of every Thoughtful venture of an overcoming of the modern age and its historical grounds. For in the *historiological* acceptance of Pascalism, the long-since accomplished repudiation of all thoughtful questioning seeks its most secure shelter
behind a supreme form of the spiritual vindication of faith.

Yet insofar as this awakening of Pascalian apologetics at least extrinsically uses the means of thought and forms of speech of that
thinking which already moves decisively in another beginning of
thinking and has already left behind the modernity which is only now
properly commencing, then the modernity of this Christian apologetics will become *still more* ambiguous and insidious. Modern apologetics does not operate with the means of ordinary refutation and vindication—instead, it takes on, first and constantly, the semblance of

110

---

18. {Blaise Pascal, *Sämmtliche Schriften über Philosophie und Christenthum*, erster
Theil (Berlin: Besser, 1840), p. 198: "The spirit has its order, namely, through
principles and argumentation, and the heart belongs to another order." The formula "logic of the heart" is not attested in Pascal.}

"living" and co-living the "lived experience" of the *search* for truth. It can indeed allow itself this *semblant* | questioning without any danger,   111 because the possession of truth has already been secured. One is modern and can even use and exploit what is "modern" more effectively than modernity can do for itself, because it is immediately removed from its apparent groundlessness and strictly inserted into the "orders." One can incorporate every modern stirring of taste and change of style into a presentation of the orders, which is flexible within definite—although secret—limits. Everything is out-and-out *imitation*, yet with a cleverness stemming from centuries of practice, such that it can one day, with the ever-increasing ignorance, pass itself off as "creative." Corresponding to this modern rescue of cultural Christianity are the "struggle" against and the "overcoming" of "Christianity." These derive from an empty enlightenment or from a half-understood Nietzscheanism or from both and merely repeat the cultural Christianity in an inversion or on a much lower plane— (building in advance, for a "faith" and for a requirement of faith, a "spiritual world" mixed from all philosophies, dripping with "seriousness," and *over*flowing with "decisions," according to which everything is already decided by way of a decisionlessness). The rescue of cultural Christianity and the semblance of anti-Christian world-views—belong | together. Their dovetailing is a sign that the conscious   112 and unconditional instituting of the modern anthropormorphizing of the human being has started as a closed process. *This* dovetailing makes possible the "triumphant parade of technology."—

The other *beginning* of the history of beyng, i.e., the *break* with the metaphysically determined history of the West, must necessarily remain invisible for a long time to come, because this break is carried out by way of a *questioning* (the disclosive questioning of what is most question-worthy) and makes this questioning the ground of *Da-sein*, wherein the human being is placed back into the affiliation with being. *What is question-worthy*, however, is for cultural Christianity *and* for anti-Christianity in the same way that which is *most hated;* for only the *faith in faith* counts as rich in results, and results count as evidence of "truth." Where there is faith in faith, one day it becomes inconsequential *what* one still has faith in—but this day can once bring into its own light that which has eventuated in the anthropormorphizing of the human being and in cultural Christianity. The human being does not then stand before the now ever more loudly detested, ever less grasped, ever more negative, and ever more formless *nothing*—instead, he stands, *above all*, before the whole "of life"—himself included therein—| and knows he cannot "start" anything with all this—be-   113 cause he has long ago forgotten everything inceptual and because his own "lived experience" has become for him the "lived experience" of boredom. Pascal makes Christianity fit for modernity.—

64

Every true historical overcoming which is not misinterpreted as "prog-ress" finds its culmination in the fact that it alone liberates what is "overcome" for great reverence. Only such overcoming will teach us what metaphysics has been.

65

If the word "existence" ["*Existenz*"] as *existentia* did not belong entirely to metaphysics, where it signifies presence, being at hand, extantness, and *if* furthermore the word were *not* misused with extreme confu-sion by the "philosophy of existence," then it could unfold its splen-did nominative power into an essential characterization of the human being: humans ex-sist—their being is grounded in the assignment to the truth of being. Humans are ex-sistent—"standing out" toward beyng and so are in-sistent within a clearing of beings. Yet no "phi-losophy" can be built on this, I in case here a philosophy may in the future be built at all. *This* existence of human beings—they them-selves in their essence—is such only on the ground of beyng, and beyng appropriates humans into that assignment and makes their es-sential plight the grounding of Da-sein, the grounding of the insistent standing out of the "there." The "philosophy of existence" is always still anthropology and metaphysics and does not ask the basic ques-tion of the truth of beyng—it poses no decision and, above all, *is* no decision.

66

Nietzsche's *Untimely Considerations* is excessively overrun by what is all too timely. Indeed even the untimeliness of the considerations is grounded in an extreme timeliness, for *modernity* more and more de-cisively determines their essence, which is: the anthropormorphizing of the human being—the sovereignty of "life"—the helpless subjec-tion to metaphysics in the form of a mere inversion. Yet insofar as Nietzsche attempts to gather this confusion in an uncompromising decisiveness as regards its essentials, and to endure therein and to sur-mount the confusion, then through him everything is shifted into the form of a convulsion and thus into an impetus. But one can all the

more easily avoid this impetus, if one so to speak I co-affirms in a   115
crude way Nietzsche's "yes" to "life" and makes a "virtue" out of his
plight and his distresses or perhaps turns them merely into a loud
amusement and a self-secure faith. One is thereby also secured against
the almost unendurable element in Nietzsche's thinking—i.e., against
that simultaneous volition to overcome and the thinking out into
something other which nevertheless, precisely in its Essential endeavor, falls back into what already was.—

66a

The renunciation of the *imitation* precisely of what is best and highest
cannot arise from a craving for "originality"; it derives instead only
from an essential plight which knows that the enduring of what is
compelling (what is question-*worthy*) is everything, such that "originality" of itself remains outside the horizon of this plight. "Originality" is a gauge of *historiological* calculation but is not a determination of *historical* being. Therefore even what is historiologically
unoriginal (i.e., historiologically demonstrable as thoroughly deriva-
tive) can very well be *historically originary*—a concealed origin of history (i.e., an attaining of the essence of beyng). The consequence is
that the historically originary eludes the investigations of historiology
and in each case comes to be expressed, I in its reticence, only in his-   116
torical dialogue.

67

Why is the *misuse* which befalls poets and thinkers, and which conditions a rejection just as much as an approval of them, always more
powerful than every appropriate relation to them? It is because the
powerful counts as the real and because the real has need of publicness. As for the poet and the thinker, however, what they say and
question stands in beyng, which is outside of power and impotence
and is not available in public. Poets and thinkers do not "effect" (at
most, in their misuse); they *are*. But *their* beyng—because it must be
the grounding of Da-sein and thus be appropriated by beyng itself—
is illuminated only now and then to ones of their own in dialogue—
poets and thinkers are merely "exceptions," if we make publicness and
power the standards, i.e., measure poets and thinkers according to
something inappropriate—in essence, poets and thinkers are the
"rule" of beyng itself—the guarantee of its uniqueness, the eventua-
tions for the history of beyng, and beyng itself, as the clearing of be-

ings, only occasionally compels the human being into the struggle over his *essence*. This essence has to be situated in relation to the gods 117 as an encounter with them, I in order to help them to an illumination of their divinity. For this history to eventuate purely and for beyng to effectuate nothing and have no capability, but only be, then in each case the misuse must expand, so much so that it does not at all appear as a misuse.

68

The recourse to Christianity seems to be a preservation of "morality," and the appeal to cultural Christianity (especially that of the Middle Ages) an affirmation and thus a furtherance of greatness—but what if all this backward flight were a neglecting and concealing of the great decisions? What is more essential: a temporary coloring over of history through evasion into the past, or a venturing of the actual plight and an acknowledging of the Godlessness and impotence, for the sake of preparing a domain of decision? The former is easier and more "beautiful"—the latter is hard and unsettling—but it *is* nearness to beyng—reverence toward what is most question-worthy—renunciation of "results" and "consequences"—yet is a leap into the clearing from which the self-refusal of beyng takes us by storm. And this storm 118 announces the close remoteness I of the possibly last god.

69

The gigantic is a mode of what is great, and indeed greatness does *not* consist in a measurable—though unusual—extension as excess; *that* "gigantism" is only the consequence of what is properly gigantic. The essence of the latter consists in the fact that an epoch calculates and secures its own present time explicitly already as a future pastness (and thus immortality). The presupposition of such a volition is that the humanity of this epoch should grasp itself and indeed completely and in every respect ("totally") as the institutable and calculable goal of itself and specifically in the sense of the relational center of all beings. That volition to the securing of the immortality of the present requires the exploitation of all the means assuring an overwhelming, a making of an impression, a taking by surprise—i.e., an extrication from what is ordinary. Also belonging here, especially in the epoch of calculability, is the numerically and physically exorbitant—the gigantic in the "quantitative" sense. This "quantitative" is nevertheless *not* the essence of the gigantic, but is only an essential consequence of that essence. (Cf. the lecture on the grounding of the modern world-picture through metaphysics.[19]) Therefore the emergence of the "gigantic" stands in an intrinsic connection to | the increasing predom- | 119 inance of *historiology,* in the essential sense of the calculative production and representation of beings as a whole *out of* and *for* the center of the self-securing of the human being as subjectum. The more powerfully historiology expands in this direction, all the more unhistorical becomes the human being. The more unhistorical his history becomes through historiology, all the more durable becomes humanity in its anthropomorphization. The more willingly this "eternity" is pursued, all the more frequently and obstinately becomes at the same time the flight into the other "eternity" of the Christian heaven. The more narrow the opposition between the two, all the more does the human being close himself off on all sides from the abyss of an essential plight and thus from the possibility of an affiliation with the history of beyng; it is by means of the thrust of beyng that the human being can first be shown in his originary essence.

70

Nietzsche's meditation on *historiology* touches an essential question of modernity—but Nietzsche does not attain an intrinsic overcoming of historiology out of the essence of history—he simply protects historiology from science. The consequence of his | reckoning with histori- | 120 ology is the elevated power of "historiology" in the sense of a forward-directed historiology that calculates the future. Nietzsche's determination of historiology makes historiology only *still more* modern—i.e., definitively subservient to "life" as such, to the self-securing of the human being.

Historiology: the technology of "history."

Technology: the historiology of "nature." (Cf. earlier.)

Inasmuch as historiology and technology are *metaphysically* the same, this sameness corresponds immediately to the sameness of nature and history in the sense of "life" as an importunate, self-configuring force.

The abandonment of beings by being, as the unneediness for being, is becoming consummated. The human being is able still to see only what is of *his own* making; "the" human being as modern, however, is necessarily individuated into encompassing "subjects."

Even what previously was great—is only a preliminary stage of the great itself—and of its "eternity," which everything earlier—*because* it had to become something past—was not able to reach. The prelimi-

---

19. {"Die Zeit des Weltbildes."}

nary stage is background of the still more decisive delineation. The human being is becoming ever more unjust and therefore smaller; he will be smallest when he has secured his smallness (i.e., the abandonment by being and the decisionlessness) as greatness. This process is irresistible, not because it is an "organic" one—but because it is a *historical* one—i.e., unleashed by | beyng itself as the concealed self-refusal having no need of force.

All "cultural politics" is already the slave of this unleashing in service to the instituting of a gigantic semblance into which all beings enter. This semblance is the concealed protection of beyng and does not allow the times of its truth to be calculated in advance through the machination of beings. Yet knowledge of this history of beyng already belongs to Da-*sein*, to the already paved, yet unrecognizable, grounding of the essence of the human being out of the summons of beyng: to experience modern humanity's lack of a sense of plight as the genuine and deepest plight, to be able to arise out of the necessitations which can be endured only as necessities of being and in that way to guarantee for the human being the freedom toward the essence of beyng, namely, to venture the path, perhaps even to venture the gods—to ground a site for the essential flight of their divinity. *This* history of beyng is the "longest" and it bears everything—but there is no historiology of it—only in each case the *May it happen!*: Da-*sein*.

{Index}

PONDERINGS XI

a   "Philosophy that is close to life"—is like a bridge submerged in a river. So can there be "a" philosophy that is *remote* from life? No. For the appraisal of philosophy in relation to "life," whether according to closeness or remoteness, is always a destruction of the essence of philosophy. Why? Because philosophy has to think beyng, has to fathom for beyng the ground of the truth *of beyng*. But beyng is the unique—what *is* only if *it* is; no beings are adequate to it—yet beyng is never the highest—instead, it is the "between"—the abyss for height and depth.

How something essential, i.e., something offered up to the simplest decisions, is "effective," how it must remain altogether ineffective and only thereby first brings beyng to determination in beings—of all this we have no knowledge. We also do not need to know it here, since only one thing matters: to *be* essential. Nevertheless the essence, i.e., how the truth of beyng eventuates, rests with beyng itself, whose summons becomes sayable as word or else gets drowned out in the noise of what are already beings and are "real."

The courage for philosophy is the knowledge of the necessary down-going of Da-sein. Philosophy, since it can be borne only in the disposition of such courage, shares with everything essential (everything appertaining to the grounding of the truth of beyng) the privilege of rarity. Philosophy does not stand related to the "intelligentsia" or the "believers" or those who calculate or the never-too-populous throng.

The modern human being has based the assurance of his essence on his becoming some day a cog in a machine, so that in service to the impartiality and calculability of the running of the machine, he might find impulses, pleasure, and effortless security. This involvement with the machine is essentially other than the mere use of "technological" possibilities; here commences the extreme adaptation of the human being to the calculability of beings. With all this the *spirit* (i.e., rational and calculative animality) first comes to its highest power; the sovereignty of the machine is neither "rationalism" nor "materialism"—not the devastation of empty reason and not the consecration of sheer matter. Rather, in this adaptation to the machine, there is carried out a self-releasement into beings which no longer has need of "images" ["*Bilder*"] for its "meaning" ["*Sinn*"]—because the intuitability has unfolded to complete calculability and is constantly present in it, since the "meaning" has entrenched itself in the ever self-genera-

2 tive planning I for a unique motility. The modern human being needs no further symbols [*Sinnbilder*], not because he renounces meaning but because the meaning is something he dominates as the empowerment of the human being himself to the calculative center of all institutions of every machination for beings as a whole. The modern human being no longer needs the symbol, because he has compelled the intuitable and visible entirely into the power of his production of everything makeable (and nowhere impossible). The symbol is possible and necessary only where metaphysics places being over beings and must present the former through the latter—; but as soon as—for instance in the age of the consummation of metaphysics—beings themselves take over all being and recognize beings only in their representation and production, i.e., as soon as the "*real*" and the "living," the "fact" and the result, constitute the "truth," then every possibility and every necessity of a symbol fall away. Whoever would again introduce such a thing in the modern era—i.e., on the path of histori-

3 ological calculation and imitation—is feigning shallow I pensiveness and is not recognizing the genuine essential depth of his own epoch.

"Symbols" are now manifoldly impossible: 1. because that which is their essence happens in a deeper sense and more decisively (the identification of meaning and image in the institutable calculation of beings, i.e., of the calculability of their being); 2. because maintaining that the creation of symbols is necessary presupposes an image-less *meaning* which requires an image—i.e., it presupposes an essential determination of being which would require that being first present itself in the total otherness of *a* being. (But precisely this presupposition is no longer posited and can no longer be posited if the human being takes himself as animal (race—blood) to be the goal of himself and has taken the planning of his history into his volition. Where meaning is placed into what is meaningless, where beings make all being superfluous, there every source of a power to *symbolize* is lacking.); and 3. because even if (impossibly) a trace | of a power for   4 *symbols* and for the creation of images is conceded to what is meaningless and is abandoned by being, the creation of images could never be awoken and carried out through a historiological excavation of past symbols and symbolic worlds in the manner of folklore. Those who are supposedly of today do not know anything of the present time of their history; instead, they "romantically" invent for themselves with the romantic means of historiology ("folklore" and "prehistory") a past as the ideal of a future.

One constantly makes "intellectualism" contemptible and at the same time totters in the orgies of an unusual historicism and closes oneself off from a knowledge of what genuinely *is*.

One preaches "blood" and "soil" and yet pursues an urbanization and a destruction of the village and farm to an extent that could not have been surmised a short while ago.

One talks of "life" and "lived experience" and yet everywhere thwarts all growth, all venture, and all freedom for erring and foundering, every possibility of meditation, and every necessity of questioning. One is acquainted with everything, knows everything, appraises everything | according to results, and takes as real only what   5 promises results.

2

The consummation and very long ending of *historiology* are reached when "sensation," "propaganda," "psychology," and "biography" determine and bear all "interest." The fact that "sensation" and "propaganda" [*"Sensation" und "Propaganda"*] are Latin-Romance terms cannot be thrust aside as something accidental. But why are we making this that is counter-German the essence of Germany?

3

Ignorance can reach a level at which, without effecting anything, it immediately becomes destructive.

4

One who has no anxiety is not thereby shown to be a hero; on the contrary, he merely proves to be a coarse person who also entirely lacks, along with fear, the possibility of reverential awe and thus the power for deeming worthy and so a sense for what is most worthy, i.e., most worthy of questioning.

6

5

The mechanicism of practical and "people"-oriented representation and "thinking" eliminates all standards by which an intrinsically prevailing essentiality could still become visible. We possess only the one averting piece of information: such a claim is "abstract" and "intellectual." We are not able to reconcile ourselves with the thought that a grounding of the realms of essential decisions can be more "popular" than all people-oriented institutions taken together, assuming that the essence of a people can never be grounded historiologically, but only historically, i.e., in projections. We are no longer and still not able to tolerate the apparent aloofness and disdaining of the masses on the part of self-compelled questioning and creating, and we have no patience for preparing decisions long into the future, all of which testifies that we have not in the least become certain of the essence of a people, i.e., of the definition of humanity. Instead, we merely continue to avail ourselves of superficial calculations and expedients whose gigantic extent can but poorly cover over the essential emptiness.

6

Prototypes—as illuminating and clever as they may be—can accom-
7 plish nothing without a previous education | in *how to take something as a prototype*. And that also requires an inner liberation for the riches and venturesomeness of humanity and its history. To take as a prototype means to place oneself into the open domain of what is question-worthy and to let oneself be cast over into an essentially transformative position. But where one already fancies oneself in the possession of all "truth," every prototype is an absurdity or a "facade" behind which one merely seeks to place oneself in a brighter light and play a fast and loose historiological game with history.

7

At times of transition, indeed perhaps at all times, must the essential questioning first enter into the effectiveness of its opposite, before what is essential to it comes to stand in its proper standing room and indeed in a way that has no need of effectivity?

8

Caspar David *Friedrich* is not a "romantic"; he is equally distant, i.e., infinitely distant, because essentially separated, from everything romantic as is *Hölderlin*. Yet, like Hölderlin, he remains—in a richly mysterious simultaneity—a peak protruding into the Godforsaken spaces of the divinity of the sometime God. But precisely in their Godlessness | Hölderlin and Friedrich cannot be compared to each other, assuming comparisons could be justified here at all. Each is respectively a forerunner of those future ones who venture "only" so far into the truth of beyng and yet first ground the essence of beyng in its truth and who stand at once on this side and that side of beings and in this stance endure down to their own day as misunderstood ones who ground. Meanwhile, the modern human being needs beyng ever less and makes his "God" beings and things already present-at-hand, from which he can calculate, to the satisfaction of his reason, the origination of his own presence at hand.

9

Subjectivism (that the human being is the subjectum of all things) must first expand into the gigantic, into what can be communally pursued and understood as of equal concern to everyone; everyone must first be allowed to partake in the blessings of the promotion and imitations of culture and thereby find his mediocrity confirmed as indispensable; taste must first have gained by struggle a priority for an average benevolence and for what is ordinarily "healthy" and "powerful"; the elapsing of the previous Western | history must first have become quite broad and shallow, such that anyone at all can stand therein and thus show himself as a "personality" and a "willing" contemporary—and all this must first be assured in a gigantic turning back on itself (prehistory—folklore—doctrine of race and heredity) to a "lived experience" that can itself be the object of a "lived experience"—before the human being as the rational animal *can revolve round about himself* "restlessly," the loss of every possibility of an essential questioning can

be registered as a gain and a success, and the compulsion into this revolving can create the impression of freedom.

The instituting of this historical age and the education of the human being to this "subjectivism" of human*kind*, not of the "individual," are peculiar undertakings, unthinkable without historiology,
i.e., without technology. This revolving round about oneself—now
commencing and scarcely to be represented in its speed and certainty
and (because ineluctable) unanimity—makes the modern Western
human being himself disappear into the void which can no longer
admit of anything impossible or unimaginable but in which the pre-
10   vious human being swirled ever more surely | and contentedly. Who-
ever does not go along with this revolving goes down.

The downgoing can take two forms: 1. whoever does not go along
is abraded away, without ever getting to see the historical necessity
and gigantism of the age; 2. whoever does not go along with the revolving—is not "tractable" to it—is flung centrifugally out into spaces
which first open up thereby and require of the human being a quite
different compliance whose plight within the vortex could never be
experienced or grasped. Such downgoings have—and must have—already happened, because indeed the revolving—the history of modernity—has for centuries occurred in slow and hardly perceptible cur-
rents. The imperceptibility of the revolving and of its increase even
entrenches itself, insofar as it therein resists and opposes the revolving
round about himself of the "individual" in order to dispose all powers toward the revolving of "life" round about itself.

The knowledge of this revolving arises already from something external to it; and because the revolving turns beings as such toward the
11   abandonment by being, and in the vortex again | requires in each case
only beings and their pursuit, supposing this can be effectuated
without being, then that externality must have granted a place for its
space by way of an appropriation by beyng, an appropriation that liberates us to experience the fact that no beings are capable of anything,
except for beyng, to which the human being is able to oppose "nothing,"
unless he brings a resoluteness to the displacing of his essence into the
arena of historical decision.

10

Neither Hölderlin nor Nietzsche visited Greece. Therefore, it is quite in order that those on *K. d. F.* trips[20] now gain a "lived experience of Hellas."—Something indeed inconsequential, and yet a sign.

Historical *destruction* does not consist in the elimination of what was hitherto and has already fulfilled its essence and now only conceals itself in the persistence of its distorted essence. Destruction exists only where the *possibility* of essentially free origins and of still undecided ventures is obstructed *already in its conditions* and is so from an intention | to belong to a constructive era and to be obliged to it. Yet such destruction can still—against its own will—contribute to the first onset of a beginning of essential becoming—provided the destruction has not turned into devastation.

11

The highest danger for human*kind* is the unquestionability of itself within a deeming of being as unworthy of questioning.

12

The "temporality" of Da-sein (in *Being and Time*) is read and taken as a determination of the "transitoriness" of the human being; in this way, it receives an "anthropological" and even "Christian" interpretation, and no one sees that "anthropology," "Christianity," and metaphysics have all come to naught through the question—*indeed already through the attitude that raises the question*—of the truth of being. This truth must first be made graspable as "time" (in recollecting the interpretation of being as beingness within the entirety of Western metaphysics). The "temporality" of Da-sein names rather the truth of being; standing in this truth, the human being transforms his essence from animality to the steadfastness in Da-sein, and Da-sein is the stewardship for this truth. "Temporality" | names the "relation" of the human being to beyng (a "relation" grounding his essence) and thus places the human being before a completely other history. We know of this history "only" the abyss over which it must move, in distinction to the constantly shallower superficiality of subjectivity in which humanity has been seized and which has ascended to become the do-

---

20. {K. d. F = *"Kraft durch Freude"* ["Power through enjoyment"], a suborganization of the German Labor Front, which organized vacation trips, etc.}

main and measure, the center and the form of fulfillment, of all "beings."

Those who are knowledgeable know first of all that they do *not* know what is being prepared in the commencing consummation and ending of modernity as regards the determination of the essential configuration of the human being. This ignorance is not a lack, because the originariness of the *historical* human being must unfold precisely therein, so that he might overcome historiology and with it, technology, and so that both in one might in due course fall away from the humanity in Da-sein and forfeit every essentially configurative power. For "temporality" does not mean "transitoriness," but just as little is it the name of something nontransitory; it refers instead to a completely different domain (steadfastness in the *truth* of beyng (care)). Therefore even the question of death has a quite peculiar meaning within a meditation on the grounding of the truth of beyng—; every "ethical," "anthropological," and "eschatological" interpretation remains superficial and I does not surmise that what matters is to grasp the essential occurrence of the *truth* of beyng—the spatiotemporal field of the "there"—in its character as event, in its affiliation to beyng itself. This holds necessarily, because nothingness, casting itself about as the most proper essence of beyng, requires death as the extreme possibility of temporality.

Thought in terms of the history of beyng, the essence of death is the abyss in which death in the usual sense is founded. Yet death as understood by the interpretation of the human being as animal could never be grasped in its essence according to the history of beyng and does not need to be so grasped there. Death is the most extreme, most solitary, and thus highest outpost of Da-sein within the current history of Da-sein's stewardship over the truth of beyng. To understand death means—thought in a way appropriate to Da-sein and to the history of beyng—to let its essence be incorporated into the *projection* of the truth of beyng. And this projecting never thinks to explain death, since indeed beyng itself essentially occurs outside every requirement of explanation, for explainability is a dubious privilege relegated only to beings. No "biology" or "anthropology" but also no "ethics" can attain the essence, or the counteressence, of death as understood in the history of beyng. That counteressence is not "birth," but is instead conception and I procreation—provided these also are taken in their essence as thought and secluded in the history of beyng.

The human being of the transition from metaphysics to the disclosive questioning of the truth of beyng stands in face of unsurmised mysteries still to be passed over in silence. Even here the poet (Hölderlin) has founded in advance, and no one of today may venture an interpretation that would raise into the light what is still preserved, because there is no one who could already stand in such a clearing of beyng. The usual notions of "time," in all their historical configurations, are essentially *insufficient* to determine the essence of temporality—it is quite the reverse: the latter, as spatiotemporal field, is the ground of the possibility of those notions. That is also the reason no one seeks to surmise the essence of temporality as the ground of the historicality and truth of beyng. The main motive of this resistance, however, consists in the lack of a sense of plight, which prevents a genuine compulsion toward the originary question of being.

13

Who are the futural ones? Most people in their masses, or the fewest ones, or the *beginning* ones, who indeed harbor an entire time in themselves and have no need of the future? But who are the beginning ones? Those who come out of the plight I of beyng.   16

14

If historicism becomes complete, it will take over even the calculation of the future, so as to get "eternity" into its power. The lack of freedom with respect to history is becoming unconditional. What in a present can precisely not be numbered is taken as dispatched—"for all eternity." Everything that is not an originary action and pursuit, everything that is without beginning, requires this delusion, because it must avoid everything abyssal and in advance has taken refuge in what can be calculated.

16[21]

That the spirit of the trenches [*Frontgeist*] gathered itself up and compelled the political distractedness into an order is an important yet merely superficial effect of the great fighter in the world war. Yet we have not at all made headway in experiencing for once things which are inconceivable about that Da-sein and in adhering to them for long, in order to know that something happened here which is still withholding its "effectivity" until the human being has returned to a depth of essence which would prepare him to encounter such mystery. Ernst Jünger is the first and only one to carry out a meditation—*but* the question remains as to whether this meditation co-grounds for itself

---

21. [This misnumbering published as such.—Trans.]

17   its idiosyncratic domain and I its ground of truth at the same time or
     whether it does not indeed lapse into a mere raising up to the level of
     the unconditioned ("total mobilization"[22]) what was already at hand
     (technology—worker)—raising what had been the particular into the
     total—and thus still lies on the path of the modern way of thinking
     and does not attain an inceptual question-worthiness—and is still
     metaphysics.

     As the incapacity for thinking increases, and so do the aversion to
     meditation, the powerlessness of questioning, and the impotence for
     essential decisions and ventures, to that extent the greatness of his-
     tory falls into the hands of those who are small, whose "products"
     necessarily protrude, as incomparable creations, over the need and ca-
     pacity of those who are smallest. It is no wonder that the grounding
     of what is essential and the venture of what is most question-worthy
     remain absent—it would be a miracle if such became everyday occur-
     rences of regulative planning. That grounding is rare, and only
     modern historicism, which surveys and calculates everything, has
     filled in the broad fissure between what is rare and what is essential
     and inceptual—filled it with the great variety of things that can be
     compared, wherein even what is unique was leveled down. The ab-
     sence of the essential grounding is also not a doom—instead, for those
18   who know, it is only the plight of patience and I silence. But what is
     indeed frightful is the entanglement of what is small in the semblance
     of greatness—yet to their "good fortune," which is the main point,
     those who participate in this entanglement have no inkling of it. In
     the presumably long duration of the consummation of modernity, this
     entanglement can become an uncanny, totally unnoticed destruc-
     tion—which, because it is a destruction of the truth of beyng, will in-
     finitely surpass every annihilation of beings, such as in a new world
     war.

     This destruction has been in progress for a very long time—all those
     who begin and prepare are assigned the task of knowing about it. But
     to them the disdain of the wretchedness of what is small must still be
     something contemptible and must not concern them. Meditation on
     this process of the consummation of modernity must not be led astray
     into an attempt to "contest" and "refute." Yet anxiety in the face of
     meditation and the powerlessness to question are not—as the "reac-
     tionaries" and "conservatives" and even the "Christians" would pre-
     tend—consequences of the prevailing political worldview—but rather
     arise out of the unfolding and consummation of the modern essence

---

22. {Ernst Jünger, "Die totale Mobilmachung," in *Krieg und Krieger* (Berlin:
Junker und Dünnhaupt, 1930), pp. 9–30.}

of the human being—for whom the *self-certainty* of his self—even if this self may be defined as subjectum—is I the first and only truth. 19 Every placing of oneself in question—every tinge of meditation—endangers this basic truth—every hint of danger therefore requires all the more decisively the unassailability of the certainty of one's self and thus the elimination of every attempt to question. The conservative way of thinking and certainly also the Christian one have for a long time been living in anxiety over what is question-worthy. Therefore, they present a "grotesque" spectacle when they now pretend to be guardians and saviors of the "spirit." The historical necessity and proper greatness of the commencing era of the consummation of modernity are essentially degraded if party politics or ecclesial politics or any other contemporary "points of view" are allowed to provide the standard.

Meditation on our history does not judge about what is historiologically encounterable, historiologically present—instead, this meditation, as inceptual, is a preparation for what is most deeply and originarily still undecided—the relation between being and beings. A thoughtful advance into the history of beyng—and only this—is the task here, a task that is unavoidably aloof, strange, and useless—and therefore is also constantly exposed to misuse on the part of what is only in appearance untimely. The essence of the vocation of the I Germans is not a mere conditional essence—one among others—but is 20 unconditional, in the sense that through the Germans the essence of beyng itself will be gained by struggle—which is not equivalent to a mere new configuration of beings in the sphere of the historical consequences of modernity and of its human race.

15[23]

"To live philosophically"—does not at all mean to follow the doctrines and rules of a philosophical "system" and carry them over into everyday "praxis." Does it not rather mean only to carry out the praxis of philosophy itself—i.e., to remain on the course of an originary, relentless, and unsupported meditation and to venture the essence of truth itself as what is most question-worthy? This questioning and discourse do not require any "effectivity"—because they in themselves essentially already surpass all "effectivity" insofar as they merely and simply *are* and thereby, without effectuating anything—startle beings and whatever counts as a being and perhaps also unsettle them.

---

23. [This misnumbering published as such.—Trans.]

17

The simplest philosophical cognition in the age of consummated modernity is the knowledge that and why philosophy had to become impossible and still remains unnecessary for this age.

21

18

Everything that effectuates and transfers itself into its results and has need of such effectuation in order to justify itself from its results—is unessential, i.e., deprived of essential force.—

Neither the deformation of *historiology* into *historicism* nor historiology itself is overcome by a flight into the super-historiological; instead, these are overcome only by history, by the human being becoming essentially historical—by his renouncing all imitation and responding only to the plight of what is originary.

19

The consummation of modernity consists in the human being grasping himself completely as a "subject" and, above all, comporting himself in that way. But the culmination of the subjective does precisely not consist in "individualism"; instead, it consists in the human being (*along with* all that is at his disposal and is proper to him) uniting *everything human*—the community and the inherited humanness—into that which lies at the basis of all valuing, planning, and acting—and in letting measures, goals, and plans be the domain that does provide the basis. The human being knows himself as human when he comes to terms with these possessions, exploits them, tolerates nothing

22   else, justifies all effectuating | by its results, and everywhere confirms himself as this subjectum. Such unconditional craving for the subjective must be able to pass itself off as the "most objective"—because "objectivity" means nothing other than the binding, without exception, to that subjectivity, and such binding supports itself and asserts itself through the unconditional demand for the unquestionability of humanity. Because what is mediocre and decisionless is what is least dangerous, and also remains what is least endangered—therefore it rightly guarantees for itself the prospect of the longest duration and can most readily stake a claim to "eternity." And if the habituation to the mediocre can once be entirely effective, then the assurance of life will seem to be triumphant. But that habituation operates most successfully where and when it has also taken possession of what is "great" as what it itself fosters and makes accessible.

20

Nietzsche's "effect" on modernity depends on what is modern in Nietzsche himself; that comprises what is essential to him and is already expressed very early in his attachment to Schopenhauer, which is not sublated by any | liberation or inversion but is only entrenched.					23
Nietzsche's statement (1873) "We are *human* in virtue of what is entirely *subjective*, which is the accumulated inheritance wherein we all have a share" (X, 212)[24]—contains his permanent basic philosophical position—precisely where the "body" becomes the Prescriptive subjectivity of the "subjectum."

Only what is timely is "effective"; the untimely is not only ineffective but—assuming it is originary and thus genuinely untimely—is what has no need of effectiveness—and is that *from* which nothing follows but which once must be followed—though this following cannot mean being "effectuated."

21

"Temporality"—the essentiality of Da-sein—the ground of the historicality of the human being and at once the ground of his assignment to the truth of beyng—is not a truth available to just anyone—it is aloof not only from common opinions and values but also from the prevailing habits of the highest Western thinking up to the consummation of this thinking in Nietzsche. For the projection of temporality is not based on a detection of previously overlooked properties of the human being or of "time"—but instead arises in | the question of the					24
truth of beyng.

22

The thoughtful return to the first beginning cannot merely aim at securing and renewing an old inheritance in order to gain prestige and a belated justification. That is for many reasons "impossible." The more originary and inceptual a grounding and what it grounds, all the more exclusively will the grounding belong to itself and deny itself any imitation or "repetition" in the sense of bringing forth once more something that had already happened and therefore endures incontestably. But every beginning requires, as what is appropriate to it, only *again*

---

24. {Friedrich Nietzsche, *Nachgelassene Werke: Aus den Jahren 1872/73–1875/76. Werke*, vol. 15 (Leipzig: Kröner, 1919).}

the *beginning; this* repetition (cf. *Being and Time*[25]) is the most pitched battle of the beginnings, that battle which remains outside all calculative *"historiological"* confrontation and which finds no assistance or support in a return to what already occurred, nothing wherein it could vindicate itself and nothing it could now offer up anew—. The return encounters what is abyssal of an opposition which retains its own most proper law and requires from the opponent only an extreme 25   alienation versus itself as the other opponent—this | battle rages outside of the clashing of violence and force—. The battle of the beginnings is a dispute over the liberation of the law (concealed in them) of their incomprehensibility. What is contested is to the highest degree again only the plight of another beginning—"beginning" is here meant essentially and never merely as what is first and most proximate for what properly *follows*—precisely that remains inconsequential for the beginning—since it is of the essence of the beginning to place the grounding purely into the essence of that grounding. What thereby "develops" depends always on an abandonment of the beginning. Only those who are in the process of beginning can think inceptually; for the others, who already want to go further, "over and beyond" the beginning, inceptual thinking becomes simply an expression of a peculiar "historiological" "interest."

23

The current generation is not hard and will not become hard—despite what might be pretended—but only obtuse. Hardness derives solely from the clarity of the highest meditation; obtuseness, however, belongs to what is dull and to the numbing which is taken to be "life" itself. Yet dullness can very well go together with a consummate "rationalism."

26   ### 24

A long back-and-forth thinking is necessary before we can break the silence over Nietzsche's thought of *"justice,"* which is an echo of δίκη ["right"] in the inceptual questioning of the Greeks—. But can we think essentially enough what Nietzsche, on the basis of "life" and in connection with truth as an illusion of constancy, an illusion necessary for life, means here? Does Nietzsche, without posing the question of beyng, perhaps brush up here against the decisive character of

---

25. {Martin Heidegger, *Sein und Zeit*, GA2 (Frankfurt: Klostermann, 1977), p. 509f.}

beyng? How justice constitutes the essential structure of both the will to power and the eternal recurrence, how justice yet is named merely *in addition*—these issues can be decided only if Nietzsche's metaphysics is thought through on the basis of an essential knowledge of metaphysics, i.e., on the basis of an intrinsic overcoming of metaphysics. How wretchedly are we equipped for this armed conflict! And, above all, how lacking in every necessity is such a thinking everywhere! Justice is Nietzsche's attempt to extricate himself from the empty "relativism" of the doctrine of perspective, and yet: is relativity to the "subject" now simply called relativity to the "will to power"—wherefore then not still relativism?? Because not an absolutism! What then?

25

27

Truth.—From what do we take the essence of truth? What guarantees us the destiny to find and watch over the essence? Perhaps only the venturing of our own essence? Whence this *necessity of venturing?* Is *this*, in advance and above all else, already the essence of the human being, which he constantly and unwittingly conceals to himself and acknowledges only in misinterpretations which present no danger to his entrenched animality? What does it mean that we mostly and straightforwardly appeal to our presence at hand and the unproblematic opinions about it and find satisfaction in the alluvium of the pursuits that merely crave for life? (Cf. p. 79f.)

26

The "sovereignty" of the human being, the machination of beings as realities (things that are effective), the oblivious disregard of any question-worthiness of beyng, the sheer evasion into sham deliverances (Christianity)—all this is unitarily driven to the extreme limit, such that the human being could no longer hope to find his way out of this state of affairs through a mere withdrawal from the "world"—as if there were still offered somewhere or other something tranquil and untouched, on which one could rely. No—the human being must I first set an extremity of the question-worthiness of beyng in opposition to this extremity of the abandonment by being—indeed not merely set it in opposition but actually set it up and venture it from himself and come to surmise something of the essential ineffectiveness of beyng and its unneediness for effectivity. What distinguishes the age of consummated modernity is that in this age no pretexts or compromises or immediate solutions are possible. Only those who are of the beginning can overcome, indeed they no longer need to be over-

28

comers if they are beginners. Revaluations, revolutions, and rebellions are stuck in the chains and circuits of the past and remain essentially behind what is needed: that the human being venture his essence, and in such venturing disclosively question this essence as that to which a first name is lent with the stewardship of the truth of beyng.

27

Beginnings never need effectivity, and to issue forth in something is always inappropriate to them. Beginnings *are;* without effecting, their
29   being compels a beginning again. Such compelling I happens beyond power and impotence and is determined by the interplay of the origins, which place themselves reciprocally into freedom.

28

Hölderlin—*historiologically* "positioned" and calculated, this poet belongs to the age of German Idealism, where absolute thinking in part carries out, in part prepares, the consummation of Western metaphysics. The calculation can be expanded to include Goethe, Schiller, romanticism, and much else, in order to make the historiological obstruction of Hölderlin complete. But of what concern to us is historiology, for which Hölderlin must count as a herald and an ending? In *historical* meditation, meditation on the history of beyng, meditation which places metaphysics in question in the entirety of its essence and history, Hölderlin is a beginning, i.e., a concealed demand of the beginning—and of the future as a beginning—and thus he is anything but an ending and a renewal.

The "inner" presupposition for a historiologist—in case such a one has an "interior"—as expert in the past is obliviousness with regard to history. For the public, he makes up for this lack (which indeed
30   cannot be experienced or recognized) I through the abundance of ever new "results" and "conceptions"; i.e., these themselves justify a "human-scientific" pursuit which in the compass of the historiological era is unavoidable and immediately also merely tiresome. Each cannot too quickly overtrump each in individual areas and with respect to the favored "problems" and "themes" of the day, i.e., in regard to what lies in the atmosphere of publicness (from which nothing escapes) in order to repeat it a little bit earlier (even if only by the length of a nose) and so a few degrees more carelessly ("dashingly") and bring it to market, so that people in the "information" and "commentary" services are not without material and "interested" parties do not lack

opportunities for idle talk. Overnight, another new publication is then already the "center" of "interest."

Yet all this can be important for meditation only in order to see in it the power of the essence of "historiology" and to startle those who are capable of knowledge—even over and against the "not bad" accomplishments from which much is to be learned. For the concern is no longer with mere learning and with the faith built upon it; instead, what matters is the knowledge that *only* the venture of I what is most question-worthy will once again cast the human being up to the height of the task of grounding.   31

If an education is now necessary, then it is the education into meditation, and meditation is at the same time untouched by what must be recognized as unpleasant, deplorable, and ordinary, but which also knows of its own provisional character, in that it feels the winds of that storm which is already gathering far in the future, the storm of the decision between ineffective beyng and the priority of the machination (power *and* impotence) of beings.

A difficult to bear and not at all publicly available measure with which those who are knowledgeable may be infallibly distinguished from people who merely bustle about is the following: *whether one can not only keep distant from what is inessential but can precisely remain silent about the essential (about the disclosive questioning of the essence) and can restrain oneself to the confines of a very small preparedness.* Who will measure with *this* measure? And who will experience anything of the fact that *such* a measure is used? And that these stillest decisions bear history (the grounding of a truth of beyng)? And that in the "space" of these decisions those who ground are conceived and engendered? And that all "blood" is a nullity *without* I the clearing of the affiliation to beyng?   32

29

No age can be grasped by way of the portrayal of a "present situation." We never know the history of an age immediately. The question of the essence of its historicality (and unhistoricality) asks how the age decides about beings as such in general and as a whole, in which truth this decision becomes prescriptive. Yet all this holds in an even more exclusive sense as regards the age of modernity, especially when that age is transitioning rapidly into the phase of its consummation, i.e., into the unconditional unfolding of its essence. The unconditional dissolution and destruction of everything hitherto is depreciated (from the already standardless horizon of the "hitherto" and as a consequence of "cultural ages") in the sense of a decline. It is then not seen that in the "dissolution" and "destruction" the essential is not the mere elimination of what previously had been valid; instead, the essential is the unconditionality, calculability, planning, and inner mutability of the destructive process itself. That means: the beingness of beings—machination as such and its unconditional lawfulness—determines |

33   that which *is*. All that was "real" until then and is still taken to be so, such as "culture" and its assets, does not disappear, but only moves into the foreground of what must supply the pretext for not letting that destructive process step forth in its genuine being. For this, like all being, can be known and endured only by a few—here, in the age of the consummation of modernity, only by those who stand *in* the machination of beings and are required by it as its directive executors.

Since such a consummation of an age / and here of the modern age / can no longer play out only in partial domains of human activity, but instead must embrace all, i.e., the modern massiveness of humanity, therefore required are essential views and institutional forms which raise the masses out beyond a mere herd character. This is not so that the masses are introduced to a higher culture, previously denied them, and experience the "blessings" of prosperity and happiness. Instead, it is so that in the luster of these institutions, the masses will become unconditionally available to machination and will no

34   longer | offer resistance to the course of the destruction. For everything that in the preceding centuries of modernity counted as "culture" in individual effective domains and strata of humanity, and contained uniform goals of creativity and enjoyment, is now undermined and without a proper determining force. It is best suited to be introduced now to the masses as the semblance of their higher vocation; in this semblant lived experience and frenzy, they keep themselves ready for an unconditional—conditionless—task of all the claims to sovereignty over an era.

Thus, e.g., all well-intentioned disinterring of earlier social assets, all worthy fostering of custom, all celebration of countryside and soil, and all glorification of "blood" merely constitute a facade and a pretext, and indeed necessarily, so that what properly and only *is*, the unconditional sovereignty of the ostentation of destruction as an intrinsically lawful process, might be kept free for the genuine full consummation of its essence, i.e., so that it might conceal itself to the many. This concealment behind a facade, however, is now not a mere delusion and certainly not a swindle or mere spectacle produced by |

35   those who remain the executors and legislators of machination. Instead, this pretext, as one already completely let loose by the genuine occurrence of the destruction, is required in the process of the consummation of machination by the executors of that consummation

themselves—they stand in an obligation which gives them that certainty which in each case becomes a sign of "greatness." This obligation of executorship contains knowledge of what in this process at any time has become unavoidable in the peculiar forms of leaps (impeding of the destruction but equally the preparation of one far in advance by means of the most inconspicuous dissolution)—the greatness of this knowledge—as a peculiar certainty, in which the *ego cogito*—*sum* of Descartes is consummated within beings as a whole and *for* them—has here its intrinsic configurative limit in that it is unable to know the essence of its own historicality.

This inability, seen in terms of the sovereignty of machination, is not a lack; instead, it is the genuine strength of the capacity to act without hesitation. Yet an essentially otherwise grounded and constituted knowledge, i.e., thoughtful knowledge, I recognizes that here,   36
in this process of the consummation of modernity, the beingness of beings, as machination, brings into the unity of the unconditional essence and distorted essence only what lies predelineated in the Western history of being—the history borne by "metaphysics." The unconditional sovereignty of beingness over beings in *such* a form that everywhere these beings, as the effective and operative, "have" the priority over "being," which gives itself out as the last vapor of mere thinking.

This sovereignty drives unwittingly toward a decision regarding beyng—a decision it itself can no longer make. It is no longer capable on its part to create a projective space for another questioning or a "time" for the question-worthiness of beyng itself as what is most question-worthy. Simultaneously, however, it becomes clear to those who know (in the manner of the executors or otherwise to these, in the manner of the thinking of beyng) that all conventional, emotional, sentimental pursuit of ethnicity and folklore—is a detached and merely utilitarian facade, an "abstract" lived experience which never has—and never *should* have—a lived experience of what genuinely I occurs and *is*.   37

The opinions (ones which would like to see the genuine reality in such pursuit of blood and soil and of what is presumably obtained and lived therein) do in fact not only mistake what *is*, what only is, but these opinions, if they step forth precipitously, are a degrading and trivializing of the unique being of the age and are a diminution of beings, which admittedly is pursued by beings themselves and is held to be desirable. At the present time, it is perhaps impossible to imagine a greater opposition than the one between, e.g., the world of Wagner's *Meistersinger* and the genuine being of the age, although the opposition is borne and endured only by very few and is grasped in its truth

as regards the history of beyng only by the rare and individual. But the fact that *this* knowledge can be thrust aside on any occasion, perhaps as a "grand abstraction," in favor of the "closeness to life" of the historiologically retrieved ethnicity and custom—this fact belongs likewise to the effective sphere of the inevitable blinding and deluding of everyone and, more or less graduated and mediated, must serve
38   the task of executing the machinational being | of modernity.

It is no wonder that in this inevitable servitude the "sciences" surpass all other knowledge in triviality and obliviousness. The "sciences" are the true-born descendants of the incipient modern spirit and are also abraded mercilessly in something they themselves unwittingly promote, namely, the essential sameness of historiology and technology; in other words, the "sciences" disappear into mere instrumentality. In all this, something which has arrogated the name "philosophy" even seeks to gain prestige, and that testifies to the complete triumph of the obliviousness. Today, as previously in the Middle Ages, the "name" philosophy is claimed as a pretense for the facilitation (pursued for the most part unwittingly) of the complete renunciation of thinking and of the capacity to think in the sense of contemplative thinking. On the other hand, *calculative* thinking—*logos*—has attained a height, a certainty, and a power which *essentially* surpass everything hitherto. Compared to this calculative thinking, the "pseudophilosophy" which is gladly admitted into the pursuit of culture amounts merely to a feeble clamor over borrowed words and concepts, and into
39   these no one | seriously inquires any longer, because here it is already very easy to see how completely this remains merely an accessory sideshow in relation to folklore, historiology, and biology, which for their part do indeed, although unwittingly, play their role simply as pretexts.

Yet there is a knowledge of being, stemming from the disclosive questioning of the history of beyng and of the history of the *essence* of truth, and this knowledge likewise knows the essence of the age and is already a preparation for the future of the age, though it would not be a picture of that future or a plan for it in the sense of the still-prevailing calculation. Under the cover of folkish [*völkisch*] and national assemblages, the history of the West carries out a veiled and essential assemblage upon the last unfolding of the *machinational* essence of beingness—that assemblage which finds its essence as the represented self-production in the exceptionless, instituted, and calculable disposability over all things as a whole and over the whole itself, and, in what is unconditioned and blind, places on itself the last demand to make disposable and to emerge in machination—a demand in itself already offering the first and definitive fulfillment. Beingness over-

powers itself here, in order to raise itself to the highest power I and to   40
expand this process of the ever and ever self-overpowering constancy
of power as its own essence in beings such that a question about the
truth of this essence and about the grounding of that truth becomes
groundless and motiveless. The human being of this era comes to
stand in a Truthless domain, since already the overpowering of the
one situation by the next contains precisely so much of justification
that even the directionality toward this justification of the unfolding
of the power is eradicated and forgotten.

There is no contradiction in the fact that the highest sovereignty of
being as machination spreads round about itself a complete forgottenness of being. And supposing it were a "contradiction," what would
that matter in this domain of sovereignty? The contradiction could
count only as an already too late "thought" which still attempts, by
way of a subsequent or accompanying representation, to keep its distance from the process of the self-overpowering constancy of power—
an attempt which succeeds only in appearance. Nevertheless, an age
for which—on the basis of the priority of what is real and effective—
the truth can no longer be a need and consequently for which the lack
of truth does not have to be a loss, but is even a gain, immediately
makes every adherence I to previously believed "truths" a vain com-   41
mencement which perhaps still furnishes superficial individuals the
expedient of reassurance, admittedly no longer has anything to say
about the sovereignty of being as machination, and even less shows
itself suited to prepare the transition.

The age of the lack of truth must, however, at the same time cover
itself with a complete semblance of the unconditional possession of
truth, and this semblance makes it seem superfluous and importunate ever to interrogate the age itself with respect to its essence and
its place within the history of beyng. Extensively and on all sides in
this age, there still can be felt a floundering of those who are unable
to see what is and of those who for their part take refuge in making
believe that what they merely champion would already on that account possess historical force. The age of the complete untroubling
forgottenness of being and lack of truth resides so uniquely in its historical essence, because here the boundless breadth of the claim to
power by beingness unites with a shrinking of being into the merely
null and truthless nothing. All that the age has available for its self-
characterization are historiological comparison as a calculation of its
incomparability and technological planning as the hindering of every I standstill which, considering the essential priority of the over-   42
powering and of its self-certainty, could immediately press forth as an
uncertainty. The most profound destructive force of an age (its "weak-

ness" hidden in the semblance of strength) consists in its inability to resolve itself in favor of truthfulness over and against its most concealed and essential plight.

But what if *this* irresoluteness, as the affirmation of what is unproblematic, constituted the essence of an age—modernity in its consummation? Then we must not speak here of a "failure" and a "lack"; we must knowingly recognize here the proper greatness—the gigantism—of a historical destiny and repudiate every demand of myopic condemnation due to bad temper and unreasonableness. For more decisive than the contentment of those who have long been satiated, because they were never genuinely hungry, and more essential than the preservation of those who have long been superfluous, is the *uprising of the knowledge* of that which *is*. For this harbors the promise of a knowledge of the other truth, the one toward which the human being of the future must set out.

The *seriousness* of a thinking is not distress and complaint over the allegedly bad times and the threatening barbarity; instead, it is the
43   decisiveness of the interrogative | perseverance in what is incalculable, genuinely occurring, and in itself already futural. If someone dispenses with publicly asserting and expanding the many often-traversed ways of a *seeking* for the same as things already found, then all his way making unites in a simple standpoint whose unique spacetime expands on account of the duty of persevering in the questionworthiness of what is still unproblematic: beyng and the grounding of its truth.

30

Self-interpretations of the human being and of his volition least of all provide "the truth" in itself, because they are most readily determined by the current moment and by its specific capacity for truth.

31

Hölderlin.—The most disastrous misinterpretation inflicted on this poet and still reserved for him consists in making him the one responsible for "Hölderlinian Germanity," not only because this Germanity must be very extraneous and transitory, but because Hölderlin is thereby deprived of what is essential to him, namely, to be the beginning of the deepest convulsion of Western metaphysics—i.e., of the
44   Western history of being. This poet can | be known only by someone who has in advance experienced the question-worthiness of being and

has grounded this experience as the ground of Da-sein. Anything else about Hölderlin is the expression of a historiological, literary, or perhaps even political arrangement of something already suppressed as past.

32

Self-consciousness as interrogative knowledge of the retained essence and of its history is one thing. Self-consciousness as rejection of all question-worthiness on the basis of a presumption of complete certainty and authoritativeness in all plans and opinions is quite another.

33

Although it is said that essential meditation remains absent because it is prohibited and suppressed, in fact this absence stems from a self-refusal of the originary plight which is all that can engender the power of meditation. The alleged prohibition of meditation is itself due to the lack of power for the essential decisions; they are made only in the space of what is most question-worthy.

34   45

Nihilism is that basic position in the midst of beings which does *not* know nothingness—and does *not want* to know it—and instead takes "truth" to be beings themselves and also the continual pursuit of beings precisely as pursuit.

35

But what if everything depended on the fact that in doctrinal activity (whether in any way merely academic or indeed public) never should or could the essential (the most appropriately experienced and questioned) be spoken of, because everything concerned with doctrines and opinions has turned dreadfully against the essential, even where and when the often-invoked "seriousness" might learn what is essential.

36

More originarily than all metaphysical questioning, the question of the truth of beyng could indeed be a mere "flourish" ["*Pfiff*"] of a

"new" wisdom; indeed this question *must* be so for all historiological opinion, which holds fast to its position and consequently can never know that the transformation of the questioning here is not a mere alteration in the "posing of a problem," but on the contrary is an es-
46   sential change in the human being | out of, and in, his "relation" to beyng—thus is the reception of a thrust of beyng itself.

It is sheer confusion to think that Nietzsche's planned "magnum opus" would exist in an elaboration corresponding to—though certainly not the same as—that of Hegel's *Logic*. "One" could then indeed establish historiologically what Nietzsche thought and meant—but his thinking and questioning would be displaced into inaccessibility, if not actually suffocated. Did Nietzsche know that? Certainly—and indeed he knew it with his knowledge that stands in a law of structure, a law we are not acquainted with and are not supposed to be acquainted with. Every essential philosophy, according to its destiny, follows its law of structure: e.g., Kant's *Critique of Pure Reason*, Leibniz's brief treatises, his letters, and his summary §§, Descartes's *Regulae*, Plato's *Dialogues*.—In which form should we then take up Nietzsche's "magnum opus" and preserve its sketches, drafts, and fragments? The proposal to leave it, to "bring it out," just as Nietzsche left it behind—even to print a facsimile of it—contains something valid and "true"—and yet thereby we are not in the least | guaranteed that we
47   would learn in its inmost and essential unity what, for the interrogative and mediative Nietzsche, organized this "material" in advance and held it in its structure and never could be "material." The numerical articulation is only an extrinsic expedient. If we see clearly that neither *one* single chosen "arrangement" can be forced onto the "whole," nor can merely leaving the extant texts in the form they take in the notebooks by itself preserve the "actual" thinking, precisely then the question of the type and mode of the handing down of *this* legacy shifts into a domain of surpassing difficulty. For even the purely chronological ordering of the individual parts works seductively—insofar as it engenders the opinion that an essential thought would first be there when it is recorded and repeatedly annotated. In truth—the essential, that which bears the meditation, incites it, and disposes it, is always pronounced later and is revealed as the incidental—and as apparently what alone is treated in the proper sense.

So then the attempt at an adequate publication (adequate for what
48   and | sufficient for whom?) of Nietzsche's attempt at a magnum opus is perhaps altogether guided by a perverse intention, inasmuch as this publication could never be destined for the public, "general" reader

and for the "people," as little as for aloof "biographers" and connoisseurs—but *only* for thinkers. And to these it is a matter of indifference which form the publication takes. For even Hegel's *Logic* or Schelling's treatise on freedom or Kant's *Critique of Pure Reason* must in each case be interrogated originarily out of its ever more essentially grasped origin, and the presentation itself *is* indeed in each case primarily an imposed one and comes to be so out of this origin. The mere technical mastery of the arrangement does not signify anything at all—especially since each of these thinkers has at some time experienced, even if not enunciated, the necessity of presenting in an entirely *different* way precisely that which has been structured *one way,* merely in order to say exactly the *same,* i.e., to say that which was uniquely questioned and thought. Hegel required the vastness of his *Logic* in order to say, in his own way and doing justice to the essence, his most simple thought; Schelling says his just as originarily and perhaps I still more   49
essentially in his incomparably "smaller" "treatise on freedom," and Nietzsche often says his most simple thought *in a single* felicitous "aphorism." Yet in each case this most simple thought is inexhaustible for those who think after Hegel, Schelling, and Nietzsche and with them and out of them. The truth is independent of the extensiveness and form of the presentation just left behind, in case one takes the presentation as what is first and merely reckons up its meaning—without ever previously standing in the origin out of which the meaning *and* the type of presentation are taken.

What should then happen with Nietzsche's posthumous work? Those who are capable of questioning into the essential—having first recognized it as such—must be aroused and ordained to create "merely" a first basic disposition of preparedness, out of which an age becomes strong in questioners and knowers so as to be struck by what happened in this consummation of Western philosophy on its first path out of its first beginning.

37

"Harmonious natures," as some individuals are called, seem at times to embody the divine itself; but this "semblance" merely covers over their lack of a relation I to the gods. Fissured human beings, whose   50
very essence is riven by a fissure, are on the other hand split apart in such a way that this kind of open domain holds ready an abyss into which the nearness and remoteness of the gods and the unrest of their undecidedness can radiate.

38

A "miracle" is now precisely what depends entirely on planning and calculation and can be reproduced at any time with ever increasing precision. Such a "miracle" today is for instance the guidance system of an antiaircraft battery. Only *such* miraculous things are "real"—are beings—so that the "world" is now, as never before, full of "miracles." What then are all artificially, historiologically produced "symbols" and customs striving to attain? The "miracles" of technology in the widest sense enchant the human being, such that he arrives at the opinion that *he himself* dominates the miracle, whereas he has become merely the most submissive cog in a machine. One can speak today of a "dominance" of the human being "over" technology only if one has at the same time failed to recognize the machinational essence of being in the modern interpretation and | is incapable of knowing anything of the essence of the modern human subjectum, an essence incorporating calculation as well as animality. Yet the human being has also not simply fallen into the hands of technology; on the contrary, technology *and* the human being are *equally* carried along in the sweep of being as machination, so that neither from the one nor the other could an overcoming and a decision be possible, as long as the decision is not placed in the question of the truth of being itself and in the grounding of that truth: "totality" is only an escape into meditationlessness.

39

To be *busy* (with "philosophy") is still not to *work;* working remains far removed from *creating,* and the latter is never a *grounding.* The differences are in each case infinite—i.e., essential. In the foreground appearance of every unbounded pursuit, each is similar to each. Moreover, this similarity can indeed still be grounded "scientifically," inasmuch as all doing and acting is conditioned "biologically," and everything thus stems equally from "life." Insofar as this recognition also still counts as a discovery, such "truths" have an enchantment for those who are thoughtless. Yet what is essential remains, namely, that the human being is in this way drawn off the path of any *meditation.* | Do we surmise what sort of destruction of "life" is thereby taking place? The destruction is like that silting up and desertification of our all-too-calculated and all-too-managed soil. And let us not ask what kind of problematic "biology" is this "science" on which such a "life intuition" is founded! Would anyone know what the much-invoked dependence of all activity—thus even "biological" "thinking"—

on "life" signifies for this "biology"? Of course not—cast off the path of meditation, one completely avoids the leap into this circle like the plague—not from indolence, but because the sovereignty of being as machination no longer liberates humanity and beings for a leap into an open domain of essential disclosive questioning.

40

Now, since fortunately even "solitude" is supposed to become a public institution, it could be demonstrated that the disintegration of all previously essential human attitudes and dispositions as well as their dissolution into the indiscriminate pursuit of lived experience has become complete. Indeed in such a way (through the instituting of solitude into an | organizable, publicly distributable, and calculated   53 condition) one intends to escape the all-too-great pursuit of mere communal work and to secure "the other." In truth, however, in this way all that happens is that the last islands are inundated by the floods of irresistible massification and universalization. For one cannot "make" or even "will" solitude—solitude is most rare and is a necessity of being—insofar as being, in its abysses, bestows itself on the Dasein of the human being. Therefore what "one" can "make" is at most a preparation of *knowing* that only a transformation of being as such, i.e., an overcoming of the age of the complete abandonment by being, will open up the *possibility* of solitary humans as ones who ground and essentially bear. On the other hand, to turn solitude into something public and an institution is to remove the last dams holding back the surge of the machination of being. That process—perhaps inconspicuous and like the flashing up of the belated romantics—is merely the sign of a process in the history of beyng, against which all temporal-historical "world history" remains child's play.

And the most remote gods smile at this pandemonium.

41

54

The philosophical ignorance (not mere unacquaintance) of today's German "scientist," especially in the rising generation, has assumed a form which shows that here no question of a "lack of refinement" helps any longer but that already something is unfolding which can neither be stopped nor impeded through an eventual increase in "philosophical" instruction. This absence has nothing at all to do with "barbarity," because "culture" is not the issue here. Instead, what is coming to light here is a sign pointing to a complete dissolution of "science," and thereby of "knowledge," into the machination of being itself. The enigma is that now, however, the "sciences" are not in the least capable of seeing how *in* their activity *as such* (not merely on the basis of the "results" of that activity) what is entrenching itself and preparing for its unconditional development is what alone *is* and will be in this age.

Why in the "sciences" ever again a "romanticism" of the "spirit" and a "mysticism" of "culture"—? Because the sciences [*Wissenschaften*] have no *knowledge* [Wissen] and are unable to question, since 55 they cannot see the severity of the | incomparable brutality of unbound being and, if they could see it, would not want to acknowledge its presence.

42

That which in the future will have to be called by the (not accidentally Latin) term *brutalitas,* namely, the unconditional machination of being, has nothing to do with a disparaging and bourgeois "moral" valuation of some superficial incidents on whose "condemnation" those who remain behind from the past and the Christian temperaments intoxicate themselves in order thereby to repay their own value, in which they indeed no longer entirely believe. The *brutalitas* of being is a *reflection* of the essence of the human being, a reflection of the *animalitas* of the *animal rationale*—thus also and precisely a reflection of *rationalitas.* Not as if such *brutalitas* were the effect and transference of a *human* self-comprehension into the domain of nonhuman things—on the contrary: *that* the human being had to be defined as *animal rationale* and *that* the *brutalitas* of beings will one day drive forth to its consummation—these have one and the same single ground in | 56 the *metaphysics* of being.

This essence of what now in the age of consummated modernity counts as a being and as a whole is *known* today, in respectively very disparate ways, only by: on the one hand, those essential human beings (i.e., humans who unconditionally and undisturbedly are assigned to and belong to that essence) who configure the age through their acting and planning, and on the other hand, by those equally few who have already on the basis of an originary knowledge leapt ahead into the question-worthiness of being itself. What "goes on" apart from *these* knowledgeable ones is unavoidable and is in its massiveness becoming more and more unavoidable—of course without ever contributing to the determination of being.

All these *never-too-many* need the romanticism of "empire" ["*Reich*"], of ethnicity, of "soil" and of "camaraderie," and of the promotion of "culture" as well the romanticism of the "flowering" of the "arts," even if that refers only to the artistes and danseurs of the Berlin Winter-garten.[26] All these never-too-many need perpetual opportunities to gain "lived experience"—for what else could they do with their "life," if they did not have a lived experience of it? Moreover, there are still "Christians" who, I because they surmise nothing of what actually is,   57 believe that they live in "catacombs," whereas they recently knew they were in "heaven" since there were opportunities everywhere for shar-ing in political power. The Phariseeism of Karl Barth[27] and his adher-ents surpasses even that of ancient Jewry by those measures posited necessarily with the modern history of being. These adherents believe that the loudest possible screaming about the long-since-dead God would lead at once into a domain of decision regarding the divinity of the gods. Because these adherents flee into the past while speak-ing "dialectically," they believe themselves to be lifted out of time into "eternity"—whereas they merely, qua the genuine destroyers, under-mine "the future" (but not the progress) of humanity. In truth they are nevertheless the quite aloof and ignorant promoters of the *brutal-itas*—they belong in their own way to the indispensable ones by *con-tributing to the prevention* of essential knowledge and to the opening of the path for the *brutalitas* of being.

A *consequence*—not at all the basis—of the *brutalitas* of being is that the human being makes of himself, as a being, explicitly I and thor-   58 oughly a *factum brutum* ["brute fact"] and "establishes" his animality by means of the doctrine of race. This theory of "life" is therefore the most plebeian form in which the question-worthiness of beyng poses as something self-evident—without this theory surmising it in the least. The elevation of humanity through the flight into technology—explanation on the basis of race—the "leveling down" of all "appear-ances" to the basic form of the "expression" of something or other—all this is ever "correct" and is "illuminating" for everyone—because there is nothing here to question, since the question of the essence of truth has become inaccessible from the start. This "theory" is distin-guished from other "natural scientific worldviews" only in that it ap-parently affirms everything "spiritual" and indeed first brings it into "effectiveness," and yet simultaneously and at the deepest level *denies* the "spiritual" with a denial that drifts toward the most radical nihil-ism—for it is "in the last analysis" (i.e., already at its commencement) an "expression" of race. In the framework of this teaching, everything

---

26. {Famous variety theater in Berlin, destroyed by bombing in 1944.}

27. {Karl Barth (1886–1968), important Protestant theologian, co-founder of the "Confessional Church" critical of National Socialism.]

can be taught according to need, and this in turn must be recognized as a consequence of the *brutalitas*.

"Total mobilization"—but never as a freely grasped and knowingly mastered consequence of the machination of beings—but only as an 59 unavoidable sign of the times next to the Wagnerian | cultural politics and the scientific worldview of the nineteenth century. Yet this "syncretism" is only a superficies of the proper greatness of this age, whose tacit principle is complete meditationlessness; corresponding in the theory of the human being is the principle of race as the basic truth. This latter principle is now first acquired by the human being and postulated for his humanity as time and ground—a principle—out of which the animality of the animal lives "on its own." "Humanness" and "personality" are themselves only expressions and properties of animality—the predatory animal is the primal form of the "*hero*"—for in the predator all the instincts are left unfalsified by "knowledge"—and at the same time are tamed by the predator's ever racially bound urge. But the predatory animal endowed with the means of the highest technology—completes the actualization of the *brutalitas* of being, so much so that in the haze of this actualization even all "culture" as well as historiologically reckoned history—the picture of history—is posed. Then is there once again for the "sciences" a "joyful" time of successive discoveries? And then? Which convulsion is essential enough to let a meditation arise? Or does the *brutali-* 60 *tas* have the last word? Has it | perhaps already spoken this word, such that everything is still only an empty tottering on into the long ending—into the *absence* of a downgoing, which means into a malformation of "eternity"?

43

It is a childish opinion to suppose a thinker could ever want to maintain that the "*sciences*" arose *out of* philosophy (like a stream of water out of a well pipe) and thus that modern philosophy at its commencement (Descartes) let the sciences leap forth out of itself. *Out of* a philosophy—if it is a philosophy and the more decisively it is such—arises altogether nothing; only mediately do the sciences (conditioned by τέχνη and work) come forth "out of" metaphysics, insofar as they make claim to the current essence of truth and thus also already fall away from that essence. Admittedly, still more comical is the intention of the "history of the spirit" to refute that alleged opinion of the philosophers. How many misinterpretations have already arisen from the constantly sought coupling of philosophy and the sciences, and indeed on both "sides"? This conjunction became a disaster for Western

history; philosophy no longer found its essence I in the question of be-	61
ing, and the sciences fell into servitude to every "master" that rose up.
And meditation on the essence of truth remained alien, if it did not
indeed all too commonly become perverted into "epistemology."
Knowledge of the domains of the essential decisions was suppressed.
All opinions became dissolute and unbridled, and people quickly took
recourse in faith—since the pursuit of "culture" is indeed secured on
other paths.—

The "sciences" *never* arise *without* philosophy—because they must
necessarily make claim to an essential positing of the essence of truth
and thus first of being—; but sciences never originate *out of* philosophy
and *through* it. Sciences are "philosophy"—insofar as they could *not*
exist *without* philosophy, even though this existence, as modernity
shows, becomes all the more "secure" the less the "sciences" bother
about philosophy and the more extrinsically they do so. But the "sciences" are never "philosophies" in the sense that they could themselves "philosophize"—precisely that is what they must in advance
repel so that they can release themselves into beings and into the pursuit of beings. Every historiological investigation into the history of
the sciences therefore in advance questions in the wrong direction by
attempting I to show the "sciences" arising *out of* a philosophy—	62
whether ancient or Cartesian. Yet precisely because this questioning
cannot be essentially justified, meditation must aim at grasping how
the "sciences" could *not* be what they are *without* philosophy—this
conditioning of the sciences by philosophy is essentially deeper (—because touching the essence of the sciences—) than the dependence of
the emergence and pursuit of science on conditions lying outside of
philosophy. Whereby it must of course be borne in mind—that these
*non*philosophical conditions are indeed not philosophy itself—but
nevertheless are grounded within a definite sovereignty of an essential interpretation of truth and being—and therefore once again reside within philosophy. The usual perplexity of scientists with respect
to philosophy has its *secondary* ground in the lack of a consideration
of the various, though interconnected, possible relations between "sciences" and philosophy. The main ground of the perplexity is of course
the great indifference with regard to everything "spiritual."

44

The sciences are borne and stimulated by the unlimited prospect of
ever new discoveries. For even *what* has already been discovered (es-
pecially in the "historiological" I sciences) can be newly discovered	63
through a change of "viewpoint," and the earlier discovery can be

proved "false." Accordingly, the viewpoints never stem from science itself. They are always brought into it—often in a form that makes the scientists believe they themselves have arrived at the viewpoint on their own; thus the *childishness* of such people. This prospect of over-trumping gives the average scientist in his own eyes his otherwise missing importance and the importance of his activity. In the great scientists, the sciences "live" precisely on the possibilities of discovery—never on an attachment to *what* has been discovered; for the latter itself can never bear a human Dasein—but only can perhaps bear the discoveredness of this Dasein—as prestige and "fame" or as simple accomplishment and as fulfillment of duty in the service of "truth."

Matters are otherwise in *philosophy:* that which is to be disclosively questioned itself—it—beyng—in its question-worthiness is in advance what is binding (or, better, *unsettling*) for the thinker. What is question-worthy here never counts as the "object" of endless "questioning" that is thus always rich in prospects and never finished. Instead, the disclosive questioning is in itself already the leap into an abyss, and *every* instant of contemplative thinking is a convulsion of Dasein. All this has of course nothing to do with a "psychology" of the philosopher—because the philosopher is indeed, precisely through the unsettling which derives from beyng, constantly *torn away* from that to which even he is referred, namely, his anthropomorphizing in everyday humanity.

64   If a thinker ever had to "live" among scientists and was taken | for one of their kind, then would this be the best of all maskings of "philosophy" and even the easiest? Must a thinker be to scientists something gloomy and dreadful—a useless abomination—or only an amorphous oddity?

45

"Objectivity."—To let beings be does not signify indifference toward them, apathy, but instead is grounded in the originary projection of being and can therefore also not be understood through an idealistic interpretation of objectivity as subjectivity. However that may be, every sort of objectivity which lets the object in itself fly right at humans, as it were, is impossible—if accepted, then a delusion, and if extolled, then boring and sterile, though indeed also harmless. If on the other hand something is surmised, at least roughly and unclearly, of the fact that all objectivity depends on the "subject," and if this becomes a doctrine and a commonplace, such that each and every person can put on airs as the legislator of objectivity, and if the "people" and its "taste"

(simply because it is that of the "people") count as the tribunal of ǀ
judgment, and if any knowledge of the difficulty and rarity of the need   65
and ability to judge is lacking, then the apparently more correct conception of objectivity becomes utterly untrue and its superiority over
the alleging of a "pure" objectivity becomes untenable.

But today matters stand thus: on the one side the previous claim
to pure objectivity, and on the other a decree of the meditationless
masses, who take the present for the eternal and for the measure of
history. Between the two equally groundless positions, there is no
mediation; in other words, a confrontation is altogether impossible,
because all questioning and meditating—all dialogue that releases
itself into question-worthiness—is rejected as mere "debate," as "par-
liamentary."

Who is yet able to see that that releasement toward question-worthiness—is the highest binding into which humanity can bring itself?

46

The main enemies of all meditation are the universal truths: e.g., that
all human activities, all work and all accomplishment, are expressions
of "life."—Such a declaration is the renunciation of all truth—i.e., a
renunciation of ontological knowledge as the steadfastness of the human being in the ǀ open realm of beings. Everything is to be justified   66
by the appeal to life; i.e., what thereby enters into opposition can be
maintained only as "life" against "life," or in this interpretation, as
self-preservation against self-preservation, for which in turn all means
are right and justified. In confirmation of this "philosophy," appeal is
made to the dictum of Heraclitus about "strife" as the "father of all
things," without an inkling of how this dictum is saying something
altogether different. Yet the absence of meditation is indeed not a consequence of a particular heroism which "enforces" its conviction; it is
only a consequence of the fact that this valuation of life has long been
in servitude to the machination of being and can only put into effect
something of which it can never be master. Therefore, every "cultural," "political," "moral," or "religious" critique is not only always
too myopic but is already as a "critique" a misunderstanding, because
to the consummation of machination in being there corresponds and
must correspond the unconditional *brutalitas* of humanity.

But it is indeed to be asked: what is this machinational essence of
being itself? Meditation must be directed to the history of being, because only out of ǀ being can beings as a whole and (as assigned to be-   67
ings for the sake of being) the human being be brought up for deci-

sion. Of course, it will presumably require a long time until we grasp the necessity of such meditation and thus also grasp the unavoidability of the venture to question inceptually, *without any* of the previous standards and prototypes.

47

Why should not the purifying and securing of the race be destined for once to have as a consequence a great *mixture:* the one with the Slavs (the Russians—on whom indeed Bolshevism has merely been forced and is not something rooted)? Would not the German spirit in its highest freshness and strength have to master here a genuine darkness and at the same time recognize it as the ground in which it itself is rooted? In this way would a humanity first become *historical,* be equal to a grounding of the truth of being, and be summoned to a capacity for the divine? What if the political consummation of modernity had to prepare this unification, at first on many detours and in apparently extreme oppositions? Does it not speak in favor of such possibilities that we seemingly still (how long still?) so entirely abide in the opposite?

68 | But then the Germans, through the deepest appropriation of the Western history of *being* and of knowledge, would have to be equipped for a πόλεμος ["war"] that would by struggle gain for itself a domain of decision within which an incalculable essence of the gods and of humans might find its way to its abysses; but then, in order to be equal to this collision of what is assigned, a power of meditation in the Germans would have to have arisen, and for this power conceptual clarity and brilliance could never be sufficiently penetrating or sufficiently anticipatory in questioning. ("Rational" and "irrational" would only be a superficial, sham distinction—and never an equal match to what then in the essence of beyng itself—as the event of appropriation—delivered itself over to the unique encounter in juxtaposition and succession.)

And how should this Western future—which alone would be equal once again to what is Asian—not proceed along at the margin of its *greatest danger*—that that unification of Germanism and Russianism would amount only to the most extreme intensification of the consummation of modernity—that the inexaustibility of the Russian earth would be taken up into the irresistibility of German planning

69   and ordering, | and each would have to hold the other in suspense on account of their unsurpassability, while such suspense would in itself become the purpose of a consummation of the gigantic in machination.

And how should not, if this greatest and closest danger were dispelled (and it *can* be overcome only out of the concealed essence of the Germans as struggle for their own essence against all denial to possess the truth already)—how should not at the same time and inceptually the supreme victory of beyng—namely, the *downgoing*—already be won?

Of course, we still and ever more obstinately see in all downgoing only ending, stopping, succumbing, and perishing, rather than the highest testimony to, and history of, the uniqueness of beyng—and this fact gives an ever new impetus to meditate on the depth of the abandonment by being in the modern age and to come to know which inceptuality of questioning must face up to this abandonment. And thereby this questioning is only the harbinger sent ahead by beyng itself into the scarcely illuminated domain of its truth and destined to be a mere transition, a harbinger that grounds lonely abodes for the future of Assigned beyng and surrenders to a long stewardship. | The   70 everyday judgments about everyday phenomena are then merely the always newly deposited flat shore of a sea whose currents no one knows and for the traversal of which the simplest boat has not yet been constructed and cannot be constructed as long as the human being considers and altogether calculates the traversal entirely in terms of the shore—away from the shore or toward it.

Yet those who stand in the service of machination and pursue their superficial affairs are the ones who least of all know what is thereby happening to them. Nor should they know it; instead, they believe that they are the bearers of truth and that their pursuits are indeed alone the cynosure of everything. Nevertheless, with time, "romanticism" must recede and give way to the relentlessness of the equipping in arms. The main supports of every genuine—i.e., forceful and today even *gigantic*—dominion are indeed the hypocrisy of promoting universal well-being (happiness and beauty for all) and that relentless arming which can immediately and definitively strike down every attack. Necessarily following in the wake of this are romanticism, enthusiasm, and the fullness of lived experience.

Yet these supports of dominion must never be deprecated "morally"—they *are* what they are qua effective forms of machination and | leave just as much room for the integrity of personal convictions and   71 sentiments as for the despicableness of mere careerism. Therefore, history must never be evaluated in these respects, in case history itself ever wants to be experienced. Falsely, and only from the arrested standpoint of the democracies, the executors of the consummation of modernity to its highest essence are called "dictators"—; but their greatness consists in their capacity to be "dictative"—in their sensing the concealed necessity of the machination of being and not letting themselves be drawn off course by any temptation. (Cf. p. 109.)

48

Publicity is not a measure of greatness, if greatness means the inceptuality of something unique in being. But publicity itself can indeed determine the *essence* of greatness, and this essence can appear in the form of the gigantic—everything concealed is small in the regard of *this* greatness but certainly not altogether null. You need to know which essence of greatness an age has in each case chosen for itself; otherwise, all valuations are confused. The only guarantee of the consummation of modernity is a humanity that already denies itself instinctively every meditation on that I which bears and guides an age in its apprehension of being, of truth, and of the human being himself.

72

49

The dangers of everything untimely lie, on the one hand, in the fact that it is inordinately overgrown and curbed by what is timely—i.e., by the binding opposition to the timely. On the other hand, the danger is that the untimely, although free from the timely and therefore already no longer un-timely, yet presses on to the *wrong time* and does not know *its own* time and is unable to wait for it. Moreover, the *times* of poetry, of thinking, and of acting are again different in each case. As long as historicism dominates us and history is calculated in one way or another—in sheer onlooking or in planned action—then ultimately there still exists the danger that even genuine meditation will degenerate into the shallowness of mere comparative analysis, will avoid being, and will not be selected for downgoing as the preparation of a beginning.

50

In the "Western democracies," ["*westliche Demokratien*"], so-called geographically-politically, for a long time already and specifically in their spoken and unspoken "*metaphysics*," I "modernity" has come to a standstill. The step into the consummation is lacking in force and above all in an essential calling. Everything happening here is compromise—attempt at vindicating and coping, no anticipatory configuring or guiding. From here, no decisions are made—above all, not ones of essential meditation on the inceptual and basic form of an-

73

other history of being. Yet an apparently external power, great wealth, inherited "culture," a spirit of mere resistance, and a vast amount of hypocrisy—place something like a barricade in front of the transition to the consummation of modernity—a barricade that can delay but is incapable of stopping the essential consummation of modernity, because everything contributing to such a barricade is only a surpassed preliminary form of the consummation—in the modern sense, but without the courage for the unfolded essence and for the extreme essential consequences. Accordingly, even precisely there a remarkable religious-commercial-"political" vindication of Christianity—accordingly, even there an utter incapacity to grasp in its abyssal character the metaphysical beginning of Western history in the Greeks—accordingly, as the already long-extant consequence, an evasive escape into "humanism."

51   74

Because the "consummation" of modernity does indeed not amount to a mere finishing of something already underway, since a consummation is always the last and authentic grasp of a previously hidden essence, therefore such consummation necessarily takes on the character of a new start. This gives rise, however, to the often long-persisting ambiguity as to whether this start launches the consummation or whether it does not already reach forth beyond the consummation to another beginning. The two are not mutually exclusive—they can exist simultaneously but can *never* be brought about by the same basic relations of human creating and suffering. Why does the consummation of modernity pertain to "politics" qua unconditional "technology"? Why does the transition into the other beginning pertain to an already—precedent—poetry (Hölderlin)? And why does this poetry above all need a long—poetryless—thoughtful meditation on the beginning of Western history, i.e., on the still ungrounded truth of beyng? How few recognize the simultaneity of what is essentially different and of the historical destiny of "acting" and of thinking? How few are able to know that this simultaneity is necessary and are able to affirm (not merely acquiesce in) the sovereignty of what is public and at the same time tolerate, indeed demand, the passing over and overlooking of the genuine I transition as essentially justified? Who   75 surmises that beings as a whole are, in concealed tremors and unnoticed strokes, twisted free from the abandonment by being? Yet we all too readily "think" in terms of the historiological comparison and planning of history, without recognizing history itself as a course of the event of the truth of beyng. This course ultimately generated the historiology through which the gods were indeed driven to flight, specifically such that at the same time the semblance of a substitute was offered in *aesthetically* experienced "art"—which for its part bred the "lived experience" that then ultimately, as "religious" lived experience, feigned to possess what is "divine."

52

Nihilism (cf. above, p. 45) resides not where *being* qua machination is displaced and instituted in its unconditional power, but where, under an appeal to proven "ideals" and "cultural assets" (as ineffective goals), it is held fast by the accident of a handed-down state of affairs. Here are carried out the proper and most covert thwarting of all decisions and the disavowal of beyng and thus also of nothingness. On the other hand, where machination has become unconditioned, there indeed nothingness is likewise rejected as nugatory—but at the same time is unwittingly sought out as unrecognized abyss—by way of an evasion from it.

76

53

Thinking purely "metaphysically" (i.e., in heeding the history of beyng), during the years 1930–1934 I saw in National Socialism the possibility of a transition to another beginning and interpreted it that way. Thereby I mistook and undervalued this "movement" in its genuine powers and inner necessities as also in the extent and kind of its greatness. What starts there, and specifically in a much more profound—i.e., more comprehensive and drastic—way than in Fascism, is the consummation of modernity—. The consummation had indeed more or less started in "romanticism"—with respect to the anthropomorphizing of the human being in his self-certain rationality—but the actual consummation requires the decisiveness of what is historiological-technological in the sense of the Complete "mobilization" of all the capacities of self-reliant humanity. One day even the opposition to the Christian Churches must be carried out in a Christianityless "Protestantism," one which Fascism of itself is incapable of supplying.

Full insight into my earlier delusion regarding the essence and the essential historical force of National Socialism first resulted in the necessity of affirming National Socialism and indeed on | *thoughtful* grounds. But also said thereby is that this "movement" remains inde-

75[28]

---

28. {Heidegger makes a mistake in numbering here. The mispagination has been allowed to stand, so that the cross-references will remain correct.}

pendent of its respective contemporary configuration and likewise independent of the duration of these directly visible forms. Yet how is it that such an essential affirmation is considered less important, or even of no importance, versus my earlier mere acquiescence, which was mostly superficial and at the same time distracted or even simply blind? In part, the blame rests on the vacuous presumption of the "*intellectuals.*" Their essence (or distorted essence) does indeed *not* consist in their vindication of knowledge and refinement over and against mere action and vulgarity; instead, it lies in the fact that they take "science" to be *the* authentic knowledge and the basis of a "culture" and want to know, and can know, nothing of essential knowledge. The greater danger of intellectualism is that it threatens the possibility and seriousness of *genuine knowledge*, not that it weakens action. Action can fend for itself. But the battle for knowledge and against science is today hopeless, because scientists do not have a sufficiently essential knowledge of themselves, of science, in order to place themselves seriously into an opposition.

Therefore, all fronts are thoroughly mixed up with one another: the universities manifest the purest form of this mix-up, and that is where the ground of their impotence is to be sought—and I also is the cause of their misguided claims. They themselves condition the irresoluteness which impedes the one single step which now must be taken: their explicit abolition and replacement by research activity and technical schools, i.e., chemical and Alemannic "institutes." A further delusion was thus my opinion that the university could indeed still be transformed into a site of essential meditation, could assert an essence wherein Western knowledge might place itself back into its proper question-worthiness, and could thereby contribute to the preparation of another beginning of the history of beyng. A concept of "science" devised on this basis, both as seen in terms of the university and as appraised in terms of historical reality, is a pure "phantom." Delusions—thought through and suffered in all their abysses—are paths to that which "*is.*" (Cf. p. 110.)

54

How many victims will historicism still devour, i.e., how many people will it still seduce to the unprofitable opinion that because they as latecomers now have definitively behind themselves that which preceded themselves, they could claim they I have *put* it behind—as if the gaze backward were already a gaze that overcomes? Essential history is in this way thoroughly concealed, because the historicists of thinking and of poetizing maintain that their respectively current timeliness is already a justification to offer critiques and thus to bypass the first task, which is to grasp the past in its originariness—i.e., to ask an originary question oneself. The fact that one can, in renouncing such meditation, nevertheless present something with an extravagant display of "literature" gives ever-renewed confirmation to historicism.

55

The first and thus all-inclusive and constantly self-intensifying insight of contemplative thinking must be: every thinker who has established a basic position in the history of Western thought is irrefutable. In other words, the mania to refute is the first fall from authentic thinking. By that measure, all philosophical bustle, especially the "National Socialistic" one, remains outside the domain of essential knowledge. This does not prevent such bustling about from attempting to make itself publicly respectable by means of boundless, noisy, and—thievish "literature," one which I corresponds down to a hair with the pen pushing that, as "Catholic philosophy," has created an entry for itself among the "intelligentsia" of all "confessions" and "stations." How long can this bustling about still endure? Or is its time only now arriving with the consummation of modernity?

78

56

Finally, however, through and for contemplative thinking—as the asking of the question of beyng—there dawns the time of a long meditation that has no results; unaffectedness by what is public; that all *knowledge* would reside in questioning what is most question-worthy, that all biological-characterological analysis and reversion to such presuppositions still amount only to a shirking of the decisions—the last flight into an extreme anthropomorphizing of everything—the last avoidance of the venture of that which is pre-posed to the human being—whither he is assigned—whence he has to abandon the past. But at the same time there rages what the human being himself as human—as animal—as "life"—pre-poses or, better, post-poses as the place of refuge of his calculations, all of which are valued according to "utility."

79

57

The basic error: that the practical is the useful and is determinable by use! That it is only the application of a (promptly to be abandoned) "theory."

Can a people lose the power of meditation as its essence, or indeed never find it? What is meant here by "a" people? Does it not first become this out of and through that passion for its essence? And does that not depend on a disposition toward meditation on the *human being*? Does the human being seek his essence and know that essence as something still concealed and self-concealing—or does the human being pursue his present-at-hand things and provide himself with "happiness"? Who decides here? Not the human being—but rather the beyng refusing itself to him.

Only if we can see that *thinking* in the sense of essential-contemplative thinking is the highest form of the most decisive *"action,"* one that must be equated with the enduring of humanity as something essentially gained through struggle, only then might the time arrive in which we grasp *philosophy.* Until that moment, we will totter in the mishmash of a "thinking" which is partially philosophical, partially scientific, and partially directed to everyday concerns—but is wholly intent on calculation and certainty and unwittingly undermines every basis of possible decisions—indeed does not even allow such a basis to emerge. But perhaps the | experience of essential thinking   80 must remain infrequent and protected from everything "common" and "communal"—so that there still might be within humanity a place for a rank to hold sway and to be able to hold sway without needing the assistance of those hailing ones who never seek what is other to themselves but only the validation of their own wretchedness. To "rule" at the expense of this throng of followers[29] is perhaps power but is never dignity. The latter bestows itself only onto the venturing of what is most question-worthy—(cf. p. 27).

58

Nietzsche endeavors to overcome the *subjectivism* of Descartes but still thinks of the human being too crudely as *subiectum* and merely interprets this *subiectum* as "body" rather than consciousness. The "subjectivism" of animality in the sense of the communal—is the "most extreme" "subjectivism," over and against which the "subjective" behavior of "private" "existence" is a formless play and mostly even very "objective." (Cf. above, p. 8f.)

The *Myth of the Twentieth Century*[30] is the supreme *consummation* of the a-mythical rational subjectivism and liberalism of the sixteenth

---

29. [Reading *Anhängerschaft* for *Anfängerschaft,* "throng of beginners."—Trans.]

30. {Alfred Rosenberg, *Der Mythus des XX. Jahrhunderts* (Munich: Hoheneichen-Verlag, 1930). Thus on the dust-jacket. On the title page: *20. Jahrhunderts.*}

century. *That is why* only in the twentieth century does there com-
mence the consistent and complete essential unfolding of modernity—the intrinsic consequences are the *"world wars"*—as the compe-
81   tition of the now "free" "subjects" of the mere desire to "live." | The
crudest—clumsiest and most violent—"knowledge" is the one that
claims to "explain" all things and in its "explanations" relies on something inexplicable which is nevertheless held to be self-evident. (Cf.
p. 90.)

59

Crashes are now often observed as regards airplanes and their technical mastery, but no one wonders about or even finds crashes happening in the sovereign domain of poetic discourse and thoughtful
questioning. This apparently indicates that in the latter domain, in
case it is not something else, for a long time no flying at all has been
carried out, no heights attained, and no depths ventured. Seen in
order of rank, crashes would indeed have to be more frequent here
than in the sphere of the operation of a machine, even though the machine is already no longer a tool and has transcended the character of
a mere means, because it is stamped and employed by being itself and
by the essential consummation of being qua machination.

82   ## 60

The new torrents of historicism.—Even already the increased possibilities of pictorial "reproduction," the speed of distribution and delivery,
the cleverness of "reportage," and the catalogued compendium of
what is known and can be arbitrarily assembled—all this ensures every intention of a historiological play with the tradition. One of the
most productive fields for historicism is the historiology of art, which
then also works itself out "typically" in many ways. Here everything
(even if said ever so effervescently and flashily, and described ever so
glitteringly and yet garrulously, and if each thing is compared to every other ever so ingeniously and penetratingly, and all things are calculated against one another) remains a backward-glancing evasion
into the past, even when now—as the present day requires—all art-
works as "expression" and "testimony" are sunk into the "primal
ground" of the "life" of the "people" so that these works can presumably be disinterred by historiology. This historicism is the inability to
see what *is* (what excites the historicism and drives it on to "activity"),
because historicism has available all registers of a gigantic pipe organ
of describing and portraying. Historicism is a witches' kitchen without

the witches, wherein only intelligent bloodhounds newly cook up the tradition for what is timely, in the opinion that timeliness will by itself guarantee | "life." Those who calculate are also enchanted— namely, by what amazes them, i.e., by the fact that suddenly new possibilities of *discovery* are given and again a generation is supplied, in its time to come, with *"new"* tasks of "exhuming" and "seeking" that which the "previous generation" has overlooked, for which the earlier generation was as little capable as the present generations should be credited with the fact that *they* now can discover something "new" and be eager for "new sights."

Folklore of whatever kind and extent never finds the "eternal people," unless such a people, in its particulars of essential questioning and discourse, is assigned in advance to those who seek the God of the people and who cast a decision for or against Himself into the essential core of the people. For first and only in that way has the people also found itself, i.e., found the necessity to acquire something of the future, instead of retrieving the past and becoming conceited through historiology, and to know that the essential, qua the ever most unique, never recurs and all regression is less than standstill, because it is only a covering over of the essential, if in advance and definitively in intention the eyes are sealed shut and denied a view into the unbounded machination of being, a machination that alone determines the space-time and levels of height for that which | now *"is."* But a crude "biologism" (justified within its own purposes) of the folkish [*völkisch*] ambition for power now seduces the "sensitive" and even more "empathetic" Germans onto the erroneous paths of folklore through which (who could deny it?) there opens up a new and broad field for curiosity, for the pleasure of vicarious "lived experience," and for imitation.

And yet—the historicism of the *pre*historical is even more disastrous than the one of history. For this latter historicism always requires (as its reverse side and complement) action, whereas the former one harbors the intention to "live" again the "primal life" and "life" in the "primal" itself, only because people "occupy" themselves with the ancient "symbols" as multifariously and exclusively as possible and prepare a "cognition" of them—as if the automobile, simultaneously racing right past such an occupation or even utilized in it and for it, as if the thundering of the dive-bomber, as if the loudspeaker bellowing out from some corner of the world, as if the gigantic movie poster, as if the concomitantly clattering typewriter—as if all this were nothing or could be measured by this "life" or could be absent even for a second. As if *"the* life" which *is* could be mastered or even merely led by averting the gaze into the certainly stimulating

83

84

obscurity of the presentiment of the prehistoric world, of which world |
85   those who come afterward always know only the externals and the
operation of the attempts directed at penetrating into it and interpreting it. Historicism leads necessarily to a *"romanticism" of romanticism,*
and thereby romanticism is "classisistically" elevated to *"classicism."*

61

A thinker can do what he must do as a thinker, namely, hold fast to
his *single thought,* only if he has the courage to take in stride every
overtoppling and thereby prepare the next one instead of equalizing
everything after the fact. What is strange, namely, that the *same* things
stand ever again in question as if they were unprecedented, testifies
to a certain familiarity with the ways of thinking. In "historical confrontation" with thinkers, we adhere, insofar as everything is taken
historiologically, either to the manifold content of their doctrines or
to their psychic-spiritual "lived experiences"—or to both at the same
time. We are scarcely able to see that *prior* to all this a basic position
toward being is holding sway, a position belonging to the history of
being itself. Accordingly, for historicists, among whom is to be included anyone who "considers" a philosophy from the outside, either
86   everything is a matter of "influences" or | else thought is a psychic "ex-
pression" of a "people" or of an all-encompassing "life."

Even more often do we come across the opinion that what a thinker
thinks and says can be measured according to what he has and has
not "read." This curious notion that a thinker would, as it were, strike
up against being through and in "reading" derives from a conception
of philosophy as a form of erudition concerned with books and writings. Why do we nevertheless stress so decisively the simple *"learning
to read"* in the education toward a rethinking of truly thoughtful
ideas? Because genuine "reading" is precisely liberated from the "letters" and from all "literature" and places itself exclusively under the
requirement of thinking only a few things, and among these only the
rarest, and of these only the simplest and most suitable. It is easy and
moreover diverting and at once a confirmation of being continually
"busy" to "read," or even to produce by oneself, a book containing,
e.g., an extensive "metaphysics" of modern physics. On the other
hand, it is difficult, and often "inconsequential" for a long time, to
think through a fragment of Heraclitus or Kant's thought of the "transcendental" or Hegel's thought of "negativity" or Schelling's thought
87   of "freedom" | or Nietzsche's thought of "truth"—and to think them
always together, even as the *same*—i.e., not as something thought, but

rather as the essentially occurring word which hovers freely in beyng qua abyss and fades away into the silence of the truth of beyng.—

62

How long must a person be enraptured with the sciences and traverse them by working in them, so one day he will learn that and why they must remain merely superficial knowledge? Today's "youth" seem to possess simpler ways; these young people grow up already distrusting the "sciences" and find themselves justified always and everywhere in turning away from them. But do these young people thereby arrive more quickly and more surely at some essential knowledge? Do they really have simpler ways? Or is this semblance spreading only because a knowledge of the domains of decision has become altogether useless and because these domains are no longer even "questioned"? What is the meaning of this unneediness, which is quite different than the increasing unrefinement whence in the first place an extensive breakdown has developed, specifically in "praxis"? Is this unneediness saying that the modern human being is now completely swallowed up by beings and | by the pursuit of beings (Who makes this bargain?—as the unshaken basic question of the "great politics"[31]) and that being has withdrawn from beings, whereby a καταστροφή ["catastrophe"] has become unrepresentable in the abyss of beyng?

Beyng itself is "tragic"—i.e., it begins out of the downgoing qua abyss and tolerates such beginnings only as that which does justice to its truth—the knowledge of beyng is therefore always reserved to the unique ones and specifically to those of them that *necessarily* must remain unrecognizable in all historiological cognition. The limit even of genuine historical meditation therefore does not lie in the extent of the capacity for confrontation—but in the essential misrecognition which spreads over those unique ones, expanding out from a determinate circle of solitude.

88

63

That which an age, indeed perhaps an integrated series of ages (such as the history of the West), has to endure in the ground of its history is seldom put into words and known by that age. For, an age always moves within the language and the thought of what it has attained

---

31. {Friedrich Nietzsche, *Jenseits von Gut und Böse: Vorspiel einer Philosophie der Zukunft. Werke*, vol. 7 (Stuttgart: Kröner, 1921), p. 156.}

89   and what is its "victory." The age remains back behind itself and does
so most of all when it makes progress. Therefore, I contemporaries as
well as those who follow cannot see beyond the nearness to what is
real and effective, i.e., beyond the nearness to beings, and so see
nothing of the abandonment of beings by being and certainly nothing
of what is "eventuating" therein: the fact that Western history is driving on *toward* a turning point—indeed the decisive one—indeed perhaps has been already driven right past it—a turning "point" which
is the decision regarding the distinction between being and beings:
will the decision be in favor of the truth of beyng, i.e., in favor of the
ending of the machination of beings?

64

The "tragic" is what takes its ascent from its descent, its downgoing,
because in the abyss it has taken on the task of grounding. The "com-
prehension" of what is tragic, i.e., primarily the traversal of its respective essential depth, is determined by what the tragic itself has at any
time acquired of the truth of beyng. The tragic is a preeminent assignment of the human being to the essential occurrence of beyng, in accord with the current openness of the human being for what is essential. The unclosedness toward what is question-worthy belongs to the
essential character of a "tragedy." In the Middle Ages, why was "tragic
drama" (not taken as a poetic form) impossible? Why does such drama
become ever rarer in modernity and can only be a gift to those who
90   in their own time are futural? How does I silence belong to the
"tragic"? Why does the mere freedom toward beings exclude the
tragic? Whence could the freedom toward beyng arise in an age of the
abandonment by being?

65

Need to know *little:* the highest distinction as the decision of the event
of appropriation in Da-sein.

66

Why is the level of human comportments and standards sinking?
Not because the previous standards have been abandoned and can no
longer be maintained; for merely to maintain is here already to sink—
the most peculiar and most insidious sinking down under oneself,
without being able to know of the sinking. The sinking sets in when
the ascent is absent, and that is unavoidable when what is question-

worthy gets denied—i.e., when the *possession* of "truth" becomes self-evident and at the same time also inconsequential.

67

To mature—to grow into the proper necessities of decision against beings and against oneself and into the knowledgeable domination over those necessities.

68

Those who are intent on "reality" and are close | to "life," who now   91
suddenly have become innumerable, never grasp that which *is*, because the "real" constitutes only the side of beings given in objective representation, and "life" is only the overlying factuality of beings on the human level. To totter in the objective and factual as the "wholistic" (a whole of what??) which can always be instituted, and which pursues all pursuits beyond themselves, is to let everything become a "happening" indiscriminately. The unconditional instituting of such "history" is the consummation of "historicism," whose particularity within historiology qua "science" remains, however, transient and contingent. Historicism, equipped with all the resources of the rapid and comprehensible procurement of the necessary "images" of what has happened, claims to be the prescriptive remembrance even of the past. Nothing which since then was ever held to be the essential—out of a genuine capacity for deeming worthy and for a more originary appropriation (all that still remains of the preservation of this deeming worthy is a historiological report, but not the deeming worthy itself)—nothing of all this can withdraw from the "clutches" of historicism, whose craving for the discovery of possible "commemorations" is becoming ever more ingenious and shameless. But the mode of the "remembrance" in historicism corresponds to the | way historicism in   92
advance and everywhere knows beings only in the pursuit of their representation. This remembrance remains a fire of straw, quickly kindled, quickly extinguished, and illuminating only the "recollective" organization and the mode and extent of the instituting of that organization. *What* is thereby commemorated remains remote and alien, and it sinks into indifference until the next "datum" of the next "commemorative hour." But through the timely kindling of these straw fires, historicism is covered over, and its capacity for "culture" is publicly attested. Just how completely historicism sequesters modern humanity from history (from the event of the singularities of the truth of beyng) is demonstrated by today's "youths"; they are neither "old"

nor "young"—they are unacquainted with a racing on to a maturity, they never and nowhere find their way to what is unsaid and not yet wished for, and, above all, they are unacquainted with the *passion of errancy*. But they do know and love the enchantment in the machination of the "machine," and to them everything else is—whether acknowledged or kept concealed—a "swindle."

93   But what if they are *right*—if they indeed *in this way* precisely are youths and thus lacking in comprehension but indeed surmising | with sureness the groundlessness of historicism? Yet this historicism could very well be necessary as the shield and smokescreen behind which an agitating and gathering of the peoples must proceed, whereby perhaps an essential condition of future history is provided. If we do not "see" with the gummed-up eyes of our usual consideration of culture and peoples, then there bursts forth everywhere that which is uncanny and is passed over obliviously by the human being inasmuch as he possesses all truth already. And this could become the first tidings of *being*, the tidings wherein everything objective and factual for once trembles and perhaps again takes refuge in the resting position of its self-certainty. But whether or not a poet is reserved for the founding of *these* tidings of being—such a founding is still infinitely distinct from the wretchedness of the orators who stress the factual and objective and enroll themselves at the "front" of those who want to hear from them only a confirmation of what is present-at-hand. Yet even here the "external" incident is still not worth attention; quite to the contrary, the process itself is to be grasped as the self-defense of historicism, and in this process the uncanniness of the machination of being is to be recognized. It is an uncanniness that *in this way* is de-

94   nied, so to speak, | every space in which it could be said and raised into transformative knowledge. From the netherworld of bad temper and small fears, of indolent indifference and zealous embellishment— an attempt must be ventured again in each case to know the simplest of this uncanniness and thereby expand it into its essence. Historicism as the executive power of the unity of historiology and technology is the aftermath and essential consequence of a decision made long ago about being—i.e., the metaphysical decision through which being, assigned qua beingness to beings, was subject to the calculability of beings and was thereby spoken out into forgottenness.

This forgottenness is the consummation of the untruth (representation as the form contrary to the clearing) of being, and, if grasped out of the essential occurrence of beyng, is the refusal of beings insofar as they have in the Western history of humanity withdrawn from a grounding of the truth of beyng in virtue of their falling away from the beginning, which has increased the ignorance about the es-

sence of all beginnings to gigantic proportions. But how is a thoughtful directedness into the history of beyng supposed to become the tid-
ings of the essence of the uncanniness to which we have grown all
too acclimated?

Why then do those who are near to "life" and are drunk on "re-   95
ality" know *nothing* of being—which alone "is"? To what extent are
they the complete nihilists and thus the ignorant co-preparers of something already from afar risen up toward what is approaching?

69

Why is meditation with so much difficulty and so rarely equal to the
decisive insight: that beyng in its truth can never be derived from beings? It is because this insight demands a transformation of human
beings which infinitely surpasses everything hitherto and at the same
time elevates what is simplest and unique into what is most worthy,
out of whose restraint in relation to all power and impotence the anthropomorphizing of the human being into animality is negated. The
enduring of that insight is the other beginning of philosophy; in order
to satisfy this endurance all the way to the bold clarity of the essential questions, the preparation of philosophy must renounce everything doctrinal and do so out of patience for a concealed maturing.
What does the lush waving of the golden spikes of grain in the radi-
ance of the summer sun know of | the night of the enclosure of the   96
seed in the hard earth?

70

It is not an accident and also not a personal exaggeration on the part
of Nietzsche that in the consummation of Western metaphysics, whose
basic character involves defining the human being on the basis of an
at hand (present) animality and vitality, now also this animality is
emerging in the consummation of the predatory nature of the roving
beast. The predatory animal, covetous of victory and power, corresponds to the inversion of "Platonism" carried out in Nietzsche's metaphysics. That the human being as this predatory animal becomes the
more or less explicitly affirmed and divulged "ideal" of humanity is
only the fulfillment of the essential requirement that one day the human being, identified as an animal, would lay claim to his essence—
which is animality—as an ideal. Therefore it is no wonder that Christian theology now does itself the favor of completely acknowledging
the "biological" conditioning of all human thinking; for the entirety
of Christianity is possible only | as "metaphysics" and can therefore   97

accommodate all forms of it. To "accomplish" that is indeed the "cultural" mission of Christianity.

71

Edward Thomas Lawrence, *Die sieben Säulen der Weisheit*[32] [T. E. Lawrence, *Seven Pillars of Wisdom*].—The first, bravest book of great reticence. Anyone who reads here only depictions of characters and the telling of "stories" and discovers only the most modern Karl May[33] and believes that these pages only treat of Arabia and Arabs and historiologically relate an episode of the world war and who seeks only for the "psychology" and the "lived experiences" of the author, such a reader surmises nothing and does not see a single one of the seven pillars of wisdom. What occurs in the book is the overcoming of the machination of beyng in a deliberately disinterested suffering of the compulsions and enchantments of that machination—all this on the basis of surmising the closure of other possibilities of being, for which every essential futural human being must become a poetizing-thinking questioner who has refused all expedients and from grave distrust already destroys all substitute forms of humanity, ones concocted out of things bygone.

98

72

The fact that "imperatives" ("Live appropriately to your species!") are preached still and repeatedly and more loudly than ever demonstrates the complete entanglement in "morals," i.e., in metaphysics and thus, for modernity, in "subjectivism." If the common interest comes before private interest, then something is gained "morally"-"politically"—but not metaphysically—instead, through the common interest the *selfishness* of humanity is all the more set into law and the decisionlessness with regard to the human being and his essence is turned into a principle.

73

A rare or indeed merely strange occupation is the concern for the "metaphysical" grounding of "heroism"; presumably a very unheroic

---

32. {Thomas Edward Lawrence, *Die sieben Säulen der Weisheit* (Leipzig: List, 1936).}

33. [Karl May (1842–1912), prolific and very popular German writer of adventure novels.—Trans.]

expulsion of "time." People even occasionally claim that the treatise *Being and Time* has initiated (although of course only from a distance and provisionally and altogether insufficiently in relation to today's demands and advancements) a grounding of heroism; for evidence, appeal is made to the concept of "resoluteness" [*"Entschlossenheit"*] in the book.

That such an absurd intention does *not* guide *Being and Time* can be deduced by any thoughtful person (but *who* is still able to *think*?) from the first sentences of the treatise, which is completely unheroic. Instead, *Being and Time* merely points very | soberly and very unilater- 99 ally (to be sure, from the "side" of what is Solely necessary) to one thing—to *the* decision before which is to be brought the thinking of the future, the thinking that still harbors beginnings. That, above all, did not succeed. Now the treatise is employed as an opportunity for endless, boring, and oblivious prattle about the "philosophy of existence" and suchlike.

Yet there are now in fact "heroic thinkers," i.e., scholars of the third and fourth degree, who believe that when they prattle on *about* heroism they are already heroic or even heroes themselves. All of these things are trivial inconsequentialities and would never be worth the least notice *if*—indeed if they were not peculiar, really peculiar, signs of a destructive process that is working itself out not in an annihilation but rather in the establishment of a gigantic semblance to the effect that everything "lives" and all "creative" sources are bubbling up and that we shortly will, or indeed already do, possess "the truth" and merely need to elaborate that possession. What will happen to young people, already weak in thinking and indolent, who grow up in such an atmosphere?

74

The genuine magnification, as an epistemic condition for grasping what is great, does not ascend upward | but rather comes *from* what is 100 up above. But how and when did it get up there? It never got there, but rather comes from there according to its *inceptual* essence.

75

Folkish [völkisch] thinking—which thinks out toward the first necessities and the genuine plights—exists only where the history of Western and especially modern humanity shifts into an Inceptual space of decision, wherein the grounders and founders speak of that which transforms the human being in his affiliation to beyng and lib-

erates him from the machination of beings. Such poetizing and thinking do not aim at a papering over of differences, and they do not divide the kinds merely according to peculiarities—instead, they move
the *essence* of history into the enclosed spaces of a grounding of the
truth of beyng. Any mere desire to preserve on the part of the "higher"
human being—the one that bears culture—against a sweeping up into
the herd is a self-delusion, unless goals of decision are set up, ones
101   which are not I "ideals," but quite to the contrary, are passages for the
downgoings. The modern human being wants to secure and preserve
for as long as possible the human being taken precisely in the guise of
the cultural animal and the mass animal. The urge to secure is already in advance a sequestration against unknown and transformative decisions.

76

Chaos and χάος are not the same. Chaos mostly refers to the disorder
which is a consequence of a loss of order; thus chaos, as the interpenetration and mishmash of all claims, measures, goals, and expedients,
is completely dependent on the precedent "order" which still operates
on it as its nonessence—(cf. Ponderings XII, p. 3f.). In contrast, χάος,
chaos in the original sense, is nothing nonessential and "negative"—
instead, it is the gaping open of the abyss of the essential possibilities
of grounding. An experience of this kind of "chaos" is reserved for the
one who is decided and creative—*this* "chaos" cannot be brought into
order, but "only" into an unfolding toward an extreme and ever freer
opposition. The essentiality—the nearness to being—of a humanity
102   can at times be gauged *by what* it takes, I and can take, to be "chaos."

77

Most people require "convictions," the confirmation of stubborn persistence in an arrogated questionlessness. *The few* reside on the moun-
tain of what is question-worthy rather than on the plain of opinion.
The former are the pursuers of beings, the latter few are the stewards
of beyng. A "struggle" *between* them is impossible; the decisions occur
in gaining by struggle that which can be pursued and that which is
question-worthy, in their struggle to separate, to struggle away from
each other. We believe, however, that these struggles had to be transferred in advance *onto the level of most people.* Then the struggle already became impossible, the abandonment of beings by being became decided, the essence of history lost, the being of beings quite
overshadowed, and the artificial light of historiology and technology

the only illumination. And in this illumination neither the human being nor the gods, neither a world nor the earth, can become visible, but in such illumination all the ever still-too-few "most people" have a "lived experience" of "life."

78

What is great goes down [*geht unter*, "sets," "perishes"]; what is small remains eternally. That we still preserve historiologically what is great and in any case I behave historiologically constitutes the most rigorous   103 proof of the already transpired downgoing [*Untergang*] of what is great.—Historicism as the destruction of history. (Cf. pp. 89, 107.)

79

Why should not the "era" of a second Wilhelmian "culture" also have *its* sorts of Eduard von Hartmanns?[34] Therefore it is not remarkable, but merely foolish, if people, after having "rejected" Nietzsche, offer his basic metaphysical position—the interpretation of beings qua beings as "life"—in a wretched trivialization and devastation, offer it as a "philosophy" with which "the sciences" are supposed to comply, ones that have become completely subservient to the mechanicism of the machination of beings. In relation to this "mechanicism," the so-called mechanistic interpretation of nature presents a mere sideshow. Is it an accident that the invocation of "life" is accompanied by the most highly developed mechanicism of the planned and calculated instituting of everything—of the whole of "life"? No—for the word "life" is here merely another name for precisely that mechani-   104 cism, a name cut to the measure of the *needs for lived experience.*" I The interpretation of the "world" as "life" permits a duplicity: making the "values" of "lived experience" "labile" and at the same time carrying through the most relentless mechanicism.

80

In the way of thinking characteristic of Catholic-ecclesial domains of faith, the proof by appeal to tradition plays an essential role, i.e., the demonstration that certain "dogmas," invented later, were "already" taught in the Scriptures and by the Doctors of the Church. Such proofs then carry on, not without forgery, what lies in the essence of all historiological proofs. This proof by appeal to tradition, as occurs in the

---

34. {Eduard von Hartmann (1842–1906), popularizing philosopher.}

Church, then undergoes a remarkable renewal and adoption in anti-Christian "thinking"; e.g., the interpretation of beings qua beings as "life" is always proved by demonstrating that Meister Eckhart, Nicolas of Cusa, Leibniz, and so on had "already" thought in that way. The *German* thinker Lessing[35] already knew that this is no proof of the truth. Of what avail then is this historiological deception for the pur-105 poses of proving a worldview which I moreover does not need to place any importance on its truth—but only on its impact and its appropriateness to needs? These "intellectual" pastimes of miscarried elementary school teachers are therefore not at all taken seriously, either by the "opponents" of the political worldview or by its own supporters; for *the latter* know, as well as do the popes, that such scribblings cannot "prove" anything. Perhaps, however, the semblance of proving something here and of promoting "culture" with such pedantry is quite useful at times and within definite limits. What is fatal of this activity consists in its now completely withholding the great German thinkers from the people. Yet this too might be in order and a sign of insight, namely, the fact that one no longer speaks of the people of poets and thinkers—but of poets and soldiers,[36] whereby this has a peculiar appropriateness to the "poets"—i.e., pen pushers.

"Catholic" thinking and "total" thinking *must* be the same; the designation is merely Greek in the one case and Latin in the other—106 where thinking and questioning are I excluded, the "proof by appeal to tradition" commences. And the much-abused ones who are eternally of yesterday? They are *too little* at home in the things of yesterday—all who are "near the present" must recognize this—the knowledgeable ones pass by: they have definitively transcended what seems likely to those of today.

81

Ethnology, paleology, and sociology [*Rassenkunde, Vorgeschichtskunde und Volkskunde*] constitute the "scientific" foundation of the folkish [*völkisch*]-political worldview. On the basis of previous thinking, one might account for these unitary "-ologies" ["*Kunde*"] as "rationalizations" of something "irrational" and thereby see in them an attempt to create a "mythos" "intellectually," through an extreme rationalism. But such an interpretation would be superficial and far removed from the essential Historical processes grounded metaphysically in

---

35. {Gotthold Ephraim Lessing, *Über den Beweis des Geistes und der Kraft* (1777).}

36. {Baldur von Schirach, "Vom musischen Menschen," in *Revolution der Erziehung: Reden aus der Jahren des Aufbaus* (Munich: Eher, 1938), p. 187.}

the interpretation of beings as "life" and of the human being as the "predatory animal." The decisions regarding this interpretation of being have been made long ago, and one must not falsely turn their executors into originators and think to decide even the least through "struggling" against them.

82

For what is "great," downgoing is neither a lack and loss, nor above all something that subsequently befalls it, as if the great could be such already in itself, *prior* to this incident. Downgoing—that something begins out of the uniqueness of an essential decision in favor of the question-worthiness of beyng and has in advance drawn its end into the uniqueness of the beginning, whereby an end "for itself" is impossible—constitutes the grounding of what is great. "Greatness" is, however, only a misleading name for the uniqueness of a grounding of the truth of beyng, a grounding that eventuates in every case of something great. The name mistakenly suggests evaluation and calculation or mere astonishment—and covers over the connection to the event—i.e., to what is *essentially historical*. Something "great" is rare and yet in each case is *the same* unique thing.—And this uniqueness has already surpassed every "eternity" we calculate as a sort of duration and find "consolation" in.

83

Refinement, in its essence (developed formation of "life") *and* in its distorted essence ("affectation"), is not a need and is a phenomenon of modernity. The Greek παιδεία ["education"] cannot be immediately connected to it—and can be mediately connected only where παιδεία moves | (as does all refinement later) in the domain of an explicit or   108 assumed "metaphysics" and is directed to an ideal (ἰδέα). The modern age of refinement becomes transformed into the age of "education" and thus necessarily turns into the age of *unrefinement*. Unrefinement is not a *preliminary* stage of refinement; it is rather a *consequence* of refinement. As an essential consequence, unrefinement is also not a lack, but is only the recasting of "refinement" into an institution of "education," and this institution for its part is determined in its "standards" and "goals" by the complete planning of an establishing of the subjectum (human being) upon the unconditional mastery over beings as a whole. Therefore we are witnessing an essential misunderstanding of the essential reality (i.e., a misunderstanding of the machination of beings as such) when the "intelligentsia" and the advocates of "democratic" "cultures" complain about the growing unrefinement and the deterioration of "culture." Such complaints are merely the helpless cries of those who are even *less* equal to beings as such than are the ones who try to keep pace with the still opaque "planetary" process of the unconditional consummation of modernity.

109   The talk of "dictatorship" is idle talk arising out of the horizon of a "freedom" which I has forgotten—or rather never knew—that whither its freedom liberates, namely, to the self-assurance of the human being as subjectum. Yet this assurance can "take hold" only where it in its essence sees uncertainty draw near. The taking hold then consists in holding down every uncertainty and threat, i.e., in the unconditional warding off of that which, by essence, must remain unassailable for all assurance—namely, the *essence of being* which, although completely concealed and dispelled, nevertheless qua machination prevails in all beings. Any warding off of the assurance of modern humanity is radically defenseless against the essence of beyng and its essential occurrence—because the enemy remains by essence invisible in this "case"—since the most intrinsic presupposition of the consummation of modernity consists in the planetary meditationlessness, i.e., in the universally homogenous and altogether unnoticed forgottenness of being, being which has long been pulverized into "nothingness" through the unquestioning attitude of metaphysics. The alleged "dictatorships" therefore do not amount to a *dictans* ["the saying"] but intrinsically already to a *dictatum* ["the said"] of that essence of being from which modern humans cannot withdraw, because in order to
110   become themselves they must affirm that essence, even in all I its essential consequences (cf. above, p. 79).

Therefore, what appears in this age is a concurrence of "states of affairs" and "situations," to whose evaluation no *standpoint of refinement* is adequate and a fortiori no comportment of "Christian" faith: the unacknowledged but now everywhere firmly established bewilderment of the youth—the absence of every creative venture. The mere execution and imitation of something planned and calculated; the impotence for convulsing previous opinions and expressions—the indifference to history—the compelled interest for presently required historiology; the lack of every arousing sphere for the upsurge of meditation.

84

That the various specialties can be ranged under a unitary concept of "science," indeed that this concept must exist, is precisely the presupposition for the "dissolution" of the universities into trade schools. The commonality of such a concept does in no way impede this dissolution, and above all does not create an originary unity which could work against specialization. Mere "unity"—as the easily encounterable abstractum of that which has long unified the modern sciences—cannot ground a new *unitas* of the uni-versity, | but can only vindicate the earlier one in its definitive form as the *diversitas* of trade schools. As long as "unity" remains merely the empty, generalizing accessory to something already present-at-hand in the content of modern science as research, a content almost running out to its end, and as long as only this unity is still sought, and is not even done so with the courage for meditation on that which "*is*," for so long an originary university remains unthinkable. For the "unity" of *that* university is never "knowledge"—or rather would have to be a knowledge that demands another truth and new decisions in favor of beyng.

Nonetheless—this knowledge will never be able to occupy the abode which is configured by the university—; that is the *real mistake* of the rectoral address of 1933, the attempt to relocate essential decisions (which drive toward the highest *individuation* of questioning and of meditation) into the domain of an *institution* and to transform that institution thereby. This attempt had to lead to an entire network of absurdities and entanglements and to the most intrinsic menace and depletion—without the possibility that any of those who are closest or remotest, allies or enemies, could be able to surmise what was transpiring. Thus the university retains, in some form or other, an essential confusion; yet this circumstance does not prevent "one" from feeling quite content with one's "science" in one's respectively assigned pursuit, even if "one" | must renounce the earlier "societal" acceptance—but one gives much away, so that only the placidity of the "spirit" is saved and everything question-worthy is kept far distant. Consequently, there should be no surprise at the lack of all courage to see the university *just as it is*—and at the expedient of taking refuge in the old "ideals" (thinly painted over with the "new" "ideal") of a "unity" of the "sciences," which is in truth only the uniformity of the flight from meditation, i.e., only the appropriate contribution to the planetary meditationlessness. The *university* as *universitas* of the concealment of the long since actual *diversitas* of trade schools, ones which are completely intermixed in the hodgepodge of the institutions and plannings of the complete equipping of what is merely to be equipped—which latter is *power*, however, solely in virtue of this equipping character—a power whose essence consists in the unrestricted overpowering of itself.

In the entirety of the equipping, the university can no longer set the standards, but instead can only be subservient, and this subservience—wholly in order—must at the same time be subordinated and

111

112

fading, in accord with the *unavoidable* insignificance of the "intellect," and therefore the university has inexorably become what it should have expected least of all: *rich in propaganda.* Yet the complete spine-
113 lessness I of so-called researchers has even here long since overcome the last restraints and thus places itself "without reservation" in the service of the very propaganda that preaches the insignificance of those same researchers.

NB: what is repugnant about this process does not consist in the state of the university, inasmuch as the essence of the age demands that state; instead, it lies in the conduct of the "scientists," who still act like representatives of what has been but on the other hand never want to come too late, whether in "engagement without reservation" or in equally remarkable "opposition" in alliance with the "Christian" rescuing of the "Churches." Let us silently pass over the nearly con-stant mediocrity of the accomplishments. It would almost seem that around 1890, amid all the wretchedness of the "worldviews" and of "interests," the university still showed a face, which is now merely a grimace of spiritlessness and decisionlessness, a grimace thinly cov-ered over with catchphrases but at much greater expense and with much more cleverness and noise. Back then, the questionlessness about what is decisive still had some legitimacy—now the thin con-cealment of the aversion to meditation is a sign that one no longer wants to know what are the characteristic pursuits in the horizon still left open to such pursuits.

114   *85*

How can *Nietzsche* give himself out as a nihilist? Why is he the first complete nihilist? How is that even thinkable, since his basic attitude presents the most extreme opposition to every "no" and "not" and nothingness—the *"yes"* to "life," and the latter not as mere present-at-hand animation and vital functioning, but as *enhancement of life,* as *liv-ing up to life*? Or does Nietzsche call himself the nihilist only because he thinks of himself as the first overcomer? To be sure. But Nietzsche *spoke* in a way that is truer than his own grasp of the matter—for that *"yes"* to life is merely the most extreme nihilism; thereby nihilism does not simply refer to the absence of all goals and the affirmation of the nugatory—it especially does not refer to what the guardians of a with-ered "democratic" "Western" ["*westlich*"] "culture" mean by the term—namely, the negation of what these guardians would still like to main-tain and what they take to be threatened, whereas it has long since been shattered already. Thought in terms of metaphysics and at the

same time in terms of the history of beyng, *nihilism* signifies the abandonment of beings by being and thus does not name an attitude of humans and of political rulers and of proclaimers of a worldview—nihilism in the essential sense is—not at all a process of Western historiology but is instead I an event of the history of being itself—   115
that beings in their machination eclipse all beyng—; the lack of "goals" is only *one* possible (not necessary and indeed quite remote) consequence of nihilism in the proper sense. This latter nihilism very well permits extraordinary plans and goals in executing the machination of beings.

Because Nietzsche makes the affirmation of "life" his basic position, and because "life" here means beings as a whole and indeed in such a way that "life," as the domain, measure, and fulfillment of all beings, becomes everything from first to last, whereby any question of being is excluded as groundless and senseless, and the abandonment of beings by being is still justified in the forgottenness of being on the part of the human being as the consummate subjectum, therefore "nihilism" in the proper sense commences with Nietzsche. By essence, *this* "nihilism" masks itself in the semblance of its opposite. Nihilism in the proper sense, however, is *extrinsic to the affirmation or negation* of every sort of "thinking" that is concerned with "culture," worldview, politics, or religion. It cannot be maligned as valueless, "dangerous," decadent, or the like—instead, it is the first product of a very broad and very remote appearance of beyng—that the still-concealed sovereignty of beyng is grounded in an unneediness for power and in impotence.

86   116

Spinelessness is intrinsic to the essence of all historiological sciences and is most prominent in "literary science," which leaps from one fashion to another overnight. Yesterday the "history of the spirit" was still the rage but was in the meantime replaced by the "existentiell" fashion; today the fashion is "ethnic" and "tied to race," tomorrow it will be "heroic," and the day after that perhaps "Christian" once again. In each case, there is much to do, and in each case someone can refute the precedent "literature" and the status of specialized research and can exhibit "new" cognitions. Why is this so? Because historiology is emerging more and more as that which it was designed to be, namely, the *technology* of "history." Through this technology, history becomes objective and relates to the past that is supposed to be produced and can be produced in one way or another from every present and from every "current" flowing within the present.

Historiology is the destruction of history—the undermining of the decision in favor of beyng—through the pursuit of past beings. In accord with this *necessary* flight from every necessity of decision, historiology is denied every possibility of an essential stamp—it is "spine-
117   less"—is illustrationism taking itself to be "life itself"—| and offers endless opportunities for "spiritual" occupations. The growing influence of publishing firms, the influx into them of miscarried "scientists," and the need for a rapid and manageable "orientation" regarding spiritual "affairs" lead to the planning of new handbooks and surveys. "Historiology" is only now reaching the distinct stage of "total organization"—the question no longer concerns that which one of the "researchers" has accomplished, insofar as something could still be accomplished here; what matters instead is whether he is included, is accounted one of the firm, and his views are "solicited." The "personalities," especially the "young" ones, involved in research do not any longer notice which leading strings are pulling on them. And should they indeed notice it, they have already been steeped so far in indifference that it does not matter to them what they employ as opportunities and means to gain "validity." None of this is to be judged "morally"; essential is again only the process—insofar as in it now the *metaphysical* essence of historiology as "technology" inevitably comes to the fore. And of course this holds not only of historiology in the
118   "form" of "science"—but applies to every | sort of representational and productive presentification of the past into the current state of the human being as the *subjectum* of all beings—, which subject thereby unmasks the human being (*animal rationale*) as the *historiological animal*, though without ever recognizing this unmasking as such.

The historiological human sciences, which today fancy themselves superior to the allegedly decisionless and "relativistic" "historicism" of the previous decades (how *short-sighted* is the thinking of these researchers, if indeed they do "think" at all), are the genuine executors of historicism, insofar as this latter term refers to what is metaphysically essential, namely, that the human being has placed himself in the public limelight as the productive predatory animal that has only something inconsequential to prey on and lacks opponents for its victories.

In accord with its *technological* essence, historiology always advocates what is timely or else (merely the other side *of the same coin*) suspects what is timely—in either case dependent and without the freedom to make a decision—for then it would have to decide against
119   itself—this | double impossibility gives historiology the tenacity of

something groundless, something ever again bobbing up and down; and with *that* "motion," historiology takes on the semblance of "life."

87

Nietzsche's *super-man* [Über-mensch] is the first and ultimate determination of the still not completely identified *animal*, "human being"—an extreme affirmation of metaphysics in its inversion as its consummation and as its ending reversion into the ended—*not* inceptual—beginning of the history of Western humanity.

88

Rainer Maria Rilke.—People again and again press me for an interpretation of the "Duino Elegies"[37] and for my "position" on them. People conjecture a kinship and even a sameness of attitude—all this remains extrinsic—the "Elegies" are *inaccessible* to me—even if I do sense and revere their poetic power and uniqueness in the midst of these poetryless decades. Three essential circumstances *separate* my thinking from this poet, i.e., make a dialogue very circuitous and today still premature:

The first is the a-*historicality* of his poetry—i.e., the immersion of the human being in corporeality and animality, whereby the human being remains one who has merely escaped from this sphere. The second is the anthropomorphizing of the *animal*—which does not contradict the first circumstance—. The third is the lack of essential *decisions*, even if the Christian God is overcome. Rilke stands, although more essentially and more poetically in his own proper course, as little as does Stefan George on the path of the vocation of the "poet," a vocation grounded by Hölderlin but nowhere taken up. Rilke has not—and even less has George—surmounted Western humanity and its "world" in a poetic-thoughtful way—Rilke bears *in himself* (more "heroically" than many of today's loud "heroes," who confuse heroism with the mere brutality of a street fight) an inexplicable fate, one seeking back—into the prehistorical—the childlike. Nevertheless, his "work" will remain, even if much of the artistry (which in the case of George proliferates quite differently) must fall away. If only the importunate "interpretations" of our contemporaries would turn toward other pursuits!

120

---

37. {Rainer Maria Rilke, *Duineser Elegien* (Leipzig: Insel, 1923).}

121   At first, Rilke's poetry is taken up more for the sake of sheer escape
and refuge, whereby it is deprived precisely of its seriousness, and what
has not been endured about it is made into a pleasure as something
merely obscure. This poetry has no place today, and that is essential
to it. A sign of this is that in its own proper way it joins in the struggle
to win for humans, out of a transformation of their essence, a more
originary standpoint. This poetry does not decide, but it does belong
to the future history of the decisions. It must first be placed back into
its proper historical limits through an inceptual knowledge of beyng.
We thereby strike up against a process which is suited only to the future of an overcoming of historicism—that everything effective
changes—is "effective" neither contemporaneously nor on the past
"historiologically"—but instead enters into the history of beyng and
out of this history first stands forth into the future of this history—
the essential *historical* isolation (not the historiological-personal-psy-
chological one) as the ringing in of the simple attunements toward
122   the assumption of the stewardship of beyng. Therefore, a | determi-
nation of my "view" of Rilke would be of no significance at all here—
since the history of beyng does not "happen" in a marketplace where
views are bartered and the historiological reports on them are com-
pensated.

Yet for now all silence is still taken only historiologically as mere
reserve, avoidance, seclusion—one continues to measure it up to the
public pursuit of publicity and thus cannot know the fact that silence
has already become the rescue of the sought-for word, the one naming something simple, and has become the assignment of this word to
the grounding of beyng. Yet how much must first fall victim to how
complete a destruction before the plight of *beyng* takes the place of the
needs and desires of life, in order thereby to transform the earlier
place, the "world" of human beings, into the site of a struggle which
perhaps does not exclude wars and times of peace but is never determined from what is merely "bellicose." The latter is now first becoming
exposed in its modern form as a *consequence,* not as the mastery, of the
machination of beings. Through the exclusive priority of the machi-
123   national—bellicose-technological—| historiological "struggle," the age
necessarily distances itself in an *essential* breadth most widely from
the essence of struggle as the multidoored portal of beyng toward the
acquisition by strife of the clearing in which what is most alien encounters its essence—bestows itself in refusing itself and binds itself
out of the supreme mildness. Yet thereby even the most remote word
of the poet is an intimation of what is ungrounded—and still to be
named—and thereby this intimation is history, i.e., the future and advent of a plight which draws beyng itself into the "beings" that have

become nonbeings. Thereby we need foreign heralds and should not reckon them over into the flatness of what is timely and divide them into the useful and useless and in that way submit ourselves to the inevitable devastation.

89

Provided it is carried out essentially enough, a history of the literary-scholarly *plunderings* from poets and thinkers could make us wonder about the history of the "spirit" and would be the antithesis to the history of isolation, which indeed could never be written since such | a　124 communication is opposed to solitude. Therefore, the history of the plunderings would not be a "companion piece," but instead the sole form of the history of the isolation in which we must see only one mode of the essential occurrence of beyng, the mode turned toward humans and incorporating them. But *plundering* refers to the arbitrary and unprepared snatching up and amassing of things that were said Essentially and to the bandying about of them in idle talk that reports and compares, wherein what was snatched up is at once cast away into forgottenness like junk that appears out of nowhere. Nevertheless, this forgetting assumes the insidious form of the historiological recording of the past—and looks like recollection—but is without memory, since everything proceeds outside of meditation. This remarkable domain of the history of the "spirit" encompasses the hunting field of the historiological sciences and of journalism. The latter is now starting to determine the definitively modern forms of the "life of the spirit"—and does not thereby "avail itself" of "technology"—but on the contrary is itself a form of it.

The planned "alignment" of the faculties of even the "spiritual" and　125 "cultural" sciences is today still only a question of cleverness and the correct harnessing of the "rising generation"—which to be sure has no longer arisen and especially will never again arise, because it itself must become a product of planning. The planning of human-scientific and "philosophical" research must be carried out immediately, if this sort of "science" is to be able to secure for itself any "justification" at all. Thereby the question is not so much about a fostering of ethnicity, countryside, and the like as it about an assignment of the previous history to the power projects of the unfolding of political power. Such planning necessarily touches on only a particular selection of its matters and pursues a disregarding and forgetting of the domains that are valueless in an "essential" respect—above all, this planning leads to a journalistic, abridged, easily accessible "treatment"—which is then called a new interpretation. The place of essential questioning is usurped by the quick and efficient survey and by the productivity of the exhibiting of what is attractive and timely. The operation of the human sciences has now been so recast that one day "newspaper science"[38] and "radio science"[39] will no longer be appendages to the basic sciences but, instead, will themselves be the basic sciences. Yet this is not the deterioration of the modern age, but its consummation.

---

38. {The first institute for "newspaper science" was founded in Leipzig in 1916. In Freiburg, such an institute was established in 1925. "Newspaper science" was the precursor of "communication science."}

39. {The first and only "Institute for Radio Science" was founded in Freiburg in 1939. Cf. *Schriften des Instituts für Rundfunkwissenschaft an der Universität Freiburg im Breisgau* (Berlin: Decker, 1941).}

{Index}

Editor's Afterword

This volume 95 of Martin Heidegger's Collected Works [*Gesamtausgabe* (GA)] comprises "Ponderings VII–XI," five of what he himself called the Black Notebooks [*Schwarze Hefte*]. From the early 1930s to the early 1970s, the notebooks were the philosopher's constant traveling companion on his course of thought.

"Ponderings X," included herein, contains a remark on the character of these "ponderings" that unfold in fifteen notebooks. They are not a matter of "aphorisms" as "adages" but of "inconspicuous advance outposts—and rearguard positions—within the whole of an attempt at a still ineffable meditation toward the conquest of a way for the newly inceptual questioning which is called, in distinction from metaphysical thinking, the thinking of the history of beyng." "Not decisive" is "what is represented and compiled into a representational edifice," "but only how the questioning takes place and the fact that being is questioned at all."[1]

Heidegger also refers in a similar vein, in his "backward glance over the way," to "especially notebooks II, IV, and V," that is, to the respective "Ponderings." They are to capture "in part ever the basic dispositions of questioning and the directives into the extreme horizons of attempts at thinking."[2] The emphasis on the "basic dispositions of questioning" reinforces the indication that the Ponderings are a matter of "attempts at thinking."

Following this up, I have inserted as an exergue to the first published Black Notebooks (GA94) a later remark (presumably from the early 1970s) to the effect that at issue in the "black notebooks" are not "notes for a planned system," but rather "at their core" "attempts at simple designation."[3] It is striking that in all three characterizations of the Black Notebooks, the word "attempt" claims an essential significance.

As "inconspicuous advance outposts—and rearguard positions," that is, as pre-ponderings and post-considerations in the basically confrontational thinking of being, the Black Notebooks assume a form not yet seen in Heidegger's many already published writings. If what

---

1. "Ponderings X," p. a. The page references correspond to the pagination of the original manuscripts, which is printed in the margins of the published volumes.

2. Martin Heidegger, *Besinnung*, GA66 (Frankfurt: Klostermann, 1997), p. 426.

3. Martin Heidegger, *Ponderings II–VI*, GA94 (Frankfurt: Klostermann, 2014), p. 1.

is indeed "decisive" is "how the questioning takes place," thus how the question of the "meaning of being" finds expression, then we are encountering in these notebooks a new writing "style," a concept often mulled over in the "notes."

Besides the published work of the 1920s, the courses, seminars, essays, lectures, and treatises on the history of being, we become acquainted in the Black Notebooks with a further way of expression on the part of Heidegger. The question of how all these various modes of speech cohere does perhaps belong to the most important tasks of a thinking which would seek to understand Heidegger's thought as a whole.

The Black Notebooks present a form which in style and method is possibly unique not only for Heidegger but also for all of twentieth-century philosophy. Compared to generally known sorts of texts, it comes closest to an "idea diary." Yet if this designation thrusts the writings that come under it mostly to the margin of the total work, the significance of the Black Notebooks in the context of Heidegger's "way for inceptual questioning" will still need to be examined.

According to the literary executor, Hermann Heidegger, and Friedrich-Wilhelm von Herrmann, Heidegger's private assistant between 1972 and 1976, the Black Notebooks were brought to the German Literature Archive in Marbach around the middle of the 1970s. On the occasion of the shipment, Heidegger stated that they were to be published only at the very end of the Complete Works. Until then, they were to be kept "doubly secret, so to speak" (von Herrmann). No one was to read them or look them over. The literary executor has decided against this directive, because delays in bringing out the still-unpublished volumes of the full project of letting Martin Heidegger's thought appear in due form should not prevent the publication of the Black Notebooks at this time.

Why did the philosopher want to have the Black Notebooks published only as the last volumes of the Complete Works? The answer might very well be related to an already familiar stricture according to which the treatises concerned with the history of being were to be published only after all the lecture courses. For these courses, which intentionally do not speak about what is contained in the writings on the history of being, prepare for what these latter are saying in a language not accommodated to public lectures.

The Black Notebooks are thirty-four in number. Fourteen bear the title "Ponderings," nine are called "Annotations," two "Four Notebooks," two "Vigilae," one "Notturno," two "Intimations," and four are named "Provisional Remarks." In addition, two further notebooks with the respective titles "Megiston" and "Basic Words" have come to light. Whether and how these belong to the Black Notebooks must still be clarified. Volumes 94 to 102 of the Complete Works will in the coming years make available the thirty-four manuscripts first mentioned above.

The writing of the notebooks spans a time frame of more than forty years. The first extant notebook, "Intimations x Ponderings (II) and Directives," bears on its first page the date "October 1931." "Provisional Remarks III" contains a reference to "Le Thor 1969," so that the notebook "Provisional Remarks IV" must stem from the beginning of the 1970s. One notebook is missing, namely, "Intimations x Ponderings (I)," which must have been composed around 1930. Its whereabouts are uncertain.

*   *   *

Toward the end of "Ponderings VI," Heidegger refers to a speech delivered by Baldur von Schirach in Weimar in June 1938.[4] Whether "Ponderings VII" attaches thereto cannot be determined conclusively. In any case, Heidegger mentions a publication of the Germanist Richard Benz from the year 1937 and also refers to his own lecture course on the Basic Questions of Philosophy (GA45) from the winter semester 1937–1938.[5] Since it is highly improbable Heidegger was making entries in more than one "Ponderings" notebook at the same time, we must assume that a reference at the outset of "Ponderings IX" to *Meditation* (GA66), a treatise on the history of being, indicates that the composition of "Ponderings VI" also began in the late summer of 1938. A remark in "Ponderings XI" concerning a possible "new world war" is evidence that the last Black Notebook of the present volume ended before the start of World War II.[6] Compared to the "Ponderings" comprising volume 94 of the Collected Works, in approximately one year (1938–1939) Heidegger filled substantially more black notebooks than in the previous years.

In the entries of "Ponderings VII–XI," Heidegger deepens his confrontation with the National Socialist worldview and with the everyday reality of that worldview. Thereby it becomes clear that Heidegger distinguishes the "Germans" from this reality.[7] The "Germans" are the "people" of the "other beginning." The further Heidegger develops this thought, all the clearer does it become to him how little

---

4. "Ponderings VI," p. 143.
5. "Ponderings VIII," pp. 28 and 40.
6. "Ponderings XI," p. 18.
7. "Ponderings VII," p. 11f.

the National Socialist "revolution" shares in this thought and how the German reality of the 1930s developed otherwise.[8]

The role of "Hölderlin and Nietzsche" in the history of being is what above all demonstrates to Heidegger that the "Germans" are the "people" of the "other beginning."[9] Hölderlin and Nietzsche—each in his own way—constitute for Heidegger the genuine reference to the task of the "Germans" in the history of being. Yet Hölderlin and Nietzsche remain misunderstood by necessity. Everyday history has not yet carried out the step into the "other beginning."

According to Heidegger, further evidence for this is a politics devoted more and more to the actualization of "culture." For him, such politics is a "parrying" of the "thrusts of beyng,"[10] that is, an institutionalizing of technology, the latter thought in regard to "machination." The confrontation with this phenomenon forms a leitmotif of the "Ponderings," especially before the war, and is accompanied by a vehement repudiation of "cultural Christianity"[11] or the "Christian cultural God."[12]

In this context, Heidegger frequently and critically considers the significance of Richard Wagner, whose "abdominal music"[13] becomes the center of a machinational art of lived experience wherein "music"[14] in general plays an essential role. These passages quickly make obvious the uniqueness of the "Ponderings" within the Collected Works. Nowhere as much as here is Heidegger exposed to the presence of "machination."

In the course of these occasionally bitter confrontations, there also appears an interpretation of "Judaism" in terms of the history of being.[15] In the age of "transition" to the "other beginning," there breaks out a "groundlessness" preventing any essential "grounding" in history. This "groundlessness" would by no means be exemplified only by "Judaism" but instead determines all domains of the world. Yet perhaps in this moment of the history of being, "the greater groundlessness that, not being bound to anything, avails itself of everything (Judaism)" would have a greater influence.

---

8. Ibid., p. 23.
9. Ibid., p. 97.
10. Ibid., p. 2.
11. Ibid., p. 3.
12. Ibid., p. 9.
13. "Ponderings VIII," p. 28.
14. Ibid., p. 61.
15. Ibid., p. 9.

Nevertheless, for Heidegger the "greater groundlessness" actualized by "Judaism" is not the property of a "race." On the contrary, the "worldlessness of Judaism" is first "grounded" by "one of the most concealed forms of the *gigantic*, and perhaps the oldest," namely, the "tenacious facility in calculating, manipulating, and interfering."[16] Like "National Socialism," however, "Judaism" is a futile attempt to use "machination" for one's own goals. "Machination" remains the real "power."

The background of these utterances regarding "Judaism," as well as of the interpretation of National Socialist everydayness, is formed without a doubt by all the thoughts we are familiar with from Heidegger's contemporaneous treatises on the history of being: *Contributions to Philosophy (Of the Event)* (GA65, 1936–1938) and *Meditation* (GA66, 1938–1939), as well as the later *History of Beyng* (GA69, 1939–1940), *On the Beginning* (GA70, 1941), and *The Event* (GA71, 1941–1942). The "Ponderings" are often reminiscent of these previously published writings.

*   *   *

The "Ponderings" appearing in volumes 94 to 96 of the Collected Works comprise fourteen of the thirty-four (or possibly thirty-six) notebooks with black oilcloth covers. The pages are in an unusual format: 5¼ × 7½ inches. The originals reside in the Heidegger literary remains at the German Literature Archive in Marbach am Neckar. I as editor had available copies bound in blue linen, with the titles printed on the spines.

The present volume 95 brings together the following texts:

"Ponderings VII," 127 pages;
"Ponderings VIII," 128 pages;
"Ponderings IX," 127 pages and 19 supplements from the 1950s and 1960s;
"Ponderings X," 124 pages;
"Ponderings XI," 127 pages.

Added to these pages are indexes Heidegger provided at times for the notebooks. When available, they are published at the end of the respective text.

The manuscripts are fully worked out. They display hardly any slips of the pen. There are no inserted sheets.

---

16. Ibid.

Detlev Heidegger prepared, and Hermann Heidegger checked, a typed transcription of all the "Ponderings" in this volume. In addition, Martin Heidegger's literary remains include three older typescripts, no doubt produced roughly at the time of the composition of the manuscripts. These typescripts are simply extracts from "Ponderings VIII–X":

"Ponderings VIII," 51 pages;
"Ponderings IX," 54 pages;
"Ponderings X," 53 pages.

It is impossible to say definitely who produced these transcriptions.

I transcribed everything once again from the manuscripts, while constantly looking at the already prepared typescripts. Then I proofread the typescripts. Finally, the galleys and page proofs were checked both by me and by my collaborator and student, Sophia Heiden.

Heidegger numbered the individual entries in the "Ponderings," perhaps imitating his own treatises on the history of being, perhaps following the example of certain writings of Friedrich Nietzsche. This changes, however, beginning with "Ponderings XIV"; it and all further Black Notebooks no longer display such numbering.

Letters ("a," "b," "c") with which Heidegger sometimes designated the first pages of a notebook, as well as the page numbers that begin thereafter, are reproduced here in the margin of the text. The vertical stroke in the middle of a line indicates a page break. A question mark within braces ("{?}") flags an uncertain reading. All cross-references in the text are to notebook page numbers. Heidegger uses the symbol "□" for "manuscript." All underlinings found in Heidegger's own text have been changed to italics; underlings in cited texts, which would be italicized on their own, have been printed in bold.

More than in other volumes of the Collected Works, certain of Heidegger's remarks, especially ones referring to historical events, were supplied with an editorial explanation. Thereby the reader can see at which time Heidegger composed which of the "Ponderings." Also with regard to persons and institutions, ones which might be unfamiliar to younger readers, I have attached concise clarifications. There could obviously be no completeness here, in an edition that is supposed to come "straight from the author's hand."

In some cases, though very sparingly, I brought Heidegger's idiosyncratic spelling as well as his characteristic syntax into conformity with current rules. At the same time, I intentionally retained certain peculiarities, for instance that of occasionally capitalizing adjectives (e.g., "Last god,"[17] or "Self-consolidating development"[18]) or writing *Gebahren* [for *Gebaren*, "behavior"].[19] Also, Heidegger's notorious coinage of hyphenated words was not standardized but, instead, with a few exceptions, is reproduced just as it appears in the manuscripts.

*   *   *

I thank Hermann Heidegger for the trust with which he conferred on me the task of editing the Black Notebooks. Thanks are due Jutta Heidegger for proofreading the present volume and for checking the page proofs. I thank Detlev Heidegger for making available the first typescript. I express my appreciation to Friedrich-Wilhelm von Herrmann for many discussions in which various editorial issues were decided. Such gratitude is also owing to Arnulf Heidegger and to Vittorio E. Klostermann. Anastasia Urban, of the Klostermann publishing house, always offered me capable and friendly collaboration, for which I am grateful. I am indebted to Ulrich von Bülow of the German Literature Archive in Marbach for assistance with regard to questions concerning the availability of the manuscripts. Finally, Sophia Heiden deserves my gratitude for her careful proofreading.

Peter Trawny
Düsseldorf
Dec. 13, 2013

---

17. Ibid., p. b.
18. Ibid., p 56.
19. Ibid., p. 119.

Lightning Source UK Ltd.
Milton Keynes UK
UKOW04n0724101117

312504UK00010B/496/P